We Made It

Sylvia Moss

First published by Busybird Publishing 2025

Copyright © 2025 Sylvia Moss

ISBN:
Paperback: 978-1-923501-52-2
Ebook: 978-1-923501-53-9

This work is copyright. Apart from any use permitted under the *Copyright Act 1968*, no part of this publication may be reproduced, stored in a retrieval system or transmitted in any form or by any means, electronic, mechanical, photocopying, recording or otherwise, without the prior written permission of Sylvia Moss.

The information in this book is based on the author's experiences and opinions. The author and publisher disclaim responsibility for any adverse consequences that may result from use of the information contained herein. Permission to use any external content has been sought by the author. Any breaches will be rectified in further editions of the book.

Cover Image: Pixabay

Cover design: Busybird Publishing

Layout and typesetting: Busybird Publishing

Busybird Publishing
2/118 Para Road
Montmorency, Victoria
Australia 3094
www.busybird.com.au

Chapter 1

I was born in Prague, Czechoslovakia just before World War II. My name is Sylvia, and I had a sister 3½ years younger. We were very close. Her name was Lydia. This story is based on what I remember from when I was about four and a half years old. My aunt and my cousin, who is four years older than I, have told me how my mother and father met, and what happened. I do remember my mother clearly. She was lovely. I have a photo of my mother, my sister as a baby, and me, when I was about 4½. This is the only photo I have of her and of us children.

My mother was German, but not Jewish, which means that I am not Jewish either. You have to have a Jewish mother to be Jewish. Her Christian name was Charlotte. She came from poor parents. My grandfather owned a little shop. He lived above the shop, with no garden, and the family's house was in a small town near Breslau (then in Germany, now called Wrocław, and in Poland). In his leisure time he wrote poetry, which he loved doing. A well-to-do lady offered my mother a job as housemaid. My mother's parents were told also that Charlotte would soon have to live in, and come home on weekends. My mother travelled to work on foot, passing a lovely park, with some small statues in it. This took about 40 minutes there and back. From the house Charlotte was working in you could see a cathedral spire in the distance. Poland has some beautiful churches and gardens. The job was offered to Charlotte, as she was the eldest. It was a large house, two storeys high, and nicely furnished.

There were lots of pieces to dust and many rooms that had to be cleaned when people were staying over. She did fresh linen for the beds and was kept very busy. Looking out of the windows to the back of the house, the garden was lovely, and well maintained by a gardener. The only time Charlotte was able to go into the garden was when she hung washing on the line, or brought it in. If she was on her own, she would wander around the garden. The front of the house was very close to the paved footpath. It was quite a narrow street, with trees on either side. Charlotte enjoyed working and being away from home. She was often on her own in the house, and would imagine it was hers. She was happy working in her job.

Charlotte had blonde hair and blue eyes. She was young and quite slim and you would say she was attractive. She would dust and clean, and would lose herself in her job. She was happy and content, and it got her away from her real life, in which things were tough, and they had to manage money carefully. One morning she was working, cleaning the house. As she had the windows open, she heard this whistling. She ran to get her duster to give it a shake, having a look to see who it was. She saw a young man walking slowly along the pavement below. He happened to look up and saw Charlotte. He called out "Good morning!" to which she answered the same, and he kept walking. Charlotte felt happy. Her heart was pounding and she kept thinking about this young man.

She wondered next morning whether he would pass by, so at the same time as she had done the day before, she opened the windows and listened, but he didn't come. This was a routine she went through every day, until the next week she heard the whistling. She could hardly contain herself. She ran to get her duster and gave it a shake. He was underneath her window. She couldn't see him, but he was whistling. Then he called out to her: "Come down. I'd like to talk to you." Her heart was racing and she didn't know what to do. She was on her own, but she wasn't sure if she should do this. She ran down the stairs and talked to him from behind the closed door. They exchanged names. He was called Kurt. He said he would like to see her and take her out, so they arranged to meet the next day, when she finished work.

Charlotte ran back up the stairs. She flew through her cleaning. She was so excited – she couldn't believe what was happening to her. That night she hardly slept, and next day she dressed as nicely as she could. She couldn't afford good clothes, but she had one or two nice dresses for best. She watched the clock and made sure she was on time as she walked to their meeting place. He was already there, and this time he had a bike with him. He said, "Hop on. I know of this nice place where we can go and talk."

She was a bit disappointed because she wasn't really dressed to hop on a bike. Still, she just couldn't stop her heart racing, it was so exciting. Holding her dress up as well as she could, she got on the bike, and he said, "Hold on!" which she did. He was so strong. She had never been on a bike before. Charlotte was a bit scared, but she was only on the bike for a short time when he said, "We are here. Hop off!', and she was glad to get off. But when she looked around there was a bridge in the distance, where a river flowed, and there were quite a lot of trees. She was standing on a little track with grass on either side. He hopped off and threw his bike on the ground. He held her hand and said, "Let me show you. This is my favourite place."

Hand in hand they walked towards the bridge and down the slope to the water. Sitting on the grass, Kurt, (my father), said he couldn't stop thinking about her, and Charlotte said she felt the same, and they kissed. Then Kurt said, "Let's walk back to the bike and we'll go and get something to eat." That was the beginning of their courtship. They saw each other every night, and Kurt said he would organise for her to meet his parents. So, a few days later he said, "My parents would love to meet you tomorrow."

They lived in Breslau. Charlotte was very nervous about this meeting. Kurt told her that he had an older brother, Heinz. They were very close and he was cleverer at school than Kurt, whereas Kurt was more artistic. Kurt told Charlotte they were never allowed to visit fairs, as their grandfather had been accidentally killed at one. My cousin Marion and her brother Peter were never allowed to visit fairs either.

The meeting went well, and Charlotte felt she was accepted. A few weeks later Kurt decided he wanted to move out of home, and that he and Charlotte should see if they could find a small place where they could live together. As Charlotte was already living in as part of her job, it was Kurt who spent time looking for somewhere, and he decided he would like to live in Prague. When Charlotte finished work, she would meet Kurt and off they would go on the bike, looking for somewhere to live. It was exciting, and after some time they did find a small place in Prague.

Chapter 2

Now I will tell you a bit about my father. He was German and Jewish. He was handsome, quite tall, with dark hair and brown eyes – in fact he was a bit of a ladies' man. He was talented and artistic. His work was drawing scenic backdrops for operas and theatre productions, and I have a photo of a design he did. I am not sure if he ever attended art school. He was a true bohemian. I think Kurt chose Prague, as his brother Heinz and his family moved there shortly after Charlotte met them. He also had to leave Germany in 1935, when the Nuremberg racial laws made it impossible for him to continue his work as an artist and stage designer. Another reason for his choice of Prague, Czechoslovakia, was that he was hoping to marry Charlotte. Also, Prague was a Mecca for artists, and he found some work there, painting backdrops for the opera and theatres.

Charlotte continued working in her job, and Kurt would take her each day on his bike, and then off he would go to his work. She became used to the bike, and things were going well. They were so happy. Then, within a short time, Charlotte realised that she was pregnant. She and Kurt were thrilled, and it was not long after that when she knew that she would have to give up her job. No more bike rides, and she would spend her time making their little home ready for the new baby. I was born, and I believe, much loved. As I grew up, I became very close to my mum, and when I was not quite four years old my mother had another baby, a little girl. My sister was born, and they named her Lydia.

I loved my little sister and became mother's little helper. I would fetch and carry whatever I could to help my mum. We were a happy little family. This was until there was talk about a war that was coming. My father spoke with his brother, who was more knowledgeable about these things, and he said yes, it would happen very soon. They both agreed that they should get out of Prague as soon as possible. Heinz said he had contacts with people in Scotland, and would make arrangements. When Father told Mother we would have to leave soon, she was very upset, as she loved her little home, and didn't believe they had to leave. She became very unhappy and cried a lot, and I remember loud voices arguing after I was in bed, and Mother crying.

Father said we would be leaving in a very short time, and he was waiting for Heinz to finalise arrangements. He was working hard on this decor and hoping to finish it before we left. Within a few days Heinz contacted Father and said it was arranged. We would stay in Glasgow with a recently widowed lady who had a large house, and Heinz and his family would be staying with people a few miles away. We were to leave next day for Scotland.

He still had not completed his work, and said he would join us as soon as possible. When he told Mother she was to go ahead without him, and he would come on his own later, Mother said no, that wasn't going to happen, and they would all go together. Father and Heinz insisted. He wanted us to be safe, so we girls must go, he said. It would be easier for him to get out of Prague a bit later by himself when his job was finished. Mother couldn't bear the thought of leaving, and being apart from Father was even more agonising. He said it would only be for a week or two at the most, and he would be with us. It would have been so hard for Mother. She was very frightened of going to a strange country and being unable to speak the language, and leaving Father with a young baby and a toddler.

He promised that as soon as he could he would be with us as a family again. We said our goodbyes to Father with lots of hugs and overflowing tears of sadness. Because Father and Mother never married (at that time the Nazi regulations banned mixed marriages), we girls kept our mother's maiden name and were able to get out of Prague with few complications. Czechoslovakia had an agreement with Germany on the reciprocal administration of their marriage laws. Kurt's name could not be entered on the birth certificates. Kurt lived with Mother until the occupation of Czechoslovakia by German troops in 1939. It was so awful for Mother, being forced to leave against her will, leaving Father behind, even though it was supposed to be for her benefit and safety. But the unknown was so frightening for her, with two small children and going to a different country.

My cousin Marion told me that my father gave her a paintbox, her first and best, as a going away present, which she treasured, just before we left Prague. Marion also told me much later we were on one of the last planes to leave Germany before the Nazis marched into Czechoslovakia in 1939.

My mother and we girls, when we arrived, were introduced to this white-haired lady, Mrs. Jess Buchanan. I remember arriving at this lady's house. It had a lovely garden. She was very kind, and held my hand when she met us, and said, "Call me Jess". The house had a wall around part of it. It was not that high, but just the right height for me, a four-year-old, to climb on, walk around and jump off, and I was always being told to get down. In fact, Jess thought I would fall off, and told Mother, who was cross and upset with me. It is funny how some things stick in one's mind. I have the one and only photo of Mother, my baby sister and me, sitting on that wall. Jess must have taken it.

Mother was talking a lot to Jess, who could not understand her, and of course there was the language problem. It was a difficult time for communication all round. Jess was wanting me to be with her more, and not be so close to Mother, to give her some time alone with Lydia. I was just wanting Mother and was scared all the time that I was going to be left with this lady. Jess used to take me into the big garden. I had to hold her hand. She showed me lots of flowers. I had never seen flowers before. I was able to let go of her hand and run in the garden, and one day I picked all the heads off -- I had both hands full of flower heads to bring inside to give to Mother. Jess was not pleased with me, and showed me how to pick flowers, and I didn't do that again.

Chapter 3

Days and weeks went by with no news of Father, and Mother became more and more worried, scared, stressed and unhappy. She was so lonely, and could speak hardly any English. It wasn't a happy time. Mother was crying a lot and would hardly eat anything. She would go to the letter box every day looking for a letter, but there was nothing. Eventually my uncle managed to make contact through the Red Cross, who found where Father was and sent him some food parcels. Father was having difficulties leaving Prague. It was not looking good. Heinz was in contact with Mother, and asked Jess if she would drive us girls to where they were staying.

It would be a bit cramped, but under the circumstances he felt it would be the best thing for us to stay with them. Mother was pleased and happy about this, and she would be able to talk to Heinz in their own language. We left the next day, after saying goodbye to Jess. There was a little girl there, my cousin Marion, four years older than I, and we were able to talk and play together. Mother wasn't crying so much, and for a few weeks being with Heinz, she settled in, and she was not so lonely or unhappy. It helped being with family, also, being able to communicate was good for her. Aunt Alice looked after us girls. We liked her. She was kind and very caring towards us. I became fond of her and felt a closeness to her. Heinz organised a small job for Mother for a few hours per day to keep her mind off things, like she was doing before. Aunt Alice also spent time helping Mother with her English, so she could at least understand a bit of what was being said.

Days became weeks, and things went relatively smoothly. We were still waiting for news, but hoping no news was good news. Then it happened. All contact with the Red Cross just stopped. No one knew what was happening, but the war was still going on. Mother simply couldn't understand why Heinz wasn't doing something about the situation and seemed to accept it. She was devastated. This must have been horrific for her. We were all praying that Father was alive and all right. Mother was so upset she was incapable of working and looking after us girls, and she became quite ill. She had a nervous breakdown and had to go into hospital.

Mother did come out of hospital after a short time, but there was still no news of Father. She wasn't eating, and her health deteriorated, so she had to go back into hospital. While she was in there, Heinz got the awful news, and had to tell Mother that Father had been captured. It was almost impossible, and one can only imagine Mother's grief. She was already thinking the worst, but was praying that Father would be joining us really soon.

She never came out of hospital. Her heart was broken. She became gravely ill with pneumonia and unfortunately died. It was very hard for me to understand where my mother was, and it wasn't until I was older that I realised I would never see my mother again. Heinz told my sister and me, and also, I found out a bit later that my father was captured by the Germans. He was taken to a concentration camp and later gassed, along with thousands of Jews.

With no mum and dad, we were suddenly orphans. We lived with Heinz, (our only surviving relative) and Alice for a short time in Scotland, but we then went to England, where Heinz bought a small place in London. Living with Heinz was not possible on a permanent basis, as his job entailed travelling. He was a Presbyterian minister preaching the Gospel in different parts of the world, and a journalist.

When I was nearly six Heinz told me that he had organised for Lydia and me to live with other boys and girls who had lost their mothers and fathers in the war. It was an orphanage in Berkshire. I was very scared and did not want to go, but my uncle said he would come and visit us as often as he could. He also said to us that we must stay together, and I should always look after my little sister. We said our goodbyes to Aunt Alice and Marion, and Uncle took us in his car to the orphanage. We were asking questions in the car and looking out of the window. I can still remember this place out in the country, a big brick two storey building with a pointy roof, standing way back from the road, with a long driveway and lots of big trees. It had a big double gate with the name Battle written on, which my uncle had to open and close. We saw boys and girls running around noisily. Then they stopped, all watching us coming up the drive. As we got out of the car a lady came towards us. She said hello to us and spoke to my uncle. Children were running towards us to see what was happening. We could hear a train going by.

My uncle talked to the lady and then we were shown inside. There was a big entrance hall with a wide spiral staircase in front. I had never seen stairs before. These had a wide banister, brown and very shiny, on one side and the wall on the other. A girl was sliding down the banister and this lady who was with us told her off. It's funny how one remembers certain things. This lady showed us around. We went upstairs and she took us to a room which had a double bed. This was for my sister and me to sleep in. My uncle talked a bit more to the lady and then said to me, "Always look after your little sister," and told us to be good. He said the lady would look after us. He would be back soon to see us. I felt so frightened, and didn't want him to leave. Lydia and I were both crying, and we clung onto him and gave him big hugs. The lady held our hands and told us her name was Margaret, and she called out to a girl called Sarah to come and talk to us and take us outside to have a look around.

Chapter 4

We heard another train, and Sarah said, "Hurry up – follow me!" We ran across the sloping lawn to the back garden, which was huge and surrounded by a high brick wall, except that at the bottom of the grounds we could see the railway tracks. There was a big wire fence going all along the back of the property. A train came by and was going very fast. We shouted, "Where are you going?" and waved madly. My sister and I often did this and would wait and watch the trains, wondering where they were going as they rushed past. Sarah showed Lydia and me how to lie on the grass and roll down the steep embankment. This was fun. There we would wait for another train to pass. Climbing up the bank was quite hard.

A bell sounded, and that meant that everyone had to be inside – it was mealtime. There were long tables, and we children sat on benches to eat. There was a piano on the other side of this big room, and after the meal somebody played music. I looked after my little sister. I knew Mother would want me to take care of her. She never left my side, holding my hand or clinging to my clothes. It was all a bit strange and frightening. After our meal we played for a bit, and then we were taken upstairs to the room with the big bed, to get into our night clothes ready for sleep. We had the lights on, and then the ladies came to check if we were in bed. They switched the lights off. We didn't like being in the dark, and we cried. We started talking about what had happened in our day. The ladies, who had been standing outside our door, came in and said, "Stop crying. No talking. Go to sleep." When we heard them go downstairs, we would whisper. I made up a little story, and Lydia would soon fall asleep. This became something for Lydia and me to look forward to at night, and eventually we didn't mind the light being off.

After my sister fell asleep, I tried to do the same, but kept thinking of my mother and father, and my uncle and aunt. I was really unhappy.

The other boys and girls teased us as we were together all the time, and she did not leave me for one moment. I cried lots and was quite frightened. I did not want Lydia to see how unhappy and scared I was. I had to be strong for both of us. After a while I fell asleep.

I woke up hearing lots of noise in the hall. My sister was crying. A lady came into our room, saying it was time to be up and get dressed and then go downstairs for breakfast. After a few minutes we heard the bell, so we hurried up. We saw a girl standing with one leg over the banister, ready to slide down, so we thought we'd do the same. There were no ladies about. It was fun. Of course, if seen, we would be punished. We should already have been at the table, sitting in the same place we had sat the night before. It was all so strange and different from being with our aunt and uncle. We were the last to sit down, and we didn't like our breakfast, which was lumpy, cold porridge. We were told that we must eat it. We always left some on our plates. We tried giving it to some other children, but the ladies caught us and we got into trouble. Looking back, I think breakfast was one of our worst meals.

I remember one very wet day we played some games inside. Hide and seek was one. There were lots of rooms we could go into, even upstairs. We went into the big room, where my sister and I hid behind the piano. We squeezed ourselves between the piano and the wall and kept very still and quiet. It took ages for them to find us, well after the games were finished. We did get a scolding: "Do not go behind the piano!" It was difficult settling in and hard to make friends, other than Sarah, who was our only friend. She seemed to like us.

When it was fine, we could go outside to play, and run around. The grounds were so big. There were lots of trees we could climb or hide in. We would hear the bell, and that meant it was meal time. We didn't like the food much, and did not want to go inside, so we hid, and a lady would come looking for us. When she found us, she was very cross, and we were punished with a smacking and sent to bed, where we had to stay until the next meal time.

Chapter 5

At night, when we were in our room, we talked. Lydia would ask, "When are we going back to Uncle's?" I would say, "Uncle's coming to see us soon." I wanted my mum. When was she coming back to us? I remembered her going away. Father, of course, had not come with us. Lydia had been a baby and did not know our mum or dad. I had forgotten that Uncle had told us when we were in Scotland that Mother and Father had died. I did not fully comprehend what "died" meant, and it was not until I was much older that I understood we would never see Mum and Dad again. Then we learned what had happened.

Our Uncle Heinz did visit us at first, but came less often as time went by. We became upset when it was time for him to go, so looking back on it, I guess it was better for us in the long run for him to stay away, as we always wanted to go with him.

We would often run down to the bottom of the garden when we heard the whistle of a train. We called out, "Where are you going to?", waving madly, and sometimes we got a wave back. We would sit at the bottom of the bank waiting for the next train, and do it all over again.

A few weeks went by, and I was told it was time for me to go to school. I was way old enough – I was nearly seven, but because of circumstances had not started school. The children who went all walked to school, and I was to join them on the Monday. The lady in charge talked to me and my sister, telling her she was not old enough to go, and I would be back in the afternoon. This was huge for both of us. We had not been separated before. I didn't want to go, and Lydia said she wanted to come with me.

I remember how awful that day was, Lydia clinging onto me, and the lady holding Lydia, who was crying and screaming for me not to go. She couldn't understand why I would leave her behind. Never had I done that before. I was so miserable about it. The lady said that we would be together soon. I had to walk with Sarah and other boys and girls, and one of the ladies came with us for the first few days. There were a lot of us, all walking. It seemed a long way. Later I was told that it was one and a half miles there and back. We passed fields with lots of trees and a big pond before we reached the school. The lady left us there and said she would pick us up in the afternoon. It was such a long day. I felt that it would never end. I did not like it much, and wanted to be with Lydia. When the lady came to pick us up, I was happy to leave. We all had to walk back, and some of the children were taking their time, walking very slowly. We had to wait for them. The lady said we all had to walk together, and I wanted to hurry back to Lydia.

When we reached the hostel, I was told that Lydia hid by herself, and nobody could find her for hours. They had a search party out looking for her, and eventually she was found. She had managed to hide in a cupboard full of linen. She was crouched on a shelf with towels over her. They thought she had got out and followed me. After this episode they said they would keep a closer watch on her. I was so worried and scared. What if Lydia did something worse when I wasn't with her, and hurt herself? I knew she would never leave me on purpose. We were both so unhappy.

Later that afternoon, Lydia and I tried to run away. We wanted to see if we could catch a train and find out where it went. We ran to the back garden and tried to find a way out, but there wasn't any that we could see. Then we ran to the front and thought we could climb over the gate. We had to be careful because of the wire on the top, but when we touched the gate there was this awfully loud noise, which was an alarm. It was not long before a lady came to see why the alarm was sounding. Again, we were punished with a smacking and sent straight to bed until the next morning.

After the lady no longer walked with us to school, I remember a day when we had our hats, gloves and scarves on. It was a freezing cold morning and we were on our way to school. Walking down the lane, fenced all the way along, we passed fields and then saw the pond. We were not meant to go in there. A few of the children climbed the fence, and one of the girls shouted out, "Climb over, or are you a scaredy cat?" I did climb over. The pond was frozen over, and they decided to see if they could walk on it, and we did. I must say I was very scared. We were a bit late for school that day. On our way back from school we climbed the fence again. The pond still looked frozen, so we walked on the edges, and as we walked further in, the ice cracked, and two girls and I fell in and got very wet. Luckily it was not very deep, and we were able to scramble out OK.

On arriving back at the hostel, we all got into a lot of trouble. We had to change out of our wet clothes, have a wash, and go straight to bed with a smacking and without any dinner. That was our punishment. My little sister came to our room. She had been waiting for ages for me to come back. She was still upset that I had left her behind. Of course, she wanted to know what had happened. Lydia was called to come down for dinner, which she did, and she managed to bring me something to eat, hiding it under her clothes. We both looked forward so much to Saturdays and Sundays, when we could have time together.

The following Saturday Lydia and I said, "Let's try again.", to see if we could find out where the train started from and try to get on one and run away. The fence was extremely high, and we weren't able to get out. We were so unhappy. The ladies decided that as we had never been apart, I should only go to school two days a week, as Lydia was so traumatised. Margaret felt it was better for Lydia that I stay back so we could play together. I helped to look after the littlies. Sometimes Margaret played the piano and we would sing and play games. Slowly Lydia became happier, knowing that on the days I did go to school I would always come back, but she still hated me leaving her.

Chapter 6

Margaret was the lady who was nice to us. We really liked her. Some of the other ladies would shout and get cross. I was still not going to school full time when our uncle made contact, telling us that Battle (the establishment's name), was closing, and we were going to another orphanage, in London, called Doctor Barnardo's Home. Of course, by then Lydia and I had mixed feelings about leaving Battle. It had taken us a long time to settle here. What was the next place going to be like? Would it be worse? We got to know some of the girls and ladies – not that we really liked it where we were – but this news was scary for us. It wasn't just us – all the children were unsettled during those last weeks. Talking among ourselves we could not find any of us who were going to London, to the same orphanage as we were.

A few weeks passed and the day arrived for us to leave. There were still children there who would be leaving in the next few weeks. I think we were two of the first to go. Saying our goodbyes, especially to Sarah, was much harder than we thought. We shed a few tears. I can still remember this place, even now, when I think about it and close my eyes. It has left a lasting impression on me. We were there for three and a half years, but once we were in Uncle's car and being driven, we were so pleased to see him we chatted a lot. It was a very long drive, passing lots of buildings, cars, buses and trucks on the roads. It was very noisy, and late in the afternoon when we arrived. The place was huge, standing quite close to the road. A lady greeted us and took us into a room where my uncle talked with her.

Another staff member took Lydia and me and showed us around. We passed children who stopped to stare at us as we were going down the passages. We went into this long room, a dormitory, which had lots of beds all in a row. We had never seen anything like this before, and we were told we would be sleeping with the other children in one of those beds. I remember how noisy this place was. We could hear the traffic going by, and there were lots of children talking everywhere, some of whom we had seen and passed while we were being shown around.

Then the lady took us back to the room where our uncle was. He said he would have to leave us now, but would come and see us soon. Once again, we said our goodbyes. It was all so different from where we had been. There was hardly any garden, a high brick wall and a tall gate, which was very close to the road.

We went down even more passages and were taken to a dining room with tables and chairs, where we had our first meal. We had to queue for our dinner. There was lots of pushing and shoving and chatter, until we reached these ladies who put dinner on our plates. We all received the same, and had to take it back to where our tables and chairs were, and find a place to sit. Lydia became separated from me by some girls pushing into the queue, and I found I could not sit with her. While I could see her, she wasn't really eating much, and some of the girls were taking food off her plate to add to theirs. I asked one of the ladies, who told me I couldn't do anything about this. I had always looked after Lydia before and she had always been with me. Now it was not like that. I asked if she could be with me for meals and have a bed next to mine, and was told we were allowed to have a bed next to each other, but at mealtimes you sat with other children, depending on who was around. I was also told that Lydia was old enough to fend for herself – she was now nearly five. I felt awful about this.

We were both miserable, and there were some very bossy children who gave us a hard time. The food was not that nice, but you would go hungry if you did not eat it. You would eat it as fast as you could before it disappeared from your plate. I made sure at our next mealtime that Lydia stood in front of me, and I kept close behind her, not letting anybody push in. It was here that I really learnt to stand up for myself and Lydia, and gave as good as was given to me. In order to survive, I grew up determined not to let anybody push me around anymore. I became strong.

Chapter 7

At bedtime, we had a wash, got into our nightclothes, and then into our single beds. How different this was for us, as we used to sleep together in a double bed. We could talk together about anything that was worrying us, and I always made up a story for Lydia before she went to sleep. Her bed was next to mine, but there was quite a bit of space between beds, so we really couldn't talk. Lydia was asking to come into my bed, but of course the lady said this was not allowed. "You're in the bed next to hers. What is all the fuss about? Go to sleep!"

When the lights were switched off, Lydia came into my bed, and we talked. I was still able to tell her a story, and get her to go back to bed. There was a lot of talking in the dormitory, and it was some time before anybody came and checked on us. When we heard the ladies coming, we all went quiet. They would come around with a torch to see if we were asleep. If we were not, we were told to go to sleep. When they came around for the second time and we were still not asleep, we would be punished next day. So, we soon learned to pretend to be asleep, lying very still with our eyes shut.

In the daytime we were always kept inside, and missed being able to go outside in the garden and run around in the fresh air. We missed hearing the trains go by, and I guess we really missed Battle. This place was noisy, with outside traffic, and so many loud and bossy children running around. After a short time, our uncle came to visit us and took us out. He said he hoped we would not be staying here too long, as he was applying for us to be fostered, and live in a house with a foster aunt and uncle who would look after us. He told us that these foster parents were unable to have children, and it would make them very happy if we went to live with them. They were looking forward to us coming.

He told us he would come often to see us, as he was living in London, and take us out. While we were at Dr. Barnardo's there were rooms where the older children went to have lessons, given by different ladies. It was like school, so we were not missing out. A lot of this I did not understand, and found it boring. The younger children were supervised elsewhere. Later in the day we all mixed, and I could be with Lydia. What I do remember is children running around a lot inside, doing whatever they wanted to do. It was so noisy. We tried to join in with what was going on, but often there were fights amongst the children. Personal belongings would end up in different places. This would start the shouting, and set everything going again. The ladies did not seem to be able to control what was happening. It was always noisy. Neither of us liked it here.

It was really good when Uncle did come and visit us and take us out. Each time he came he would tell us a little more about where we were going to live. It was in Essex, 48 miles from London, and we would be living in a two-storey house. He said it had a garden, which he knew we would be pleased about. We thought that was great. He said he was waiting for paperwork to be finalised. He took us back in the afternoon and said he would tell us more when he came next time. He was coming every two weeks. This made it exciting, so we knew exactly when he would be arriving. We looked forward so much to seeing Uncle again. Sometimes he took us back to where he lived, and we would see our Aunt Alice again. It was good. I felt I had a connection with her. When it was time to leave, we used to get upset, and Uncle felt it was not a good idea to continue this. He would take us to a park where we had fun on swings and slides, and were able to run around. We saw trees, plants and flowers, which we never saw at Dr. Barnardo's.

After Uncle took us back, we wanted to keep together as much as we could, and stay out of trouble. Each day that went by brought us closer to when we would see Uncle again. On his next visit Uncle said, "I have good news. The next time I come you will be leaving here." He wanted us to know that all had been finalised. He told us he was our guardian and would be keeping in contact with the foster aunt and uncle to find out how we were going. He explained to us that his job was taking him to different parts of the Continent and he would be travelling a lot – he was a journalist -- so he would not be able to see much of us. He also said that this foster aunt and uncle would be like our mum and dad, but we were to call them Aunt and Uncle, and they would look after us. Then he said, "I have some exciting news, which I know you will like. We will be travelling by train to Essex." Uncle knew we had always wanted to go on a train, after seeing the trains passing by at Battle. This made us happy.

Our uncle took us back to Dr. Barnardo's, the last time for us. In two weeks, he would come, he said. "You will be leaving here and I will be taking you to your new home." We were very excited at this news, and were looking forward to leaving. Both of us wanted to leave here, and would not be sad about it. We hadn't made any friends, and there wasn't anybody we would miss. We were counting the days until we would be saying goodbye to this place. The day finally arrived and the ladies had our few belongings packed. Uncle was waiting in the same room that we had been in when we first arrived. We saw the same lady again, who said goodbye to us and hoped we would be happy in our new place.

We went in Uncle's car to the railway station. He held our hands, as we had to get on the escalator. This was something we had never seen – moving stairs. Uncle said, "This is an adventure for you." We walked to the right platform, where we had to wait for our train. We saw other trains coming in and out of the station. People were all in a hurry, except those waiting for the train with us. The train finally arrived, and we managed to get a seat near the window, and we were able to look out as the train roared past. We saw lots of gardens and fields and the train stopped at many stations. We were excited, and asked Uncle questions concerning our aunt and uncle. He said we must wait and see – they would meet us when we got off the train. It took one and a half hours to reach Colchester, and we enjoyed the journey.

It was time to get off. We walked with Uncle to the waiting room. He said our foster aunt and uncle would meet us in there. We went inside, where there were lots of people sitting on seats. As we walked in a lady and man stood up and started walking towards us. Uncle spoke to them and I knew these were our foster parents. We were introduced and left the waiting room to go to a café, where we got something to eat and could all talk together. Our foster aunt said, "My name is Aunty Jean, and that is what you must call me, and this is Uncle Stan," as she turned towards him. She did most of the talking. I noticed that she looked different to the other ladies we had had. She was older, and her hair was pulled back in a bun. She was a bit stern looking. She spoke very precisely, and I wasn't too sure I would like her. However, Uncle Stan was friendlier and chatted to us, while Aunty Jean was walking with and talking to our uncle. He said they had a dog called Monty, a cocker spaniel, and when he walked him, we could go too. "Monty lives outside in a kennel, but sometimes he's allowed inside for a treat." We arrived at the café.

Chapter 8

Uncle Stan was chatting a lot to us while Aunty Jean was talking with our uncle. She was not impressed, and asked Uncle Stan to listen to what our uncle was saying. He was telling them all about us, and Aunty Jean said that we should all be getting to know each other. After a while, when we had finished eating, we left the café and had to catch a bus to where they lived. They did not have a car. This took about half an hour. After getting off the bus we had a bit of a walk before reaching the house. Uncle Stan held our hands as we walked, while Aunty Jean was still walking with and talking to our uncle. There were lots of houses all in a row. We reached their house, the one at the end, next to a vacant block.

There was a small gate with a path leading up to the house, and a hedge on one side, where the vacant block was. On the other side of the path was a small garden with flowers and a grassy area. We opened the gate and went up the path to the front door, where Uncle Stan had the key ready to unlock the door, and we all went inside. We entered the front room on the left and all sat down. There was more talking. After a while we were shown around the house. Our uncle came with us. First, we went up the stairs to a landing where there was a small room directly opposite. We were told this was always under lock and key, and was not for us to enter. There were two more bedrooms, and ours had a big double bed, which had four black posts with a brass knob on each. So, we would be sleeping together once more. I thought this was good.

The bathroom had a bath and toilet in it. Going back down the stairs, we walked past the front room, down the hallway and into the kitchen, which was quite big. There was a wooden table with four chairs around it. The back door led off the kitchen to the garden. Outside near the back door was a kennel. Monty came out to greet us. He was a spaniel with a copper-coloured coat and droopy ears, and was very friendly. We were then shown the back garden. It was small, and there was a greenhouse at the bottom of it. Uncle Stan told us that he grew seedlings and small plants in it, before they were planted in the garden.

We went back inside and there was more talking. Then it was time to say goodbye to our uncle, which was very hard for us. He gave us big hugs and we clung onto him. We both cried. I was wondering how we would like it here. I remember Uncle saying that Aunty Jean would be like a mum to us. I felt tears come into my eyes. "She's not like a mum. I want my mum. I want to be hugged and loved." But I had to be strong and not show how I felt. We did not want him to go. He promised he would be in touch with us really soon. After our uncle left Aunty Jean said, "Now, come and sit down, both of you. There are things you need to know. We have rules here that you must obey. You must always do as you are told, and speak the truth, no matter what." Aunty Jean and Uncle Stan were religious people. Aunty Jean was a strict person, Uncle Stan less so. She would tell him what to do, and he would do it, and that is how it was. She spoke for both of them.

I noticed Aunty Jean made more fuss over Lydia, as she was tiny and cute. But it was not long before I realised that she was not too fond of me, and in fact quite cool towards me. Uncle Stan tried to make up for this by being nicer to me. He was always looking to make sure he was doing what Aunty Jean wanted him to do. Aunty Jean said, looking at me, "We must get you to school. You have a lot to make up, as you have missed out so much on proper schooling. You will have to work hard to catch up." I knew straight away how it was going to be, and felt again I was not going to get any love from her. I did not think I would feel any love for her either. What she said made me feel that this was my fault. There was no understanding of our circumstances. She then continued, saying that we would be going to Sunday school and church on Sundays. "Now go upstairs and wash your hands, and I will have dinner ready. Don't be long."

Lydia and I ran upstairs, chatting, saying, "At least we can sleep together." In the bathroom, while washing our hands, Lydia said, "Why wasn't Aunty Jean nice to you too?" She had noticed this as well. I said, "Don't worry. I'll be fine. Maybe it's only today she's like that. But I'm glad she's nice to you. Uncle Stan is nice." She agreed. We heard Aunty Jean calling out from the bottom of the stairs to us to come down. "Dinner is served." We ran down the stairs to the kitchen, where our meal was on our plates. We were told, "No running in the house."

As we picked up our knives and forks to eat, Aunty Jean said, "Please put them down." We looked at each other. "First we must say grace." Then she turned to Uncle, "Say grace, please." Then to us she said, "Now close your eyes and listen to what is being said. For what we are about to receive, make us truly thankful, Amen."

"You will be taking a turn to say grace in the future, so remember it," she said.

When dinner was finished, which was quite nice, Aunty Jean said that Uncle Stan would do the dishes, and I was given a tea towel to wipe them. I was also told that when Lydia got older, we would take this in turns, but until then this would be my job.

Aunty Jean took Lydia and went into the front room. When I finished wiping the dishes, Uncle showed me where to put them away, and said this was part of my job too. "Don't worry if you can't remember where everything goes. Just ask me. It will take you a few weeks to settle in, and it is bound to be a bit strange for you for a while." He also said that if I was worried about anything, I was to ask him.

We then joined Lydia and Aunty Jean. When she saw us come into the room, Aunty Jean stood up. I could tell that Lydia had been sitting on her lap. Aunty Jean didn't want me to see that. She went on to say, "We must take your belongings and go upstairs and unpack." There was an empty chest of drawers all ready for us. We started to get our things out of our bags and sort them out, and Aunty Jean said, "Put them all on the bed. I will show you how to fold your clothes, put them away and hang them up in the wardrobe." When this had been done, she said, "Now I'll run a bath. Then you can get into your night clothes." We went into the bathroom. We were shown where to put our dirty clothes – in a large laundry basket in the bathroom. The hot water came out of a geyser at the end of the bath. Turning on the taps, she said, "You can get in together, one at each end of the bath, and give yourselves a good wash. I'll be back soon," she said, as she was closing the door.

When we were on our own, I asked Lydia, "Did Aunty Jean put you on her lap and hug you? She said yes. This was our introduction to a bath. We chatted and said how different things were. There was a long window above the bath. I stood up to see what I could see, and as I was looking out over the front garden I noticed on the other side of the road, a bit further down, there was a tall metal frame like a tower. This stood on its own with a fence all around it. There was traffic going past, but we were high up, so nobody could see in. That was what we were both doing (Lydia really couldn't see) -- standing up and looking out of the window – when Aunty Jean suddenly opened the door, holding our night clothes. We both sat down fast, and water splashed over the bath onto the floor and over Aunty Jean, who got wet. It was not a good beginning to our first night. Of course, we did get a telling off, directed more towards me – being the eldest, I should know better: "Don't let me ever catch you doing that again!"

Once we were in our night clothes and had cleaned our teeth, we went downstairs to say goodnight to Uncle Stan. I wanted to give him a hug. Aunty Jean said, "No need for you to do that. Just say goodnight to Uncle Stan." Then Aunty Jean took us upstairs to our bedroom, and we climbed into the bed, which was quite high. Aunty Jean just stood at the door and said, "Goodnight. See you in the morning. Get dressed before you come downstairs." I noticed she had put clean clothes out on chairs, which were on either side of our bed. She turned off the light and closed the door. We heard her go downstairs. We talked about what had happened that day. Neither of us was sure we would like being here. Lydia wanted me to make up a story and tell it to her.

We were talking and did not hear Aunty Jean come into our room. She heard us. I said, "I was making up a story for Lydia." She said, "Bed is for sleeping. No more talking." With that she closed the door, and we could hear her going down the stairs again. We both knew we would have to whisper, just like it had always been, or we would be in trouble if heard. In the morning when we woke, we dressed and then went into the bathroom, before running down the stairs, where both Uncle and Aunty were in the kitchen having breakfast. Aunty said, "You have slept in." As it was our first night, she said, we had not been woken, but we would all eat meals together in future. I wanted to know what we were doing that day, and was asking questions.

It was then I realised how our time here was going to be. We were told no talking at the table, grace before meals, sit up straight, and speak when you're spoken to. When meals were finished, we had to take the dishes to the sink. Uncle always did the dishes, I did the wiping up and putting away, and Aunty Jean would take Lydia to the front room. Once we were done, we would join Lydia and Aunty Jean, and there would be a discussion of what would happen for the rest of the day. School was the first priority, and it was not long before it was organised. It was in Lexden, where we lived.

Lydia was now old enough to start school too. I was to make sure that she was all right at playtimes. She was so excited about going to school, but I wasn't. I knew it would be difficult for me, as what schooling I had had been little, and interrupted by circumstances. Now, at eight years old, I found I had a problem, because I had not been at school like other children. I was behind for my age, and became sensitive about giving my age to anyone. It has stayed with me all these years. This did not add to my relationship with Aunty, whereas Lydia absolutely loved school. I would see her at playtimes. She was always happy to see me, and I helped her to make some friends of her own age, and I would end up playing and joining in too.

I was given homework to do, and was told I was way behind other boys and girls of my age. I did not know any of what was talked about in class. Uncle Stan would pick us up from school. We had quite a walk home. He said he would help me with my homework after dinner. On our way home we passed some shops, and he stopped at a sweet shop. We all went in, and he bought us a packet each of Dolly Mixture. That was fun, and we had to eat the sweets as we were walking, before we got home. He said, "Make sure you eat your dinner tonight. It's our little secret, all right?" We agreed. We got to like him, and we noticed how different he was on his own, when Aunty Jean was not around.

Chapter 9

When we got home from school, we had to take our school shoes off and carry them to the back door. Then Aunty Jean said, "Now go to your bedroom and change out of your school clothes. There are some clothes on the chair for you to wear around the house. Hang your clothes neatly on the back of the chair, then come down to the kitchen." We chatted as we raced up the stairs, saying, "Aunty Jean will ask us about our day." Lydia was excited. She just loved school, and was glad that I was there at playtimes. I found it all too hard and did not like it at all. We hurried and changed our clothes, and ran down to the kitchen, where Aunty Jean said, "Now sit down. There is a glass of milk for you to drink." Lydia and I were talking about our day, but Aunty Jean said, "Stop. After dinner we talk about your day at school. First there are some jobs to be done."

I was told that my job was to clean our school shoes, which had to be done outside the back door. I was given shoe polish, a brush and a cloth to carry. Then Aunty Jean said, "Come out with me and I will show you how to clean them." Lydia came out with me and Uncle Stan was already out in the garden. I wanted to run and see what he was doing, but was told, "Stand still. Now watch what I am doing." Aunty Jean gave me the cloth and I had to make the shoes really shiny. That was one pair done. "Now I will leave you to do the other pair," she said. Lydia wanted to stay with me. Aunty Jean said no. She always wanted Lydia with her. I felt she was trying to separate us. "Bring them in when you have finished, so I can see if you have done them properly."

After they had gone inside, I saw Monty was watching me. I went to pat him. He was always pleased to see me. Poor Monty! He had a collar and chain, which was attached to the side of his kennel by a rod, so he could only run a short way, then back to the kennel. Aunty Jean would knock on the window. "Have you cleaned those shoes yet? Bring them in." She inspected them. This was my job every day. There were times when I was sent out again – they were not done properly, she would say. I remember one day I put the shoes and polish on the ground and patted Monty, then ran down the garden to see what Uncle Stan was doing in his greenhouse. I loved talking to him and seeing what he was doing, planting seedlings into pots, and he would tell me about them. I saw how those seedlings would grow. I took a real interest and wanted to learn about plants. It was from there that my love of gardening started. Uncle Stan asked, "Have you finished cleaning the shoes?" I said, "Oh no!" and ran back to do them.

This time, when I ran back to where I had left the shoes, I discovered I had left them too close to Monty's kennel, and he had chewed one shoe. Black polish was on his face and on the concrete. I did get a good telling off and was sent to our room with a smack. Aunty Jean said I was old enough to know better. She would have to tell our uncle I was not behaving myself. It seemed a long time before I was allowed out of the room. Lydia was sent to get me to come down for dinner. She was carrying some clean clothes in her arms and dropped them on the bed. Aunty Jean said I was to help her put them away. This was our together job, she said. We chatted. Lydia told me she had helped to fold the clothes, and her other job was to set the table at mealtimes. She said to me, "I'll help you with the shoes when I'm older. Don't leave them near Monty again." She was quite upset about it. I said, "I won't. I've learned my lesson." I had to have another pair of school shoes.

As we were going downstairs, Lydia was telling me "We are having dumplings for dinner. They are like balls. I wonder what they taste like?" Uncle Stan and Aunty Jean were in the kitchen, talking. They stopped when we walked in. Aunty Jean said, "Now sit down." Grace was said by Uncle Stan. "Have you had these before?" she asked, as she served the dumplings on the plates. We hadn't, we said. There was lots of gravy put on, with two dumplings each. They were quite hard, and as I cut into them, gravy went everywhere. I did not like them, which did not go down well. Aunty Jean cut Lydia's for her, and she didn't like them either. Aunty Jean then said we must eat them. "There are some things in life we don't like, but must do, and food is the same. You must eat, or you will go hungry." So, we had to try and eat them. Because we were really slow, both Uncle Stan and Aunty Jean got up from the table and started clearing up the dishes. When they weren't looking, Lydia gave me some of hers, and I managed to hide some of both of ours in my hanky. I put it up my knicker leg, as our dresses were quite short. We had to have a hanky with us at all times in case we needed to blow our noses. When we were still young schoolchildren, this is what we did.

When Aunty Jean turned around and saw our plates, there were only some small pieces left. She said, "Good. You have taken long enough. Just put the rest in your mouths and eat it. There are some boys and girls who haven't enough food to eat. Remember that you must eat what is put in front of you." That is how it was. There were quite a few foods we did not like, and managed to hide in our hankies. The weather was cold and frosty, and there were long icicles hanging from the eaves. When we could, we went outside and gave the food to Monty, who got rid of it very quickly. I remember this happening once, and it was bedtime. I still had food in my hanky when we got to our bedroom. What we did was very naughty. The large brass knobs on our bedposts, we found, would unscrew. We took them off and put food down there. We could not have done this too often, as it was never discovered – there was no smell.

When our dinner with the dumplings was finished, and the routine with me wiping dishes and putting them away, I then had to do my homework on the kitchen table. Uncle Stan said he would help me with it, but Aunty Jean said, "No. She should be able to do it by herself." Then they both went with Lydia to the front room. I just sat there. I did not understand any of it. I hated having to do homework. I had never done anything like this before. I was so unhappy, and I started crying. After a while Uncle Stan was sent in to check on me. He said, "Stop crying. I'll help you with it.", and he showed me how to do it. He ended up doing it for me. Aunty Jean was not aware that he was helping me that night. We went back into the front room. Aunty Jean said, "Now you can talk about your day at school. What did you do? Did you make any friends?" By then, those feelings of excitement and enthusiasm about our day had gone. But this routine, which we had to have, was so hard for us. We couldn't be children. We were suddenly made to be young ladies. We had jobs to do and could talk only at certain times. How I missed being able to talk whenever we wanted to, also playing and running with Lydia, and being around other boys and girls.

Aunty Jean said, "You will be bringing readers home from school soon. I will be hearing you read after dinner every night before bed." Looking at me, she said, "You will be getting the same reader as Lydia to start with, as you have never done any reading before, and you can help each other." I said to myself that we could help each other. I thought this was good. Then Aunty Jean said, "Now go upstairs and get ready for bed. Come down when you're in your night clothes." This was the only time we could chat – while we were going up the stairs. Lydia said, "It will be good to have readers. It will be like another story for me, and I will learn to read it by myself." Lydia was so eager to learn, and this was something I was really interested in too. As I was always making up stories for Lydia, it would be so great for me to be able to read a story as well.

Still chatting, we went into our room to get undressed and put on our night clothes, and into the bathroom to clean our teeth. We only had a bath on a Saturday night. We would have a wash using the basin every day. Aunty Jean called out, "Stop talking. You should be down here by now to say goodnight to Uncle Stan." So, we hurried and ran down the stairs, and she said, "Say goodnight to Uncle Stan." We always wanted to give him a hug – hugs were not allowed. Aunty Jean then came up with us to make sure we got into bed. As she was turning off the light she said "Goodnight. I will wake you in the morning, and remember, we all have breakfast together!" We heard her go downstairs. We started whispering to each other. I asked Lydia, "How was school?" and she said she liked it, and didn't mind too much living with Aunty Jean. I was happy that Lydia was feeling like this. She whispered back to me, "I hope you will like school soon, and make some friends. Please make up a story for me." So, I told her one of our favourites, which was: we were both in a lovely garden with lots of trees and flowers. There was a butterfly flying and then it sat on a flower, and we were running on the path, trying to catch up to it so we could see the lovely colours when it opened its wings. Then it flew away.

I looked at Lydia, and she had fallen asleep. I was thinking that I must try and accept it here. I wished I could know what other boys and girls of my age knew. I didn't have any friends of my own age, and was feeling so alone. More than anything I missed being loved, as I had been by my mum, and I still really missed her. But I had to keep this inside me and not show I was upset. Always I had to be strong. I was finding it so hard. I eventually fell asleep. We were woken by Aunty Jean, who said, "Time to get up and dress, and come down for breakfast. We are all eating together, so don't be long." We hurried up and went first to the bathroom, then down to the kitchen. Aunty Jean was serving our porridge in dishes. She said, "Sit down. You just made it. If you were any later, it would be cold, and you would still be eating it." She turned to Uncle Stan and said, "Say grace, please." We ate this hot but lumpy porridge and were then told to go upstairs to clean our teeth and brush our hair. Lydia's was short, but mine was quite long, and it had to be tied back. Aunty Jean came into the bathroom to braid it. She made a parting down the middle and pulled back hard on my hair, and I would complain. Then she made it into two plaits, tied with elastic bands.

"You will need jumpers," she said, "It is very cold and frosty outside, also your hats and gloves." She opened a drawer and got out what we had to wear. Our hats were called pixies. They had a point at the top and looked a bit like bonnets, with a tie on each side so we could make a bow under our chins. Aunty Jean walked us to school, and Uncle Stan walked us home. We carried little cases in which Aunty Jean had packed sandwiches for our lunch. These were light, and looked as if they were made of cardboard. When we arrived at the school, which was fenced off with railings, Aunty Jean left us at the open gate. We went through into the playground, and she said goodbye. When the bell sounded, the gate was closed and locked by a teacher.

Chapter 10

I went with Lydia to her classroom, and said, "See you at playtime." She seemed to have made some friends already. They were calling her. I found where my classroom was and I said to myself, "I want to try really hard to see if I can learn something." I was asked by the teacher to hand my homework to her. She said I would be getting more to take home, and she would let me know at the end of the day how I went. At playtime I found Lydia, who was happy to see me. She was playing with friends, and I joined in. Some of the children had small bags made of material, with pull ties. These bags had marbles in. Then children would roll marbles on the ground, aiming for certain ones. Some were bigger than others, and they were colourful. The teacher would blow a whistle, which meant we had to form a line. Where the teacher stood there was a large red crate containing small bottles of milk. The teacher handed them to us to drink with straws. This happened every morning. When the bell went, it meant that we had to go back to our classrooms. I would take Lydia back to hers and then run back to mine.

When I got back the teacher was handing out small readers. She said, "Look at them. Can anybody read anything from them? If so, put your hand up." There were one or two children who put their hands up and said they could read. These readers had coloured pictures with only a few words. We learned to sound our letters to make words, and I felt -- yes --I really want to do this! It was then I made up my mind that if I didn't understand something, I would be brave and put my hand up. We were told we could take our readers home and bring them back next day, and we would be taking it in turns to read aloud in front of the class. For the first time, I felt I wanted to learn to read. This was something I was really interested in, and believe it or not, I was looking forward to trying to read a few words to Aunty Jean later, in the front room. I hoped she would help me sound out the words. I felt sure Uncle Stan would.

When the bell went again it was lunchtime, and I found Lydia on the other side of the playground. We got our cases, which were hanging up on hooks on a wall, and carried them to find a place to sit. We were not allowed to be inside, so we wanted to find somewhere to sit together in the playground. If it was freezing cold, we would huddle up under the porch near the door, and sit, if we could, on the concrete step to eat our sandwiches, which had bread and dripping (meat juices) in them. Then we would play till the bell rang, and I would take Lydia back to her classroom and return to mine.

We had to learn our multiplication tables, starting with 2s to 4s. The teacher asked us to recite them. I found I could remember them all right. She said to me, "Well done." This made me feel good. I had not been praised for anything much before. At the end of the class the teacher said, "Now put your readers in your bags to take home, and bring them back tomorrow. You will read to me in class what you did at home." When the bell rang again the teacher called my name to come and see her. "I have marked your homework. It was all correct," and she praised me again. Of course, it was really Uncle Stan who had done it. "I do believe you are at last beginning to understand this. I have more homework for you. Now this will be a bit harder. See how you go with it." I fitted this in my case with my reader. She said, "Aunty Jean told me she will be helping you with your reading." She was kind to me. I was thinking I must get Uncle Stan to explain it to me so that I would be able to do it by myself, even if it took me a long time to grasp things. Then I went to find Lydia, who was waiting outside her classroom for me. She was so excited. "I have a reader to take home," and I said, "I have one too." Lydia said, "Can I see yours?" I opened my case and Lydia looked in. "Oh good. It's the same as mine. We can read together."

Uncle Stan was waiting at the gate to walk us home. It became a routine for us to call at the sweet shop. He would let us choose sweets from large jars sitting on shelves. We were allowed to have a little bag of whatever we wanted. There were aniseed balls, which we loved. We would suck them, and Lydia would say, "Open your mouth. What colour is yours now?" As we sucked them, they changed colour, and we would try and see whose aniseed ball lasted longer. I loved humbugs too, with their black and white stripes. You could also get red and white striped ones. We often had dolly mixture too. Uncle Stan said, "Remember, this is our little secret. Mind you eat your dinner." If we didn't like our dinner, we would try to give it to Monty, otherwise it would go in my hanky, and I would get rid of it as best I could.

We told Uncle Stan that we had readers. We wanted to show them to him. He said, "When you are in the front room, we will see them and you can tell us all about them." I said I had had my homework marked and it was good, and I now had harder homework to do. He said, "I will try and help you." I asked, "I want to understand it. Can you please explain it to me? I want to try and do it by myself." We arrived home. He said, "Remember, shoes off. Carry them through to the back door, change your clothes, then come downstairs to have a drink. Then you will have your jobs to do." I was actually looking forward to when we would be in the front room with our readers to show what we had learned.

Lydia told me as we were taking our readers out of our cases that she knew some words. We chatted as we were changing our clothes. This was good. I wanted to check what Lydia knew, but we had no time, as Aunty Jean was already calling out, "Come downstairs to the kitchen and have your glass of milk. Jobs are waiting to be done." So, we hurried and did as we were told. I said, "I wonder what's for tea. I hope it's something we like." When I was outside doing the shoes, I got them done quickly. I was getting better at doing them, and I wanted to play with Monty. He was always so pleased to see me. Lydia was never allowed to come outside after school, so I did not see her again until dinner time. I would spend as much time as I could with Uncle Stan, watching him and talking to him in his greenhouse until Aunty Jean knocked on the window and called to me, "Bring the shoes in to be inspected." I was not sent out to redo them as often as before, which was something.

Aunty Jean would let me run down the garden to tell Uncle Stan that it was dinner time. I would ask him what he was doing, and he would show me some of his little seedlings, which were going to be planted in his allotment. I wanted to know what an allotment was, and he explained, "It's where you can grow more vegetables, and it is a little way behind the vacant block. You can come and watch me plant them on a Saturday." I knew that this was something we would be doing on Saturdays. Once we were inside, Aunty Jean was waiting to serve dinner, and our routine would start. Uncle Stan would say grace. We knew we had to stay silent, and very little was said by Uncle Stan and Aunty Jean at meal times. We sometimes had our favourite meal, one that Lydia and I both liked, toad in the hole, (I am not quite sure why it was called that – it was batter with sausages inside), or sometimes just batter on its own, which was called Yorkshire pudding. We thought that was yummy too. We didn't always like the vegies, and I had the hanky ready just in case.

Chapter 11

I do remember the first time we brought our readers (books) home. After the dishes had been done, we were told, "Go and get your readers." We raced upstairs. I also had this homework in my case, which I brought down. Aunty Jean said, "We will wait till you have done your homework, and then you can come into the front room and we will talk about your day and see the readers." Aunty Jean took Lydia, and Uncle Stan said he needed to explain what I had to do for my homework. Reluctantly Aunty Jean agreed, saying, "Don't be long." Uncle Stan showed me what to do, and I said, "I must try and do it by myself, even if I get some wrong." He was being called, so, leaving me, he said, "Do your best and don't get upset about it. Then come into the front room." I did try, but just couldn't understand what to do. I wished Uncle Stan could have been with me longer, so I could ask him more questions. I thought I would try, as Uncle Stan said, and wished I knew how to do it. Uncle Stan was sent to come and get me. I had put something on paper. Uncle Stan looked at it. He said he would ask Aunty Jean to talk to the teacher, and get her to help me. "Now come into the front room, and let's talk about your day."

Lydia would talk first, being younger. She was so eager to talk about what she had done at school and the friends she had made. She wanted to show her reader and sound out the words she knew, with the pictures. Before that, Aunty Jean said it was my turn to talk about my day. I said how we did our times tables, and the teacher had said "Well done." to me, when we recited them. It was as if we sang them, and I could remember some. We did this over and over in class in the mornings. Aunty Jean said, "Now let me see Lydia's reader." Then Lydia was asked to read. She knew quite a few words, and was so happy and excited about what she knew. Aunty Jean said how clever she was.

Then it was my turn. I opened my reader. I knew almost as much as Lydia. Aunty Jean said, "You still have some catching up to do. Remember, your sister is three and a half years younger than you." There was no praise or encouragement for me, except that Uncle Stan said, "You will get better in time." We closed our readers and it was time to get ready for bed, so, taking our readers with us, we climbed the stairs, chatting. Lydia said, "We have to put them in our cases, but we will know more tomorrow, with the teacher." I said, "Yes. I hope I can get quicker with sounding out the words. I want to catch up with girls and boys of my own age." We were being called by Aunty Jean to come down and say goodnight to Uncle Stan, so we hurried down the stairs. A. J. said, looking at me, "We will be leaving a bit earlier tomorrow, as I will be talking with your teacher to ask if you can get extra help with your reading, and if you should be in a different class."

Aunty Jean followed us and saw us get into bed. Turning off the light, she said, "No talking! Straight to sleep!" We heard her go downstairs and the door being closed. Lydia said, "I will help you with your reading."

"Thanks. That would be good." She was so eager to help me, and picked everything up quickly. She loved school. I said, "Tomorrow, when Aunty Jean takes us to school, I wonder what she will say to the teacher, and how the teacher will be with me after Aunty Jean has spoken to her to ask for extra help with reading as well, and whether I should be in another class." Lydia said, "Don't be upset. It will be all right. Please tell me a story." Well, I did, and it wasn't long before Lydia fell asleep. I just couldn't get to sleep. I kept thinking that I really didn't have any friends of my own. If I had to go to another class, would it be so bad? Then I thought, the teacher is kind to me. I like her. I would miss her. How do I know it would be any better for me in another class? I feel so alone. I must be strong. I miss my mum and uncle to talk to. And with that I eventually fell asleep.

We were woken by Aunty Jean, who said, "Don't be long. Remember, we are leaving earlier." We hurried to the bathroom and got dressed in time for our lumpy hot porridge. Uncle Stan said grace and we had to eat quickly. After cleaning our teeth and having our hair done – I hated having my hair brushed. It was always pulled back hard and braided, and I would always complain. Aunty Jean said, "I think we should get your hair cut short, like Lydia's. It wouldn't take so long to do, and I don't need to hear you complain every morning."

"I don't want my hair cut!"

"It's not what you want. It's what will be the best thing." Once we were ready, Aunty Jean walked us to school. This time she came through the gate to go to my classroom. I went with Lydia to play with her and her friends till we heard the bell. Then I ran back to my classroom. I was so worried about how the teacher would be towards me. She asked me to hand my homework in. "I will talk to you later. Now go and sit down." She sounded just the same as she always did. We always started with our tables. Every so often the teacher would stop us and ask a child a certain table to see if they knew it. It wasn't till lunchtime that I was called to stay behind.

The teacher said she had looked at my homework, and Aunty Jean had spoken to her about my reading. She had decided to spend more time helping me. I was to come to school earlier in the mornings for a while and she would see how I went with that. Most of my homework was wrong. She never asked how I got my other homework right. "Tomorrow Aunty Jean will walk you to school early, so no more homework today. Now off you go and have some lunch." She was nice to me, which made me feel a bit better. I ran to find Lydia and told her, and she said, "It will be all right. You will be able to do it soon by yourself, and I can help you too." When it was time to go back into class, we were asked to get our readers. The teacher chose a few of us to come out and read. When it was my turn, I went through a few more words to sound out with pictures, to read and see what I knew.

After listening to others before me I wasn't so worried. I wasn't the only one having a bit of trouble. The teacher was nice to everybody. We were to take our readers home and bring them back on Monday, as it was the end of the week. We had been at school for one week. I hadn't made any friends of my own, but the teacher had been kind to me, and that made me feel a bit better, and I had no homework for the weekend. I went to Lydia's classroom to get her. She was talking with other children. When she saw me, she was happy, and told me about her reader and all the words she could read. Uncle Stan was waiting at the gate, and we chatted to him. We were looking forward to going to the sweet shop. He asked me how I went with the teacher and my homework. When I told him, he was pleased that I was getting extra help to understand it. We chose our sweets, and Uncle Stan said, "Remember, this is our little secret." He said this each time we came out of the sweet shop, and we never told anybody that was what we did when walking home from school with him.

We asked, "What will we be doing on Saturdays and Sundays?", and he replied, "Aunty Jean will tell you when you're in the front room." Once we reached home, our routine would start all over again. Carrying our shoes to the back door, running upstairs to change, we chatted to each other, saying "I wonder what we will be doing on Saturdays and Sundays?" Then I said, "I don't want to be with Aunty Jean all the time, doing jobs." We agreed we wanted to play and have some friends. Again, we were being called, and this was the routine we had to obey. I was getting very good and quick at doing the shoes. This meant I had time to spare. Aunty Jean was inside with Lydia and I was bored. I decided to let Monty off his chain and run with me up and down the garden. He was so happy chasing me and we were having fun. I took him down to the greenhouse, where Uncle Stan was. He was shocked that I had let Monty off. He said, "Go and take him back to his kennel, before Aunty Jean sees you."

"I want to play with him. Can we walk him?"

"No. Dinner will be ready soon." I ran to put him on his chain. Then I ran back to Uncle Stan, to talk with him.

Monty was making this awful noise, howling and whining. Aunty Jean came outside and found out what had happened. I got a good telling off and a smack on the legs. I was told, "You must never do that again. It unsettles him." Uncle Stan came up the garden and said, "He will get walked tomorrow." Well, I found out that was another thing we would be doing on Saturday – walking Monty. What a way to find out! It was time to come in for dinner. Lydia had set the table, and I wondered what dinner would be. It was something we had not had before. It had lots of gravy and mincemeat, with some vegies. We didn't like it much, and I managed to hide some of the lumps in my hanky to give to Monty when I could, after dinner. Aunty Jean and Lydia went to the front room. I was with Uncle Stan, wiping the dishes. He said, "You have homework to do." I replied, "No, not until Monday, when I go to school early. The teacher will help me and give me some homework then." Uncle Stan said, "Go and get your reader and come into the front room." As I ran up the stairs, I could hear him going into the front room and the door being closed. I got the reader and ran back downstairs to the kitchen. I was on my own. I quickly opened the back door and gave Monty the food in my hanky. I then went into the front room. I had my reader ready.

Chapter 12

Aunty Jean said, "Let's talk about your day. Lydia is to speak first." She did, saying she had made some nice friends at playtimes, and she liked me being there too. She loved reading and school. When it was my turn, I said how a few children read aloud in front of the class, and I did too. I was told I had done well. Aunty Jean said, "You still have some catching up to do. Now I will tell you what we will be doing tomorrow, which is Saturday. Did you know that you have been with us for one week?", and we said yes. "We all eat breakfast together, and after that I will show you how to keep your room tidy." I pulled a face. Aunty Jean saw me, and said I was being cheeky. "You need to learn these domestic skills. I have a little job I do at lunchtime, so we'll have some lunch, and Uncle Stan will look after you, and I'll be home later in the afternoon." We looked at each other and smiled, and said, "Good." Aunty Jean could see we were happy with that. I was not sure she was too pleased about it. "Now get ready for bed, and come down to say goodnight."

So, we ran up the stairs, and I said to Lydia that we might have some fun while we were getting ready for bed and chatting. We agreed that Uncle Stan would not make us do jobs. We ran down to say goodnight to him, and Aunty Jean came up with us to see us get into bed. "I will wake you in the morning." Turning off the light, she said goodnight. We heard her go downstairs and listened for the door closing. We started whispering. I said, "I know we are going to be walking Monty." We both agreed that was good. I had spent more time with Monty than she had, being outside while cleaning shoes. Lydia was a bit scared of him, and not as fond of him. Of course, I was the one giving him food, leftovers from our meals, so we became firm friends. We were looking forward to seeing what our Saturday would be like.

We had been talking for quite a while and were wide awake when we heard Aunty Jean coming up the stairs. We held our breath. She stopped on the landing outside our door, near the little room. We heard her put a key in the door, and open it. Then there was a rustling noise, and in a little while the door closed. She turned the key again and went downstairs. We both whispered, "What could be inside?" I said, "I will try and find the key when Uncle Stan is looking after us, just to see what's inside." Lydia said, "Do be careful. Now can you please tell me a story?" so I did. It was easy for me, as I had a vivid imagination and enjoyed doing it. It wasn't long before Lydia fell asleep. I was thinking how things had changed for us. I really did not like it here, but what could I do but accept it? Lydia seemed to be settling in. Aunty Jean made lots of fuss over her. She was tiny and cute and enjoyed school, which was good.

I was a bit jealous, but I did not want to feel like that. I wished someone would show me some love and affection. I was on the solid side physically, and coming into puberty. I was finding everything so hard, as well as school. Our uncle was overseas, so I couldn't talk to him. Uncle Stan was all right, but didn't show me any love, and I couldn't tell him anything, because Aunty Jean ruled the roost. I wasn't allowed to hug him, and he couldn't show us any affection, only by buying sweets for us on our way home from school, which Aunty Jean didn't know about. I missed my mum so much, and remembered hugs and being loved, but I had to be strong. Then I thought that it was good that Lydia seemed to like it here. She hadn't known what I had experienced when I was younger and she was only a baby. It had not been so traumatic for her, which was a good thing, and I always wanted to look after her. So, I thought, work it out. I must make the most of it. We have each other. My mum would have been proud of me, I knew, and my uncle too. Thinking all these thoughts, I eventually fell asleep.

Aunty Jean woke us. It was Saturday. She said, "There are some clothes on the chair. Get dressed and come down for breakfast, and then we will talk." We jumped out of bed, went to the bathroom, got dressed and raced down the stairs. Breakfast was ready. Uncle Stan said grace, and there was no talking until breakfast had been eaten. Then Aunty Jean said, "You will learn to keep your room tidy. I will show you how to dust, and then you will need to shake the dusters." We were given a rag each and told to follow her upstairs into our room. She walked to the window and opened it wide. "First we need to have fresh air in the room." We were told and shown how to do some housework. We had never done anything like this before. Everything had been done for us – we were still children. Looking back on it, it was unbelievable how we grew up. Aunty Jean was so strict and straitlaced with us, and felt she was doing the right thing. We had to learn domestic duties and be young ladies. We didn't have much of a childhood. We had to grow up fast. I wanted to run and play and be out in the garden with Lydia. It was all jobs, jobs, and rules to be kept, or else.

Chapter 13

"First we must sort out your clothes." Some clothes were lying on the floor. Shock, horror! "Pick them up! Now you should know where to put dirty clothes – in the basket in the bathroom, and the rest get hung up in the wardrobe. When that has been done, the bed needs to be made up with clean sheets." Aunty Jean went to get the clean sheets. We had to take the dirty sheets off when that was done. Aunty Jean still had not come back. So, we climbed on the mattress and did some jumping up and down, having fun. I was the instigator, being older. Lydia would do whatever I did. We were only children, which we weren't allowed to be. Aunty Jean heard us as she was coming up the stairs. She was so cross with me. "Get off the mattress! What bad behaviour you are showing!" She smacked me on the legs. "You will damage the mattress. Now watch, and I will show you how to put the clean sheets on." So, opening the sheets, we had to hold a corner each, with a struggle, and tuck it in under the mattress.

Eventually the bed was made. Aunty Jean was getting quite exhausted with us, and she found it frustrating showing us how to do things. She became red in the face and crosser than ever. Both Aunty Jean and Uncle Stan would have been in their early fifties, so it wasn't an easy thing to take on two children. They were unable to have children, and probably did not realise what a job they had taken on. They were deeply religious, and as my uncle was too, he felt it was a good thing for us to be brought up by them.

We were shown how to dust. Aunty Jean said, "You dust some, and then you need to shake the duster." This meant running downstairs, through the kitchen, opening the back door and shaking the dusters. We made it a game, running up and down the stairs. Monty thought this was fun, jumping up trying to reach the duster and barking. Aunty Jean was becoming frustrated with Monty and us, and said, "That should be enough shaking the dust off. Now go upstairs and finish your room. I will be up soon to have a look." So, we just sat on the bed and talked. I said, "It will be good when Uncle Stan looks after us this afternoon. Hope we have some fun and no more jobs." In a little while we heard Aunty Jean come up the stairs. We jumped off the bed. She asked, "Have you finished your room?" We said yes.

She came in and had a look. There were two more pieces of clothing that we had to hang up. We also had the stairs to do, which were brown, wooden and shiny. They had to be dusted and had some marks on them. We were given a special cloth to use, and another to rub the marks off. We still made it a game. Aunty Jean went off into the kitchen. We had to tell her when we were finished. She came and checked what we had done. "Now go and wash your hands and come into the kitchen. I have something to tell you." We looked at each other. I said, "No more jobs, please." I got a stern look. "Just go upstairs to the bathroom and wash your hands." We chatted as we ran upstairs. I said, "I really don't want to keep doing jobs. I think we should ask if we can see our uncle, and tell him we have all these jobs to do." Lydia said, "It would be nice to see Uncle again, so let's ask Aunty Jean." We agreed that we would ask her.

When we had washed our hands, we went down to the kitchen, and I said, "We have something to ask you." Aunty Jean said, "Sit down. Now what is it?"

"We want to see our uncle."

"That is not possible. He is overseas. He will make contact when he is back." We asked, "When will that be?"

We were told that it would be a few weeks yet. We both said, "We really miss him."

"You have only been here for one week. It takes time to settle in. Now I have something to tell you. Remember the little job I told you about that I do on a Saturday? It's nearly time for me to go. There are sandwiches on the table ready for your lunch. I will call Uncle Stan to come in. He will look after you. Be good, please." Calling Uncle Stan, she said goodbye. We were so happy to see her go. We said we should have some fun now. Uncle Stan came into the kitchen and said, "Go and put your coats and hats on. It is very cold outside. We will walk Monty before lunch." I thought this was great.

Monty was on a lead and Uncle Stan was waiting for us. "We are going to walk across the road, so we need to hold hands, and then we will be going down a lane into the woods." We didn't know what the woods were, and he told us. It was exciting, so we set off, Uncle Stan holding the lead. I wanted to, and was told I could later on, when we were in the woods. We walked for a while, with Monty pulling Uncle

Stan, who kept saying "No!" to him. Monty was taking no notice – he was in a hurry to get there. We ran. It was fun. We reached the entrance. There were lots of trees, small paths, and some long grass, in which there were some lovely flowers growing. I asked if we could pick the flowers. Uncle Stan said we could on our way back. He asked me, "Do you want to hold Monty's lead now?" Of course I did. I think Uncle Stan was glad of the rest. I ran with Monty, Lydia following and Uncle Stan in the rear. After a while Monty slowed down, wanting to sniff. I asked, "Can he get off the lead now?"

"No. He could run away and get lost. He has never been off the lead."

Lydia didn't want to hold the lead, and she had started picking flowers. I wanted to pick some too. I gave the lead to Uncle Stan. Lydia and I had bunches of flowers in our hands. He said they were wild bluebells and snowdrops. It was time to turn around and head for home. When we arrived back, Monty was put on his chain again and given clean water in his bowl. Uncle Stan said, "Shoes off." We were told to go and wash our hands and then we would have lunch. We left the flowers near the sink. He said he would find something to put the flowers into. We ran up the stairs chatting. We agreed that was fun. Lydia asked, "What will we do after lunch?"

"Uncle Stan will tell us, and it won't be jobs, which is good."

Once we were in the kitchen and sitting down, Uncle Stan said grace. We shared the sandwiches and started eating. I asked, "What are we going to be doing when we have finished lunch?"

"No talking at mealtimes. I will tell you when we have finished eating."

Eating in silence was hard for us, but this was discipline we always had to have. We just wanted to chat and be children. I remember I would eat fast and be finished first, but it made no difference to Uncle Stan. "We must wait till we have all finished before I will tell you anything." I thought it would be different with Uncle Stan looking after us, and when he was on his own. He was nicer towards us, not so hard on us, but still stuck to the rules. Eventually we had all finished eating. "We are going to the allotment. It is cold outside. Put your coats, hats and shoes on and come down to the greenhouse."

Chapter 14

Uncle Stan had a large wheelbarrow and was putting a lot of seedlings in it, and some tools. "Follow me." There was a little gate in the fence on the side where the vacant block was. He unbolted and opened the gate. We were then in the middle of the vacant block. Closing the gate and bolting it again (it was high up), he said to us, "It's a bit of a walk. Follow me." We could hear and see children playing at the front of the vacant block. We asked, "Can we say hello to them and play too?"

"No, you must follow me," which we did.

Some of the children called out to us, waving. I waved back, and just kept following Uncle Stan. We came to a hedge that had an opening that led to the allotments. There were little paths that divided different people's plots. He kept walking. There were some people working. Some raised their hands to Uncle Stan and he responded. I asked, "How much further?"

"We are nearly there." A little further on, he stopped the wheelbarrow and said, "Can you carefully help me to take some seedlings out and put them on the ground over there?" He pointed to where he wanted them. We helped him to unload the wheelbarrow. "Now I'm going to plant these seedlings, and you can watch me." We did this for a little while, and then got bored, so we ran between the plots along the little paths, playing chasy. Some of the people who were working said hello to us. There were no other children about, but we could still hear those other children playing at the front of the block. That's what we wanted to do. We ran back and asked him, "How much longer are you going to be? We want to play with those children we saw." He said no, he must be with us all the time, and he wouldn't be much longer. So, we ran around a bit more, and at last he finished. He asked Lydia if she would like a ride in the wheelbarrow, as it was empty now except for a few tools. She said yes. I helped push with Uncle Stan, and we reached the vacant block.

There were still some boys and girls playing with the ball. One tall girl ran over to us and asked if we could play with them, and she would look after us. Uncle Stan said sorry, we couldn't – maybe another time. Turning to us, he said, "When you have been here a bit longer, we'll talk about it."

"Please! You could watch us for a while. We just want to play." Then I jumped up and down, saying, "Please, please, Uncle Stan." He said, "Let me put the wheelbarrow in the garden, and I'll think about it."

"We will be good, and you can watch us."

"All right. You can play for a little while and I'll watch." We were so excited, and said, "Thank you, thank you!" Uncle Stan walked with us to the front of the vacant block. The tall girl came running up to us. She told us her name was Betty. Uncle Stan came with Lydia and me and we walked to where the other boys and girls were. They were throwing a ball to each other to catch, and threw it to me. I didn't catch it, but they tried throwing it to Lydia, and she couldn't catch it either. She was the smallest one there.

They were nice to us, talking and asking questions, wanting to know all about us, "How long are you staying in the house next to the vacant block?" We said we weren't sure. Uncle Stan walked closer to where we were and said, "I think it's time to come home now. You have had a little play." So, we had to say goodbye. Betty said, "See if you can play again soon. I don't live that far away." She gave me a ball and said, "See if you can catch it next time." I said, "I will try and see you again soon." We thanked Uncle Stan. "That was fun."

"You can play in the garden for a little while. I have some more to do in the greenhouse. Then we will go inside." So, we had the ball, and I was throwing it against the wall and trying to catch it. Lydia was watching me. Sometimes I caught it after a few tries. Lydia wanted to try too. We were having fun. I threw the ball to her so she could have a turn, but I threw it too far and it landed on the greenhouse, breaking some glass. Uncle Stan had a shock and was very cross with me and said I shouldn't be throwing it to Lydia, as she wasn't able to catch it. "Now I will take the ball off you before it does any more damage. It's too dangerous to play in the garden." I asked, "Can we play on the vacant block with it? You can leave the gate open and see us." He said no, "Time to go inside. Aunty Jean will be home soon, and I must start getting dinner ready. Do not say anything about this to Aunty Jean." – looking at both of us. We said we wouldn't. I said, "I am sorry."

"Remember, there will be no more playing ball in the garden. Understood?"

We said yes. "Also, don't say anything about playing on the vacant block with the children. I will tell Aunty Jean myself. Now take your shoes off, put slippers on, go inside and wash your hands. Then come down to the kitchen." We ran upstairs, chatting. I said to Lydia, "We did have some fun. I wonder how Aunty Jean will be with me when Uncle Stan tells her what happened? And remember, don't say anything to Aunty Jean, will you?" Lydia said she wouldn't, and I hoped it wouldn't come out. We put our slippers on, went to the bathroom, washed our hands, and on the landing, I tried the door to the little room again. It was locked. I said to Lydia, "I am going to look for the key. You go to the kitchen. I will be down soon." She said, "Do be careful." I went to Aunty Jean and Uncle Stan's bedroom and opened the door. I had not been in there before. Just inside there was a big dark wooden dressing table which had a large mirror and two narrower hinged mirrors on either side which you could move, and see yourself from different angles. I was moving the side mirrors and looking at myself. I had not seen myself in the mirror before. I was fascinated, intrigued. Then I heard the front door open and Aunty Jean calling out, "I'm home." She walked through to the kitchen. I quickly put the mirrors back like I thought they were, closed the door and ran downstairs.

Aunty Jean turned around when I came in. "Where have you been?" I told a fib, "In the bathroom." Uncle Stan had started dinner. He was washing some potatoes that had been dug up on the allotment. They were very dirty. When washed, they had to be peeled. Aunty Jean said to me, "I can show you how to peel a potato." She got a peeler out of the drawer and took a potato from the sink. We watched her peel a potato. Now, looking at me, she said, "See if you can do it." I was given another potato and the peeler. I tried, but just couldn't do it. "You must practise, and you will." I sat on the chair with the potato and the peeler, and tried, but it was no good. Uncle Stan was using the knife to do them. Aunty Jean had a stew organised, and it wasn't long before dinner was ready. There was no asking about our day or what we had been doing. We wanted to talk and tell her, but were told, "After dinner we will talk about what you have been doing." We just wanted to say we had had fun, but we had to be silent and eat our dinner.

We were brought up with this strict discipline, regimental rules and good manners. It was not until years later that I found out Aunty Jean's behaviour and personality were not the norm. She was a very hard person, but thought she was doing the right thing for us and we would grow up well behaved young ladies – and we did. However, we missed out on being given any love and hugs, and on being children. Aunty Jean showed Lydia some affection, as she was so lovable, bright for her age, and keen to learn. Aunty Jean praised her, whereas I was struggling and had problems. How I wished she would say something nice to me!

After dinner and when the dishes were done, Uncle Stan and I joined Aunty Jean and Lydia in the front room. It was then and only then we could talk about our day. I wanted to talk first. I said, "We walked Monty to the woods. It was fun." Then Lydia started talking, and we were both talking at the same time about our day. Aunty Jean said, "One at a time." I said, "We picked some lovely flowers, and Uncle put them in a vase on the kitchen table. You never mentioned the flowers at dinner time." Aunty Jean said, "Is that where they came from?" She asked Lydia, "What else have you been doing?"

"We went to the allotments, and I had a ride in the wheelbarrow coming home." I said, "It's my turn to talk now. We watched Uncle Stan put the seedlings in the ground, and played chasy running along the paths in the allotments." Aunty Jean didn't seem too pleased. She gave me a stern look. I was looking at Uncle Stan. I knew he did not want me to say anything about us playing with the children. I asked, "What are we doing tomorrow? It's Sunday." Aunty Jean said we would be going to Sunday school. Lydia asked, "Is it like school, only it's on a Sunday?" Aunty Jean said, "Yes." She told us that she and Uncle Stan would be going to church while we were in Sunday school, which was next door to the church.

All this was new to us. What was church, and what would we be doing at Sunday school? Aunty Jean said, "You will learn about God, who made Heaven and Earth. Church is where you worship God. Now off you go. It's time to get ready for bed." So, running up the stairs, we chatted. Then we had to come down to say goodnight to Uncle Stan. Aunty Jean always saw us into bed. She said we did not have to get up early on a Sunday. We were to have breakfast later, and she would call us. "Sunday is a day of rest." She said goodnight and went downstairs. We talked, and I thought, that's good – no jobs! I said to Lydia, "I wonder if we will like Sunday school? It's only in the morning, so we won't be there that long." We talked about our day. We agreed it was fun playing with the children on the allotment, and we didn't have to do any jobs.

Uncle Stan was going to talk to Aunty Jean about the children we played with, and the broken glass. I said, "I wonder how she will be with me?"

"I hope we can play with the children again on a Saturday." I then told Lydia a story, and she soon fell asleep. I was thinking about being here, and hoping we would be able to make some friends. Aunty Jean did say Sunday was a day of rest, so no jobs – hooray! That will be good. I was looking forward to Sunday.

Chapter 15

We both woke next morning before we were called. The sun was shining through the curtains, and we were talking in bed. I said to Lydia, "There are no jobs today – it's a day of rest. We will meet some children at Sunday school. That should be good." Lydia agreed, and we felt it was going to be quite an exciting day. We were chatting when we heard Aunty Jean coming up the stairs, saying, "You can have breakfast in your night clothes, as you will be putting on your best clothes for Sunday school and church. You have some dressing gowns. Put them on, then go into the bathroom, and when you have finished, come downstairs for breakfast." We hurried and did this, and ran downstairs. We could smell something nice.

When we opened the kitchen door Uncle Stan was making toast. That was different – no porridge this morning. Aunty Jean was sitting at the table. "Sit down. We have a change on a Sunday. It's a special day." We liked our hot toast and had dripping on it with salt. There was jam that we could have if we wanted. After breakfast she said, "Let's go to your bedroom and get out some clothes to put on. These will just be to wear on Sundays." Looking in the wardrobe, she said, "I will have to buy you some more clothes." She seemed nicer to us, and I thought, I like Sundays already. Once Aunty Jean had worked out what we were wearing, it was time to get our hair done. I did not enjoy having mine braided. She pulled hard on my hair. Then Aunty Jean said, "I won't braid it today. You can just have it loose, and part it on one side, with a ribbon in it, like Lydia's, (Again I thought, I like Sundays), but then she went on to say, "Yours is that much longer. It will have to be cut short soon, and that will make it much easier to look after."

"I don't want it cut short."

"It's not what you want. It's the time factor, and it's easier to manage." Oh, I thought, and felt a bit down.

We were ready to leave, and Aunty Jean said, "We will be walking. It's quite a long way." Aunty Jean held Lydia's hand, and Uncle Stan held mine. It was much further than our school, which we passed, and still kept walking. Then we turned down another street. We could see a lot of people in the distance, standing on the footpath. As we got closer, Aunty Jean said, "We are here. Now I will take you into Sunday school. These people will be going into church soon. Say goodbye to Uncle Stan. You will see him later. Hold my hand." We passed the people. Some spoke to Aunty Jean, and she kept walking down this little lane beside the church.

As we got closer, we could hear children's voices. We came to an open door. A lady was standing in the doorway. She spoke to Aunty Jean, then, looking at us, she said she would be seeing us after Sunday school. We were then left with her. There were lots of children sitting at tables, and we were shown a place to sit with the other children. We were given some sheets of paper and pencils, and we did some colouring in. We also sang. We only had to be quiet for a short time, when the lady read from the Bible. She told us what it meant. It wasn't like school – we could talk when we wanted to.

The lady was very nice to us. We enjoyed it. When Sunday school was finished, Uncle Stan came to get us, and walked us to where Aunty Jean was standing outside the church, talking to some people. We had to say hello. She was telling somebody all about us. I found it boring. We had to stand still. It seemed a long time before we started walking home again. Aunty Jean, holding Lydia's hand, walked in front. Uncle Stan held mine. As we were walking past the shops, I noticed they were closed, and I whispered to Uncle Stan, "Our sweet shop is closed," and he whispered, "Shh. All shops close on Sunday. It's a day of rest." Aunty Jean heard us talking and said, "We will talk about your time at Sunday school after lunch."

"Can I walk in front with Lydia?" Uncle Stan thought that would be all right, and said so to Aunty Jean, who reluctantly agreed, but we had to stop when we saw a road we had to cross. So that is what we did on our way home. I was able to chat to Lydia.

Uncle Stan and Aunty Jean knew we were talking, but couldn't really hear what we were saying. I said to Lydia, "I wonder what we will do for the rest of the day?"

"It would be nice if we could go outside and play." When we got back, we had to take our shoes off and get out of our Sunday clothes and into our round the house clothes, wash our hands, and come down for lunch. Aunty Jean had made some sandwiches. After grace had been said and lunch eaten, we went into the front room. Aunty Jean asked, "How did you like Sunday school?" Then we were able to talk about our morning. We said we had really liked it, and I asked, "What are we going to be doing now?" We were told we could go and get our readers, and she would hear us read for a while. Also, she asked if there was any homework to catch up on. "We are going to have a quiet afternoon. Later on, you will take Monty for a walk with Uncle Stan."

"Can we go outside and play?"

"No. We need to do something quietly. It's Sunday, and you will be going to bed early on Sundays." She heard us read and checked our homework, which took a little while. We were then allowed to go into the back garden and wait for Uncle Stan to come out, and we would be walking Monty. While we were outside, we patted him. Uncle Stan came out. Aunty Jean didn't come. I was so glad.

We went a different way to our last walk. This time, after walking past the lane to the woods, we went down this steep hill. I was allowed to hold Monty. I ran, and Lydia tried to keep up with me. Uncle Stan was in the rear. We came to a stile, which we climbed over to go to the fields. Monty had to go underneath it. I let go of the lead, just for a quick minute, while he was going under the stile, and he ran away, with the lead still on. We kept calling him, and Uncle Stan did too, but he kept running. I nearly caught up with Monty to grab the lead, but he was too fast for me. We could see some more people way in front, walking towards us. They did help us, and got hold of the lead. When we caught up to them, Uncle Stan thanked them, and of course I was given a good telling off. I must never let go of the lead, or I would not be allowed to walk Monty again.

"It wasn't easy to climb over and hold the lead at the same time." Uncle Stan said I should have waited for him. Monty was very happy after having a lovely run. I asked Uncle Stan what Aunty Jean had said about us playing with the children, and the broken glass on the greenhouse. He said for me not to worry.

"Can we play with those other children again one day?"

"We will see." It was time to go home, and Uncle Stan held the lead this time. He said, "We need not mention this to Aunty Jean." We said we wouldn't. Monty had a great time. He looked so happy – he looked as if he had a smile on his face. We put him on his chain, and he lay down, exhausted. Aunty Jean said, "You must have had a long walk with him."

"We went down the steep hill to the fields, and I ran with Monty." Aunty Jean had dinner ready. "Take your shoes off and go and wash your hands, then come down for dinner." We ran up the stairs, talking. I said, "Uncle Stan is nice not telling Aunty Jean." Lydia agreed, "Don't say anything about it, will you?" It was fun being able to run, and we did enjoy it.

Chapter 16

Aunty Jean had dinner ready, and our routine began. Often, we didn't like what was given to us, but we managed with difficulty to hide some in our hankies, and I had to work out how to give it to Monty without being caught. Monty and I became good friends.

As it was Sunday night, Aunty Jean had got our school clothes ready for us to put on next day, and we were in bed early. We were allowed to read to each other for a short time. Then Aunty Jean would come upstairs saying, "I'm turning off the light now. Time for sleep! You have school tomorrow." We whispered to each other for a while, and then I would make up my own story for Lydia. It wasn't long before she fell asleep. I was thinking, school tomorrow. I must really try and learn. I'd love to get better at reading, and want to catch up, and know what other children of my age know. I soon fell asleep.

Aunty Jean woke us in the morning, saying, "Now off to the bathroom. Get dressed and come down for breakfast. Don't be long." We knew the routine, and it wasn't long before we were being walked by Aunty Jean to school. Leaving us at the gate, she said, "Be good.", looking at me, "See if you can catch up." We were still going to school earlier, as I was having the extra help. I had already made up my mind to try and catch up, without Aunty Jean telling me to. After taking Lydia to her classroom, so she had time for a play with her friends, I ran back to my classroom for my extra help. The teacher listened to me read, praised me, and gave me a new reader to take home. She spent time with me on new words. I was pleased with myself and I thought maybe Aunty Jean might praise me too. In class, it was still hard for me to understand some of the other lessons, but with the help of the teacher, I was starting to grasp some of what was being taught.

I would see Lydia at playtimes, and she was always pleased to see me, even though she had friends of her own age. I was running back from Lydia's play area to mine one day, to go to class, when my teacher said, "You need to start making friends of your own age." She said that Lydia seemed happy and settled. She felt that I should just see her at lunchtimes. "I'm sure Lydia will understand. Have a talk about it." Then I had lunch with Lydia, and I told her what the teacher had suggested, and she said that was fine. The teacher asked some girls to let me join in and play with them, and slowly I was accepted. Uncle Stan would always meet us at the gate. We looked forward so to that, and always managed to finish our little bags of sweets before we got home. We were getting used to our routine.

When we got home it was shoes off, and I had to clean them. Lydia was allowed to come out and watch me sometimes, depending on Aunty Jean's mood. We were able to chat together on our own about things, but other than that, it was only when we were in bed, when we would whisper to each other. We didn't get much chance at other times. We would pat Monty and talk to him, and if we had time, we would see Uncle Stan in the greenhouse and chat to him, before Aunty Jean would knock on the window. It was time for dinner. I always had my hanky ready so I could get rid of any food we didn't like.

One day it was sprung on me by Aunty Jean that I should say grace. "You have heard it being said so many times – now you can say it." With a bit of prompting, I did complete it. "You will be taking it in turns with Uncle Stan." she told me. When dinner was finished and the dishes had been done, I ran upstairs to get my homework and my new reader. Also, I remembered the teacher had given me a note to give to Aunty Jean. I knew what was in it. It was to say that I was settling in and making new friends. But first, I was to go to the kitchen, sit at the table and do my homework. I was on my own, and was more confident with what I had to do. I knew the teacher would explain it to me if I did get anything wrong. When I had finished, I went into the front room, taking my new reader and the note to show Aunty Jean. "Have you finished your homework already?" I said yes. "Well, let's hear you both read – Lydia first." She was doing so well, and also had a new reader. When it was my turn to read, I gave Aunty Jean the note, and she read it. She said, looking at me, "See what you can do when you put your mind to it!" I thought, I guess that was some sort of praise for me. Then I read to her. We were asked whether we had anything else to talk about – this was the time to do it, before going to bed. This was the routine.

I said to Aunty Jean, "It's about me playing with other children. I only see Lydia at lunch times now." Aunty Jean asked Lydia if she was happy with that, and Lydia said yes, as long as I saw her at lunch times. As long as Lydia was happy, Aunty Jean was happy. She said she had something to tell us now. "Tomorrow when we get home from school, I will be taking you and Lydia to the hairdresser, and you (looking at me) will be getting your hair cut short, and Lydia will be having a trim." I made a big fuss, saying, "Please, please, I don't want it cut. I won't make any noise when you do my hair in the mornings and you pull it back hard." Aunty Jean said, "It's not what you want. It is getting done. It will be quicker and easier to do in the mornings. Now, no more fuss. Off you go upstairs and get ready for bed, and then come down and say goodnight to Uncle Stan."

We raced upstairs chatting and I said to Lydia, "I don't want to have it cut short."

"It will look nice, and Aunty Jean won't pull your hair like she does now." I thought, that will be good, as I really hated having it pulled back so hard when it was braided. We got into our night clothes and ran back downstairs. She said, "Stop running in the house!" After we had said goodnight to Uncle Stan, she saw us into bed, saying, "Goodnight. Straight to sleep," as she closed the door. We heard her go downstairs, and of course we whispered about our day.

I had just finished telling Lydia a story. We heard this really loud noise. We were frightened, and heard Aunty Jean and Uncle Stan running up the stairs, telling us to get out of bed. Uncle Stan wrapped Lydia in a blanket, picked her up and carried her, while Aunty Jean tore a blanket from the bed in half and wrapped it around me. Holding my hand, she said we must follow Uncle Stan, who was already downstairs opening the front door, with Monty beside him. The noise was even louder than ever. We hurried down the path and out of the front garden gate. I asked, "Where are we going? What's happening?" I was frightened. Aunty Jean didn't answer. It was very dark, and there were other people all hurrying across the road, where there was a funny looking place. We found out afterwards that it was called a shelter.

We went down some stairs, and there was a wooden bench attached to the wall, running right around. We managed to get a seat and huddled together, listening to the awful noise. We were told it was planes. It was all very frightening. It seemed a long time before the noise stopped, which was a siren, we were told. The war was in its last stages. This happened a few times in our early days living with Aunty Jean and Uncle Stan. Of course, when we did go home again, it was so hard to get to sleep. We still had school next day, but we didn't want to go. Aunty Jean said, "You will be going to bed early tonight." It was not until we were older that we understood what had happened. When she left us at the school gate, she always said to me, "Be good, and learn." Lydia was happy to go and play with her friends, and I would go to my classroom. The teacher was always there, and gave me the extra help. I really liked her, and slowly I found I could tell her things. I could talk with her and tell her what it was like living with Aunty Jean. She became a friend to me. I think she saw that I was not very happy, and wanted to give me the extra time. She always praised me, as I was really trying, but was still behind with my learning in general.

I was doing well with my reading, though. I enjoyed learning new words. I often think back about how fortunate I was to have had such a caring teacher. I always looked forward to lunch times, when I would meet Lydia in the playground and we would eat our lunch together. She was pleased to see me, and would chat about what she had been doing. It was good that she had made friends, but I was happier being with her and her friends than the children of my own age. We looked forward to the weekends after Aunty Jean went to do her Saturday job. Of course, first we had our house cleaning to do. As I grew older, I was given more jobs. Lydia was allowed to be with me, but I was the one in trouble if anything was not done as Aunty Jean wanted it to be.

Chapter 17

After Aunty Jean had gone to work on a Saturday we said, "Hooray!" Uncle Stan would look after us. We did our walks with Monty, which I enjoyed, and if we heard any children playing on the vacant block, he would let us join in. He would always be there to watch us. We made some friends, and really enjoyed those times. We found out from Betty, the tall girl who first asked us if we could play with them, that she went to our school. She was older than I, and in a higher class. She said she would look for me at playtimes. That made me happy. Lydia also saw one of her friends playing on the vacant block. Uncle Stan said that we should not tell Aunty Jean about us playing on the vacant block, and we never did. Although he was strict with us, he had a soft spot.

Saturday was our favourite day, after Aunty Jean had gone to work. On Sundays we were now going to church at night as well as going to Sunday school in the morning, which meant we had to do something quiet in the afternoon. We found it boring listening to the minister talking, and didn't understand what was being said. I found it hard to sit still, and Lydia and I weren't allowed to sit together, as we would whisper to each other. We were glad when it was all finished. Then as people walked slowly up the aisle and reached the front entrance, the minister would say something to each person and shake hands. He shook my hand once and asked, "How are you?"

"I want to get home. It's boring." Aunty Jean gave me a stern look. Lydia squeezed my hand, which meant: Don't say anything more. It took so long to finish. I always wanted to get out of the door fast, and couldn't wait to get going. Sometimes it was dark when we were walking back and the street lights were on. Once we were home it was shoes off, carry them to the shelf near the back door, get out of those clothes, straight to the bathroom and get ready for bed. While we were in the bathroom, Aunty Jean would get our school clothes ready for the morning.

We always had to go downstairs to say goodnight to Uncle Stan, before running back upstairs to get into bed. Often, we made it a race, and I would give Lydia a head start. I would run and try to get in front. Aunty Jean would still be in our bedroom sorting out our clothes. She would hear us, and tell me off for my behaviour. "Just walk upstairs and be young ladies. Now get into bed and go straight to sleep," as she closed the door. We would listen for her going downstairs, but there were times when we heard her stop on the landing and put the key in the door of the little room next to our bedroom, and unlock the door, always kept locked. She was not in there for very long, and we would listen, hearing a rustling noise. Then we heard the door close and the key go in the door to lock it again. We heard Aunty Jean go downstairs. We would whisper, "What could be in there?"

"I must try and find the key again and get into Aunty Jean's bedroom to look for it, but we will have to wait until she goes to work on Saturday, and I will have another try."

We whispered for a bit longer and then I made up a story to tell Lydia. It wasn't long before she fell asleep. I was thinking how we were getting used to living with Aunty Jean and Uncle Stan, and the routine. Lydia was quite happy, and doing well, which was good. I wondered when our uncle would come and see us again. That would be nice. I would ask Aunty Jean in the morning. I didn't like Aunty Jean, but Uncle Stan was all right. I still missed hugs – we never got any, and I was not allowed to give hugs. Lydia and I gave each other a hug before going to sleep, and I would hug her before she ran to her classroom. I would see mums giving hugs to their children at the school gate. The only contact I ever had was holding hands with Aunty Jean or Uncle Stan on the way to and from school.

We really missed out on love. Looking back on my childhood, it was so cold and disciplined. We didn't play when Aunty Jean was around, but Uncle Stan would let us join in if there were children playing on the vacant block. Aunty Jean didn't know about this. She was so strict, and more so with me. I did stand up to her and answer her back a bit. I had had to fend for myself before, and always looked after Lydia. Now Aunty Jean was looking after Lydia, and she didn't like me saying anything. I didn't like the way she treated me, and I felt she was trying to stop me being close to Lydia, as we had always been. This is what I felt was happening. I felt so desperate to talk with my uncle about this. Eventually I fell asleep.

The next morning, I said to Lydia while we were getting dressed, "I am going to ask Aunty Jean how much longer it will be before we see our uncle."

"I hope it will be soon." When we came down into the kitchen I asked if I could talk, "I need to ask a question."

"Breakfast first. Now say grace, please." I was getting good at this, and remembered it without a mistake. We had breakfast and then she asked, "What did you want to say?"

"When we can see our uncle?"

"It shouldn't be much longer before I hear from him."

"Can you tell him we want to see him?"

"Why do you want to see him?"

"We just do, and we love him." I don't think she liked me saying that. "You will have to wait until he lets me know. Now go upstairs to the bathroom and clean your teeth. I will be up in a minute to do your hair."

We ran upstairs. I said to Lydia, "We will have to keep asking about when our uncle is coming, so Aunty Jean will eventually do something." When she came upstairs to do our hair, mine was easier to do. I still missed my plaits, but I didn't complain, and she was happy. Holding our hands, she would walk us to the school gate, always looking at me, saying, "Be good and learn." I was looking forward to going to class, and really enjoyed my reading. The teacher gave me more words and another new reader. Then she asked me if I had anything I wanted to talk to her about. That made me feel special, and sometimes, if I was unhappy, I would tell her things.

At playtime I looked for Betty. She said she would try and find me. I did see her, but she was talking with some children and didn't see me, so I joined in with a group that the teacher had asked to include me. I always had playlunch with Lydia and we talked about things. Lydia said to me that she liked school. I told her I was settling in. One day It was raining very hard when we came out of school. Uncle Stan was at the gate with a large umbrella. We still went to the sweet shop and chose what we wanted. Once we were home, we had to change our clothes. I would still have to clean shoes outside. It was so wet, and I would stand under the eaves as far as I could, to keep dry. I was still getting a bit wet. I was not allowed to do them inside. Monty would come out of his kennel to see me and would get really wet. When I had finished the shoes, I asked Aunty Jean, "Can Monty come inside, and sit under the kitchen table?" Aunty Jean said, "No. He has his kennel to keep dry in."

"But he is still getting wet. The rain is coming into his kennel."

I remembered Uncle Stan telling us that Monty was allowed to come inside when it was really wet. I then asked Aunty Jean, "When is Monty allowed to come in?"

"Well, it is when the weather is really bad."

"It is really bad, and he is getting very wet." Aunty Jean got really cross with me for answering back. "I will decide when Monty can come inside. Stop arguing with me."

"I'll let Uncle Stan know it's time to come in, shall I?" and before she could stop me, I ran down the garden to the greenhouse. I asked Uncle Stan about Monty coming inside, not telling him I had asked Aunty Jean. I guess I knew I was naughty doing that, but I felt so sorry for Monty, and hoped Uncle Stan would say yes, which he did. "Yes, it is one of those very wet days." He dried Monty down with an old towel, and let him come in. He had to stay under the kitchen table. Uncle Stan put another towel down for him to lie on.

Aunty Jean was so very cross with me for asking Uncle Stan. "You should not have done that!"

"But Uncle Stan said it was too wet. The rain was coming into the kennel." Poor Monty! Those were the only times when he was allowed to come inside. This happened often. I would ask Aunty Jean. She would say no, and then I would ask Uncle Stan, and he would let him in. Monty was so happy inside. He had a smile on his face and his tail would wag. When we ate our dinner, it was so easy for us to give him food we didn't like, always watching, so we didn't get caught. After the dishes had been done and I was on my own doing homework, Monty would come up to me and I would play with him. When I had finished my homework and it was time to go into the front room, Monty would make a huge fuss. He didn't want to be on his own. Aunty Jean said, "He has to stay in the kitchen under the table." I would say, "Can he not come in for a little bit?" "No." Uncle Stan would then come into the kitchen to get Monty's food ready. He allowed me to come in and watch. As I grew older, I was allowed to prepare the food and give it to Monty. I was so fond of him, and he became fond of me. He always came to me when we were walking him, and I was the one holding the lead. Of course, Uncle Stan was with us.

Chapter 18

I was coming on in leaps and bounds with my reading. I really enjoyed it. When Aunty Jean heard me read, she said reluctantly, "Well. At last, you have shown some improvement." This was praise of a sort, and I felt pleased. Always after reading we were asked if there was anything we wanted to talk about. Lydia would talk first about how school was and how she liked it. She was doing really well. I asked again about our uncle. "We want to see him." Aunty Jean was getting really cross with me for asking all the time. She said, "No. There is no need to worry him. He will let me know when he wants to see you."

"But we want to see him. Why can't you let him know that?"

"I have told you before, he will let you know when he can. Now go and get ready for bed, and come down to say goodnight to Uncle Stan." So, we would chatter while we ran upstairs. Lydia said, "Our uncle will come when he can, I am sure. Aunty Jean is getting so cross with you for keeping on asking. Don't ask all the time!" I thought that Lydia wasn't too upset about the situation. It was me, and I thought, well, I will keep on asking – I want to see him, and I'm not going to stop asking. I hoped she would let Uncle know. I so looked forward to seeing him.

We had been living with Aunty Jean and Uncle Stan for quite a few months, and it was going to be Christmas soon. Children at school were getting excited, and there was talk of hanging up a stocking on Christmas Eve. This was all new to us, and we were told our stockings would have something put in by Father Christmas during the night. In the morning, when it was Christmas Day, we could have a look. I was wondering when Aunty Jean or Uncle Stan would tell us about this. I would have to ask when it was our time to talk. Lydia didn't know anything about it either. We would whisper to each other at night, and she asked, "Do you think we will get a stocking?"

In the morning, we knew our routine, and I knew when it was the right time to talk – after breakfast, before we left the table, so I said to Aunty Jean, "I have a question." I could see Aunty Jean looking cross. "Yes. What is it now? Do not ask me again about your uncle."

"That wasn't what I was going to ask. I want to know about Christmas. Do we hang a stocking up, and if so, where?"

"We will talk about Christmas tonight in the front room after dinner."

"Have you heard about our uncle?" Aunty Jean said, "No!" and was really cross.

"Now go and get ready for school. I will be up soon to do your hair." We ran up the stairs chatting, hearing Aunty Jean call out, "Stop running up the stairs!"

It wasn't long before we were being walked to school by Aunty Jean, who left us at the gate, looking at me and saying, as always, "Be good and learn." Lydia and I would give each other a hug before she ran to play with her friends, and I was happy to see my teacher and show her my homework. I was more confident, and felt at ease talking to her. I decided to ask her about what I had heard about Christmas. The teacher told me what happens on Christmas Eve, and said there would be school holidays soon. After those holidays, I would be going into another class with a different teacher. This made me upset. I didn't want another teacher. She said, "You are doing well, and there are still a few weeks to go. Do not worry about it. All the children will be doing the same thing, and having another teacher. This happens every year, and you will have caught up by then." I wasn't too sure I would have. I wished she hadn't told me. I wanted her to be my teacher all the time. She was my friend.

I was given more homework to do, and the teacher was pleased with what I had done. I must keep trying, I said to myself, and it will be all right. Be strong. Do not give up. I told Lydia all about it at playlunch. She said, "Oh. That means I'll have another teacher soon too." It didn't upset her. She said, "As long as I still have my friends with me."

"Yes – your class will have a new teacher." This news made me think, I really must make friends with children of my own age, as I still joined Lydia at playtime with her friends, and had not made any friends of my own age. I think it was because I was behind with my learning, and when I could, I stayed behind and talked with the teacher. But I said to myself that the teacher had said I was catching up. I must try harder.

When the bell rang at the end of the day Uncle Stan was waiting at the gate. We told him what we had heard from the teacher, about going into another class. He said, "Yes. That is what happens. Do not worry about it. I'm sure you will make some friends and get to know your new teacher after a little time." We chatted and called into the sweet shop, eating our sweets on the way, always finishing before we reached home. Again, we knew what our routine was – out of our school clothes and into doing our jobs. The weather was getting really cold, and we had warm clothes to change into. It was starting to get dark earlier. I still had to go outside to clean the shoes. I was able to do them quickly and was getting better at it. When Aunty Jean checked them, they passed her inspection. I was also saying grace at all mealtimes now. Lydia was learning to say it gradually, and then we would take it in turns.

There were still meals we didn't like. We managed to put certain vegies and other stuff into our hankies for Monty. We were really getting good at it, and becoming used to living with Aunty Jean and Uncle Stan. We always looked forward to the weekends, when A.J. went to her little job. It was the best time for us. We played with the other children on the vacant land, and U.S. would watch us. He was much nicer to us when A.J. wasn't there, and less strict. He would leave us inside the house on our own a bit while he was in the garden. A.J. had told us certain jobs needed to be done before we were allowed to go outside. We hurried with our jobs. I said to Lydia, "Now is our chance. I want to find the key of the room that is always locked." We were curious about what could be in there.

Chapter 19

I opened the door into A.J. and U.S.'s bedroom to look for the key. Just inside the door was the large dressing table I had seen before. Lydia was standing outside the door keeping watch in case U.S. came inside, when she would call me. I started looking in the mirrors, seeing myself from different angles, calling Lydia to come and have a look. When she saw them, she was fascinated, seeing herself and moving the mirrors backwards and forwards at different angles. There were little dishes and jars on the dressing table that had lids on. I had a look in each of them. Lydia helped me, but there was no key. There were little drawers at the top of the dressing table, and I started opening them. Then we heard Uncle Stan call out, "You should be finished by now! Get your coats and hats on – it's time to walk Monty." So, we hurriedly put the mirrors back like I thought they were and closed the door. We raced into our bedroom to get our coats, hats and shoes, and met Uncle Stan downstairs. He was outside already. He had Monty on his lead, who was all excited that he was going to be walked. I was allowed to hold him, and we were going to the woods. I asked if we could take a basket or something so we could pick flowers and carry them home.

He gave us a small cane basket and Lydia carried it. Then we walked to the woods. There were some lovely bluebells. Lydia started picking them. I gave the lead to Uncle Stan and picked some too. We ran amongst the trees, having a lovely time. Monty started barking and trying to catch up with us. He was pulling Uncle Stan, who said he couldn't let Monty off the lead. I ran back, took the lead off U.S, and ran with Monty. He just loved that. Those times were fun and memorable. Once back home and when A.J. had returned, the atmosphere changed. We were happy. We wanted to tell her about our fun time, but we weren't allowed to. "First, take your shoes off. Go upstairs. Off with your hats and coats. Change into your round the house clothes," which we did, while chatting, "I wonder what's for dinner?" As we were coming down the stairs, we saw there was something on the small hall table at the bottom of the stairs in the corner. There were some letters and a card poking out with a picture on it. We stopped. I picked the card up and had a look. I turned it over and recognised my name and Lydia's, with lots of other writing. We looked at each other and guessed it was from our uncle. I said to Lydia, "Don't say anything. I will ask the question when we're in the front room – whether A.J. has heard from our uncle. I wonder if she will tell us anything?"

"But you will make Aunty Jean so cross again if you ask that."

"Let's see what she says." We went down the hall and opened the kitchen door. Aunty Jean was serving dinner. I said grace and the meal was eaten in silence. Then Aunty Jean took Lydia into the front room. I was with Uncle Stan, who was tidying up and doing the dishes. I, of course, had the wiping up to do. I started to chat to him, saying, "I still have some homework to do. Can Monty come in the kitchen while I do my homework? It is so cold outside, and starting to rain."

"Let's get these dishes finished and put away, and see what the weather is doing then." I had some food in my hanky for Monty, and it would be good if he was inside, where I could give it to him. I so enjoyed it when Monty was under the table, and we were on our own. I would be doing my homework, and I patted and talked to him. When everything had been done, I asked U.S., "Please can we bring Monty inside?" He opened the back door. It was really very cold and windy, and it was starting to rain. He said, "All right," and he went out to get him. Monty came bounding in, full of excitement. U.S. had to quieten him down, and said, "Under the table, or you will have to go out again." Monty settled down, wagging his tail. U.S. said to me, "Go and get your homework." I ran upstairs and got it, then put my books on the kitchen table. He said, "Well, when you have finished, come into the front room." As soon as U.S. left the kitchen, I gave Monty the food from my hanky. He was so happy – more wagging -- and I patted him. Then I started my homework.

When I had finished, I played with Monty. U.S. came to check on me, and I got caught playing with Monty. He said, "Go into the front room now. I will feed Monty, and then he needs to go outside." "Can I stay and watch, and help you?"

"Oh, all right." He got out Monty's dish and I held it while he put the food in. However, it was raining heavily, so Monty could have it under the table. U.S. left the door open so he could see what Monty was up to while we were in the front room. A.J. wasn't happy about Monty being inside. He was so good. He settled down and eventually fell asleep. A.J. asked, "Is your homework done?"

"Yes."

"Have you got your reader? I will hear you read." Lydia had already read to A.J. while I was in the kitchen. I had been a long time, apparently. I started reading to A.J. After only a little while I was told to stop. She said, "That's enough. Now let's talk about your day. Lydia first." I thought, if only she would say something nice to me. I knew I was doing well with my reading. The teacher had told me so, and I really enjoyed reading. It just would have been nice to get a little praise, or encouragement of a sort.

Chapter 20

Lydia looked at me. She knew I was going to ask A.J. about the card. I didn't want her to say anything. I shook my head, and I knew she understood. She started saying, "We did our jobs and went with Uncle Stan to take Monty for a walk. We went to the woods and picked bluebells.". I started talking, "I helped too, and I ran with Monty. It was fun."

"One at a time, please. Lydia is talking." Lydia said she wanted me to talk now. A.J. said, "You haven't finished talking."

"I don't want to say anything more. I want Sylvia to talk." A.J. said, "Very well," and looked at me. "You interrupted your sister. That was rude. Please don't do that again." Then she had a few words to say about manners, what is good and what is bad. Yes, we were brought up well in that respect, and in lots of other ways. The big thing we missed out on was being allowed to be children, playing, receiving love and being able to show it. I had to say sorry to Lydia for interrupting. A.J. then allowed me to talk, which I did, "Have you heard from our uncle?" A. J. looked at me crossly. "Not yet. How many times do I have to tell you? When I do, I will let you both know."

"There are letters on the hall table. Can I run and get them for you?"

"No, thank you. I will get them later."

"But why can't I get them?" A.J. did not answer me, but said, "Now, tomorrow is Sunday again, so that means bath night. I want you to go upstairs now and get your night clothes, and take them to the bathroom. I will come upstairs with you to run a bath." As we were going up the stairs, A.J. was right behind us. I whispered to Lydia, "We can talk in the bathroom."

A.J. went to the bathroom to run the water. She called out to say the bath was ready, one at each end. As she closed the door she said, "I'll be back soon to wash your backs." As soon as she had gone, I said to

Lydia, "She will get the letters now. When I ask her again, she will have to tell us something. We saw our names on the card. Let's see what she says now." Lydia said, "I will tell her I saw the card too." We washed ourselves. Lydia said, "You are changing." She could see that my body was coming into puberty. The door opened. A.J. came in and washed our backs. This was our Saturday night ritual. Once in our night clothes, we had to say goodnight to U.S. A.J. would come up to see us into bed. We were allowed to read on a Saturday night as well as on Sundays, then A.J. would come up to turn off the light, closing the door as she said goodnight. We started to chat about our time here. Lydia seemed quite happy, and I was accepting how things were. We were really looking forward to hearing what our uncle wrote on the card, and hoped we'd get to see him soon.

We listened. Someone was coming up the stairs. It was Aunty Jean. She opened the door and put the light on. She said, "I had better get your Sunday clothes out ready for the morning." She walked to the wardrobe and took clothes out. She put them on each of our chairs, saying, "Now, I'm turning off the light. I'll call you when it's time to come down for breakfast. Goodnight, straight to sleep. It's getting late." She closed the door again. We heard her stop on the landing. I said, "I bet she goes in that little room again." We heard her stop, and then the key going into the door. This time, she was only in there for such a short while, then we heard the door being closed and locked. I whispered, "Do you think I should ask these questions: what is in the little room, why is it being locked, and what is the rustling noise we hear? and see what she says?" Lydia was horrified, "No, don't. She will get so angry with you." She never wanted me to upset Aunty Jean in any way. "But I do wonder what is in there. I want to know. Don't you?"

"We will find out in time."

"All right. Maybe I'd better not. I don't think she would tell us anyway, if I did ask. Let's try to find the key again when she is doing her job." We chatted a bit more. I wasn't telling Lydia a story as often, as she was growing up. Now, she was reading herself. Only occasionally would she ask me to tell her one.

Chapter 21

We woke and said, "It's Sunday morning.", with the smell of toast wafting up – no lumpy porridge today, and no jobs to do. Hooray! Lydia was saying grace this Sunday. We would now be saying it in turn. After breakfast we'd run upstairs, clean our teeth and get dressed in our Sunday clothes. I didn't mind Sunday school. We were together, we could talk, and it wasn't as strict as school. We made friends with a few children. It was after Sunday school when we went into the church by the side door. We didn't like having to sit still and listen. There were three pews reserved for us children at the front. The minister would come down from his pulpit and say something special to us. Then he would return to the pulpit and say, "Now open your hymn books to (a certain number)." The hymn books were on a shelf on the back of the seat in front of us, propped up by a rail, and we would grab one and try to find the number quickly before the singing started. There were some words I could read, but lots I couldn't. We would open our mouths and make some sort of noise. Some of the tunes were nice. When the service was finished, we children could get up and look for our parents, and then walk down the aisle slowly to get out of the church. The minister was at the front, standing in the porch by the wooden front door. He would shake hands with everybody and say a few words. I made sure I just said hello, and nothing else.

As people came outside, some would stand in a group and talk. We girls would have to stand still by Aunty Jean and Uncle Stan and wait, until eventually people started moving to go home. I would stand on one leg and hop, and then the other. I just wanted to get home. A.J. would say, "Stand still." I found this difficult, and it was boring. I just wanted to hold Lydia's hand and run. After a while, A.J. said, "It's time to walk home." Lydia and I were allowed to walk together in front. This was good, and we could chat. We were often asked to slow down. We skipped a bit. A.J. said, "Just slow down! Walk and behave like young ladies."

While we were walking and chatting, I said to Lydia, "When we have had lunch and are in the front room, I am going to ask about our uncle, and see what A.J. says about the card."

"I hope she doesn't get cross with you."

"She will have to tell us this time. She can't get out of it, and we have seen the card."

"Oh, I hate it when she gets cross with you."

"I don't mind.". We were passing the sweet shop. Of course, it was closed, it being Sunday. Lydia asked, "Wouldn't it be nice if it was open? We could get some sweets."

"No. Not with Aunty Jean there. She wouldn't allow us, and don't forget, we mustn't say anything. We promised Uncle Stan, and Aunty Jean doesn't know we've been there."

"Oh, I forgot that." Once home, we had to change into our round the house clothes, while A.J. and U.S. went to the kitchen to get lunch ready. We couldn't wait for it to be finished so we could go to the front room and ask A.J. about the card.

"I wonder what she will tell us?" I said to Lydia, "And I wonder what's for lunch? I hope it's something nice."

"I expect it's that bread with some of that Spam meat I don't like. Make sure you have your hanky ready." There were lots of meals we still didn't like. We would eat slowly and A.J. would say, "Eat up. You need to eat it all." She would watch us for a bit, then she would get up and start tidying. As soon as she turned away from us, Lydia would quickly give me the food she didn't like. I had my hanky ready, and would put it up my sleeve or my knicker leg, if we had dresses on. We were becoming good at this. Uncle Stan was always finished first, and moving around the kitchen.

The hard thing was for me to hide it until we could give it to Monty, who ate everything. It was nearly time for Aunty Jean and Lydia to go to the front room. I had to help with the tidying, wiping up and putting dishes away. As Lydia passed me, she squeezed my hand. I knew what she meant. How would A.J. answer us, and behave towards us? After they had left for the front room, I chatted to U.S. "Are we walking Monty this afternoon?" He said yes. "He needs a walk. It will only be a short one. Where would you like to go?"

"I like the woods best, but is there anywhere else we haven't been?"

"I will get my thinking cap on." I laughed.

"How can that tell us somewhere else to go?"

"It's a saying one uses," and he tried to explain it to me.

U.S. was helping to put some dishes away. "Can I go outside quickly to pat Monty for a bit?"

"Oh, all right. Don't be long. We're nearly ready to go to the front room. Don't get him excited. Just walk to him." I had all this food in my hanky, most of it from Lydia. I needed to get rid of it. I opened the back door and walked towards Monty. As soon as he saw me, he jumped up. I started patting him and gave him the food, but his chain made a noise. Of course, A.J. heard it and called, "Why are you outside? You should be ready to come into the front room by now." U.S. asked, "Why do you get him so excited?"

"I didn't mean to. I just patted him."

"Now, come along. Let's go into the front room."

A.J. said, when she saw us walking in, "You have taken a long time, and we have been waiting for you. Now, both of you, go and get your readers." We raced upstairs, with A.J. calling out, "Stop running!" We chatted. Lydia asked, "Did you get rid of the food?"

"Yes. You gave me such a lot." We picked up our readers and I said, "Well, it's nearly time. I'll ask the question."

"She will tell us something."

"Yes, or she will say she doesn't know again. Let's go down the stairs quietly. We don't want to make Aunty Jean cross." When we got to the front room, A.J. said, "Well, that was better. Why can't you do that all the time?" We had our readers and Lydia was asked to read first. She was doing really well, and was told so. Then it was my turn. I thought I did all right, but within a short time was told to close my reader. "Now we can talk." I thought, I must get used to A.J. not saying anything. Don't get upset. U.S. never speaks, -- he just sits there. I wonder why he doesn't say anything?

A.J. looked at Lydia, "Now what do you want to talk about?" Lydia started to talk about Sunday school, then looked at me. "You talk now." A.J. said, "Haven't you got anything else to say?" She said no. A. J. turned to me, "Now what have you got to say?" I just blurted it out. "We want to know about the card, and when is Uncle coming to see us? Is it soon?" A.J. got really angry with me.

"I haven't spoken to him, and I did tell you, when I do, I will let you know. Do not speak to me like that. You are being rude. Also, you were looking at other people's letters."

"We saw the card sticking out of the pile, and we wanted to see the picture, then we turned it over and saw our names on it, and he said something about us." Lydia interrupted: "Please tell us what Uncle said." A. J. said, "Thank you for speaking so nicely. Yes, I will tell you. Uncle wants to know how you are, and hopes you are behaving." (Looking at me.) "He sends his love, and is hoping he can see you at Christmas."

We both jumped up and down. This made us very happy. I asked, "Can we see the picture?" A.J. said she hadn't got the card with her. I asked, "Can you go and get it? What is the place called?" A.J. said she would show it to us. Lydia said, "Can you do it now, please?" A.J. got up and left the room. We looked at each other, and then at Uncle Stan. I asked him, "Do you think Aunty Jean would have told us about the card if I hadn't asked?"

"Yes, she would have told you when we finished talking."

"But she hadn't got the card with her."

"She must have forgotten to bring it. That's enough. Aunty Jean will read it out to both of you." With that, A.J. came back and sat down. She had the card in her hand, "Now I will read it. Your uncle says he is expecting to see us at Christmas time and is thinking of you. He sends his love and hopes you are being good."

"Can we see the picture?" She showed it to us. It was from overseas, in France. We said thank you, and asked, "Can we talk about Christmas?"

"We will have to wait and see when Uncle comes here to know what we are doing."

"But I want to know what happens at Christmas."

"I have already told you we will not know until Uncle has been in contact again." I said, talking fast, "I know that, but what happens? Do we have stockings to hang up? What goes in our stockings? Is there a man called Father Christmas?"

"Slow down. You are asking a lot of questions. If you're good, you can have stockings to hang up. I'm not sure what will go into them, though. Now that's enough questions. It's time to get ready to walk Monty. Go to the bathroom and then put your coats and shoes on." We were only going for a short walk, as after dinner, in the evening, we would have to go to church again.

Chapter 22

I said to Lydia as we went up the stairs, "Uncle Stan is putting his thinking cap on for somewhere different for us to walk Monty."

"You are being silly. What are you talking about?" I told her what U.S. had said to me. She thought that was funny too. When we got downstairs, U.S. was waiting outside with Monty, and we were ready to go. A.J. never came with us to walk Monty. We were glad. U.S. was nicer to us on his own, and we were both becoming fond of him. We asked, "Where are we going?"

"There is another walk you haven't been on before. It's only short. It's on the other side of the allotments." We went out the back way, through the side gate, which U.S. unbolted, and then we were on the vacant block. Nobody was there. It was all very quiet. At the allotment, U.S. wanted to see how his seedlings were going. They were growing bigger. "We will be able to have some vegies for dinner soon." He pointed to something growing, and said they were carrots. "You will be able to come with me soon to pull them out of the ground." We kept walking to the end of the allotments, where there was another gate, which we opened, and then we were in a field.

"I want to run with Monty." He gave me the lead. Lydia and I played chasy. I let her run a fair way in front, and Monty and I raced to catch her. Monty loved running and barking. We had fun. It was such a treat not to have to sit still and behave. We enjoyed those times. We could be children. Once we were back home, it all changed. We had to be young ladies, and only speak when spoken to. Looking back on my childhood, I know that having Monty gave us an escape. We could run, talk, shout and let off steam for a short time.

When we reached home, A.J. had dinner ready, and our routine would start. We would walk to church after dinner. Neither of us wanted to go. We didn't understand it. This meant sitting still for a long time –

boring. A.J. separated us. Lydia would have to sit on the other side of her, then it was me and U.S. I found it difficult to sit still for long. It's the same even now – I'm always on the move. I would swing my legs back and forth. A.J. would hold my legs down and say, "Please keep still and listen to what's being said." I felt I would only understand what the minister was saying when I was older. When hymns were sung, everybody would stand. Lydia was allowed to stand on the seat so she could see, and A.J. had her arm around her. We made some sort of noise to the singing.

When it was all finished and it was time to leave, A.J. said to me, "Now, behave yourself. Do not speak when the minister shakes your hand.", and I didn't. We were so glad to get out of the church. It was dark outside and a bit scary. There were street lights on, but there were areas of darkness. We girls could still walk in front together, but not too far ahead, and talk, which was a relief. We were tired from all the walking we did on Sundays. Once in bed, we soon fell asleep. Often A.J. had to wake us, and we found it hard to get out of bed. We dressed as quickly as we could, and our routine would start. A.J. walked us to school, and always said to me before she left, "Be good and learn. Goodbye." We girls would give each other a hug, saying, "See you at lunchtime." Lydia would run to find her friends, and I to my teacher.

I would get my books out and sit down. The teacher had a look at what I had done, and was pleased with me. "At the end of this week the school holidays start, and when you come back to school again it will be after Christmas, and you will be in another class." She was nice. I could talk to her. She told me I would have another teacher, but she would speak with her and let her know all about me. "I am going to write a note to your aunt, and at the end of the day I will give it to you. Now go and have a play before the bell goes." This wasn't easy for me, because I really hadn't any friends, and knew I should start doing something about it. I couldn't keep playing with Lydia's friends. I plucked up some courage and asked a girl if I could join in. They were skipping. Two girls held each handle, turning the rope, and one was jumping over it. I wanted to have a try. She asked, "Can you do it?"

"I don't know. I've never tried."

"You can try when we've all had a turn." I stood and watched, and felt, I could do this.

After a while, they let me try. It wasn't as easy as it looked. One girl said, "You will have to practise." We could hear the bell, so we hurried back to class. I asked, "Can I play with you next playtime?"

"It should be all right." There was a group of us, and we all walked into our classroom together. I would meet Lydia to have lunch with her, and we chatted. She was doing well. "I'm trying to make some friends of my own."

"That's all right. I don't mind. I hope you do." It did take me quite a while before I made any friends, but eventually the girls let me join in and gradually it happened. This was my last time with my teacher. I couldn't believe that after the holidays I wouldn't be in her class again. I was thinking, oh, what are we going to do in the holidays? It's going to be so awful being at home all the time with A.J., doing jobs. I wonder how long it will be before we see our uncle?

Back in class we were having maths, not my favourite subject, but I was coping. I thought, will I get my maths homework tonight? When the bell rang, after all the children left, I was the last to leave. I went up to the teacher. She had some extra work for me, and had also written a note for me to give to A.J. I asked, "What will we do in the holidays?"

"I am sure Aunty Jean will have something nice for you to do. Now you had better go. Your uncle and Lydia will be waiting for you." When I saw U.S., I asked, "What are we going to do in the holidays?" "I don't know what Aunty Jean has planned." We were just reaching the sweet shop. "We will miss having our sweets."

"Now, not a word to Aunty Jean. It's our little secret, remember?" Lydia asked, "But what will we do all the time when there is no school?" I replied, "I hope Aunty Jean won't give us jobs all the time." Uncle Stan said, "Now stop talking like that. Don't worry about the holidays. I am sure you will find out soon enough. You have a few more days to go before you finish school." I said, "Yes, and we have to say goodbye to our teachers." Lydia spoke up, "I wonder who we will get? Will it be somebody nice?"

"I have the nicest teacher now. I don't want anybody else." U. S. said, "You get a different teacher each year. You will soon get used to that."

Chapter 23

We had reached home, and knew our routine. Once we were in the front room, we were sent up to get our readers, then I gave A.J. the note. I said, "I'm doing well."

"I will read it later. Now let's hear you read – Lydia first." After our reading, A.J. opened the note and said, "It seems the teacher is pleased with you. Now you know you will be getting another teacher after the holidays."

"Yes. I will miss her so much."

"This is what happens. You won't know who your teacher will be until you get back to school, and that's the way it is. Now Lydia, is there anything you want to talk about?" She said, "We both want to know what we will be doing in the holidays." "I'm not sure yet. You will know by the time you have finished school." I said, "I don't know why you can't tell us something."

"Now that's enough. You will know when school has finished. Is there anything else you want to talk about?" I asked, "Have you heard from our uncle again?" I could see that Lydia was holding her breath. A.J. looked crossly at me, "If your uncle wants me to tell you anything I would let you know." Lydia looked at me and squeezed my hand, meaning "Don't say any more", and I didn't. "Now, both of you, go upstairs and get ready for bed, then come down to say goodnight to Uncle Stan."

We ran upstairs. Lydia said, "Why do you keep asking about Uncle? You know it only makes her cross."

"Well, I want to know how soon he will be coming. It was written on the card that he would be coming soon, and I thought she might know more."

"She will tell us when she hears. Don't keep asking. It upsets me when A. J. is cross with you." When we chatted, I would ask her, "How is everything?" and she would say, "I'm all right. I like school, and have made some friends". I then realised that Lydia had no real problems. It was I who so badly wanted to talk to Uncle. I don't think she minded A.J. and U.S. too much. She really didn't know anything different, or the way things had been when I was young, such as our mother and father. How could she? She was only a few months old, whereas I remembered them, and still missed the love that was given to me. I also knew what had happened to them, and often thought about them. It made me feel sad. I knew I would always miss them. A.J. was not like a mum to me. I really didn't like her. I was finding my body changing. I couldn't talk to A.J. about it. She must have noticed it too, but didn't say anything. I was thinking, and unsure how to talk to my uncle about it, and it was embarrassing. This was on my mind. Lydia was asking me questions. I said to her, "When you get older, that's what happens – your body changes." I knew that much, but wanted to know more. I know – I will try and talk to my teacher about my body changing – that's what I'll do.

When we were in bed, A.J. came up, said goodnight, and turned off the light, closing the door. We whispered a bit more. Lydia asked, "Did you make a friend?" I told her about trying to skip with the rope. She thought that was fun. "I hope I can play with them again. I don't know anyone's name yet."

"You should ask them their names next time." It wasn't easy for me. I felt I should be with Lydia. I had always looked after her. It was hard for me to try and make my own friends, but I thought, I must try again tomorrow. Lydia was growing up, and this is what she wanted me to do.

In the morning, after our lumpy porridge, we were walked to school and left at the gate. Aunty Jean said goodbye. Lydia and I gave each other a hug and said, "See you at lunchtime." She ran to her friends, and I was on the way to my classroom when I bumped into Betty. I hadn't seen her for a long time. She told me she had been sick and away from school, and wanted to know how I was. "I'll see you at playtime."

"That would be great." I then hurried to see the teacher and hand in the homework she had given me. "Did you give the note to Aunty Jean?" and wanted to know what she had said. I told her what A. J. had said, "It seems the teacher is pleased with you."

"Didn't she say she was pleased too?"

"No. I wasn't sure she believed me." But that was the truth – that's how it was. If only she really knew how A.J. was towards me. When we talked early in the mornings, I would tell her things. She was a friend to me. I don't know if she really thought I was telling the truth. She would say, "Aunty Jean really cares. She wants the best for you."

"She's just not nice to me."

"I'm sure it's not that bad."
"I know that is how it is, and I can't do anything about it."
"Now go out and have a play."

Chapter 24

I looked for Betty, but couldn't find her. I saw the group of girls with the skipping rope, and, being very brave, went up to them. "Please can I join in?", and I told them my name. They said, "Sure." and told me their names. I couldn't remember them all. The one who spoke to me was called Jane. She said to the others, "Let Sylvia have a go." Two girls turned the skipping rope. I stood in the middle, jumping over the rope when it came near my feet. Slowly, I got the hang of it and was able to skip. I thought it was fun. We heard the bell ring. Jane said, "See you next playtime." She wasn't in my class, but it was nice that I knew somebody. I wondered what had happened to Betty. I hoped we would see each other soon.

I was given my last lot of homework by my teacher. Lydia and U.S. were at the gate waiting for me. "I think I have made a new friend." Lydia wanted to know all about it. U.S. was pleased to hear it. "That deserves an extra sweet. It's important that you have friends." While he was getting our sweets, I said to Lydia, "That is nice of him. I wish he was like he is now all the time." She agreed. He had the sweets in little white bags and handed them to us. As we left the shop, a group of children came in. U.S. held the door open for them, and Betty was with them. "Hello. I didn't see you at playtime." "I was looking for you too."

"I joined in with the girls who were skipping."

"Oh well, see if we can see each other tomorrow. That would be good". Lydia said, "You have two friends now." U.S. asked, "Was that one of the girls who played with you on the vacant block?"

"Yes. She has been sick for a few weeks and hasn't been to school." "Oh. We had better start walking home now. Eat your sweets. No more talking, or you won't be finished before you get home." That's what we did.

Once we were home, we had to do our jobs. Lydia came outside with me (I was doing the shoes) and chatted, patting Monty and playing with him. I went down the garden to see U.S. and asked, "Can we put Monty on his lead and run up and down the garden with him?"

"Go and ask Aunty Jean how long before dinner." I said to Lydia, "You go and ask. She might let us do it." She ran inside. A.J. was upstairs putting clothes away. Lydia asked, "How long before dinner?"

"Only a little while. Then I need you to set the table." Lydia raced downstairs and got the lead. It was hanging up on a hook. She could now reach it, and came outside with it. Monty was beside himself, so excited. He thought he was going for a walk. I put him on the lead and ran down the garden to the greenhouse. I told U.S., "It won't be long before dinner." Lydia told him she had to go in soon to set the table. We had a few runs up and down the garden, which we enjoyed, and so did Monty.

A.J. knocked on the window for Lydia to come in. U.S. told me to put Monty on his chain. Monty looked sad. It would have been nice if he could come in too. The weather was fine, and I knew there was no good me asking. I patted him and looked around. Nobody was near me, so I bent down and told Monty, "I will bring you some food later." I thought, I don't know if dogs understand what we say, but he went into his kennel and lay down. I was told, "Come inside and wash your hands – you have been playing with Monty." I ran upstairs and did as I was told.

Lydia was in the kitchen. The table was set. I was hungry, and thought, I do hope it's something nice that we like. A.J. was serving mashed potatoes and sausages. Yes, we liked that. It was my turn to say grace, so I stood up and said it without a mistake. Again, there was no talking allowed at meal times. I was thinking, I must save a piece of sausage for Monty. I looked at Lydia, who was eating well. This meant it had to come from me, so I cut a piece off my sausage and put it to one side on my plate. I ate the rest, waiting for a chance to hide it in my hanky. I made it, while A.J. had her back to me at the sink. "Have you finished that piece of sausage? It's been sitting on your plate for quite a while." I felt pleased with myself – I had done it. Now I had to work out how to give it to Monty.

A.J. and Lydia went to the front room, and I was helping U.S., wiping up the dishes. "Have you any homework tonight?"

"It's the last lot. We only have two days left with my teacher, then it's the holidays."

"Well, you won't have homework to do for quite a while."

"No, but what will we be doing in the holidays?"

"Don't start that again. Now you know the answer to that – you will be told soon enough." I thought, I'm not going to get any more out of him. I must find a way to give Monty his piece of sausage. But how? U.S. said as we were putting the dishes away, "You'd better go and get your homework and reader."

"Can I go and pat Monty first?"

"No. He is quiet. You will get him all excited."

"I promise I won't. I just want to say goodnight to him." U.S. looked at me, "You are becoming fond of Monty, aren't you?"

"Yes. I wish he could come inside more. It is so cold outside."

"He has a warm kennel."

"Please, can I just go and see him?"

"Oh well, all right. Just don't get him excited. Be very quick. If Aunty Jean hears that chain rattle, we will both be in trouble, and that will be the last time I will let you do it." I went over to U.S. to give him a hug. He just stood there. I don't think he knew what to make of me. There was no response, so I opened the back door to the garden very quietly and walked to where Monty's kennel was. He was lying down, asleep. He opened his eyes, stretched, and sat up. "Shh. Lie down." I tried to get him to do so, and he did. Then I got the sausage out of my hanky, which was in my sleeve, and gave it to him. He liked that, and was looking for more. "No more. Sorry.", and patted him.

U.S. was at the door, beckoning me to come inside. I gave Monty one last pat, then I left, hoping like mad he wouldn't make a fuss or rattle his chain. U.S. said, "You did well with Monty. He has settled down again. Now go upstairs and get your homework and reader."

He went into the front room. I got my homework and opened my books, thinking, this is the last lot I'll get from my teacher. It will be sad to say goodbye. I know she said she will be teaching another class, and will ask the new teacher how I am going, and I will probably see her from time to time, but it won't be the same. No more being able to talk to her and tell her about things at home. Oh, I must ask her tomorrow about my body and find out more. She was a friend to me, not just a teacher. I will miss her so much. I don't think she understands how hard it will be for me. I felt tears come into my eyes. I do hope I'll get another nice teacher.

I made a start on my homework. I was more confident, and it was becoming easier for me. I had almost caught up, the teacher said. "You will be able to go up into a higher class with the other children." I finished, and sat there thinking. I remember asking her what would happen if I hadn't caught up. "You would stay down and be with me and the other children I'm teaching." I thought that wouldn't be so bad. At the time, I said, "I don't mind staying down." "Now, Sylvia, don't think about it. It's important that you learn and get on, so when you're old enough to leave school, you will be able to get a good job."

"When does that happen?"

"Fifteen is the earliest, and up to the high teens." I was sitting thinking about all this when U.S. came into the kitchen to see how I was getting on. "Have you finished?"

"Yes."

"Well, why didn't you come into the front room?"

"I was just thinking about things, and how it will be when I have a new teacher."

"You must stop worrying about it. You will get another nice teacher." "I hope so."

"Come into the front room." I followed him in. A.J. was listening to Lydia read. She was reading so well and fast now – she just loved reading, like me. A.J. always gave her lots of praise. U.S. just sat there and didn't say a word. Of course, it was my turn next. I was doing quite well, the teacher had said. I only read one page, and was asked to close the book. It was our time to talk. As I was closing the book, U.S. looked at me and said, "You're really coming on." I was so surprised. "Oh. Thank you." A.J. gave U.S. and me a stern look.

Chapter 25

Lydia asked, "Can we talk now?"

"Yes – I did say earlier that it was time to talk."

"I want to say, my sister is reading as well as me."

I said thank you to Lydia. A.J. asked, "Now, have you anything else you want to talk about?" Lydia started talking about her friends and asked, "Can we see them in the holidays and play?"

"I have told you I'm not sure what is happening in the holidays. We only have two days left, and then it will be the holidays."

"Yes, I am quite aware of that, and will tell you both when I know more. Now, it's time for you to go upstairs and get into your night clothes and then come down and say goodnight to Uncle Stan."

We left the room and heard voices being raised as we ran upstairs, chatting, "Why is A.J. so mean to you?"

"She doesn't like me and I don't like her."

"Well, I stuck up for you, and U.S. thinks you're doing well." I said thanks and gave her a hug. "It's good that she likes you, though, and I'm going to try not to let her upset me." However, I thought, it hurt, though I did not say that to Lydia. We got into our night clothes. "Well, we should know something soon. One day left of school, then it's the holidays."

When we got to school, it was my last time of coming in early, and I handed my homework to the teacher. "Can I ask you a question? It's about me." She looked at me, "Yes."

"I notice my body is changing, and I can't talk to Aunty Jean. I want to know what is happening to me."

"This is perfectly normal. Not to worry about it. I should ask Aunty Jean. She will explain everything to you. Now you have done really well, and there will be no more homework from me. After the Christmas holidays, as you know, you will be in another class with another teacher.

Just keep doing what you're doing. I'm sure I'll see you from time to time." She gave me a hug. This was something she had never done before. There were no other children about, and I knew it was a goodbye hug. I thanked her, saying, "I hope I can talk with you sometimes when I see you."

"We will have to see how things are. Now go out and play with your friends."

I could see the girls skipping, and Jane called out to me to join her, which I did. I was becoming better at it, and it was fun. Slowly I made some friends. The girls were talking about the holidays and what they were going to be doing. When they asked me, I said, "I don't know." Jane said, "It might be a surprise for you, and that will be nice." I thought about that. She didn't know anything about me or our circumstances. She knew I had a sister. I thought: Oh well, we will know soon enough. It's my last day with my teacher. It was a happy time. We did some reading, which we took in turns, and then sang our tables. The teacher said goodbye to everybody: "Enjoy your holidays and have a lovely Christmas." Then there was this rush to get out of the classroom and get home. I just took my time. I felt sad, and I was the last to leave. I went up to the teacher and said, "Thank you for being nice to me and helping me."

"You're welcome. Now off you go. I'm sure you will have a nice Christmas. Lydia will be waiting for you." She was already at the gate with U.S. They both asked, "Why have you been so long?"

"I wanted to say goodbye to my teacher." U.S. said, "Now let's get going to the sweet shop. We won't be doing this for quite a while." We had our choice of sweets and were allowed to ask the lady to fill our little white bags to the top. He said, "Don't forget, this is our little secret." How different he was towards us on his own. He took a sweet from each of our bags, and we just managed to finish them before we reached home.

Chapter 26

After changing our clothes and taking our shoes outside to clean, I thought, I won't have to clean them for a long time. That will be good. Lydia came outside with me. "When we've had dinner, and are in the front room, A.J. will have to tell us something, as it is now the holidays." We were excited. We wondered what we would be told. We were chatting, and stroking Monty. I finished the shoes, and we carried them upstairs to put them in the cupboard, as we wouldn't be needing them again for a few weeks. We raced downstairs, and were told dinner was ready. Lydia was asked to say grace. We were both looking forward to hearing what A.J. would tell us. Eating in silence was not easy, as we were dying to find out about the holidays.

We both liked our dinner. There was nothing for Monty tonight. Lydia and A.J. went to the front room. I did the wiping up and put the dishes away. "It's the holidays now. We will know what we will be doing."

"Yes. Let's go to the front room."

"Hooray. No homework! It's the start of the holidays." As we opened the door, A.J. said, "Come and sit down. I have some news for you. I have heard from your uncle, and he is coming down here to see you." We jumped up and down, we were so excited. I asked, "When?"

"I am about to tell you. It's next Sunday afternoon." We started talking together, asking questions. "Now please be quiet and I will tell you what will happen. Your uncle will be taking you to stay with him, and you will be spending Christmas with him."

"Oh, that's so good. How long will we be staying with him?"

"It's not decided yet how long you will be staying. We'll know more when Uncle arrives."

Lydia asked, "Will Father Christmas know where to come, to our uncle's?"

"Yes. We will let him know. Now, is there anything else you want to talk about?" I asked, "Yes. What will we be doing tomorrow? It's the holidays."

"You don't have to get up early. I have my job to go to." I squeezed Lydia's hand and thought, that's good. "Uncle Stan will get your breakfast and look after you. Your room could do with a tidy up. I will be home after lunch." We still had our new readers to keep for the holidays, and A.J. heard us read. Then it was time for bed. We raced up the stairs, chatting. I was so excited, and said to Lydia, "Isn't it good our uncle is coming, and we're going there for Christmas?"

"Yes, I'm pleased too." After A.J. said goodnight and turned off the light, we heard her go down the stairs. No stopping in the little room tonight. We must try and find that key soon, and see what's inside. I said, "That's the best news, about our uncle. I will tell him I don't like Aunty Jean, and want to live somewhere else." Lydia became upset. "Where will you live?" Lydia asked. "I don't want you to go." and she started crying. "No, we will stay together. I would never leave you. Please don't get upset. Our uncle might find somewhere else where we can both live." Lydia kept crying. "Please don't cry. I would never leave you."

"I don't think I want to live anywhere else." It was then I knew that Lydia was settled here. It was I who had the problem. I said, "Let's get to sleep." It took some time before Lydia finally went to sleep, and I started thinking about things, and what I was going to say to Uncle.

In the morning, I was so looking forward to A.J. going to her little job, and U.S. was looking after us. We stayed in bed, waiting for A.J. to go. It wasn't long before she called out, "I have left some sandwiches for you all. Be good. I'm going now. Goodbye." We said, "Yes, we will." We heard the door close. "Good. She's gone." We went downstairs to the kitchen for breakfast. U.S. left us by ourselves. He was already outside. I said to Lydia, "Let's try and find the key again."

"We will have to be quick." U.S. saw us in the kitchen and came in to ask if we would like toast for breakfast. We said, "Yes please.", so that's what we had. It was yummy. "I will be outside working in the garden. When you have finished, put your dishes in the sink, and then go upstairs and tidy your room. Come down when it is done." We said, "Yes." It was so good to eat on our own, and we could talk. We didn't even have to say grace.

We ran upstairs. On the landing I tried the door of the little room, but it was locked. We dressed quickly and went to A.J.'s bedroom. We had another look in the drawers of the dressing table. There was no key. I asked, "I wonder where she hides it?" We saw a chest of drawers on the other side of the bed, and walked over to have a look, and pulled out the top drawer. There were a lot of little boxes, and we started looking in some. A.J. had some nice things. There were some beads and rings. We tried them on, looking at ourselves in the mirror. We were having fun. Then we heard the back door open, and U.S. came inside, calling us.

"Have you tidied your rooms yet?" I said, "We still have some more to do."

"Come downstairs into the kitchen when you have finished."

We took off the beads and rings, put them back in the boxes and closed the drawer. Lydia had moved the mirrors. I said, "That's not how they were. I'll put them back like I think they were before. I hope that's right." We went to our bedroom, picked up some clothes, and hung them up. It looked quite tidy. We went downstairs to the kitchen. "What have you been doing?"

"We were tidying our room. It is quite tidy." I asked, "Can we have a play if the children are out?"

"Yes, for a little while." We raced upstairs and put our shoes on. U.S. had Monty on the lead, and we went down the garden to the side gate. U.S. opened it. There were a few children playing, and we all walked up to them. Betty was there, and they were throwing a ball. U.S. let us join in, and stood and watched us. I told Betty, "We are going away on Sunday for Christmas to our uncle's." She said we were lucky to be going away. She was staying at home. "How long will you be away?"

"I don't know. Only a little while, I think." I turned to U.S. and asked him. He wasn't sure. "Well," Betty said, "Tell us all about it when you get home."

We had fun playing. U.S. said to say goodbye. "We are walking Monty now." I was allowed to hold the lead. We went through to the allotments. U.S wanted to see how his vegies were going, especially the carrots, to see if they were ready to pull out of the ground. I was really interested. We had a bag with us, and U.S. pulled some carrots up. We put them in the bag. They were ready to take home. We put the handles of the bag over the tap where the hose was, to pick up on our way back. Then we walked to the end of the allotments and out of the back gate. A few people said hello.

Once we were out of the gate we were in a field. I was able to run with Monty. I wished we could let him off, as he wanted to go fast and was pulling me. Lydia couldn't even hold Monty, as he would pull her over. U.S. caught up with me. I had stopped. I remembered when we got to the stile, that I had to give the lead to U.S. and I made sure Monty would not get away again. I climbed over, and U.S. passed the lead to me. There was another field leading to a lane, which we walked down. There were large trees on either side, with a few leaves on, and lots on the ground. As it was windy, more were starting to fall. There were little nuts on the ground. U.S. told us they were beech nuts. They had a diamond-like shape. We started picking them up. They weren't very easy to see, and were hard to pick up, as they were amongst all the leaves. We wished we had that bag with us. We gave some to U.S., and he put them in his pockets. I asked, "Can we come back another day and bring a bag with us?"

"Yes. We will do that." We could have taken the bag that we had left on the tap if we had known.

It was time to walk home, and we went back the same way, to pick up our bag from the allotment. "I will water before we go home." I asked, "Can I do it?"

"All right," and he gave me the hose. He turned the tap on for me, and I watered the vegies. Then I decided to have some fun and spray Monty, who enjoyed it, jumping up and down through the spray. He looked like a drowned rat. Lydia got a bit wet, but she didn't mind. U.S. looked at me, and wasn't too pleased. It was time to walk home. The children were still playing, but we just waved to them. Once we reached home, Monty had to be put on his chain, and U.S. got a towel to dry him off. I gave him some fresh water. We had to go inside. A.J. would be home soon. Shoes off! We chatted about the nuts as we ran upstairs. "We must remember to take a bag with us next time," I said. "I wonder when U.S. will empty his pockets? I hope he puts them in a dish on the table so we will be able to eat some."

We took off our coats and had to hang them in the cupboard. A.J. would check our room and in the cupboard, so we had to make sure it was tidy. When we hung our coats up, A.J. would always make us do the top button up. This was to hold the shape of the garment, she would say. When she went to the cupboard to get our school things out, she would check if we had done it correctly, and say, "If you do it enough times, it's a good habit, and you will always do it automatically." I still do this now, and often think about how we were brought up. Some of it was good, and stayed with me, but some of it I disliked. Underneath, I feel, she meant well --- she just couldn't give me any love. Our upbringing was so strict. We had to speak precisely, say please and thank you, and excuse me if I wanted to interrupt a conversation, or if I wanted to pass anybody. She would say, "Speak when you're spoken to." and, "Children should be seen and not heard."

Chapter 27

We heard A.J. come home, talking to U.S., as we came downstairs. "I hope you have been good." We said yes, and started telling her what we had been doing. "Uncle Stan has already told me. Now I will check your room, so come upstairs with me. Then you can help me in the kitchen, to get some vegies ready for dinner." We followed A.J. back upstairs to our room. We had been sitting on the bed, and the bedspread was all crumpled. We had forgotten to straighten it. That was the first thing wrong. Also, our chest of drawers wasn't properly closed, and we had left some clothes on it that had not been put away. "Now you need to fix this." She looked at me. Then she went to the cupboard. She was quite pleased we had remembered to hang a few things up, and do some of the buttons up. We hadn't done them all, but we had tried. She left the room, saying, "Come down when you have finished." We did what we had been told. "I am going to try the door of the little room. I heard A.J. go in there before." As we walked past the little room, I tried the handle. It was locked again. "I am going to ask A.J. what is in there when we are in the front room."

"I could ask her. She won't get cross with me."

"That would be good. We only have one more day, and our uncle will be here. Hooray! It will be so good to see him." Lydia agreed.

We had peas to shell. I just loved doing that, and we would eat some raw. The only thing was, there weren't many going in the saucepan. A.J. said, "Stop eating them. We will not have enough for dinner." U.S. came in with some potatoes he had dug up from the garden, and put them in the sink. I was asked to wash and peel them. Although I had been shown many times how to do this, I just couldn't grasp how to use the peeler. She became quite cross with me. "How many times do you need to be shown?"

"Sorry. I just can't do it." U.S ended up doing them. I wasn't allowed to use the knife yet, which I was glad about. I was frightened I would cut myself. Lydia set the table, then we were allowed to play outside while dinner was cooking.

We were excited. Tomorrow our uncle would be here. I was so looking forward to him coming. While we were outside, we chatted about what we would ask A.J. in the front room. It would be our last time for a while. Lydia said she was going to ask what was in the little room, as we both wanted to know. A.J. called us in, as dinner was ready. We knew what our vegies were, but wondered what the meat would be, and soon found out. It had lots of gravy with it, and was minced meat. Neither of us liked the taste much. We found it hard to hide it in our hankies, as there was so much gravy. A.J. saw we were slow with our eating. She stood and watched us. She gave us a spoon to scoop up the gravy, saying, "Now it's easier. Just stop playing with your food." We had to eat most of it, as she kept watching us. We managed to get a small amount in our hanky. After A.J. and Lydia left for the front room, I asked, "Is there any gravy in the saucepan that Monty could have?"

"No, but I could put some water in the saucepan and go around the edges with the spoon, and he would get a taste."

"That's a good idea. I can take it out to him." I thought to myself, I was so pleased that I asked, and now I could put my little pieces of meat in his dish. "One thing I will really miss is Monty."

"I'm sure he will miss you too." I gave Monty lots of pats and told him we were going away the next day.

U.S. called me in and said, "Let's get these dishes done and join Aunty Jean and Lydia in the front room." A.J. asked, "What do you want to talk about?"

"What time is Uncle coming?"

"He will be here for lunch when we get back from church."

"How long will we be staying with our uncle?"

"I'm not sure yet."

"It's going to be so good." Lydia asked, "What is in the little room?" We could see A.J. was so surprised at Lydia asking that question.

"You don't need to know. It doesn't concern you." I said, "But we hear you go in there, and then we hear this rustling noise. We want to know what it is."

"Well," A.J. said, "it's not something you need to know about." I said, "But why can't you tell us?"

"Now that's enough. Is there anything else you want to talk about? We have to sort out some of your clothes for you to take." With that, she got up, saying, "I'll come upstairs with you and get a bag out of the cupboard, and we will sort out the clothes." We went upstairs. From the top shelf, A.J. pulled down a large bag, and put it on the bed. She started opening the chest of drawers, getting out some undies and socks. We went to the cupboard and helped to put clothes on the bed, because we had to be shown how to fold them before they went into the bag.

"We have made a start. We will have to wait until tomorrow to do the last-minute things, when we come back from Sunday school. Now I will run a bath for you, and I will call you when it's ready for you to hop in."

When we were on our own in the bath, I said, "Well, we still don't know what's in the little room."

"She didn't get cross with me, but she won't tell us."

"We must find that key. It will have to be when we are back from Uncle's. Isn't it exciting? We are going to Uncle's!"

"Yes. It's been so long since we have seen him. A.J. came in to wash our backs, and said, "Out you get and dry yourselves, and get into your night clothes. Then come down with your readers, and I will hear you read." We were allowed to read in bed for a while, and enjoyed reading by ourselves. After A.J. came upstairs, said goodnight and turned off the light, we found it hard to get to sleep. I said, "I wonder if we will be sleeping together at Uncle's." We were too excited to sleep, and talked for a long time. A.J. heard us: "It's time you were asleep. Enough talking! You have a big day tomorrow." Down the stairs she went – no stopping on the landing. I whispered, "We must find out what's in there when we get back." Eventually I fell asleep, way after Lydia, as I kept thinking, what was I going to say to Uncle about myself and how I was feeling, and about so many other things?

In the morning, we woke late, and A.J. told us to hurry and come down for breakfast. I had to say grace, and we enjoyed our Sunday breakfast. Then we had to hurry to finish getting ready. It wasn't long before we were walking to Sunday school. Our teacher knew we would be away for a while, and said she hoped we would have a nice time. We had made friends with some of the children, whom we sat with, and they said they would miss us, which was nice. After Sunday school we all had to go into the church for the service. We were always glad when that was finished. There was no standing talking to anyone when we came outside. A.J. was in a hurry to get home and organise lunch. On arriving back, we set the table and helped in the kitchen.

Uncle would be here very soon. We were excited. A.J. said we were allowed to go out to the front garden and wait by the gate. We saw the bus go past and knew the stop was further up the road. Uncle would be getting off and walking back towards the house. It wouldn't be long before he came in view. We were beside ourselves. I saw him first and opened the gate. We ran up the path to meet him. He gave us big hugs. We were both talking at once. "Now, one at a time! Gosh, you have grown so much since I saw you last." I asked, "After lunch we are going straight away, aren't we?"

"I will have to have a big talk with Aunty Jean and Uncle Stan first, so it will be later in the afternoon when we leave." We reached the front gate and walked around the back. Monty started barking – he didn't know Uncle. I said, "It's all right, Monty." Uncle gave him a pat.

A.J. opened the door to let us in. She said hello to Uncle and shook hands with him. "How are you? Did you have a good journey? Nice to see you." U.S. was there too, and said, "Hello. It's been a long time." Then, turning to us girls, Aunty Jean said, "Go upstairs and show Uncle where the bathroom is. Then wash your hands." We all went up together. It was so great having him with us. We showed him the bathroom, then our room, and the clothes which we had packed. He said, "That's good. You're organised." I asked, "How long are we staying with you?"

"I need to talk with Aunty Jean about that. We had better go down now for lunch." In the kitchen, A.J. was serving our lunch and our uncle said grace. It was different from the one we knew. We all ate our lunch and liked it. While eating, Uncle was talking to A.J. and U.S. Our meals had always been eaten in silence – now we heard conversation!

Chapter 28

We just listened and kept quiet. It was so different hearing grownups talking. After lunch, A.J. said, "You girls can help Uncle Stan in the kitchen, and then, when the dishes are done, you can go to your room. Uncle Stan will be joining us in the front room." While we were helping to tidy up, U.S. said he would miss us. I said, "I might miss you too." Lydia said, "Of course we will miss you, but it's only for a short time." There was no food left for Monty. I asked, "Can we give him something to eat, as we won't be seeing him for quite a while?"

"Oh, all right. Go out quietly and get his dish, and I'll find something to put in it." I went to give him a hug, as I had done before. He just stood there. It was as if he didn't know what to do. Lydia was surprised that U.S. was going to give Monty some food. She said, "Aunty Jean wouldn't like you giving Monty food now."

"There is no need to say anything. All right?"

"I won't say anything." A.J. didn't call out, so she must not have heard us.

After the kitchen was all tidy, U.S. said, "Off you go to your room, and see if you can put anything else on the bed with your bags that you think needs to go with you. Aunty Jean will sort it out when she comes up. Be good. It shouldn't be too long." He went into the front room. We cleaned our teeth, put our toothbrushes on the bed, sat down and chatted. I said, "I hope it won't be long before we go. Let's try and find the key again." I jumped off the bed and walked to the landing. Of course, the door was locked. Lydia said, "They might come out of the front room soon. We had better not. Uncle would be so cross with us if he knew what we were thinking of doing."

"I just want to leave now. It will be fun going on the train again, and seeing our aunt." Lydia said she couldn't remember her very well. We stood at the top of the stairs, listening. We could hear voices, but couldn't really make out what was being said. I heard my name being mentioned a few times. I said, "I wonder what she is saying about me?"

"Don't worry. I'm sure Uncle will tell us."

We sat on the top stair, looking down. We could see the door of the front room. We were still listening, leaning over the banister, trying to hear. The voices grew louder. I aid, "I wish we could go out and see Monty. I'm tired of waiting."

"We had better not. Let's go back to our room." We sat on the bed and played a little game – I Spy with My Little Eye. We did that for a while, then we heard the door open. A.J. called out that she was coming up to finish packing our things. We said, "That's good."

When she saw us, she asked, "What have you been doing?" We told her we had been playing I Spy.

"Have you put anything else in your bags?"

We said no. The few things on the bed needed to go in, and she did this. She checked to make sure there was nothing left out.

"Glad you have been good. We can take the bags down."

I carried the small one and A.J. took the heavier one down. Lydia followed us. We left the bags at the door and went into the front room. I was thinking, almost time to go. I can't wait for it to happen.

Both uncles got up when we walked in. Our uncle said, "It is time to leave. Say goodbye to Aunty Jean and Uncle Stan." We said our goodbyes. Aunty Jean said, "We will see you in a few days." I said, "Oh. As soon as that?" Our uncle gave me a stern look, saying, "Yes. Your stay will not be for very long. I will be in touch with Aunty Jean." We picked up our bags and walked to the gate, waving, as we walked to the bus stop. I was asking Uncle a lot of questions, and he said, "When we are on the train we can talk. We have nearly an hour's journey." There was a wait for the bus, and he said, "No more talking." We had to wait at the station for the train. We were so looking forward to being on it. I couldn't wait to talk to Uncle and ask all the questions I wanted answered.

Chapter 29

At last, we were on the train and had a carriage to ourselves. Uncle said, "We can now talk."

"How long are we staying with you?"

"It depends on a few things, and I'm not going into details at this stage. Now I want to know, how are you finding it at Aunty Jean and Uncle Stan's?"

"I don't like Aunty Jean. She isn't very nice to me and I don't really want to live there." Then our uncle asked Lydia how she was finding it, and she said she didn't mind her, but agreed Aunty Jean wasn't nice to me, which was unfair. He asked me, "Why do you think that is so?"

"Well, I think it's because I was behind with my schooling, but I have almost caught up, and I never get any praise from her. I just don't like her."

"Aunty Jean feels you are rude to her, and answer her back a lot."

"It's because of how she is with me. Sometimes she tries to separate us. I don't like that. Oh, I just don't like her."

"I want you to try and get on with Aunty Jean. She is a very good Christian lady and is kind enough to have you both living with her. Now, you have settled into school, and it would be too disruptive for you both, finding somewhere else to live, and somebody new to live with. Well, will you do that for me?"

"I will try. I just wish she would be nicer to me." Lydia said, "I stick up for Sylvia when I can."

"That is nice of you, Lydia. Keep doing that, and maybe Aunty Jean will realise herself that she could be kinder to you, Sylvia. As you grow older you will understand that there will be people you don't like as much as others. You need to get on with them in life. You can't always avoid certain people because you don't like them." Uncle then asked me, "What about Uncle Stan?"

"He's quite nice. I get on all right with him." Lydia said, "He's nice, and does things without Aunty Jean knowing." Uncle gave us a surprised look. I said, "Yes, he is not as strict." I asked our uncle, "Why is she like that? We have to do a lot of jobs, and she won't let us play with other children."

"Because she feels it's the right way to bring you girls up, and it won't be doing you any harm for your future, her being like that. But I will have a word with her about it. Please understand, she is doing what she feels is best for you both."

"She doesn't show us any love."

"Some people find they can't show or even give love, but remember, what she is doing is giving you both a home, and you are being taught the Christian way of life. Now, that is love in a different way. Both Aunty Jean and Uncle Stan couldn't have children, and I'm sure they love you being with them. They will be missing you even now, and by having you girls living with them it is a different kind of love." I said, "Oh, it's hard for me to understand. I want hugs like you give us. Lydia and I give hugs when we say goodbye or when we have done something nice for each other. Why can't she? That's the love I know and want.

"That is so good. You keep doing and showing that, and one day it might be returned."

"But why can't they do that now?"

"We are all different, and I really want you to try to understand and see if you can get on better with Aunty Jean. I am proud of you both," and, turning towards me, he said, "You have done so well to get where you are at school. Just keep on trying. Don't ever give up. Will you do that for me?" I said, "All right." He looked at me and said, "I'm sure you'll get on better if you don't answer back."

"But I find her hard to get on with."

"It will get better with time, I'm sure. Now we are going to have some fun while you are staying with us."

"What are we going to be doing?"

"Wait and see."

Once we were off the train, Uncle carried our bags. There was a bit of a walk, with lots of traffic going past. It was very noisy. He lived in Ealing. I remembered there was a park not very far from where he lived. I could see trees in the distance, which meant we were nearly at his house. I couldn't wait to get there. I wondered what our Aunt Alice was like now, and Cousin Marion. Uncle told us on the train that we had another cousin, a little boy, whose name was Peter, who had just started to walk. Uncle said, "You must be tired." We replied, "Yes. Are we nearly there yet?"

"It's not much further." We were walking through the park, and I asked, "Can we stop for a swing?" He put the bags down and said, "That's a good idea. I can have a rest too." We ran to the swings. There was nobody on them – great. I called out to him, "Can you give us a push?" We enjoyed our swing for a while. Then Uncle said, "Come on. We had better get going. Aunt Alice will be wondering what has happened to us." So, picking up the bags, he said, "Just a bit further to go. We are nearly there."

We could see as we walked up the path that Aunt Alice had the front door open. Uncle called out to her, then she appeared, carrying a little boy in her arms. She gave him to Uncle and gave us both hugs. She was so pleased to see us. Uncle put Peter down on the floor. He started to walk a bit, then crawled. We ran after him. He was so cute. We loved him, played with him and giving him cuddles. When Marion came home, I felt she was quite grown up. It took a little while for us to get to know each other. Aunt Alice made a lovely meal. Uncle said grace and we all talked at the table. It was fun. Marion couldn't believe we weren't allowed to talk while having dinner. Afterwards we played games indoors. It was the best.

Chapter 30

When it was bedtime, we saw a big double bed, which meant we were sleeping together again. We chatted way into the night. Nobody came upstairs and told us to be quiet. I felt and wished we could live with Uncle for ever, but knew it wasn't possible, because he was away often with his work, and Aunt Alice wouldn't be able to manage four children. Lydia and I hung our stockings up on Christmas Eve. Such excitement! We woke up very early, checking what we had in them. We had some fruit and walnuts in their shells, and a book each in our stockings. From our uncle and aunt, Lydia got a soft doll, and I was given a doll that looked like a baby, made from a kind of porcelain. It had flexible arms and legs held by elastic bands. It had clothes on that I could take off, and some extra clothes with it. This doll is still in the family. We were very happy with our presents. There was a small Christmas tree on a table in the hall, with lights on. Aunt Alice, I found, was so easy to talk to.

When I was helping in the kitchen and we were by ourselves, I plucked up courage and asked, "Can I talk with you about myself?"

"Of course."

"I notice my body is changing. What should I be doing? I can't talk with Aunty Jean."

"That's a shame. She should be explaining things to you." I said I felt I couldn't talk to Uncle about it. "I understand."

"It's nothing to worry about. It happens to girls between the ages of twelve and fifteen. You could be having a period soon. This is the start of becoming a woman. You must tell Aunty Jean when that happens, and she will buy what is needed." Bit by bit, I learned the facts of life. Each night, Aunt Alice spent half an hour with me, talking about growing up, while we were doing the dishes. I had no idea – it was all very interesting. She said that if I had any questions, she would answer them. I became really close to her – we got on so well. Lydia loved playing with Peter, and Marion went out quite a bit. She was more grown up than I was, as she was four years older.

My uncle had a study and spent mornings working. At lunchtime we would all get together, either playing games indoors such as snakes and ladders, which we loved, or going to the park. We had fun. Lydia and I were so happy. We were there for two weeks, and neither of us wanted to leave, but Uncle was going overseas in two days and would have to take us back. We cried and didn't want to go. "We must not get too upset, or else we can't do this again." After saying our goodbyes to Aunt Alice, Peter and Marion, and giving big hugs, we promised not to make too much fuss about leaving. When packing our bags, we had more to fit in, and had to squash it down. We just managed to fit everything in, although we had an extra carry bag for my doll. I couldn't squash that in my bag, as it would break. We were loaded.

Chapter 31

We caught a bus to the station and didn't have to wait too long for the train. While on board, Uncle said, "I will have a talk with Aunty Jean and Uncle Stan about things. Now, you have promised me to try harder to get on with Aunty Jean, and Sylvia, see if you can control yourself and not answer back." I said, "I'll try". I asked, "When can we come again?"

"I am not sure, and will keep in contact with Aunty Jean. I will write to you too." We were so happy that Uncle would be writing to us, and we could write to him. I said, "That will be so good. Can I write to Aunt Alice?"

"She would like that."

When we got off the train, it wasn't long before we saw the bus that would take us back to A.J.'s. As I looked out of the window, the bus passed A.J.'s and the vacant block, as the bus stop was a bit further on. I noticed there were lots of children playing. We got off, carrying all our bags. It was just a short walk to the vacant block and A.J.'s house. The children were still playing and called out to us, waving. Uncle said, "That's nice. They have missed you."

"Yes, but Aunty Jean doesn't know we play with them sometimes. Uncle Stan lets us when Aunty Jean's not around."

"Oh. I will have a talk with both of them."

"Thank you. We like playing with the children, but we don't want to get Uncle Stan in trouble."

"I will say it in such a way that he won't. Now, don't worry." We reached the front door. I rang the bell and kept my finger on it. Uncle said, "That's enough."

Aunty Jean came to the door and said, "Oh. I wasn't expecting you so soon. The bus must have been early."

"How are you?" Then I said, before Aunty Jean could answer, "We had the best time."

"I'm glad." Uncle said, "It all went very well. Did you have a good Christmas? I Hope you managed to have a rest." U.S. came in from the garden. We ran to him, talking about our Christmas and what we had in our stockings from Father Christmas. We were so excited. Our bags were at the front door. We raced to get them and started pulling out our presents. Aunty Jean said, "We will see them later. How about Uncle helping you to put your bags in the bedroom? Then come down." I asked, "How is Monty? Can we run out the back and play with him?" Uncle Stan said, "Yes. He will be so pleased to see you." We could hear Monty making a noise with his chain, running up and down. Aunty Jean said, "Will you please take your bags upstairs now?" We ran up the stairs, dropped the bags on the floor, and raced down again, through to the kitchen and out of the back door. We were dying to see Monty. U.S. said, "Look how pleased he is to see you." Monty was jumping up and down with excitement. We patted him and I asked U.S., "Can he get off his chain?" He said, "Yes." Then I ran to get the lead.

A.J. and our uncle were in the front room. She called out to U.S. to join them. We ran up and down the garden with Monty, playing with him until he was tired. Then I put him on his chain and we got him more water. We went inside. We could hear loud voices. We tiptoed to the front room. I had my ear to the door and tried to listen but couldn't really make out what was being said. I asked Lydia, "Shall we open the door and go in?"

"Oh no, we'd better not."

"Well, nobody has told us what we should be doing. Monty is tired. I'm going to knock on the door and see what happens. Our uncle is there. Let's see if she gets cross with us." So, I knocked and opened the door. Aunty Jean said, "We are having a talk, and it's not for you girls to be here. Go up to your room. You can unpack your things and put them away." Ignoring A.J., I asked our uncle, "Are you staying for dinner?" He answered, "Yes. Aunty Jean has kindly invited me. Now, go to your room and do what Aunty Jean has asked."

"Yes. Goody!" Running up the stairs, passing the door of the little room, I tried the handle. It was locked.

Chapter 32

Lydia said, "We had better unpack and put some things away."

"All right then. But if they are still talking, we can have a look for the key again." We sat on the bed and unpacked, pulling our clothes out of our bags. At the bottom of the bag, we found the game of snakes and ladders. Aunt Alice must have put that in. How nice of her. She didn't tell us she was going to do that. We must tell our uncle. So, we decided to play, while sitting on the bed. When we finished, Lydia said, "We had better put some clothes away."

"All right. It won't take us long." We did that, then I leaned over the rail on the landing, listening. Yes, they were still talking. I asked, "Now what?"

"Let's play with our dolls." So, we did that for a while. I asked, "How much longer are they going to be talking for? Come on – let's run down the stairs again." We stopped at the door of the front room and heard our uncle's voice this time. We could not make out what was being said, so went out into the garden again to play with Monty. We could still hear the children playing. Oh, how we wished we could go and play too! We walked to the side gate. I tried to reach the bolt to open it, but couldn't. We called out to them, but they didn't hear us. However, Aunty Jean did. Everybody came out of the front room to the back door, and Aunty Jean called us to come up to the kitchen. I said, "We are bored. You have been talking for such a long time." Aunty Jean turned and said to our uncle, "See what I mean?" Our uncle said to me, "That's no way to talk. Yes, it has been a long while, but there was a lot to discuss."

"We were only calling out to the children. We would love to play with them." A.J. said, "Come into the front room and we will have a talk."

Lydia and I looked at each other. Our uncle smiled. I thought something good was going to happen. We squeezed onto the couch next to our uncle, who said, "Aunty Jean will speak to you both." A.J. said, "We have had a long talk, and I know you would like to play with the children sometimes. When I'm working on a Saturday and you have done your jobs, and when Uncle Stan is looking after you, that can happen, and maybe after school, when you have done your homework."

"That would be so good."

"Your school work must be finished first."

"It will be." I gave our uncle a hug and said thank you.

"Now thank Aunty Jean." We said thank you. Our uncle said, "You know you could be in a different class this term, so it could take a little while to settle in and make new friends."

"We might have the same friends as we had before."

"Well," A.J. said, "You won't know until you're back at school. You will have to wait and see what happens."

"We should still be able to play with our friends." Our uncle said, "Yes, but you might find you make new friends. This is your last year at primary school, before you start secondary school."

"Oh. Unless I stay down. I don't want to go to another school."

"Now, please don't talk like that. You must keep trying with your school work. You have done well. It's all part of growing up."

"But I won't see Lydia!"

Aunty Jean interrupted, "You will be together after school. Now, why don't you show your uncle the back garden, while Uncle Stan and I organise dinner?" We got up and took our uncle's hands to pull him off the settee and went through to the kitchen and out of the back door into the garden. Monty was beside himself– he was so excited. I called out to U.S., "Can I put him on the lead, and go to the vacant block to show Uncle?"

"Well, all right. Dinner will take about twenty minutes." We were excited and ran to the back gate. Our uncle reached for the bolt and opened it. Some children were still there. They came running towards us. Betty was one of them and was so pleased to see me. Our uncle spoke with her, and then we told her about our holiday and that we would also be able to play on Saturdays, and sometimes after school. "This is really good." We had one more week of the holidays, and then we would be back at school. Lydia talked to some of her friends and said she was looking forward to going back. I said to Betty, "Wouldn't it be nice if we were in the same class?" She said yes. Oh well, I thought, we will have to wait and see.

Our uncle said, "We had better make our way back. Aunty Jean will have dinner ready." On our way, he said, "Now, Sylvia, I want you to promise me that you will try very hard to think before you speak, and not be rude to Aunty Jean."

"It's not easy. I don't mean to be rude, but it just comes out, and it's because of how she is with me." Lydia said, "Yes, she isn't as nice to Sylvia as she is to me." Our uncle said, "Like I said before, I'm sure if you are nicer towards her, things will get better."

"I will try, but I still don't like her."

"Just speak nicely, then Aunty Jean won't have anything to be cross about." I thought, he really doesn't understand, or see how she is with me, but I will try, and see if it makes any difference.

We came into the kitchen. A.J. said, "Dinner is ready. Go to the bathroom and wash your hands." We ran up the stairs, saying how we would do our best to do what he wanted. "Hope it's something nice for dinner."

"Well, I won't be able to hide any food, if you give me any. They will be watching us. We will just have to eat it." We sat round the table, our uncle sitting between us, and A.J. asked him to say grace. It was the one he said when we were staying with him. It was a nice dinner, but there was just one thing I didn't like, cabbage, but I swallowed it. Our uncle made conversation with Aunty Jean while we ate, and she actually told him, "We don't talk at meal times."

"Oh, sorry." I put my hand under the table to try and touch Lydia, but I couldn't reach her. Uncle looked at me as I touched him instead. We ate in silence. I wondered why Uncle didn't stand up to her. After dinner we all went to the front room. Our uncle only had a short time before he had to leave. I was feeling sad. There was more talking, then our uncle got up and said, "The time has come to say goodbye." We all walked to the front gate. He gave us big hugs and whispered in my ear, "Don't forget what you promised."

"I will try." It felt good, as if Uncle and I had a little secret, and I did want him to be proud of me. I wasn't sure I could do it, though. A.J. held Lydia's hand to walk back inside. I stood by the gate until Uncle was out of sight and started to cry. U.S. was standing near me. "Don't be upset." He held my hand. "You will see him again soon." We walked along the path to go inside. A.J. said, "Now these dishes need to be done."

"I will do them and the girls can help." I wiped and Lydia put away. A.J. said,

"I'm going upstairs to check on the clothes you put away. Come up when you've finished."

We had done that, but A.J. said it had not been done very well. She fixed it up. I asked, "Can we play Snakes and Ladders?" as it was still lying on the bed.

"I think it would be a good idea for you both to have an early night. It's been a big day."

"I'm not tired." Lydia quickly asked, "Can we show you our presents?" She said yes, and we started pulling them out of our bag. I asked, "Can we call Uncle Stan to come up?"

"All right." So, I ran to the top of the landing and called him. I think A.J. was surprised at what we had been given, and she had to find room on a shelf to put them on. When U.S. saw our game he said, "We must play it with you." A.J. answered, "Not tonight. It's getting late. Time for bed." Once in bed, after A.J. had closed the door, I heard her go downstairs. We whispered. Lydia said, "I think A.J. will let us do more things, and she will be nicer to you."

"I hope so, and I will try to be nicer to her, but I still don't like her." We whispered for a while and did go to sleep quite quickly. A.J. was right – we must have been tired. When came down to the kitchen, A.J. said, "Good morning. There was no need to wake you." It was later than usual. U.S. was already in the garden, and A.J. made our breakfast, saying that she had made some sandwiches for lunch for all of us, and would be leaving soon to go to her job. I thought, that's good.

"Can we play with the children if they are on the vacant block?"

"Yes, but first there are a few things that you need to do."

"Thank you." A.J. gave me a surprised look, as if she couldn't believe I said thank you. She told us what she wanted done. Lydia nudged me. We ate in silence, put our dishes in the sink and raced upstairs, chatting. "I told you A.J. would be nicer."

"We'll see. Let's get our jobs done quickly. Hope the children come out and play." After cleaning our teeth, we made a start on the jobs. It wasn't long before A.J. said she was leaving. She seemed nicer to us and said, "I will see you later. Uncle Stan is in the garden, and sandwiches are on the table for your lunch." We said goodbye, then heard the front door close. I said, "Come on, let's hurry and finish." We had the stairs to dust. We quickly got dressed and made cleaning the stairs into a game, then hurried through the rest.

There was nobody to check on us. We hadn't seen U.S. yet. I said, "I want to try and find the key. Let's go into A.J.'s bedroom." We wanted to start looking but were always being distracted by the dressing table mirrors just inside the door. Lydia loved turning them to different angles to look at herself and calling out to me to come and have a look. We thought it was clever and were fascinated by what we looked like when we moved the mirrors. Then we heard the back door close. U.S. called out, "What are you both doing?"

"We have just finished our jobs."

"Good. Put your shoes and coats on and come outside." We hurried, putting the mirrors back as we thought they were, and did as we were told. We opened the back door and could hear the children's voices, and Monty greeting us with funny noises. U.S. said, "He would love a walk. We will do that first." I asked, "Then can we play?"

"Yes."

We did our favourite walk, to the woods. We loved running and would take it in turns, holding Monty. U.S. would hold Monty while Lydia and I picked wildflowers. Bluebells were my favourite. Lydia and I put our bunches together to make one big bunch. U.S. would carry them back. He said we could go and play. He would take Monty back. It was fun to join in and play without U.S. standing and watching us. He said he didn't need to stand and watch us anymore. He would call us when it was time to come back. We would run back to eat our sandwiches. There were only the three of us. How different it was! We felt more relaxed, even though we were still not allowed to talk while eating. Afterwards, U.S. would ask us how we were feeling. He was friendly and would smile. We felt happier being with him, and he seemed happier too.

When A.J. came home, the atmosphere changed. As I grew older it became more obvious, and I would feel uptight. I really tried hard not to answer back, and for a little while after our uncle returned home, things were a bit better. It didn't last, and I became unhappy again. It was the way she spoke to me, and I could tell she didn't like me. I was always glad when she wasn't around. I said to myself, I will do my best. I promised our uncle.

School was starting in the morning. Our clothes were to be put out ready and we had to be in bed early, as we needed to be up in time. We talked in bed, wondering what our teachers would be like. It took a while for me to get to sleep. Aunty Jean woke us and told us to hurry and get dressed, then come down to the kitchen for breakfast. She walked us to school and inquired where we had to go, and to what classrooms. Lydia and I were going to see each other in the playground at morning break. We gave each other a hug and Aunty Jean said, "Goodbye. Be good and learn." I felt a bit nervous when I arrived in the classroom. Children were standing and chatting, and I couldn't see anybody I knew. Then the teacher, a lady, came in and told us to find a desk and sit down. She said, "Good morning. It will take me a little to get to know everybody." She seemed nice. We started with times tables, which were written on the board. At morning play, I looked for Lydia. I couldn't see her, but she saw me first. "I've got a nice teacher, and one of my friends is in my class." She was happy, which was good. J hadn't seen anybody I knew. "Why don't you have a look around and see if you can find some of your friends? I am fine. I will see you at lunchtime." So, I left her with her friend while I went looking for someone I knew. I was feeling a bit lost.

Then I heard someone call my name. I turned around. It was a group of girls I had played with previously. "Come and join us!" they said. I thought that was nice. When chatting to them, I asked whether they were in my class. Two of them were, which was good. I still hadn't seen Betty, though. When the bell rang, we went into our classrooms. It all went well and I felt I was doing all right. Lunchtime came and I caught up with Lydia. We ate together, then she ran to join her friends. I left her knowing that she was happy. It took me a while, but eventually I saw the group and joined in with them.

I was still feeling a bit disappointed, as I couldn't find Betty, and wondered why. Back in class again, all went well. At the end of the day the teacher gave us homework, which was to be handed in next morning. I was wondering if I would be able to do it. She did not speak to me on my own, and I just put it in my bag. The bell went and everyone, including me, rushed out of the classroom. I was to meet Lydia at the gate with U.S., who was walking us home. Lydia was at the gate with U.S., waiting for me. She was very chatty and had had a lovely day, having made some new friends as well as seeing those she knew. U.S. asked me how my day had been. "It was all right, but I couldn't find Betty." He was glad my day had gone well, even though I hadn't made any new friends or seen Betty. "Guess where we are going?" Lydia said, "The sweet shop." U.S. answered yes. We thanked him and held his hand. I already knew what I was going to choose. It seemed a long time since we were there. Our paper bags were full of sweets. We were on our way out as a few children were coming in, saying hello, but there were none we had played with. While walking home, U.S. had a sweet out of each of our bags and said, "Now, you know this is still our secret." "Yes. We haven't even told our uncle."

"Well, that's what a secret is. You don't tell anybody." We knew we had to finish eating before we got home. Talking with U.S., I told him, "I have homework."

"Oh. I hope you will be able to do it." Lydia didn't have any, only her reader, which I had too. "We will have to get into the routine of doing it after dinner, homework and reading." We knew the drill. A.J. wasn't home when we arrived. We quickly changed and ran outside. Monty was excited. We said hello and patted him. I asked U.S., "Can we have a quick play?" He said yes. He unbolted the gate. We ran to the group of children. Betty still wasn't there. No one knew where she was, but one of the girls said she would find out, as she lived near her. We had a play and it was fun. U.S. called us. We said goodbye to the children and ran back. He said, "Now, quickly do your jobs." My job was cleaning the shoes, and Lydia went inside to set the table. U.S. made a start on dinner. While I was cleaning the shoes, I patted Monty. When I had finished, I just got the lead and ran up and down the garden with him. No A.J. yet!

I quickly got Monty some fresh water and went inside, asking, "Where is Aunty Jean?" and Uncle Stan said, "She had to go to a meeting and won't be home until late."

"Oh, that's good." Lydia gave me a look. I knew what she meant: "Don't be rude." U.S. didn't say a thing. It was the first time we had had dinner without her. It was so good. U.S. had left some dinner for her when she got home. We talked about things while wiping the dishes and putting them away. I had homework to do and U.S. took Lydia into the front room. I hadn't even looked at it. I pulled it out of my bag and put it on the kitchen table. I was surprised I was able to do it, and pleased with myself. I was excited and ran into the front room, telling U.S. He said, "That is good." He heard us read from our readers. "Now, please go upstairs and get ready for bed. I will be up shortly." We were in the bathroom when we heard A.J. come in the front door, calling out to us to come downstairs and see her. I said, "We haven't finished in the bathroom yet." Then, to Lydia, "I wish it was only U.S. looking after us."

"She will be nicer to you. Just be careful how you talk to her."

"I just don't like her. It's so hard for me to do that. She always finds fault with me." We ran down the stairs to the front room, where A.J. asked how we got on at school. We told her about our day. She said she was pleased it went well. Turning to me, she said, "You need to make new friends, like your sister has done."

"I hope to soon." We settled into school quite well. I got most of my homework correct. At playtimes I joined the group and became part of it, although I still hadn't made any new friends, and hadn't found out about Betty. I wondered when she would be back, and if she would be in my class. How good that would be.

It wasn't easy for us to have a play, once we were home from school. A.J. always found some reason for us to stay inside. I was dying to get outside, because I wanted to know from this girl who lived close to Betty, why she wasn't at school. I hadn't seen her, and felt sure this girl would be playing on the vacant block.

Chapter 33

I was looking forward to Saturday, when A.J. would be going to her job, and U.S. would let us play. We would chat in bed, whispering about everything. Lydia loved school, and had just started to get a little homework. She was growing up. She joined me after dinner at the kitchen table. We would sit opposite each other, and A. J. and U.S. left us on our own. This was great. We would talk and help each other. A.J. would come into the kitchen every so often, saying, "You shouldn't be talking. Have you finished yet?" Of course, Lydia didn't have as much homework as I did, so I was left on my own. I now found some of it more difficult, but the teacher didn't say anything to me when I handed it in, and I did get some wrong. I was just given more each day, like all the others. We would talk amongst ourselves, and I found out that others were, like me, getting some wrong. That made me feel better, so I was not worried. I knew what subjects I liked, of course. They were the ones I was good at, and I was happy with that homework. Nothing more was said about the ones I got wrong.

The weekend came at last, and A.J. left us with a list of jobs that needed doing. We did them as quickly as we could, always making it a game to see who could finish first, or sometimes we finished together. I said, "We are going to find this key. No looking in the mirrors." I held her hand and we walked past the dressing table to the other side of the room, where there was a large chest of drawers. The drawers were long and heavy. I held one handle and Lydia held the other. We pulled, and managed to open it a tiny bit. It was hard to do. We pulled again, and eventually we got it open wider. It was full of clothes. Lydia said, "It won't be in there."

"It might." and started pulling clothes out and passing them to Lydia, putting my hand in, stretching my arm and reaching the bottom. "Oh", I said, "I can feel something hard, but I can't reach it to take it out. Help me take more clothes out!"

"We can't do that. We haven't got any more time. U.S. will be calling us. We'd better put the clothes back. We will get caught."

"Oh, all right. Pass the clothes to me. I will put them back. Be careful."

As Lydia was passing them to me, some fell out of her hand. I was trying to fold them neatly. I said, "Have a look out of the window. Can you see U.S. in the garden still?" She said no. "Oh, that means he might be inside. I will do this. Go downstairs and see." Lydia ran downstairs. I could hear her talking to U.S. I quickly put the clothes back and tried to close the drawer, but couldn't. I heard Lydia come running upstairs and into the room, saying, "U.S. said to put our coats and shoes on."

"Help me close this drawer first, please." It was hard, but we managed it. We ran into our room, put our coats and shoes on and went downstairs. U.S. was in the kitchen, having a drink. He said, "That's good. You're all ready for walking Monty. I'll meet you outside, and you can put him on the lead, ready. I won't be long."

We chatted outside. I said, "That was exciting. I wish I could have reached what I felt. I wanted to see what it was."

"We were lucky we didn't get caught. Hope you put the clothes back all right." U.S. came outside and we were ready to go. I asked, "Where are we going?"

"To the allotments, to see how the vegies are growing. We might pick some to take home, if they're ready." He had a bag with him. Once we were outside the gate, the children were calling to us. I asked, "Can we play when we get back?" He said yes, then I asked, "Can we just do a short walk? Monty could come with us when we play, and I will look after him."

"We will see." It was sunny. Monty was in a hurry. Soon we were walking down the lane. U.S. was trying to keep up. He called out, "What's the hurry?"

"It's Monty, and we would like time for a play too."

"Please wait at the stile, and I will take Monty." We waited and then got over the stile. U.S. took Monty, who went under it, and we started running. It was fun. We hadn't got far before U. S. called us, saying, "Time to go back and look at the allotment. Hopefully we will get some vegies, and then you can have a play."

"Thank you. That would be good." When we reached the allotment, we picked some peas and greens, put them in the bag and started walking home. Yes, the children were still there, and U. S. said we could run and have a play. He took Monty. I found out that Betty wasn't well, and hoped to be at school on Monday.

Chapter 34

Uncle Stan called us and we ran home. After giving Monty a pat, we went into the kitchen. "Who is going to help me shell the peas?"

"We will. We love doing them." We would eat a few, while shelling them, and were always told, "There won't be enough for dinner. Put them in the saucepan." We rushed upstairs to take our shoes and coats off and wash our hands. Then we helped with the peas. The front door made a noise. It was A.J. coming home. She wanted to know how our day had been. We told her, and I asked, "Can we play a game inside while dinner is being cooked?" She said yes. We said thank you. Since our uncle had had a talk with her and U.S., we were allowed to do more things, which was good. We ran upstairs and got out our game of snakes and ladders, which we loved. We were called when dinner was ready. I asked, "Can we all play a game after dinner?" A.J. said yes. Lydia nudged me. I said, "Thank you. That will be fun." A.J. looked surprised. There were fewer things we didn't like eating. We were getting used to different tastes, but Monty missed out a bit and was always looking for food when I went outside to say goodnight. I would try and find something in the cupboard that I could sneak out and give to him. On Saturdays we were allowed to stay up longer, and it became a routine to play a game, or sometimes we were allowed to read in bed.

We liked Sunday school and had made a few friends. There was this girl whom I had seen at school, who came. I found out her name was Sylvia too. She had really blonde hair, almost white. We became friends. A.J. knew her mother, and Sylvia also joined Sunday school. We would sit at the table together. There would be coloured pencils and sheets of drawings for us to colour in. Before we did that, we would have to listen to a story about the pictures.

Sometimes we had a different teacher. Her name was Miss Miller. We really liked her. When Sunday school was finished, it was she who took us into the chapel, and would sit with us. The minister would give his little sermon especially for us. Then, when he was finished, we would stand and sing the hymns listed on the board. Our teacher had an unusually shrill voice, and when she sang, she would move her head up and down, and her neck would turn red. We girls would get the giggles, and found it hard to stop. It was really funny. We thought she looked and sounded like a cockerel. We would get stern looks from the congregation. When we reached home, A.J. wanted to know what was so funny. When I told her, she said I was being very rude, and should know better. I was sent to my room. A.J. came up after a little while with the wooden spoon and used it on my legs. I had to apologise to Miss Miller, who was understanding about it. We children did like her, but found it really hard not to get the giggles when she sang. That's how it was.

As we grew older, we went to the evening service as well and would have to sit still. We found it difficult getting up the next morning and would often have to be woken. We would have to hurry and get dressed and have a quick breakfast before walking to school. We always gave each other a hug before we went to our classrooms. I couldn't believe it when one day Betty was in my classroom, standing amongst a lot of children. The bell went and we all had to go to our desks. Betty was still standing when the teacher came in. She spoke to her, saying, "You can find a desk at the back." It was so good to see her. I couldn't wait for morning recess. We ran outside, asking, "Where have you been? Are you well? I have missed you". She told me why she hadn't been at school. It was because she had been seriously ill and had missed a few weeks. How great it was to have a friend!

Chapter 35

I wanted to see how Lydia was. Betty came with me and I found she was happily playing with her friends. "I don't need you to check on me. I'm all right. You go and play with your friends." She had met Betty before, when we played on the vacant block. I said to Betty that Lydia was becoming more independent, but I still wanted to make sure she was all right and happy.

Betty and I had so much to talk about. We joined in with the girls playing with the skipping rope. At the end of the day, we were given more homework. Again, the teacher didn't say anything to me about the ones I got wrong. She wasn't like my other teacher, who would contact A.J to let her know what was happening. A.J. was unaware of the situation. I would just answer the ones I knew. Nothing was said to me. I hadn't seen my other teacher since I was in her class, and wanted to tell her what was happening. I told Betty, who said, "Don't worry about it.", so I didn't.

One day, Lydia and I were sitting at the kitchen table on our own, doing our homework. I could hear a man's voice talking in the front room. I asked, "I wonder who that could be." Then we heard a lady's voice. Lydia asked, "Did you see anyone come inside?" I said no. After a little while, U.S. came out to the kitchen. "Come into the front room." We looked at each other. When he opened the door, nobody was there, but we could hear a lady speaking. Looking around, we wondered where the voice was coming from. Then we saw on the floor a little black box-like object. We were told it was called a wireless. A.J. said, "Listen to the lady who is talking." The lady said a program was coming on for children now. A.J. said, "Sit down and listen," It was exciting. It was called Anne of Green Gables. Both of us liked it and were told it was a serial, and would be on again next week. We looked forward to that.

There were other programs we were gradually allowed to listen to. At the weekends we still had our jobs to do, while A.J. was doing hers. We couldn't wait for her to go. That was when we did our exploring to find the key. It was I who desperately wanted to know what was in the little room.

"Let's have another try," I said to Lydia.

We raced to do our jobs, then, standing on the landing, we tried the door again, which was locked. We looked out of our bedroom window to make sure U.S. was in the garden, in his little greenhouse, which he was. Then we went into A.J.'s bedroom, going straight to the chest of drawers to have another try, walking past the mirrors. I passed clothes to Lydia, till I could feel the bottom of the drawer. I couldn't feel anything. I asked, "What happened to the lump I felt?"

"Take these clothes and let's put them back." I was really disappointed. Hurriedly, we put everything back again and with difficulty, got the drawer closed. We went into our bedroom and talked about it. "I did really feel a lump before."

"It could have been just buttons on some clothes that were squashed up."

"I don't know if we'll ever find the key."

"Well, she doesn't want us to know what's in there. We will find out one day, or A.J. might tell us."

"I really want to know now. I want to keep trying to find the key."

U.S. had no idea what we were up to, and never checked on us or our jobs. He would only ask, "Have you done what Aunty Jean asked you to do?" and we would say yes. When A.J. got home, if things had not been done correctly, and often they weren't, she would be cross, and I, being the eldest, would be punished. I knew I was the instigator of everything. Lydia only did what I asked her to do, and that's how it was.

When I told Betty and some of the other children about everything, they said they didn't have any jobs to do, like we did. I found out as I grew older that it wasn't the norm. A.J. was extra strict, and expected a lot from us children. I confided in Betty that I was having pains in my tummy, and she said I could be getting my period soon. Did I know about that? I told her my Aunt Alice had told me a bit about things. "You must tell Aunty Jean."

"It's going to be hard for me to do that."

"It happens to us girls. Nothing to worry about." Betty said she was already having her period. I was surprised. She told me more about it. Lydia knew I wasn't feeling so well, and said she would come with me to tell A.J. We were in the kitchen. It was dinner time, but I wasn't even hungry. A.J. said, "That's not like you. What's the matter?"

"I have a tummy ache."

"Oh", she said, and served me a small amount. "You must try and eat something, and I will talk with you after dinner. Come to the front room."

Lydia and U.S. stayed in the kitchen. Lydia gave me a look. Would I like her to come with me? she meant. I shook my head.

"Now what is wrong?" A.J. asked. I told her, "I think I might be going to have a period."

"That could well be. I will buy you something when I'm shopping. You are growing up, and you will have to get used to what happens to your body. It is a natural thing." I told her I had heard a little about it from Aunt Alice. I thought A.J. might explain more to me about it. She only said, "That's good, so you know what to expect."

"I just want to go to bed now."

"Yes. Oh – have you got much homework?"

"Only a little."

"Well, see if you can get that done first, then you can go to bed."

As soon as we were in bed, Lydia asked about what A.J. said. "How did you get on, and what did she say?" I ended up telling her about everything I knew. She was surprised, and I knew she was worried about me, as I really had problems and so much pain. I couldn't go to school for a few days. A.J. said, "You will get used to it as you get older." I thought, I'm glad Aunt Alice had explained things to me, as A.J. didn't have a talk with me about any of it.

It was over a week before I went back to school. While I was away, I lay in bed, thinking about what Betty had said, "We are in our last term of primary school, and next year we will be going to another school." I felt upset and sad, and didn't want to go without Lydia. What if she needed me? I wouldn't be there for her. Besides, I would really miss her. A.J. had told us when our uncle was here at Christmas, "It's all part of growing up, and there's nothing you can do about it. That's how it is." I thought, I don't like this growing up much. Betty had said that there would be two schools one could go to, it depended on our school reports and marks, but you wouldn't find out about that for a few weeks yet, till the end of term. All this was on my mind. I would spend my mornings in bed and U.S. would make lunch. We would have it together. I would chat to U.S., and found him easy to talk to, when there were just the two of us. He said not to worry so much about things. He said I was doing quite well with my school work. "Keep doing the best you can. That's all anybody can ask." I thanked him. He hadn't spoken to me like that before. I decided I'd ask, because he was nice to me,

"Can I have Monty inside for company, please?"

"Oh, yes, for a little while." I think he felt sorry for me, and from that time on I felt we became closer. I don't think A.J. knew anything about those times, and U.S. always made sure Monty was outside on his chain before she came home.

Chapter 36

After a week home from school, I was feeling better, and soon got back into the routine. Lydia was pleased that I was walking with her. A.J. wrote a note for me to take to the teacher. I was given homework at the end of the day. Betty was pleased I was back, and told me a bit about what I'd missed. I was wondering how I would go with the backlog that would be given to me. I thought, I'll ask Betty if she can help me. Then I remembered what U.S. said, "Do the best you can." The teacher gave me the same homework as Betty had – no extra to do. We talked after class about it. "If you have problems, you should let the teacher know. If I can, I will help you."

Lydia and U.S. were waiting at the gate. Lydia asked, "Why were you so long?"

"I was talking with Betty about homework." U.S. asked, "How did you go?"

"I must let the teacher know if I can't do it."

"Yes, she is right. You do need to let the teacher know. Now, let's get walking to the sweet shop. We are running late." We enjoyed choosing what to have and just managed to eat them before arriving home. Once home, we knew our routine and got our jobs done. The weather was colder and it was becoming dark earlier, but I still had to clean the shoes outside. After dinner, it was nice to have Lydia sitting at the table with me doing homework, as she had just started having some. A.J. would say, "No talking.", and would check on us from time to time. When U.S. and A.J. left us on our own and went to the front room, we would talk a bit. Lydia was happy doing her homework. She found it easy and got hers done quickly. She tried to help me, but I was three and a half years older. She really didn't understand what I was doing. Of course, once A.J. knew Lydia had finished, I was left on my own. I was struggling, but did not want to tell A.J. I knew she would be cross, and would feel I should know it. So, I never said anything.

Next morning at school I would show Betty my homework before the bell went and we had to go into class. She helped me a bit before we handed it to the teacher. I was no good with my maths, but my other subjects weren't too bad. It was so good to have a friend like Betty. We became inseparable. At lunchtimes, Betty would come with me to see Lydia and we would all have lunch together. The term of primary school was coming to an end. I had really settled into school. It made such a difference to have a close friend and we all got on well. At the end of the day, I was getting more homework, but nothing was said to me about the ones I got wrong. Sometimes the teacher would talk to all of us and explain a certain aspect from our homework, but it was not done individually.

Chapter 37

It was a Friday night when, after dinner, we were in the front room. A.J. said she had something to tell us, "I have another little job you will help me with, and I will show you what needs doing." I asked, "Do we have to do it?" A.J. looked cross. "Yes, you do. It will be good for you, and if you do it well, you will get paid. It will be pocket money for you and you can save it in a money tin." Lydia looked at me asking, "That sounds good, don't you think?"

"Can we buy ourselves what we want?"

"No. It will go into a money tin. You will have one each, and when you're older, you will then have some money to spend." I thought, that's good.

"What is the job we have to do?"

"I will show you tomorrow. It is in a chapel, and you will be dusting and putting hymn books out on the back of the pews, behind the rail."

"Is it our chapel?"

"No. It's just around the corner from our street. We will go tomorrow. Now, let me hear about your day." We took it in turns to talk about school, then were told to get ready for bed. We ran up the stairs, talking. I said, "Well, I wonder if we will still have our jobs to do as well."

"She will tell us more soon."

"More jobs? I just want to play after A.J. goes to her job."

We got ourselves ready for bed, then went down to say goodnight to U.S. A. J. would come up to see us into bed. She turned off the light and said, "Goodnight. Straight to sleep." We heard her stop at the landing and unlock the door of the little room. We listened. We heard the rustling noise, the door being closed and locked, and her going down the stairs. "What do you think it could be?" I said to Lydia. "I don't know. She might tell us one day."

"Well, she knows we hear her doing it. I think it's not right that she won't tell us what she's doing." We talked about it before we went to sleep. We were woken by A.J., who said, "Get dressed as quickly as you can and come down for breakfast." When we were in the kitchen, we were told we would be leaving very soon to do the job. We walked. It wasn't far, just around the corner, as she said, in the next street. There was this small chapel with houses on either side.

A.J. got out of her pocket a large wooden ring with lots of keys on. She had the largest key to unlock the wooden door. I thought, I bet the key to the little room is on that key ring. She unlocked the heavy wooden door that made a squeak as we went inside. It was quite dark. A.J put some lights on and we walked to the front, where there was a little room called the vestry. A.J. gave us some rags and we were shown what to do – the dusting of the pews. I did one side and Lydia the other. A.J. went up to the pulpit, dusting. After that, we were given hymn books to distribute. When we had finished, U.S. came to pick us up and we walked home with him. A. J. was going to her other little job she did on a Saturday. We still had our jobs to do at home. U.S. would go into his greenhouse and we were told to let him know when we had finished. "Let's hurry and do our jobs. Then we can explore to find the key." We had less time now. We had another little look on the dressing table, in the knick-knack pots, but no key. Lydia said, "There's nowhere else for us to look. She must have the key with her all the time on that bunch of keys she has." I ran and tried the door again. Yes, it was locked. "Oh. We will just keep trying when we can."

Chapter 38

A.J. had bought money tins, and each Saturday, when she came home, she would give us a penny to put in. If we had been really good, we would get a threepence. We loved doing that, hearing them drop in, feeling the tin getting heavier each week. We would shake the tin to see if any would come out, but nothing happened. We couldn't wait for it to be full, so we could count how much money we had, hoping A.J. would let us spend some on things we liked. We didn't mind doing our chapel job, but found doing our chores at home no fun. We still walked Monty with U.S, after lunch, and he would let us have a play when we were back. I asked each time, "Please, can Monty come with us on the vacant block while we play?" It was always "No." He would put him on his chain. Then, one Saturday, I asked. "Oh, all right, just for a short while." I still had the lead in my hand, and raced to where the other children were. They patted him, and he was jumping up and down, having a lovely time. I ran with him and we had fun. When U.S. called us, we ran home. He had left the gate open and was checking on us from time to time. Everything went well, and this was something we did every Saturday. Monty would come with us. Before we went inside, I would put him on his chain and run inside to find a little biscuit to give him. A.J. never knew about those times. U.S. said not to say anything, so this became another little secret we had.

We came home from school one day. U.S. unlocked the door, and there were a lot of letters on the mat. I picked them up, and recognised one from our uncle. "This is from our uncle."

"It's for Aunty Jean."

"Do you think she will tell us about it?"

"Of course. If she thinks it is something you should know about."

"Our uncle did say he would write to us. We wrote a letter a long time ago and haven't heard anything. Did A.J. send it?"

"Yes, she would have sent it."

"Why can't you open it?"

"No, it's for Aunty Jean. You will just have to wait until she opens it."

"Oh, I wish you could open it."

"No, I can't do that. Go and get out of your school clothes and do your jobs." Once we were on our own, we talked. Lydia said, "She will tell us. Maybe he is coming for a visit. That would be great. I can't wait to ask her when she gets home." We were excited. After we had done our jobs, we were in the kitchen. U.S. was getting the dinner ready when we heard the front door, and A.J. came in. U. S tried to stop me as I ran to meet her with the letter in my hand. "What is all this about?"

"It's from our uncle. Please open it. He might be coming to visit us, and we really want to know. We did write to him, and we haven't got a letter back yet."

"Please slow down. I will read it when I can. Dinner is first, and you know when it's time to talk about things – after dinner, in the front room."

"You are mean and unfair. Why are you the way you are?" I couldn't help it – it just came out. I knew I would be in trouble as soon as I said it, and I was. "Go to your room and stay there. You are being very rude." I could hear Lydia asking her, "When can Sylvia come down?" I was thinking, why is A. J. so mean? I really don't like her. I wish she was different. It seemed a long time before Lydia was sent to come and tell me I could come down. Lydia asked, "Why did you do that? You know how she is. She gets cross. We can only ask about things after dinner in the front room. You know that." I found it so difficult to stick to these rules.

Once we were in the kitchen, my dinner was on a plate and I was left on my own. They all went into the front room. U.S. came to see me in a little while and said how disappointed he was with me. "Now do your homework, and when you have finished, come to the front room." I did the best I could and then did so. A. J. heard us read before we were allowed to talk about our day and ask about the letter. I was bursting to find out what our uncle had said. "Please can you tell us about the letter?" A.J. gave me this look. "Your uncle is wanting to make a time to visit. I will contact him." We jumped up and down. "That would be so good. Hope it's soon."

"Is there any letter for us?"

"No, but he said to thank you for the letter you wrote. He has been very busy." Little more was said. We would be told when he was coming. "Now get ready for bed."

Chapter 39

We ran upstairs. I said, "It will be the best thing." We were excited. A few days passed before A.J. told us that our uncle was coming. It was going to be on a Sunday, and he would be giving a sermon in our chapel. We counted the days, and at last, the time arrived. We were told to be on our best behaviour, especially me. He arrived very early in the morning. He gave us big hugs and we all walked to chapel together. Each of us held his hand and he was in the middle. A.J. and U.S. walked behind. The three of us talked all the way there. We had Sunday school first. When it was finished, we went into the chapel and saw our uncle in the pulpit. He spoke to all of us children first, giving us a short sermon, saying he had two nieces sitting here listening. We felt very proud. Some of the children were whispering, "Is that your uncle?" When he had finished, he spoke to the congregation, and we had to sit still and listen. Then it was over, and our uncle walked down the aisle to the front porch, shaking hands with everybody as they went out. As we got closer to the porch, I whispered, "What do you think he'll say to us?"

"I don't know." When we reached him, he shook our hands and said, "I'll see you soon."

"That's good." Once we were outside, it was that wait again. A.J. and U.S. were talking to people. We had to stand still beside them. Eventually, our uncle came out of the chapel and he started chatting to different people. More waiting! I became restless and we whispered to each other. "Hope it won't be much longer." A.J. heard us, "Behave!" At last, we were walking home again, Lydia and I in front with our uncle. He asked us about the service. "What did you understand about it?"

"It was about Love One Another." I asked him, "How can you do that if you don't like someone?" He looked at me. "You must always try and find the good in someone." I pulled a face. "Sylvia, behave yourself.

There will always be some good to find in people and you need to look for this. Try to understand, and always be kind."

After arriving home, we ran upstairs to wash our hands, while everybody else went to the kitchen. Then we ran down to the kitchen. A.J. was on her own. U.S. was showing our uncle the garden and his greenhouse. We had to set the table, and I was asked to run down and say that lunch was ready. Our uncle said grace and we had a nice lunch. A.J. went to a lot of trouble. We all ended up in the front room, chatting. Of course, our uncle wanted to know how I was going in my last term at primary school, saying how important it was for me to do well, and if I didn't understand anything, always ask.

"I don't want to go without Lydia."

"We have spoken about this before. You are growing up, and you won't be able to continue being with each other all the time." Lydia said, "Sylvia, I can look after myself now." Our uncle said, "When you are home again, that will be your time together."

"But I have always been able to be there if Lydia needs me, and besides, I will miss her."

"You have done well, and it will be hard for you at first, but Lydia will be fine. She has learned to stand up for herself, and this is how it is now. You have both grown up more, and this is the next stage of your lives." I was thinking, this growing up – I don't really like it. Lydia took my hand, saying, "I am really fine. Please don't worry about me." A.J., who had been very quiet, listening to the conversation, spoke, "You will adjust, Sylvia. This is how it is now. Why don't you both ask if Uncle would like to come and take Monty for a short walk, while Uncle Stan and I tidy the kitchen and do the dishes?"

Our uncle said, "That would be nice." We each held Uncle's hands, pulling him up from the settee. I ran to the back door to get the lead. That started Monty making lots of noises and rattling his chain. I managed to put him on the lead, calling out to Lydia and Uncle, "We are ready. Come on!" It was good having Uncle to ourselves. We conversed while walking and skipping to the woods. I knew the way, saying, "This is our favourite walk." On reaching the entrance, we could see that all the bluebells were out. He said, "This is lovely."

We will pick some for you. Please hold Monty's lead." We each picked a bunch, then put them together, which made a big bunch, and gave it to him. He thanked us, "I will take them home for your aunt, and she will love them."

"When can we see her and Peter again?"

"I'm not sure. I will try and arrange something." I held the lead walking Monty home. Uncle would be leaving later in the evening. We didn't have very much time left together. He told us that he was going overseas soon, and wouldn't be in touch for a while. We loved it when we were all together, and found it hard to say goodbye. We felt sad.

Having to get into our routine, and knowing that this was my last few weeks at this school, I felt uptight. I did really try hard, hoping and wanting to go with Betty to the same new school. At recess, she helped me with work I didn't understand, and I found I was able to catch up a bit, and was feeling more confident. After school, going to the sweet shop, I said to U.S., "I'm going to miss this."

"I'm sure Lydia will save you a few." Lydia said, "Don't worry. We can get some for you." U.S. said, "It might not be that easy." Lydia replied, "Oh, then I will save some for you. You won't miss out, but it won't be the same without you being here." I asked, "What time will I get out of school?"

"It depends on what school you are going to. We'll just have to wait and see. Just enjoy what you have, and remember, this is still our little secret."

"Thank you. We won't tell anybody." When we were on our own and changing out of our school clothes, "Lydia, I wish I could stay at the same school with you."

"I do too, but we will be together when we come home, and then we'll have lots to talk about. Please don't worry about me. I will be all right, and I can really stand up for myself now." I thought about what she said. Yes, she had grown up a lot and had many friends, but it would be hard for me, as I had always been there. This would be a big adjustment and separation. I would miss her so much. Deep down, I knew that Lydia would be fine. She was strong and loved school. It was I who was finding things difficult, and I was the one who had to get used to new things.

In a few weeks I would know what school I would be going to, and if I would be with Betty. Since our uncle had visited, A.J. was being a bit nicer towards us, me especially. I hoped it would last. One Saturday, A.J. said she would teach us to sew and knit, "Every young girl needs to know how to do these things." She was armed with wool and knitting needles, going into the front room after dinner. We were given needles and different coloured balls of wool. We could choose a colour we liked, and were told that we would be knitting a scarf each. It didn't take either of us long to grasp it. It became a race. We enjoyed it. When it came to the sewing, which she showed us another time, we found that harder. I really didn't like learning to hemstitch. A.J. said, "Another thing you need to know is how to sew on a button." Another time, we were shown how to darn socks. There was this plastic toadstool or mushroom we had to push into the sock where the hole was, and with the same colour thread or as close as, we were taught how to darn. We were kept very busy after school, and it became our only playtime with other children when A.J. was away working or at a church meeting.

The last weeks of primary school I really enjoyed. I made the most of that time, as I knew it was coming to an end. It went so fast. The day arrived when the teacher said she had an announcement to make. She called out the names of those who were going to certain schools. I held my breath. Would I be going with Betty? Listening to the names being called, I heard Betty's name, then others. At last, my name was called, and a few more after mine. The teacher was saying she would be giving us notes to take home, with information explaining details. I felt so relieved. I was going to the same school as my friend. How good was that! I barely heard anything else. I was starting to feel a bit excited. I couldn't wait for it to be time to go home so I could talk with Betty. After we were handed our notes to take home and had left the classroom, Betty and I gave each other a big hug, squeaking with excitement, saying, "We are going to the same school! This is the best!" Then we met Lydia and U.S. and told them the news. They were happy for me, and it was celebrated by U.S. buying me extra sweets. Lydia said, "Now you won't mind going to another school, will you?" I gave her a hug. "You're right. It will be better now that we are going to the same school, but I will still miss you."

Chapter 40

Walking home, talking about the situation, I said, "I have a note from the teacher."

"Show it to Aunty Jean. There are only a few days left. Enjoy your time together and then it will be holidays." I asked, "What will we be doing in the holidays?"

"You will have to ask Aunty Jean about that." I wasn't sure if I was looking forward to them. We arrived home and ran upstairs to change our clothes. Lydia said, "Don't forget to take the note out of your bag to show A.J." We did our chores, then helped U.S. in the kitchen, with getting the dinner ready and setting the table. A.J. still wasn't home. I asked, "Can we take Monty to the block?"

"No. Aunty Jean won't be long, but you can run him up and down the garden. Don't take him off the lead, though." We ran to get the lead and played with Monty. It wasn't long before A.J. knocked on the window, asking us to come inside. We raced upstairs to wash our hands. I grabbed the note from the bed to show A.J.

Dinner was served. A.J. said, "Now is not the time to talk about the note. You know we do that in the front room." I was asked to say grace, then dinner was eaten in silence. I knew I only had a little homework, and was looking forward to sitting with Lydia at the kitchen table. It was so good now Lydia had homework. We were alone. We would talk about school before joining them. A.J. had opened the note and said, "First, let me hear about your day. Lydia first." Just before Lydia finished, she said how good it was for me to have a friend to go to the new school with. A.J. didn't comment, and only said, "Sylvia, what have you got to say?"

"Have you read the note?"

"Yes."

"Well, the teacher did tell us that we would be visiting the new school and would be shown around. It was in the note – you didn't let us know." I asked, "When are we going to see my new school?"

"I will tell you when I feel it is the right time for you to know."

"But why can't you tell me now?"

"I have already said when you will be told."

"Well, you know I'm going to the same school as Betty. We are so pleased that we will be together."

"That doesn't mean that you will be in the same class." I thought, why does she have to be like this? Well, even if that happens, I'll see her at playtimes and on the bus. I asked, "What are we going to be doing in the holidays?"

"There will be a lot to organise – uniform, shoes -- you will need books, and something to carry them in, and your jobs still need to be done." After she heard us read, it was time for bed. When we were upstairs, Lydia said, "I'm glad you kept quiet about A.J. saying you might not be in the same class as Betty."

"I'm trying not to be rude to her, but it's like she can't be happy for me. I don't know why she's like that."

"Don't let her upset you. I think you are strong. Just keep doing what you are doing, and then she can't get cross with you." It was great that Lydia was growing up and could see how things were and we could talk about it. She was helping me to manage what to say to A.J. This wasn't easy, but I knew I would be worse off if I didn't hold my tongue sometimes, much as I wanted to say what I felt. Once we were in bed, we would talk heaps about things.

When the last week of primary school came, I was making the most of it, spending lunchtimes and playtimes with Lydia. I knew that this was all coming to an end, and I felt sad. I was even teary. Lydia would say, "You will have some good times at your new school."

"I hope so." She didn't seem to be upset.

I said my goodbyes at the end of the week to some of the children as I walked through the playground for the last time with Betty. "I'll see you in the holidays." U.S. and Lydia were waiting at the gate. We were going to the sweet shop for the last time. He said, "You can choose whatever you like." We both had a larger bag than usual. "Now, no talking, or you won't finish before we get home."

"I will miss this."

"We will work something out. Let's just wait and see."

"But when will I eat them?"

"Now remember, this is our little secret." We both said, "Thank you. We won't tell anyone."

Chapter 41

In our school holidays, A.J. worked in the mornings and we could get up late. We went down to the kitchen and got our own breakfast. Sometimes, U.S. would see us and come in from outside. He would make sure we were all right, and do breakfast for us. We had a few chores and then U.S. would let us take Monty to the vacant block. Often there were children playing and we would join in. Once A.J. came home our afternoons were organised, with finding out what was needed for my new school. One day after dinner, in the front room, A.J. announced, "We will be visiting the new school tomorrow and catching the bus."

I was excited and wanted to tell Betty, but hadn't seen her since we left school. I asked A.J. if all those who were starting at the new school would be attending. "I expect so."

"That's good. I will see Betty. What time do we get the bus?"

"It's in the morning, so you must be up and dressed, breakfast finished, as if you were going to school. I will be taking you and making sure you are ready."

"Can Lydia come?" She said yes. Lydia said, "Good. I want to see your new school too."

We talked in bed about visiting the school next day. I was feeling a bit nervous and it took a while for me to get to sleep. We were woken by A.J.: "Your clothes are on the chairs. Hurry up and get dressed and come down for breakfast." It wasn't long before we were ready to leave to catch the bus. As we walked towards the bus stop, we could see there were a lot of parents and children waiting, and the bus was pulling in. We hurried to catch up. I could see Betty, and waved to her. She waved back. She waited for us and we all got on the bus together. I said to A.J., "This is Betty." She said hello to Betty, and A.J. started talking. The bus was fairly full, but we managed to get a seat as I looked out of the window, wondering how long before we got there.

It took about 20 minutes before we went down this big hill, and the school was at the bottom. When we got off, a teacher was there to meet us. She said we should follow her. We walked to a big hall with a stage, with chairs set up in front of it. There was a lot of talking. We were divided into groups and shown around the school. Betty was not in my group and I hardly saw her to talk to. This school was very different to my last one. There was a courtyard which had plants in the middle of this big square, and classrooms led off that. It had a big gym at one end, with ropes hanging from the ceiling, and other equipment. We were shown inside, and there were ladders up on some walls. There was also a canteen at the other end of the square, where you could buy lunch. There were lots of fields where you could play hockey, cricket or basketball. We were also shown where the headmaster's room was and were told that if you misbehaved you would be punished. I had never seen anything like this before.

Lydia said the school was grand, and she hoped she could go there too. A.J. seemed impressed. We ended up back in the Assembly Hall. There was more talking about books, uniforms and a starting date. I could see Betty and called out to her as she sat in the front. A.J. said, "Behave. You can talk to her later." Once we were on the bus, we managed to find seats together. We tried to talk. Everybody was talking and it was quite loud. We really couldn't hear each other. When we got off, A.J. wanted to get going. I said to Betty, "We will see one another soon."

"I hope so." As we walked home, A.J. said, "It will be good when you are at school," and started talking about it, asking what I thought of it, which was nice. I told her, "I think I'll like it." Lydia said, "I can't wait to get there."

"You have three more years before we think about that."

Later, as we talked in the front room, U.S. wanted to hear all about it. I was excited about going. We talked lots in bed about things. A.J. went out to work in the morning and we were left alone in the house. U.S. was outside. We made our own breakfast and did our jobs. We knew our routine and I hadn't forgotten about finding the key to the little room. I still wanted to look for it. Lydia said, "It doesn't matter. She will have the key with her. We have looked everywhere for it." I was not giving up, so I went to A.J.'s bedroom by myself and had a look, but found nothing. I heard Lydia calling out for me, "Come on! Let's ask U.S. if we can take Monty for a walk."

"That would be a good idea."

We raced outside. U.S. said we could do that. There was no-one outside – all was quiet. We were now allowed to go walking in the woods by ourselves, and we loved that. U.S. said I was now considered responsible. We would run – it wasn't far. We took it in turns to hold the lead. U.S. had lunch ready for us when we came home. The afternoons we really didn't enjoy, as A.J. came home, and we would either knit or sew. I was counting the days until I would be starting my new school, and was looking forward to seeing Betty. When the weekend came, we heard children playing, and U.S. said yes, we could join them. We took Monty, and he was so happy when he could get off his chain. We ran with him. We knew most of the children, but Betty wasn't there. I hoped she wasn't sick. Nobody knew where she was. U.S. often took us to the allotment, and we would take a basket and pick some vegies to bring home. Also, it needed watering. We both wanted to water, often sprinkling Monty, who loved getting under the hose. It was such fun. Monty would then shake himself, wetting us all. U.S. wasn't happy about that.

Chapter 42

Our holidays were coming to an end, and this was the last weekend before the Monday when school would be starting. A.J. had everything organised, ready to go for the big day. When I was at Sunday school, I asked if anybody would be coming to my school. There were a few who said yes, so that was nice. I would be seeing some faces I knew. My friend Sylvia said she wasn't – she would be going to the grammar school, which was a shame for me, but I would still see her on Sundays.

It was hard getting to sleep on Sunday night. Lydia and I whispered for a long time about what the next day would be like. I was so nervous. Eventually I fell asleep. A.J. woke us, "You must hurry up. Bathroom first, then come down for breakfast. I don't want anything spilled on your uniform." We ate breakfast in silence. When we were finished, A.J. said to me, "You have a bus to catch now. No talking. Clean your teeth, get dressed and do your hair. When you are ready, come downstairs, Lydia too. We will walk to the bus and make sure you are on it, and I will then walk Lydia to her school." When I was upstairs getting dressed in my uniform, Lydia said, "You look so grown up." I had a look in the mirror. I did look older and different. Well, I thought, this is it. My life is going to change. I wonder if I will like it? We ran downstairs. A.J. was waiting. She handed me a satchel and had made lunch. Lydia was given hers. We said goodbye to U.S., who said to me, "Have a nice day. I'm looking forward to hearing all about it." A.J. said, "We must hurry up. No time to talk. You will miss your bus." She hurried out of the door and walked fast up the street. We kept up with her. A lot of people, children mainly, we could see, were waiting. On reaching the bus stop, Lydia gave me a hug. "I hope you like it." A.J. said, "Now be good and learn. Uncle Stan will be at the bus stop when you get off." I said to Lydia, "I will miss you. See you later on."

"Me too." A.J. said, "Come along. We are going now." She took Lydia by the hand and walked off. I could see the bus coming. When I got on, I couldn't see Betty. A few girls said hello. I got a seat near a window. I looked out and thought how strange this was, feeling very much alone. I wondered what had happened to Betty.

I found my first day a bit scary. We all went to the Assembly Hall, where the headmaster welcomed us. We sang the school anthem, Jerusalem. Then we said the Lord's Prayer. After this, names were called out for our classes. I found it difficult not knowing anybody. I had a young lady teacher. We had our own desks and used nib pens. There was a hole in our desks where an inkwell fitted. Using it was not easy. I had a lot of ink on my hands and smudged my work. We were given blotting paper and told we would get used to this.

At playtime, we went to the fields, where we stood around in groups, talking. I found out the names of some other girls in my class. We went to different classrooms for some lessons. We had lunch outside sitting on the grass, joining a group of girls, talking about our first day. It went very fast. Sitting in the bus going home, I was talking to a girl in my class, which was nice. This made me feel less lonely. I was really looking forward to getting home to see Lydia so we could talk about our day. I wondered if she had missed me as much as I missed her. It was so different for me. As the bus stopped, I could see U.S. and Lydia. I couldn't wait to get off. I ran to join them, asking, "How are you?" Lydia ran up to give me a hug. It felt so good. I had missed her heaps. She asked me so many questions. She had some sweets for me. I thanked U.S. Trying to eat them and talk at the same time wasn't easy. Lydia told me about her day. She was happy. She did say she missed me, but had had a good day. U.S. said, "Hurry up and finish your sweets. We are nearly home. You can talk later." It was so nice being together again. I couldn't wait to tell her how my day was. When we were home, we ran upstairs. I got out of my uniform while we talked nineteen to the dozen. It was really good. A.J. wasn't home.

We asked U.S. if we could take Monty for a walk. He said yes. We grabbed the lead and took Monty off his chain. He was a happy dog. Oh, how good it was being on our own with Monty, running to the woods and being able to say what we liked without having anyone to stop us. Feeling free as a bird was wonderful. When we reached home again, A.J. was back. We could see her through the kitchen window as we put Monty back on his chain and filled his bowl of water. A.J. knocked on the window, saying, "Come inside!" Lydia and I looked at each other. She said to me, "Be careful. Don't make A.J. cross with you."

"Don't worry. I won't."

Once inside, we had jobs to do. A.J. said, "We will talk about your day in the front room." Dinner was served and I had grace to say, then we ate in silence. This was a mincemeat dish Lydia didn't like, and she gave me a nudge under the table to let me know. She got her hanky out and gave a little cough. I knew what she was doing. A.J. said to Lydia, "Now eat up." As she got up to clear the table she said, "You should be hungry." I managed to eat mine – not that I really liked it either. When U.S. took my plate and had his back to me, Lydia gave me her hanky with food in. Now I had to give this to Monty. I was always wanting to go outside to pat him and talk to him. Also, I was allowed to give him his dinner sometimes. So, I asked U.S., "Can I give Monty his dinner?"

"Yes, after we have done the dishes." This is good, I thought. It's much easier to get it to Monty than it used to be.

I had no homework and neither did Lydia on the first day back. We helped U.S. with the dishes while A.J. went into the front room. She said, "When you are finished, come and join me and we will talk." Then, as soon as she had gone, I asked, "Can I get Monty's dinner ready?"

"Yes. Show me before you take it out to him." I knew what to do and how much Monty was allowed to have, and U.S. said, "That's fine." I was able to give it to him, and adding the meat from dinner was easy. He really enjoyed it and wagged his tail. We all joined A.J. in the front room, and I knew the routine. Lydia went first and I was really interested in what she said. It sounded as if she managed well without me around, although she did say she missed seeing me, and liked her new teacher. A.J. was happy about all that. When it was my turn, I said I found it a bit difficult and missed Betty.

"I did say to you that you won't be able to see Betty or talk to her, now that you are at high school. You must make new friends and grow up." She didn't understand that I found it difficult. I had hoped for a bit of caring. I knew deep down that she was right, but wished she could show a bit of understanding. I knew I was on my own there with A.J. U.S. didn't say anything while I was talking. When we had finished, A.J. said, "Make the most of having no homework tonight. It will start very soon. Now go and get ready for bed. You can read in bed for a while tonight." We raced up the stairs. I said to Lydia, "That's good. We will have time together to chat." Once in our night clothes we ran downstairs to say goodnight to U.S. He said, "Sleep well. See you in the morning." A.J. said, "I will be up in a while to turn off the light." In bed we just talked. I asked, "See if you know anybody who can tell you why Betty wasn't at school." She said she would see what she could find out. I really hoped she wasn't sick again. It wasn't long before A.J. came up to say, "Time for sleep." and turned off the light. "Goodnight. No talking." With that, she closed the door.

Chapter 43

We listened for her going downstairs, but no. We heard her turn the key to the little room. I whispered, "I want to get out of bed and go and see what is happening." Lydia grabbed me. "Don't be silly. You can't do that."

"That's what I want to do, but I won't. Let's listen for how long she is in there for." It seemed longer than it had sometimes. The door was being locked again. Then there was a rustling noise and the sound of her going downstairs. "How can we find out what she does and what the noise is?"

"She will tell us one day." I asked when. "I don't know, but we will find out." After us talking together, I really wanted to know. Lydia fell asleep, but it took much longer before I did. The next morning, A.J. had to wake us again, and it was a rush to get organised. We made it. A.J. said, "We will talk about this tonight." We were walking fast to get me on the bus. I just made it, with a quick goodbye to Lydia as I got on, with me waving and Lydia waving back and A.J. not looking at all. Again, there was no Betty. I sat with somebody new who didn't want to talk. I followed everyone to the assembly hall. "This is what we do each day," we were told. The headmaster spoke, then we sang the school anthem, and finished with a prayer before going to our classrooms. Everybody had to walk – no running, we were told. I was managing the work and liked the teacher.

Our desks were quite close together. There was a girl next to me. She said her name was Angela, and she had auburn hair. She was being friendly to me at playtime and started talking to me. Some of the other girls weren't very nice to her. I asked one girl, "Why are you being mean to her?" and was told it was the way she looked, with the colour of her hair, and she was a big girl. I felt sorry for her and thought, that didn't make any difference to me, and what was happening was wrong. So, because I was friendly with her, they didn't want to talk to me either. I wasn't sure what to do about it. By the end of the day nobody would talk to me. Angela would try and sit near me and be with me whenever she could. This made it not so nice for me. Should I tell the teacher or not? I was feeling miserable. I couldn't wait to get home and talk to Lydia about it. I wondered what A.J. would say. U.S. and Lydia were waiting at the bus stop, and I was given more sweets. Lydia asked, "What's wrong? You don't look happy." I thought, do I tell her now as well as U.S.? I did – it just came out. U.S. said that was really unkind, what was happening. Lydia said, "Why would they do that? What difference does it make?"

"I know. That's why I'm friendly with her. It shouldn't matter at all."

"But what can I do about it?"

"Well," U.S. said, "You'll have to report it to the teacher."

Lydia understood that would make it hard for me. U.S. said, "Finish your sweets." We were just about home.

"We will talk about it in the front room with Aunty Jean." While we were upstairs changing out of school clothes I said to Lydia, "Oh, I hope Aunty Jean will be understanding about it."

"Well, she can't be cross with you. Don't worry, it will be all right." After dinner, neither of us had any homework yet, which was good for me. We helped U.S. while A.J. went to the front room. While wiping the dishes, I said to U.S., "Can you tell Aunty Jean what is happening to me? It would be hard for me."

"Let's just wait and see what she says when you start talking." Lydia was putting the dishes away and said, "You could explain it to Aunty Jean for Sylvia." He said, "I will if there is a problem and you're not explaining it well."

"Oh. I wish you would do it for me," I said. A.J. came into the kitchen, saying, "I can hear a lot of talking. What's going on?" U.S. said, "We are nearly finished here and will join you soon." With that, A.J. went back to the front room. U.S. said, "No more talking. It will be sorted soon." We didn't say another word. Lydia and I looked at each other. When we were in the front room after Lydia had told us about her day. she was settling in well with her new teacher and happily making new friends. A.J. said she was surprised she hadn't any homework yet. Then it was my turn to talk. I told it exactly as I had done to U.S. and Lydia earlier. A. J. said, "Well, you should have told the teacher. That is ridiculous." U.S. spoke, saying it was a difficult situation. A.J. said, "Well, it won't get any better if left alone." I asked, "So should I tell the teacher in the morning when I go into class?"

"Yes. You need to say, "Can I talk to you, please?" and she will tell you when it is the right time to do that."

"It's going to be hard for me."

"That's part of growing up. Sometimes you will have difficult things to sort out. But you can do this, and you must. Do you understand?" I said yes. "Now, don't you have homework either?" I said no. "Goodness me. This is the second day without it. Well, I want you both to go to bed early and have more sleep. This having to try and wake you in the morning has to stop. You nearly missed the bus, Sylvia. Do you both understand?" We said yes. "Now go and get ready for bed." We raced upstairs. Lydia said, "You'll be all right. Just tell the teacher how difficult it is for you. I'm sure she will understand."

"I hope so. I wonder what she will do about it?"

"Don't worry. It will get sorted." I thought, I am not looking forward to doing this. After A.J. turned off the light, I couldn't get to sleep, thinking all the time about what would happen. I wished I could talk to Betty. I must have fallen asleep eventually. Lydia was awake before me and woke me, saying, "Let's get up before A.J. comes in." As we jumped out of bed, we heard A.J. coming up the stairs. "Good. You're up. Don't be long coming down for breakfast." We ate in silence and were told to go and get dressed and ready for school. We were walking to the bus in plenty of time. A group of children were waiting. Still no Betty. A.J. said, "Goodbye. You know what you have to do today." I said yes. Lydia gave me a hug, saying "Good luck." I thanked her. We could see the bus coming. A.J. said, "We are going now. Goodbye." As she took Lydia by the hand and walked away. I thought, I'm on my own. This is it. There was lots of chatter on the bus, but I didn't really know anybody to talk to. Once off the bus I followed everybody to the assembly hall.

I was beginning to know the routine. I walked to my classroom from there. Angela was already sitting at her desk, wanting to talk. A lot of chatter was going on as the teacher came in. Everybody stopped talking when she said, "Quiet please. Good morning, class." We all said, "Good morning." Then it was straight into maths, with her using chalk and writing on the blackboard. Maths was my weak subject, and I was finding it hard to follow what she was saying. I thought, at the end of the class I would ask her to explain it, and I could tell the teacher what was happening to me. Angela was whispering to me and I wished she wouldn't. I didn't want to talk and get into trouble. After maths it was morning recess. Angela said, "Come on." to me as I sat there still, waiting for everybody to leave. I said, "I want to talk to the teacher, so I will see you afterwards."

"Oh, what if I come with you?"

"No, I'll find you before we go to our next class." As everybody was leaving, the teacher asked, "Have you got a problem?" I asked if I could talk with her. The room was now empty. She closed the door and asked, "What can I help you with?" I said I was finding maths difficult. She spent time explaining it to me. I thanked her, then told her what was happening to me about Angela. She was nice to me and said, "This must not continue. I will speak to those who are doing it," and asked for names. I said, "I really didn't know all their names."

"Well, I will speak to the class. Now don't worry--it will be sorted out. Go out to recess." As I went out to the playing fields, I wondered what would happen. Angela found me straight away and asked, "What's wrong?" I ended up telling her. She couldn't understand why they were being like that, and I again told her. I felt awful about it and thought she should know. She got quite upset, and I said I didn't mean that to happen, but the teacher was going to talk to the class about it, so she would hear it from her, and would wonder why I didn't tell her. She said she understood, but was upset about how things were. It wasn't until later in the day, before we were back with the same teacher, that she spoke about the problem with Angela. If anyone was still being unkind, I should let her know, and they would be dealt with. "This is not how we behave. We must learn to get on with one another and others in society. We are growing up into adulthood." At the end of class Angela asked me if I would still be her friend. "Of course I will, yes. See you tomorrow." It was time to catch the bus.

I felt much better, even though there were some girls who avoided talking to me. I saw U.S. and Lydia waiting for me and knew they would want to know how I had got on, and I couldn't wait to tell them. U.S. said I did well, and Lydia gave me a hug, "I knew you could do it." It really felt good – it was nice to get some praise. When I thought about my day and how I managed to handle it, I knew I was growing up. This was my first experience of doing something by myself as I began high school. Later, when we were in the front room and it was my turn, I told A.J. wondering what she would say. "Well, you listened to me and spoke to the teacher, and now it's been sorted out." She said, "Yes, now you know what to do in future, I hope." She asked, "Have you got homework?" I answered no. "What, another night with no homework?" Lydia still didn't have any either, so we were allowed to read in bed. We spent our time discussing school. It was good to hear all about Lydia's friends and how she was getting on. She did tell me that she had heard that Betty was sick again. She said she would give the girl a message for Betty, that I was thinking of her and to get well soon. "That would be great." A.J. came up to turn the light off, saying, "Straight to sleep." We heard her go straight downstairs – there was no stopping on the landing that night.

Chapter 44

My first week at high school was bumpy, but I got through it, and a few more girls were talking to me, not so much to Angela, but she didn't seem to mind. We became close friends. She was good with maths and helped me to understand it. We were told that we would be having homework the next week. A.J. was happy with that and we still had books to read from our teacher. I was looking forward to the weekend and hoped Betty would be around on the vacant block. I had so much to tell her about school. We did our jobs on Saturday morning as fast as we could, so we could go outside. We heard voices, as we had our bedroom window open, and we could see U.S. in his greenhouse. I said, "Let's tell U.S. we are finished." We raced each other down the stairs and outside. "You have been quick. I hope you have done all your jobs."

"Yes. Can we join the children playing and take Monty?"

"All right, for a little while." I was disappointed, as Betty still wasn't there, and again no one knew what had happened to her. We played for a while, then went home. I asked if I could walk Monty. U.S. said, "I will walk with you, as I want to take some shoes to the cobbler's. Just wait for me." We knew where the cobbler's shop was, as we passed it when walking to Sunday school, but it was always closed on Sundays. U.S. came out with a bag with shoes in it. This was different. We walked in front, taking it in turns to hold Monty.

When we arrived at the cobbler's we watched for a while as he mended some shoes. He said, "Sorry to keep you waiting." U.S. showed him the shoes in the bag. Monty was becoming restless and wanted to get going. U.S. was talking about the weather with the cobbler. I took Monty outside and ran up the road. Lydia ran out of the shop and came with me. We bumped into a boy riding a bike, who stopped and said hello. I recognised him from Sunday school. He said he lived just a few doors up the road. We were talking when U.S. found us. He spoke to the boy for a while and introduced us to him. U.S. told us he was his sister's son and his name was Dennis. We were surprised – we had never been told anything about his family. "We are only a few houses up the road. Would you like to meet my father and mother? They are quite elderly, and live next door to my sister." We said yes. "How come you haven't told us about them?"

"I don't see them that often, but we could call in, as we are so close." There was a long pathway to go up, off the road, before we reached the house. We could hear birds making a noise, then we saw a chicken. Monty saw it first and pulled me towards it. The chickens ran, making lots of noise as we approached. We saw more chickens, half running, half flying, to get away from us, to go further up the garden. U.S. said, "Let me hold Monty." We walked towards the back door, which was opening, and a large, elderly man said, "Oh, it's you, son, causing a lot of commotion." When he saw us girls, he said, "Come inside."

"We are not staying long."

"You never do." Monty was not allowed to come in, and U.S. tied him to a post.

The room was quite dark, and a little old lady was sitting in an armchair. "Come closer. I can't see you. I won't eat you." Lydia held my hand and we walked to where she was sitting. "I'm your grandma and that is your grandad."

"I don't think that's right."

"Don't argue with me. You are being cheeky." Before I could say anything else, U.S. said, "I will explain things to the girls. I thought I would just call in to see how you are, as I was at the cobbler's dropping off some shoes." Monty was whining, making lots of noise. U.S. said, "I think we should go." We started walking to the door and his father grabbed me, saying, "Give me a cuddle." I pushed him away. U.S. said, "Dad, don't do that." He was cross, saying, "We are going now." I couldn't wait to get out of the door. Nobody had done that to me before. U.S. untied Monty, saying sorry to me. "My dad was showing his affection."

"I don't like it. I don't know him and it frightened me."

"I understand. It shouldn't have happened."

"I don't want to go there again." As we walked home, I asked U.S. about them being my grandma and grandad. He explained, saying, "They are your step-grandparents."

"Is it just because you are looking after us?" and he said yes, and went on to explain a few things. Lydia was very quiet. When we got home, we ran upstairs to our room and talked about it. Neither of us had seen anybody that old, and Lydia asked, "I wonder if he will tell A.J.?"

"I will, when we talk in the front room." U.S. was calling us, saying, "Come downstairs, and you can help to get dinner ready." I had carrots to wash. "I will tell Aunty Jean about our visit, so there is no need to say anything." We looked at each other. I said, "If she asks us, what shall we say?"

"You leave it to me to talk."

"All right," and started asking him questions. He told us he had a younger sister, and we would meet her one day. Sometimes, she went to church, but she was not a well person. They had two boys, and we had met the older one, and they lived next door to his parents. Lydia asked, "So you have no brothers?"

"Yes, I have two brothers. One is younger than me and goes to our church, and the other is older and I don't see him much." I asked why not. "We won't go into that. I think that's enough for you both to get to know in one day." I asked if A.J. had brothers or sisters, and he said no. "Now, no more questions." Dinner was already cooking when A.J. came home. "I hope you have been good. We will talk about your day after dinner in the front room." While we were having our meal, it was raining hard. We could hear it. I asked, "Can I let Monty inside?" A.J. said, "It's only a shower, and he does have his kennel to go into."

"But he is allowed to come in if it's wet, that's what you said. That made Aunty Jean get cross with me."

"Monty will be all right. Stop worrying about the dog and eat your dinner."

"I don't think you like Monty much, or you wouldn't be like you are to him." Lydia gave me a look. I knew I had said too much, and A.J. said, "You are being rude. Go to your room. I will deal with you when I've had my dinner." I quickly had another mouthful and stood up. I walked upstairs and sat on my bed, thinking. I felt I had only spoken the truth. Why can't Monty come in? A.J. is the one being unkind. When she came up to see me, she had the wooden spoon. I knew what that meant. She asked, "Have you anything to say?"

"I didn't mean to be rude, but why can't Monty come in when it's wet?"

"You have been told many times not to answer back. Do you understand?" and with that, she used the wooden spoon on the back of my legs. I was told to stay there until I was called to come downstairs. I looked out of the window, and wondered if it was still raining. Poor Monty – he just loved being inside with us, but there was nothing I could do. I thought, I will ask U.S. (when I am allowed to go down without A.J. hearing me) if he can say something to A.J. about Monty needing to come in when it was really wet. I could hear Lydia coming up the stairs to get her reader. "Why did you say anything? You know how she is."

"I feel sorry for Monty."

"But you get yourself into trouble."

"Yes, but sometimes I can't help it. It just comes out. It upsets me."

"Then you get into trouble. You should think about that." She gave me a hug and went downstairs with her reader. It always upset Lydia when I made A.J. cross. She didn't like me being in trouble, but I found it harder and harder to keep quiet. As I was growing older, I really didn't get on with her, and simply didn't like her. A.J. called me to come down to the front room. U.S. was there. Dinner was finished and the dishes had all been washed and put away. I was still hungry, but knew I wouldn't get anything until breakfast. Lydia was asked about her day, and then it was my turn. Neither of us said anything about our walk to the cobbler's. We thought U.S. was going to say something, but he didn't mention it then. He just sat there, twiddling his thumbs and saying nothing. A.J. said, "Tomorrow is Sunday. I will be up to get your clothes out. Now go and get ready for bed." We raced upstairs, talking about me being in trouble. Lydia said, "You remembered not to say anything about the cobbler's. Do you think he will tell A.J.?"

"I wonder that. I think sometimes he is afraid to say things." Lydia agreed.

When we were at Sunday school the next day, Dennis, the boy we saw, spoke to us, "Now I know who you are, and you are living with my uncle."

"Yes. We didn't know anything about Uncle Stan's family." Dennis said, "I don't see him much." It was a surprise to find that out. When walking back from church, Lydia and I talked about it, saying, "Do you think we should mention that we saw Dennis when we are in the front room?" We agreed that we would do that. Lydia said, "You can do it, but let's talk to Uncle Stan first. He might not want us to do that." It wasn't easy to see U.S. on his own, to tell him what happened, but I managed it later in the day. So, I asked, "Why can't I?"

"I don't want you to. It could cause problems."

"All right, I won't, then." When I told Lydia, she was surprised. We talked about it and both of us decided that U.S. didn't want A.J. to know about us seeing his family. We wondered why. What could his reason be?

Chapter 45

I was settling into school quite well, and now we were given homework. I wasn't sure how I would go. On the first night, when A.J. knew about it, she said, "That's good. You have homework." She left us, and we talked when Lydia had finished hers. It wasn't long before A.J. came in to check. "Have you finished yours?" she asked Lydia. "I see your books are closed – you have finished. Now come into the front room." Turning to me, she said, "Just get on with it. When you have finished, come to the front room."

"Yes." Some of the work I was able to do and felt pleased with myself. There was just a bit I did not understand. I went into the front room. Now there was our usual routine of talking about our day and what we had done. Neither of us mentioned anything about seeing Dennis. U.S. just sat and listened. Hardly ever did he make any comment.

When we were in bed we would talk about things. On Sunday nights we had to go to sleep straight away – no reading or listening to the radio. That was only for Friday and Saturday nights. We were managing to wake up in time for me to catch the bus. Sometimes it was a rush and A.J. would get cross with us, mainly me, saying, "You must have been talking in bed instead of going to sleep." There was still no Betty, which made me sad. I really missed her. A few girls talked to me, but they were not my friends. Not only did Angela sit next to me, but she followed me wherever I went. I think I was the only one who talked to her. I did feel sorry for her, but it became difficult for me to make more friends, as they didn't want to include Angela. At least they had stopped saying unkind things to her.

After lunch it was sports, and we had to change into our sports clothes. We were learning to play netball, and the teacher explained how to play and what was involved. I really enjoyed it, managing to put balls through hoops and score goals. Angela was unhappy. She was unable to run much because of her size, and wanted to sit out. The teacher said we all had to participate unless a note was given to her. Because I scored, I became popular and was spoken to more, but Angela was feeling left out. It wasn't easy for me and I tried to make her understand that I was still her friend, but I enjoyed sport and it was fun. It was all a learning time, finding out how to handle it. Angela was studious and got good marks. Sometimes she would help me and we would talk. At times I was snubbed and on my own, but then other girls would include me at playtimes. I really didn't know from day to day who would be talking to me. I would talk to Lydia about it and she helped me not to get upset. She said, "Do your best," and I said I would try. I never mentioned this in the front room.

I was still struggling with my maths and sitting at the front of the class next to Angela. The teacher saw me whispering to her and gave me a warning: no talking in class. Before class finished, we were whispering to each other again. I was told to stay behind when everybody left for recess. I had to sit and write lines – I must not talk in class, and the teacher decided I was no longer to sit next to Angela, and I had to swap places with another girl. I felt this was a bit unfair, as it was Angela who was talking to me. It turned out that when our lunch break came, children were talking to me, and I joined them in playing. From then on, I had problems in maths, with no Angela helping me. A note was written to Aunty Jean, and I was in trouble. I knew how it would be in the front room. I told Lydia when we were changing that I was not looking forward to telling A.J. Lydia said, "You will just have to get help. Don't worry – you can't be good at everything." Well, I thought, I guess that's true.

When our time came and it was my turn to talk in the front room, I said, "I have a note to give you."

"Well, what's that about?" I told her. She looked at the note and said, "I will have to see your teacher and see what's to be done." She was cross, saying, "I wondered how long it would be before the teacher contacted me. I will write a note for you to give her." I didn't tell A.J. that I no longer sat with the same girl in maths. When we were in bed, Lydia and I discussed things. "Well, you will get help from your teacher with your maths."

"Yes. I wonder if Angela will talk to me?"

"I'm sure she will." The next morning, A.J. said, "Now I have put a note in your satchel with your lunch. Make sure your maths teacher gets it, and please learn. You are growing up. It is important. Do you understand?"

"Yes. I will try." I said goodbye to Lydia at the bus stop. I couldn't believe it. Betty was there. We clambered onto the bus, getting a seat together. We were so happy, and she still had more to tell me when we arrived at school. She had been sick again and lots had happened. We were hoping she would be in my class, but it wasn't to be. We said, "We should be able to see each other at recess."

Chapter 46

When we were going into my maths class, Angela caught up with me and said, "Sorry, I can't help you any more now you're not sitting next to me."

"I have a note for the teacher, so I should be able to get some help from her." I thanked her. I handed my note in at the beginning of class and the teacher said she would talk with me at the end. I tried, but knew I wasn't following how to do it, so I just sat there. After the class had gone, she called me to come up and see her. She spent time with me and said, "You will have to stay behind each time after class and we will go through this work until you understand how to do it." I was looking forward to seeing Betty at recess. I hoped we could catch up at lunch time. I was given homework to bring back next day. I didn't see Betty all day. It wasn't until we caught the bus that I saw her. We didn't stop talking until it was time to get off, saying that we hoped we would be able to spend more time together the next day.

U S. and Lydia were waiting and they had some sweets for me. U.S. said, "Now enjoy them. Eat up. No talking. You can do that once you are home." I thanked him. I couldn't wait to tell them my news, that Betty was back, and about my day. It wasn't long before we were home and changing. A.J. was still out. We had our chores and talked to each other the whole time. U.S. was making a start on dinner. We ran out to play with Monty and were allowed to put him on his lead and run with him up and down the garden. We had only a short time, then A.J. came home and we were called to come inside. "Now go upstairs and wash your hands. We will talk after dinner." Lydia said to me, "I don't have much homework. Show me what you have." I did so, and she said, "I think I can help you when we are at the kitchen table." It was my turn to say grace and then our meal was eaten in silence. We helped U.S. with the dishes. A.J. was in the front room.

I was allowed to feed Monty, and I gave him a little extra. U.S. did not ask me now to show him what I gave Monty. I just wished I could bring him inside more often, but the weather was dry and I knew there was no chance of that happening. Once A.J. and U.S. left to go into the front room, we were on our own doing homework. I showed her mine and she said, "I think I can help you, but I'd better do my homework first." It wasn't long before U.S. was sent to check on us to see if we were doing homework. Then he left. Lydia grabbed my homework and said, "Let me help you." She was explaining it to me when A.J. came in. "I can hear talking. You must have finished. Lydia, why didn't you come into the front room?"

"I was seeing if I could help my sister, and it would be good if I could."

"That is not a good idea. You cannot be expected to know this."
"Why can't Lydia see if she can?" I asked.

"You are being taught by the teacher and I don't want Lydia being confused. She has her own work to do. You should know what to do. You need to concentrate more." I was left on my own. Oh, I thought, I wish A.J. wasn't like she is. I sat there, looking at it. I could do a little, but wasn't sure about it. I said to myself that I must try harder to understand when I was with the teacher. I wished I were clever like my sister. I knew she would still help me if she could.

When we were on our own in bed, we would talk about everything. Lydia said, "Don't worry. You will pick it up. Just ask the teacher."

"Yes. I am going to try harder. Thanks." We talked and eventually fell asleep. Next morning, I said goodbye to Lydia, whispering, "I hope when I see you later that I will know how to do it."

"Come along," A.J. said to Lydia, "Let's get you to school." She said goodbye to me and "Please learn!", and off they walked. As I waited for the bus, Betty saw me and we talked about my homework. I told her I was finding maths hard. She agreed, "You must ask, and the teacher will have to go over it with you." I was looking forward to school that day, as we had been told we would be doing PE and using the gym. I had to take my clothes with me to change into later that morning. Betty said, "I wish I was in your class. I haven't had PE yet. Talk to you later. Hope you like it." PE was after recess. First came maths, and this time I could follow what the teacher was telling us. I felt pleased with myself, hoping that when the class had finished and I saw her for my extra lesson, that I had done it correctly. There was more talking and at last the class had finished. After everybody left, the teacher said, "Close the door and let me see what you have been doing." She looked at the work I had done. She was pleased that I had done it correctly and had understood. "Now, let's go over this other work." She explained it to me and I asked her about it, as I still didn't understand fully. After talking some more with her, letting her know what I was stuck on, I felt better and was given some homework. She was nice to me. I thought, I hope I can remember how to do it tonight. I was told to go and get changed for PE, which was next.

Chapter 47

The class were all waiting in the passage for the teacher to turn up. There was lots of chatter. Angela said she didn't want to do PE, and had a note to give to the teacher. I asked, "Why don't you try? You might find it fun," but she did not want to do it. When the teacher arrived, we were put into groups and told to climb the bars against the wall, and reaching the ropes hanging from the ceiling, then working our way down to the floor with the ropes, then had to do it in reverse. I enjoyed it. It wasn't easy, but it was fun. Then there was the horse, a piece of gym equipment. We had to run up, jump onto it, do a somersault and land on the mat on the floor, on our feet. It was really difficult for me and I couldn't do it. There were only a few who could, in our first lesson. There were other things that we did. Angela and a few others sat and watched. I was enjoying most subjects, managing so far in maths, but with help I was able to understand it.

At afternoon recess I looked for Betty, but could not find her. Angela wanted to spend time with me. I did feel sorry for her as she didn't seem to have any friends except me. I wished she would mix with the other girls at recess, but she just wasn't interested. I said, "I can't always be with you only," as I did want to join in with some of the other girls sometimes. She couldn't understand that, and got upset. I said to myself that I would take it in turns and see how that went. The only times I could catch up with Betty were when we were waiting for the bus, or on it. We had so much to talk about. Later, when I was at home telling Lydia about my day, I said, "I hope I remember how to do it."

"Do your best. The teacher will know you have tried."

"You are right. I am really trying."

"I will have a look when we are doing our homework. I have more to do now, so we will be together longer."

"That's good."

We ran downstairs. U.S. was in the kitchen starting dinner. We asked, "Can we go outside and play with Monty?"

"Yes, for a short time." I grabbed the lead and U.S. called out, "Stay in the garden. Aunty Jean will be home soon." We didn't have long playing before we were called to come in. It was starting to get dark and cold. I ran inside and asked if I could get a biscuit for Monty. "Yes, just one, then. Hurry up and wash your hands. We will be having dinner soon." A.J. was home and coming down the stairs when we went in. We were going up to the bathroom to wash our hands. She had something in her hand. I asked, "What is that you have?"

"You don't need to know." Lydia tugged at my top. I knew she didn't want me to say any more. A.J. said, "Now go and wash your hands. Don't be long. Dinner is ready." We were passing her on the stairs. I tried to see what was in her hand, but couldn't. I said to Lydia, "It made a noise."

"Yes, I heard it."

"A.J. must have gone to the little room. If we had come in earlier, we might have seen what was in there. I wonder what it could be?" On our way from the bathroom, I tried the door of the little room again. It was locked. We tried to guess what it might be. After dinner, at the kitchen table, I showed Lydia my homework. "I think I can work it out."

"Let me see if I can remember first." I was pleased with myself and found that I was doing it, hoping that I was doing it correctly, "See, you're doing it." Now that she was older, she was having more homework herself. We were able to sit and talk while doing homework together.

U.S. came in and could see we were still working. It wasn't long before Lydia finished and went into the front room. I finished soon after. A.J. was pleased to hear that I understood how to do my maths. "About time,". I spoke about having PE and what we did. Lydia said, "That sounds like fun."

"I really enjoyed it." A.J. said, "Well, you are at school to learn, not to have fun."

"But I'm still learning when I have PE and having fun."

"That's questionable." It was time to get ready for bed. I didn't say another word. When we were racing upstairs, Lydia said, "You're getting better at not answering back. See, you then don't get into trouble."

"Well, sometimes I can't help it. Oh, but I'm really trying to hold my tongue." My Sunday school days were finishing, and it had been organised for me to go to youth group, held on Friday evenings in a hall not far from where we lived. Again, we were separated. After listening to a Bible lesson and singing hymns, we had some time when we could play and talk amongst ourselves. I knew most of the children and enjoyed going. We were also given something to eat and drink. U.S. would take me. Lydia would come for the walk but was not allowed inside. When it was finished, he would pick me up. On Sunday mornings I would have to sit in the front pews with the youth group, and later the children from Sunday school would come in. I would leave a space for Lydia. We would whisper, often getting black looks from the teacher, and she would put her finger on her lips. We knew this meant "No talking." The minister gave a short sermon for us children. Then the hardest thing for me was having to sit still and listen to the adult sermon. At the end of the service, he would announce coming events. In a few months (no dates yet), we were told that an Evangelist minister was coming to Colchester. He was an American, and young. His name was Billy Graham. The minister said he would invite him to our church, but, failing that, we would be told where in Colchester he would be preaching. He attracted large crowds. There was a huge interest in him, and lots of people followed his preaching. In the front room, A.J. spoke about it. She said she didn't approve of the way his preaching was being done. I asked, "What do you mean?"

"It is different from how our minister preaches."

"How is it different?"

"If he comes to our church, you will see." Lydia asked, "Is it because he is young that more people come and see him?" A.J. said, "That could be. We will have to wait and see."

"It can't be just because he's young, if he says the same things. What else is different?"

"It's how he goes about it."

"Well, it could be more interesting for me, because I find the sermons boring." A.J. was shocked -- "That's no way to talk. It's because you're not concentrating on what's being said."

"It's the same talk over and over again each week."

"I think you have said quite enough. I'm very disappointed in your feelings and attitudes."

"I think it's just for the older people who like that kind of talk." Lydia said quickly that she didn't understand the sermons either. "You are not expected to at your age, but I had hoped for far better from your sister." She said that I needed to make more of an effort to understand what was being preached, now that I was a teenager.

Chapter 48

On Sundays we were allowed to read and go for walks – no playing. Sunday was a day of rest, and it was good not having to do jobs. We were going to church in the mornings and evenings, so it was only the afternoons that were free. I would have loved to walk Monty and go into the woods – that was my favourite thing to do.

When it was wet, we would read. One of my favourite books was given to me by our uncle. It was Anne of Green Gables (by L.M. Montgomery). It had also been on the wireless as a serial each week. Lydia loved it too, and often we would have a quiet evening reading, before it was dinnertime, then off to church once more. We were quite tired by the end of the day, as we did a lot of walking, and it wasn't long before we were in bed on Sunday nights. We fell asleep straight away. Mostly we woke up early on Monday mornings, for school, without being woken up.

One morning I was in the bathroom and happened to look out of the window. I saw Dennis riding past on his bike. I ran to the bedroom to tell Lydia. She said, "Are you sure it was him?" I answered, "Yes. He's older than me. When we talked that time, he said he wasn't at my school. I must ask U.S. when he's on his own." Lydia said, "He might know. You will have to wait until U.S. picks us up at the bus stop after school."

I was finding that I was becoming more confident and joining in activities at school. I was starting to enjoy most of it. We had a young man as our history teacher, my first experience of having a male teacher. He was very good looking, and a lot of us girls would talk about him after class at recess. I have to admit I had a crush on him. History was a subject I found interesting, not only because of liking Mr. Turner, but because he would often say something that made the class laugh. He was always happy. Everybody seemed to like him. He made the class interesting, and you always wanted to know more. We never got any homework from him – it was always maths and English. I was coping with my English quite well. I loved reading and it became one of my favourite subjects. Then we were introduced to Domestic Science. We were allowed to take an apron to school and some money. We would be learning how to handle food and do some cooking. This sounded exciting and I was looking forward to it. I couldn't wait to tell Lydia, and wondered what A.J. would think about it.

On arriving at the bus stop, my first question to U.S. was about Dennis. I told him I had seen him riding his bike early that morning. U.S. was surprised and said he knew he had left school, but wasn't sure what he was doing. I chatted away, telling Lydia about me: "Tomorrow I will be learning about food, and might do some cooking." She said, "That will be good. I wonder what you will make.? Will you bring it home? Don't eat it all. I want to try some." I said, "Of course I will leave some for you, if we are allowed to bring some home." U.S. said, "That's good. You will learn to cook! Then you can help to make dinner."

"I would like that. Can I choose what we have, if I'm going to do the cooking?" U.S. said, "I don't know about that, but we will work it out." Later, in the front room, when I told A.J., she was pleased to hear it. I said, "I have a note to give you." She said, "Not another note. What is it this time?" I replied, "It's about what I have just told you."

"Oh, that's all right, then, as long as it's nothing else you are having problems with."

"No, I'm enjoying school."

"Well, that's good to hear, as long as you are learning. It's not a place to go and have fun."

"But why can't I do both?"

"You always have an answer to what I say, and want the last word, and it doesn't work like that."

I knew I had better not say any more. Later, in bed, Lydia said, "You are doing well at not answering back." I told her more about my history teacher, and she laughed and thought it was funny that I had a crush on him. "But," I said, "It's not only me. There are other girls feeling the same. I think he knows how we feel, and often he has the class laughing. It's still about history. He makes up a little story, and it's how he puts it over. I don't know anyone who doesn't like him." Lydia said, "You have never talked about anyone like that before." "Well," I said, "I have never liked anyone like that before." She answered, "You are funny. I am glad you are happy. We had better go to sleep now." It was a while before I fell asleep.

In the morning A.J. gave me one of her aprons, which was way too big for me, and some money in an envelope for Domestic Science. I was excited, and looking forward to what I would be making. Lydia said, "Good luck." as we said our goodbyes. I told Betty on the bus, and she commented, "I haven't heard about Domestic Science, and you are lucky to be doing it. You do more stuff than I do." After lunch, for our first lesson, we all went to a classroom on the other side of the courtyard. It was huge, like a big kitchen. It had sinks, benches and an oven, also desks we sat at. The teacher collected our envelopes and asked, "Have you all brought an apron?" We were told to put them on.

We had a talk about cleanliness, certain foods and were put in groups of eight and told that we would be making some scones, which were quite easy to make. We had to line up first to wash our hands, then we were given a bowl with the right amount of flour and margarine. We were standing by the benches. The teacher showed us how to make a crumble mixture. Then she came round and put some milk in our bowls. We each had a wooden spoon with which to mix it into a big ball. The next thing was to put some flour onto our board and knead it with our hands until it was about an inch thick. We had to share a circular cutter, pushing it down, and we had a scone that needed cooking. While we were doing this, the other half of the class greased some oven trays, ready for our scones. With our oven at the right temperature, while they were cooking, we had the dishes to do, for the other half of the class to make their scones. I enjoyed doing this. It was really easy, and we could smell them cooking. All we wanted to do was to taste them and see what they were like.

We were told we could take them home at the end of the day. They would be in bags for us. The teacher said, "You can have them with butter and jam, or even cheese." I was feeling hungry, but we all had to go to our next lesson, which wasn't easy. This was another subject I liked doing. I was thinking that it came close to being my favourite – reading. At recess, we all talked about our cooking class. We were looking forward to collecting our bags when the bell rang. There wasn't anybody I knew who didn't like doing it. Angela said, "Yes, I will make some at home now I know how." I wondered if I would I be allowed to. The teacher did say we would have four scones to take home. That was good. It worked out well for us. It was hard to concentrate on our next subject, English. It was nearly time to get the bus, and enough time was allowed for us to collect our scones. We had to line up and walk to the Domestic Science room. The teacher walked with us. There was a bit of chatter and pushing to get in the front of the line. Those who were doing it were sent to the back. We were excited to collect our bags. Our names were called. When it was my turn, I grabbed the bag and hurried to where the bus would be waiting. Betty was already there, saying, "Let me see. How about we have half each of one?" I said, "I think I'd better not. Sorry. We'll wait so we can all have them together at home." She said, "Aww."

"Anyway," I said, "We don't have anything to put on them, so they won't be that nice." We chatted about our day. She said she hoped she would be having Domestic Science soon. I raced off the bus, to where Lydia and U.S. were waiting. I opened my bag, showing them my scones. Lydia said, "Oh. There is one each." I replied, "Yes. Isn't that good?" U.S. said, "They look good enough to eat." I said, "Of course they are, and I can't wait to try them." He said, "I will take them to the kitchen, and it will be nice to have them after dinner." I thought, I hoped A.J. would be all right about that. When we heard A.J. arrive home, we were talking as we opened the kitchen door. I said, "Have you seen the scones I made? Can we have them after dinner?" She said, "Yes, they look nice. We will try them then."

"Have we some jam to put on them?"

"Yes. We will talk in the front room."

"Can we go outside to see Monty for a little while?" I grabbed the lead. We both ran out into the garden. Lydia said, "A.J. is nicer to you now." I thought about that. "I think you're right. I wonder why?" Lydia said, "It's because you're not answering back." I replied, "Well, I am really trying not to." "You're doing well."

Chapter 49

Monty was pleased to see us, jumping up and down and wagging his tail. I took him off his chain, saying, "Let's run down the garden without putting him on the lead." Lydia said, "That would make A.J. cross. Why do you want to do that?"

"I don't want her to be cross. I just want Monty to be free." With that, I ran down the garden. Monty followed. When I got to the bottom, I quickly grabbed him and put him on. "You were lucky A.J. wasn't looking."

"See how happy he looks!" She agreed. "You put him on his chain. I'm going in to get a biscuit for him." I ran inside to the cupboard and grabbed a dog biscuit. A.J. had her back to me. She called out, "What are you doing?" I said, "I'm getting something for Monty. I am allowed. Uncle Stan lets me." Then I ran out of the kitchen, leaving A.J. having words with U.S. Lydia said, "That wasn't very nice to do that to U.S."

"I didn't think about that. I was only thinking of Monty, who needs a treat."

Once inside, we raced to wash our hands. Then we went to the kitchen. I asked, "Is there anything I can do to help?" A.J. looked surprised. "You can help your sister set the table. Dinner is almost ready." We did this and watched dinner being served. I could see it wasn't my favourite, but I was hungry and would eat it all. I knew Lydia didn't like the mince balls, and was ready if she gave me some, but hoped she would eat most of them. It was her turn to say grace. Looking at me, she pulled a face. I knew what that meant. We ate dinner in silence, and I got kicked by Lydia under the table, letting me know, be ready. She was going to pass me some of her mince balls. I was ready. A.J. said, "We have Sylvia's scones, when you have both finished." She got up. U.S. was putting them on a plate, and A.J. was getting a knife to cut them and spread some margarine and jam on them. I had finished my meal. Lydia quickly gave me some in her hanky. A.J. said, turning round from the bench, "Lydia, you still have some on your plate. Hurry up and finish, so I can take the plates away and put the scones on the table." We were given one each. I really liked mine, but wished there was more jam on it. I was looking and waiting for somebody to say something. We had all finished. Lydia said, "That was nice. Will you be able to make some more?" U.S. said, "Very nice." A.J. said, "Yes. You have done well."

"Thank you. Now I know how to make them, can I make some more here?"

"That was a treat, not something you make all the time."

"But it's nice to have treats. Why can't we have treats sometimes?"

"You have to earn treats. Now, no more talking." She got up and went to the front room. We helped U.S. with the dishes, and I asked, "Can I feed Monty? Is there some gravy left in the saucepan?"

"Not really, but you can put some water in the pan and stir and see if something comes out."

"We should leave some for Monty."

"He has his special food."

"But why can't he have a treat too?"

"Well, you are now giving him one, which is nice."

I did get a little gravy out and took it outside, and quickly added the bits of meatballs that Lydia gave me. I watched Monty. He ate it so quickly and was looking for more. He did enjoy it. U.S. said to me, "It's too cold to stay outside."

"Can Monty come inside?"

"You know the answer to that. Please, let's hurry with the dishes. Go and get your homework." We were on our own at the kitchen table, talking about the scones. Lydia said, "I wonder what you will make next?"

"I don't think A.J. is going to let me make any."

"Well, now you know how to make them, and you never know, one day she might." We got into our homework. Lydia wasn't long before she was finished and ready to go into the front room. She asked, "Are you O.K.?"

"Yes, I can now do this." It felt good, knowing and understanding what I was doing. At last, I was grasping it.

The next morning, when I was in the bathroom, I kept looking out of the window, in between washing my face and grabbing the towel. Again, I saw Dennis. I told Lydia -- "He must be working somewhere. We could ask him when we see him on Sunday."

"Yes. U.S. doesn't know much, and he is family." We were talking about it when A.J. called out, "Time you were down for breakfast." We hurried to the kitchen. Our porridge was already in our bowls. A.J. said grace. "Now, eat up, before it gets completely cold. Too much talking, and we will be running late again." Not another word was spoken. Once we were finished, it was a rush to catch the bus. Saying my goodbyes to Lydia, I gave her a hug. Betty had saved me a seat on the bus and we spent our time chatting about how everybody liked my scones. She said, "I don't think you will make something every time."

"Oh, I thought we would. Well, we'll find out soon, I guess."

As I arrived at school, I could see Angela walking to the assembly hall. I caught up with her. She was telling me she had two notes – no netball or PE. I asked, "Why?"

"I just can't do it, so I will be able to sit out." I thought, well, I'll be able to join the other children. I asked her, "You don't mind missing out?"

"I'd hate to have to do it."

"Well, I would feel the same if I couldn't." She didn't understand that. She thought it was a waste of time. Our first subject was maths. Angela asked me, as we were going into the classroom, "How are you going with it?"

"I feel I am understanding it at last. I am hoping this homework I have done will be right." She was pleased. Staying behind after our class and having my extra help, I was feeling happier about things. When the teacher looked at my homework, she asked, "Have you done this by yourself?" I answered yes. "Well, this is all correct." She was pleased, and felt I was understanding it. She asked, "Are you worried about anything?"

"No. If I need to ask some questions, and get stuck on any of it, is that all right?"

"Yes. You shouldn't need any more extra lessons. Let's see how you go in the next few weeks." I thanked her and went out to recess. I was happy at last that I was getting it.

Angela was waiting for me at the playing fields and we chatted. There was only a short time of recess left. Some girls were practising putting balls through the hoop. I wished I could join them, but knew it would be unfair for Angela, who had been waiting for me all this time. We talked about what we might be doing in Domestic Science. She asked, "Do you think we will be making something to take home?"

"I hope so, but it's not till the end of the week, and we haven't been told anything yet." It was PE next, and I had to go and change. Angela pulled a face, saying, "I am glad I can sit out."

"See you later," joining the others, who were waiting for the teacher. It was good being able to move and exercise. I really enjoyed it. Yes, there were more subjects I liked than I disliked. I was happy at this school.

Chapter 50

When it was time to go home, Betty was already waiting for the bus. She was excited. "We are having Domestic Science tomorrow, and guess what? We are making scones."

"That's great. We haven't heard any more about what we will be doing." We were still chatting about our day as the bus stopped for us to get on. Lydia was pleased to see me, telling me about her day. U.S. handed me some sweets, saying, "Eat up. You can talk when you are home." I just felt like giving him a hug, and stretched out my arms, saying "Thank you." and walking towards him. He stepped back, not sure what to make of what I was trying to do, and my bag of sweets got knocked over. I managed to save some. U.S. said, "What are you doing? You have lost a lot." Picking them up, he said, "These will have to go in the bin." I tried to explain and said sorry. "Just eat what you have. No more talking." He was getting cross with me. I thought, I didn't mean for that to happen, and ate what I had left without another word.

On arriving home, U.S. unlocked the front door. There were letters on the mat. We both started picking them up. I said, "Look, this is one from our uncle." U.S. said, "We will have to wait for A.J. to open it."

"I wish you could do that."

"You know we have to wait for A.J. You will find out in the front room. Please behave." We ran up the stairs to get changed. Lydia asked, "Why did you do that with your sweets?"

"I just wanted to give him a hug, and it all went wrong."

"You know we can't show or give hugs."

"You're right."

"I just had this feeling I wanted to do it. Oh, I can't wait to hear what our uncle says in the letter."

"I hope we find out today." We could hear A.J. coming in. She was talking to U.S. We hurried out of our school clothes. Lydia said, "Be careful how you talk. Don't get yourself into trouble." I gave her a hug. "I will try hard to do the right thing." We walked down the stairs to the kitchen. A.J. called, "Hello. Now do your jobs, while we get dinner organised." I said, "Our uncle has written to you. Have you seen the letter?"

"Yes. We will talk about it later, in the front room."

"Yes, it's nice to hear from him. I can't wait to hear what he says." I quickly left the kitchen to get our shoes to clean, going outside with them and talking to Monty. He was pleased to see me. I gave him plenty of pats while making a start on the shoes. Lydia was inside setting the table. She should be coming out soon, I thought, as I had nearly finished. The door opened. It was Lydia, saying, "Thank you for cleaning my shoes." She was about to take them inside. I asked, "Please take mine too, and find out if we have time to take Monty off his chain." Lydia came back with the lead, and Monty was so excited. We took it in turns to run and play with him. I asked Lydia, "How is A.J.? Is she in a good mood?"

"Sort of. It's something I like for dinner. Guess what?" We chatted about this, but I couldn't guess what it was. Lydia told me. I said, "Good. I like it too."

"So, you will eat it all?"

"Of course."

When we were all in the front room and had talked about our day, I asked A.J., "What did our uncle say in his letter?"

"He wants to organise a visit." We both jumped up and down, "That will be so good."

"I will be writing to him. It has to be worked out. He said he hopes you are both behaving, and sends his love."

"Did he write us a letter?"

"No. He has been away and very busy."

"I hope we see him soon."

"We will have to wait and see." We were told to get ready for bed. I said, "I wonder if we could stay with our uncle again?"

"I hope we find out soon when he is coming." We were excited to know we would be seeing him again. It had been a long time since we heard from him. "Until I write, we don't know the answers to these questions. Now, please go and get ready for bed." She was becoming cross. We quickly left, closing the door of the front room. We raced upstairs feeling happy, chatting.

Chapter 51

The next morning, we were in the bathroom together. I said to Lydia, "Look out of the window. Dennis will be going past soon. You watch with me." She could only just see out of the window, as it was high up, by standing on tiptoe. We waited. After a little while, he rode past on his bike very fast. Lydia said, "Yes, it is him. I wonder where he goes?"

"We must find out on Sunday." A.J. was calling us. "Your porridge is on the table, getting cold. It's time you were downstairs." We raced into the kitchen. A.J. said, "Too much talking going on. We will have to hurry up. The bus waits for no one." We quickly ate our porridge and got ready for school. The bus was at the stop already. I said a quick goodbye to Lydia and got on. Betty had saved me a seat. "Why are you late?" I told her what had happened. She was excited, as she was having Domestic Science, which would be cooking, that day. "We will be making scones."

"I'm sure you will enjoy doing it."

"Yes." We got off the bus and walked to the assembly hall, where we all went to start our day. I loved singing "Jerusalem". After that, everyone left to go to their classrooms. I said goodbye to Betty and walked to mine. A few girls talked to me on the way. I didn't feel so alone. Then I saw Angela, already sitting at her desk. She said, "See you at recess. I will wait for you while you have your extra lesson."

"You should join in with some of the girls. I will find you when I have finished."

I walked to my desk and sat down. I was looking at my homework when the teacher came in and our morning started. More new work! After a while, she was asking questions, calling out different names to give her the answers. I was hoping that she wouldn't ask me. I listened to what was being said. I knew some, but not all, and she didn't ask me.

I was glad. At the end of class, after everyone had left, I walked up to her table, showing my homework. "How are you finding it?"

"I know it better now." When checking it, she said, "Yes, I am pleased. You have improved. Let's see how you go without my help for a while."

"But I really didn't understand the new work you were talking about." She explained it to me and said, "I want you to try and do it on your own. When I mark your work, I will see how you're doing."

"But I'm not sure I can do it without your help." I was nervous and unsure. "You can do this. You cannot rely on me to help you always. You must concentrate. I know you can do it."

"If you really think so." She handed me some homework like the other children were given, and said, "Have some confidence in yourself."

"I will try."

"Now, off you go to recess."

Chapter 52

Angela was waiting when I reached the playing fields, standing on her own. "Nobody will talk to me, only you."

"Just try and join in." I told her I had no more extra work. I was on my own now. She was pleased. "We can go out to recess together."

"I will help you to join in with the other girls. You don't want to be on your own all the time."

"I have you."

"It would be nice if we could all mix and talk together sometimes."

She wasn't interested. The rest of my day went well, and when it was time to catch the bus, I could see Betty already there, waving. When I reached her, she showed me her bag. There were some scones she had made. I said, "They look yummy."

"It was so good making them, and I'm taking them all home."

"Yes, you should." We chatted about our day, and she was pleased I was doing well with my maths. As we were getting off, I hurried to where Lydia and U.S. were waiting. Lydia was telling me about her day. They had some sweets for me. I said thank you and got into them. U.S. said, "That's good. Eat up and talk later." I did manage in between mouthfuls to talk about my maths. U.S. said, "You should be pleased." Lydia commented, "You are doing well. That's great." It was only I who was feeling unsure about not having any extra help. It was good there was no school the next day. It was the weekend, and I was looking forward to it. "We can stay up later, although we'll have to make a start on our homework."

Chatting to Lydia when we were on our own, I said, "Hope we can listen to our serial on the radio tonight." It was always on Friday night. We enjoyed it. "Hope A.J. has written to our uncle."

"It's a holiday soon."

"Yes, I know. I wonder what will happen, and what we will be doing? If we ask A.J., she always says we will have to wait and see." Lydia agreed, "She does say that a lot." We came out of our bedroom, passing the little room. I tried the door. I did it every time I passed. Lydia asked, "Why do you do that? You know she always locks it."

"Well, one day she might forget." We ran down the stairs. A.J. wasn't home yet. We were allowed to help get the veggies ready for dinner. My favourite – shelling the peas. We were both eating some each time we opened a pod. U.S. also let me try peeling a potato with the peeler again. I was starting to get the hang of it, but was slow. We heard the front door close. A.J. was home, saying, "Hello. I see you are helping with dinner."

"Yes, we are."

"Have you done your jobs?"

"Not yet. We will do them after."

"You can go and do them now. I'm home to get things organised." U.S. said, "Thank you, girls." So, we dropped tools and left the kitchen, grabbing our shoes and going outside. Big greetings from Monty, who was making lots of noise, wanting to get off his chain. We quickly cleaned our shoes. "You take them in and ask if we can take Monty off his chain."

"All right, I will." It wasn't long before she came out with the lead, saying, "Dinner won't be long, so we must hurry." Quickly getting Monty onto his lead, we ran up and down the garden a few times before we were called to come inside. We hurried to wash our hands. Dinner was served. It was my turn to say grace. We ate in silence. I managed to save some sausage for Monty. I looked at Lydia, who was eating all of hers. We both liked this meal. A.J. got up from the table, saying, "You can go and get your homework. We will clear the table. I will call you when it is time for your program on the radio." We said, "Thank you." A.J. looked surprised. I said to Lydia, "Hope A.J. has gone into the front room when we get downstairs. I have some sausage for Monty and I want to feed him."

"You are taking a risk. U.S. might have fed him already. Then what will you do?"

"Oh. Then I'll have to eat it." Lydia laughed. "Be careful. We want to hear our program." We came downstairs.

The table was cleared. A. J. was in the front room. I asked U.S., "Can I feed Monty?"

"Yes, I have left that for you to do. It's all ready. Just take it out to him. Don't be long."

"Oh good. Thank you." I picked up the bowl and walked outside, grabbing the piece of sausage out of my pocket and putting it in his dinner. I watched Monty for a little while. He was enjoying it. Lydia was already doing her homework. I quickly came inside and got my homework out. I sat thinking – see what you can do. I surprised myself, finding that I was mostly working it out. A.J. called us. It was time for our program. We hurried into the front room and sat down. We so enjoyed it. This was something we always looked forward to. When it was finished, we would talk about it, and our day, what we had been doing at school. I was also going to youth group on Friday evenings. It was a busy time for me. I had to hurry and get ready. U.S. would walk me there. Sometimes, Lydia would come for the walk, and at other times A.J. would want Lydia to stay with her. This time, I was on my own with U.S. I asked, "Do you know if A.J. has written to our uncle?"

"I'm not sure. He will be in contact soon."

"Well, it's the holidays very soon."

As we arrived, he said, "Enjoy your time. I will be here when you finish."

"Goodbye," I called, and went into the hall. I couldn't believe who was there. It was Dennis. He said hello. I wanted to talk with him. I had to wait till it was our time, when we were allowed to mix, talk, play games and have something to eat. He was with a few boys who also hadn't been before. We were introduced to the newcomers – there were two new girls as well. I really didn't really get to talk with Dennis. He was never on his own. When it was time to leave, he called out, "Might see you Sunday." I came out of the hall. U.S. was standing there. I told him about Dennis. He said, "I did see some boys go past, but didn't recognise anybody." I asked more questions about his family, but found out very little. Lydia was still up when we got home and said, "Did you enjoy it?"

"Guess who was there?" A.J. said, "I'd like you to go and get ready for bed now." She wasn't interested.

Lydia and I ran upstairs. She asked, "Who was there?" I started telling her all about my night. "I wonder what A.J. will say when U.S. tells her."

"That's if he does."

"You will have to try and talk with him on Sunday."

"Did you find out if A.J. has written to our uncle?"

"I asked, and she told me she had, so that's good."

"I hope he writes back soon." We talked a bit more about everything.

Chapter 53

On Saturday, after doing our chores, and when A.J. had left to do her work, we could hear the children playing. We raced down to the greenhouse. I asked, "Can we join them for a little while?"

"A.J. will be home early, and you will be helping her to do another job at the church."

"Why is she coming early?"

"They are having a special service before another one later, and there will be more to get ready."

"Oh. What more will we have to do?"

"A.J. will tell you when she comes home." We ran as fast as we could to get the lead for Monty. We went to the vacant block and Betty was there. We were able to talk lots and play games. We had fun. It wasn't long before we were called. Quickly putting Monty on his chain, we ran upstairs to wash our hands. We could hear A.J. coming in. She went into the kitchen. Lydia and I hurried down for lunch. U.S always had sandwiches ready. A.J. said, "We will be leaving early. There was a function last night, so the church will need a good tidy up and clean. There will be a christening early in the morning. Lots to get ready for that." I started asking questions and was told to sit down and be quiet.

Lydia was asked to say grace and then we started eating our sandwiches in silence. It wasn't long before we were walking to the church. On our way there, a lady across the road in her garden called out to A.J., asking about the christening and giving A.J. a big bunch of flowers for the church. I asked, "Is that someone you know?" A.J. introduced us to her. Her name was Lena. She said, "I'm sure I'll see more of you." Lydia and I looked at each other. I was asking questions. A.J. said, "That was Uncle Stan's brother's wife." Then she started walking really fast. "Now, no more questions. We have a lot to do."

We arrived at the church. She got her bunch of keys out of her bag and opened the big wooden door. It was dark inside. She turned on the light and we could see it was untidy, with lots of stuff on the floor. A.J. soon had us organised, picking rubbish off the floor and putting it in bags. She swept and we were given rags to dust with. We were also given hymn books to put in the rails at the back of the pews. She arranged the flowers at the altar. It looked really nice when we had finished. She was pleased and thanked us. "You have done well, and you can have extra pocket money to put in your money jars." It was still quite early when we got home and we were allowed to walk Monty. I asked Lydia, "What did you think about the lady who gave A.J. the flowers? She is U.S.'s brother's wife."

"Yes, she seems nice."

"When we talk in the front room, I'm going to ask about her. I think we should be told more about the family."

"Yes, I agree, but be careful how you say things. I wonder if U.S. will talk about it if I ask him?" We chatted a bit more, then ran to the woods, having fun. Arriving home, we could see U.S. working in his greenhouse. We ran to talk to him, telling him about Lena. Yes, he said, he knew she was getting the flowers for the christening. "We want to know more about your family," I said.

"Dinner is ready. Time to go inside."

"Well, I'm going to ask when we are in the front room and can talk." We ran up the garden, leaving U.S., who was walking behind, not saying a word. Lydia said, "I wonder if he will tell us anything." After dinner, she asked A.J. about the lady who gave her the flowers. "Can we know more about the family?"

"You will, in time."

"But why can't we know now?"

"Until you meet anybody, there is no need to."

"But when will we meet them?"

"I can't tell you that. No more questions." U.S. didn't say a word, just sat twiddling his thumbs. I was looking at him, thinking, do I ask him more, then thought better of it. I didn't want to get punished for asking. When we were in bed and able to talk, I asked, "Why doesn't U.S. say anything? It's his family."

"He just goes along with whatever A.J. says."

"You're right. It doesn't look like we will meet them all at once." "Unless they tell us, how do we know if they are family?" We chatted a bit more. "I might find out something if we get to talk to Dennis tomorrow." It wasn't long before we fell asleep, as we did have a busy day.

Chapter 54

Next day, when we were walking to the chapel, we both said we would try and find out things from Dennis. I said, "We might not be together when we see him, but we'll talk later about it." I said goodbye to A.J. and Lydia, who went into Sunday school, and I went into the chapel by the side door. I sat in front with the youth group. Later, when Sunday school had finished, Lydia came and sat next to me. I always saved her a seat. She whispered, "I haven't seen Dennis." After the service, when we were walking home, talking by ourselves, we caught up with a lady pushing a pram with a baby in it who was trying to sit up. A.J. stopped to speak with her and called out to us to wait. We ran back and A.J. introduced us to her. "This is Mrs. Taylor, and the baby's name is Elizabeth." We said hello, then there was more talking with A.J., and we started walking home. Later, in the front room, I asked about Mrs. Taylor. We had seen her before after school. She was out walking when we were coming home. A.J. said she was not a well person and was having to go to the doctor's often. I said, "The baby is cute, and she seems nice." A.J. agreed, "She doesn't live very far from us." Lydia said, "The lady we saw yesterday, who gave you the flowers, she put her hand up to me and waved as we were coming out of church." A.J. said, "That was nice of her." I then asked U.S., "Why don't you talk to each other, if you are family?"

"It's just the way it is."

"I don't understand." A.J. said, "You don't need to."

"But I want to."

"You can't always do what you want."

"But if it's family, why don't you get together, and we could meet them?" Lydia interrupted, "That would be a nice thing to do." A.J. said, "It's not going to happen."

"What do you mean?"

"This is the end of the discussion."

"But why can't you explain?" She was becoming cross with me. "No more talking on this subject." I looked at U.S., hoping he would say something, but he just sat there, looking down at his lap. Lydia was looking at me, and I was thinking, I'd better not say another word. It all went very quiet. Lydia asked, "Are we allowed to go outside and take Monty for a walk?"

"Yes, that's a good idea." We jumped up fast, saying thank you, and hurried out of the room, closing the door. We could hear them talking. We ran to the kitchen and grabbed the lead. I said, "So glad to get outside." Monty was jumping up and down, pleased to see us. We ran down the garden and out of the side gate. Lydia said, "U.S. doesn't join in on any conversation."

"I think he's a bit afraid of A.J. He is so different when she is not around, than when we see him on his own."

"I am going to ask why he doesn't join in. It's his family – and why we can't we meet everyone and have a get-together?"

"Maybe A.J. won't let him."

"Do you really think that could happen?" We both thought it was strange. I said, "Maybe they don't want to meet us." We spent our time talking about it until we reached home. No more was said, but A.J. and U.S. were very quiet. We were all quiet. I was glad when bedtime came, saying to Lydia, "Maybe they have had an argument." She agreed, "Glad that it's school tomorrow. Remember, it's our last week before the holidays."

"I wonder what we'll be doing for them?"

"Yes. I hope we hear from Uncle soon. We must ask again."

Next morning, A.J. seemed her normal self, telling us to hurry, "We are running late." U.S. said, "Have a nice day." Hurrying, we left the kitchen. A.J. had our lunches ready and put them in our bags. "Come along. You will miss the bus one of these days, and you will not get to school." She took Lydia by the hand, walking fast. We could see the bus was already there. A.J. said a quick goodbye. Betty called out to me, "Come on! Why are you always running late?"

"I'm not sure. We must have woken up late." We talked about our weekend. Arriving at school, we were told at assembly about the holidays. They would be for two weeks, and we would be finishing earlier on the Friday. A note would be given about it. My day at school went well and I was enjoying most subjects. I was coping much better. Girls were talking to me. Angela just tagged along, but still wanted us to be by ourselves. I felt I needed to join in with others sometimes, and it sort of worked out without any upsets. Everybody was talking about the holidays. "What are you doing?" I had to say, "I don't know," which was true. I was thinking, I must find out from A.J. She hadn't told us anything.

Even Betty on the bus was asking me the same thing. She said she was going away for one week. I said, "We should know soon what is happening." U.S. and Lydia were waiting as we got off. She was full of chatter. They had little school work. Her teacher was away. They played games, which was fun. U.S. gave me some sweets. I said, "Thank you. Can I ask you a question?"

"Of course."

"Are you going to do something so we can meet your family?"

"There's nothing I can do. It could be that that you will meet them gradually, over time."

"But why can't we meet them all together?"

"It just can't happen." Lydia asked, "Don't you want it to happen?"

"It's not as easy as just wanting it to." I said, "They're your family. You should do something, if that's what you want. You're so lucky to have your mum and dad still alive."

"I know. It must be hard for you to understand. We are nearly home. Eat up. Now things are the way they are, and you must accept them."

"Well, it looks like you have." Lydia said, "Your family could meet us and we won't know if they are family unless we are told."

"That's true. I'm afraid that's how it is."

Chapter 55

We arrived home. I finished my last sweet. We raced upstairs, chatting, with me saying, "Well, it looks like nothing is going to change."

"U.S. can't change things about his family."

"I wonder what's happened to make it like it is. Do you think we will ever find out?" After more talking, we agreed we wouldn't say any more about it. I said, "A.J. must know from our uncle about our holidays. I'm going to ask when we're in the front room."

"Yes. She should know what's happening now." We heard A.J. come home and go into the kitchen. We hurried downstairs and opened the kitchen door, saying hello. A.J. said, "We will talk later. Now go and get your jobs done." We went outside with our shoes to clean. "Oh, I think A.J. is cross about something."

"Well, it's not us, so that's good. Be careful how you talk when we are in the front room." We cleaned our shoes. Monty was waiting to get off his chain. I said, "You ask if we can walk him."

"All right. I'll take the shoes in. You stay outside while I ask." I could hear Lydia asking as she went inside. She came outside with the lead and A.J. said, "Dinner won't be ready for a while. Stay in the garden." She sounded cross. We played with Monty, who was happy. I said, "I wonder if we will find out what she is cross about?"

"Just be extra careful what you say."

"All right, I will. Hope it's something nice for dinner that we like. Try and eat it all." It did seem a long while before we were called, and it felt tense between them. It was a dinner we both liked, which was good, and of course, there was no talking. A.J. went into the front room. We helped U.S. with the dishes, and he was very quiet. I asked, "Is everything all right?"

"Nothing for you to worry about," he said. Lydia asked, "Are we allowed to know why A.J. is cross?"

"That is between Aunty Jean and me." We had finished putting the dishes away. "Now go and get your homework." Lydia said, "I don't have any." I still had some, and went upstairs by myself to get mine. U.S. and Lydia had already gone into the front room. I sat down by myself and looked at what I needed to do. I was getting into it. U.S. came to check on me, saying, "It looks like you know what you're doing."

"Yes. I think I have it." It wasn't long before I went into the front room. A.J. asked, "Well, let's find out about your day. Lydia first." She talked about her teacher, who was sick, and they had somebody else. "We played games, and it was fun." A.J. was not impressed. "You have a few more days before the holidays." I was in the good books, because I still had some homework, and thought, I hope it will be correct. I said, "It's the holidays at the end of the week. Have you heard from our uncle?"

"Yes. He will be here on Saturday morning, really early." We were so excited, jumping up and down. "Is he staying with us?"

"No. He wants you to be able to stay with him for a few days." We could hardly believe it. I said, "That will be so good." Lydia said, "It's been a long time since we have done that." We were so happy. I said, "It will be a real holiday for us." A.J. said, "There is a lot to sort out, and very little time to do it."

"Oh, you sound cross."

"It would have been nice to have more notice."

"Well, you should have written earlier to him."

"Do not tell me what I should have done. You are being rude."

"Sorry. I didn't mean to be rude." I just remembered I had a note in my satchel, "Can I go and get the note I have for you?"

"Yes. It's no good leaving it in your bag, and I hope there are no more problems." I left the room and ran to get the note. I knew what it was about. I read it. It said we are finishing school at lunchtime on Friday, and the times of the bus. I thought it wasn't up to me to tell A.J. what was in the note. I went back into the front room and gave her the note, "So, you will be finishing school early on Friday." Lydia said, "I think we will be too, but I haven't got a note yet." A.J. sounded cross again, "There is a lot to sort out, to work out your clothes, to pack and be organised." I said, "We can do that."

"You can help. That will have to be done on Friday, after school. Now go and get ready for bed." We raced up the stairs, saying, "That's great. We will be staying with our uncle again."

Next morning, we were very excited going to school, telling our friends that we would be going away, staying with our uncle in London and going on a train. Betty asked, "Can we see each other sometime in the holidays?"

"We are not away for all of the holidays." When I told Angela, she was impressed, saying she hadn't been on a train before, and said we were lucky. She didn't know that I had no parents, or anything really about me. No one at school did, only Betty.

Chapter 56

Our maths teacher collected homework after class, and we were not given any more, because of the holidays. The next day was our last. I wondered if the teacher would have marked our maths by then. I just wanted to know if I got it correct. I guessed I would have to wait and see. There was excitement about, because we would be finishing school the next day. My day went well. Talking with Betty on the bus, I said, "I will let you know when I find out." U.S. was waiting with Lydia as we got off. "I have had a fun day and I have no homework." U.S. handed me some sweets. "Thank you." and asked him, "Will you miss us?"

"Of course. It will be very quiet without you both." Lydia said, "It will give you time for yourselves." I said, "It will be like a holiday for you too." He went very quiet, only saying, "Eat your sweets – we are nearly home."

On the other side of the road, we saw Mrs. Taylor again, pushing the pram. I called out, "Hello." She waved to us and kept walking. U.S. said, "That was nice. She is not a well person." We arrived home and ran upstairs. I explained, "I have no homework." "Nor do I. I wonder what A.J. will say about that? Maybe we can read or chat in bed." We quickly changed and went down to the kitchen. U.S. said, "A.J. has a meeting tonight, so she won't be home till later. It's just the three of us." I said, "That's good," and quickly asked, "Do you want any help?"

"No, thank you. Monty would love a walk." We could hear him making lots of noises. I grabbed the lead. We always had a big welcome. He was pleased to see us. We ran out of the side gate, chatting. I said, "I wonder what U.S. will make for dinner? It is great that it's just the three of us."

"It is different when that happens."

"Yes, I won't be punished if I say or do something wrong."

"He's not as strict."

"But try not to upset him."

"Of course, I won't do it on purpose." We had a lovely run with Monty. When we got back, U.S. had dinner ready, and we really enjoyed it. After helping with the dishes, we both said, "We don't have any homework tonight, and we come out of school early tomorrow."

"Yes. I will pick you up." Once we were in the front room, Lydia started talking about her day. U.S. listened, but didn't comment, then I spoke, and after that, I asked, "Could you tell us more about your family?"

"What would you like to know?"

"Well, why don't you have a get-together so we can meet them all?" "There are too many of them."

"But how will we meet them and when?" Then Lydia said, "They will know us, and unless they talk and tell us, we will never get to know them."

"That's just the way it is." I said, "You could change it if you wanted to."

"You might think that, but it's not possible." I asked why. "It's not something I can explain. I did tell you that before. You will have to accept what I'm telling you."

"That's really hard for us to understand. You are lucky you have a big family and you still have your Mum and Dad alive." We heard the front door opening. A. J. was home. U. S. said, "No more talking on this subject." She came into the front room, saying, "I thought you'd be ready for bed by now." Lydia asked, "How was your meeting?"

"Very good, thank you. Now, how about getting ready for bed?" I asked, "Don't you want to know about our day?"

"Uncle Stan will tell me. You still have school tomorrow and need to be in bed early." We ran out of the front room. A.J. called, "No running. Come down to say goodnight when you are ready."

We could hear her talking, and she sounded as if she was still cross. I said, "I feel sorry for U.S."

"I wonder how it got like that, and why things are the way they are?"

"Why doesn't he stand up for himself?"

"But it's not easy. I found it hard."

"You do that really well now, and sometimes you're in trouble for it." "I know. Like I said, it's not easy to know when to speak up."

"You've shown me how to stand up for myself."

"Yes. You can do that well now. We'd better hurry and go downstairs. We'll talk more in bed." After we had said goodnight in the front room, A.J. came upstairs with us to turn off the light, saying, "Straight to sleep, as it's a big day tomorrow. We have to get your clothes ready after school for your holiday." We could hear her going downstairs and chatted – we were excited. I said, "It's going to be so good to be with our uncle again." Eventually we fell asleep. It was a rush in the morning, saying our goodbyes at the bus stop. A.J. grabbed Lydia's hand. "Come along. I have a busy morning, and I will be home when you get out of school. Goodbye."

Chapter 57

The last day of term for me was easy. Lots of chatter. Hardly any work. We even had a game with our maths teacher, asking questions and putting our hands up when we knew the answer. Guess who came up with the highest score? It was Angela, of course. We talked about it afterwards and she told me her mother gave her maths lessons. She was a teacher at a boys' school. No wonder she is clever, I thought. We said our goodbyes at lunchtime and wished each other a good holiday. Other girls came up to me, saying the same. I felt I had made friends and settled into this school.

When we got on the bus, Betty saved me a seat. I didn't talk with her that morning. She was sitting at the front and I was late getting on. She asked, "What happened this morning?" We had a good talk and Betty said, "I hope you will be back for some of the holidays."

"I don't know how long we will be away. I don't think it will be that long, though." U.S. and Lydia were waiting as we got off. He handed me a bigger bag of sweets, saying, "Enjoy. You won't be getting more for a while." Lydia said, "A.J. will be home when we get there. No more talking. Eat your sweets."

"Thank you." As soon as we got through the door, A.J. was calling us. "I'm in your bedroom." We ran upstairs. A.J. had little piles of clothes out. "These will have to be packed. Your uncle will be here early. We need to be organised. Go and wash your hands. Then you can pack some of these things." We did as we were told. Our bags were on the floor. Looking at my pile, I asked, "Do you know how long we will be staying?"

"No. I expect it will be for a few days."

"Well, we might need more clothes."

"That should be enough, and you will just have to make do. You only have these bags." I started putting my clothes in and Lydia did the same. We had a bag each.

"There will be last minute things to pack in the morning." We still had our uniforms on. She said, "We are having dinner early, then you're going to bed, as it will be a very early start." I said, "Can we go and see Monty and take him for a quick walk?"

"Just on the vacant block. I will call you when dinner is ready." We raced downstairs and grabbed the lead from the hook. U.S. was organising dinner. I said, "We can just take Monty to the vacant block."

"Oh. But you still have your uniforms on. You haven't changed." "Aunty Jean told us not to. We are going to bed early and up early." He said he knew that. We put Monty on his lead. He was so excited. We went as fast as we could out of the side gate, running round the block. No-one else was about. It wasn't long before we were called, and had to put Monty back on his chain, giving him some fresh water.

We had our favourite dinner, which was sausages and mash. I managed to save a piece of sausage for Monty in my hanky and gave it to him when I took his food out. We all went into the front room together to have our talk about our day. Lydia had had a happy day doing little work, and I said the same. A.J. thought it was still school, not the holidays, so we should still have been working. I thought: can you believe it? We were so excited. I asked, "How early will our uncle be?"

"Seven thirty. That is early."

"That is why you are going to bed now. Please go to sleep and don't keep talking. In the morning it's breakfast, and you need to be dressed and packed before then. You will be leaving straight after that to catch a bus and train to London." We were surprised that it would be so early. Once we were in bed, A.J. turned off the light. "Straight to sleep. Goodnight." We said goodnight. After we heard her go downstairs, I said, "I wonder why it's so early?"

"Our uncle will tell us when we see him. We had better try and go to sleep. A.J. will wake us early."

"I know, but I'm too excited."

"Well, I'm going to sleep now." and she gave me a hug, "Goodnight." I lay there for quite a while and was almost asleep when I heard A.J. coming up the stairs. I quickly closed my eyes. She opened the door and checked on us, then closed the door again and went to the little room. I heard her unlock the door. It was quick in and out. I heard her locking it again. I listened, but didn't hear any noise, only A.J. going down the stairs. I was thinking: what is in there and what does she do in there? I really wanted to know. I eventually fell asleep.

A.J. had to wake us. It was hard getting out of bed and we were told to hurry. "To the bathroom first, and then come down in your night clothes for breakfast." Our clothes were all on the chair ready for us.

Then we had to clean our teeth, so we didn't put anything on our clothes. A.J. was in the bedroom putting our last-minute things on our bed. We were asked to help carry our bags down to the front door, then wait in the front room. It was only a little while before the bell rang. We ran to the front door with A.J. following. She opened the door and there stood our uncle. With excitement, we gave him hugs. He said, "You have done well to be ready so early." He thanked A.J. and said, "I can stay for a little while, before we have to leave." We were asking him questions. A.J. said, "Let your uncle come inside to the front room and we can all have a talk." We all sat down and U.S. went to the kitchen to get a drink for our uncle. He told us, "There was a meeting I had to attend to and I stayed in town last night. That's why I'm here so early." He wanted to know from A.J. how everything was, and if we had been behaving. She said, "Yes. All is going quite well." -- looking at me. "Glad to hear it." our uncle said. After having a drink and a bit more talking, he said, "We had better make a move. We'll see you in a week." We were having a week with our uncle. That's nice, I thought. "Enjoy your time by yourselves. It will be a nice break for you too."

We said our goodbyes. "Oh." I said, looking at U.S., "Can I run outside and give Monty a pat and a biscuit?"

"Yes." A.J. gave me a look. I quickly ran to the kitchen and grabbed a handful of biscuits, which I gave to him. I patted him, saying, "Goodbye." He wondered what was happening. Then I ran back inside. Everyone was at the front door, waiting for me. A.J. opened it, saying, "Goodbye." U.S. said, "Have a nice time." We said thank you, then ran down the path to the gate. We opened it for our uncle, who was following. He said, "You are in a hurry."

"Yes, it's so good to see you. I can talk, and don't have to be careful what I say."

"What do you mean by that?"

"Well, I find it difficult. I often say something and I'm in trouble. I always have to be careful and think how to talk. It's hard for me." Lydia said, "A.J. often finds fault with what Sylvia says or does." Our uncle said, "We will talk about things on the train." We caught a bus which was almost empty, then walked to the station. It was so good going on a holiday. We could see a train coming in on our platform. "This is it," our uncle said. We got on, and had a carriage to ourselves. There weren't many people about. We sat on either side of him, both of us talking. "One at a time, please. Who is going to talk first?" I said, "I will just explain what I meant earlier about having to be careful. I feel whatever I say, Aunty Jean tries to find fault with it. I always have to stop and think, and be careful, or I will be punished." Lydia said, "She is very strict on Sylvia, and it seems unfair. She's not like that with me."

"Sorry it's happening, but look at it this way. At the same time, it can be a good thing. It is preparing you for when you are an adult. You will have to weigh things up before you speak. How do I say this, or should I even say it at all? Is it the right thing? Try and look at it like that, and think hard before you speak. It can affect the person, and it's not always easy to make things right."

"I find it difficult and I don't like her."

"It's all part of growing up, and Aunty Jean can sense that you're not fond of her." He gave me a hug. "Just try and understand what I am saying, and see the good side of people. You have done really well with your school work, and looking out for your sister. You have become a strong person through what has happened to you in your life. Now you need to learn how to manage another strong person who is an adult, and whom you are not fond of." Then, turning to speak to Lydia, he asked, "How are you getting on with Aunty Jean?"

"It's mostly all right. I do think she likes me more, and is nicer to me, which isn't really fair, but what can I do about that?"

"Very little. Again, it's partly circumstances that has made things how they are. One must try and make the most of it. You haven't had setbacks with schooling, and you are a fast learner, so what is there not to like? That makes it easy for Aunty Jean to get on with you."

"But I feel upset when she is so strict on my sister, and it's unfair. I try and help Sylvia and say to be careful how you say things, and sometimes it works." Our uncle gave us both hugs, and said, "It's a learning process. I'm proud of you both. You are doing well."

Chapter 58

No one came into our carriage, but we could see more people about when we stopped at stations. Uncle asked, "What about Uncle Stan?" We both said, "He's much easier to get on with, and we both like him.", and we chatted, telling him things. "But he can't, or doesn't, stand up for himself." Our uncle asked, "What do you mean? Explain, please." We both started talking together. He said, "One at a time, please." Lydia said, "You tell." I told him that U.S. had a large family, and he even has his mother and father alive. "How lucky is he? I wish we did. And he hardly sees them. That's because of Aunty Jean. We found that out." Lydia asked, "Why do you think he doesn't stand up to her?"

"It's difficult to know. Again, it could be circumstances way back in their relationship, when they first met, and how it grew over the years. Still, he might be happy with the way things are." We both said, "He's not. We can tell." I said, "He'd like to see more of his family, but things can't change, he told us, and won't say why." Lydia said, "He's not as strict as Aunty Jean, and is nicer to us. He gives us –" I quickly interrupted her. "It's a secret, remember? He told us not to tell anybody. Oh, sorry. We promised we would not tell." Lydia said, "It makes us happy. I can say that, can't I, Sylvia?"

"Well, you don't have to tell me, in that case. I'm glad you find him easier to get on with."

The train stopped and we had some people came into our carriage. I asked, "Are we nearly there?"

"Just a few more stations." We kept quiet and looked out of the window. The train was going very fast, passing through stations. I was excited. It would be so good to see my aunt again. I was looking forward to talking with her about girly things. Now the train was slowing down. People were standing up. Uncle said, "We will be getting off now." We were walking along the station with a lot of people. Then we had to go up the escalators. It wasn't easy to get on. Lydia was holding onto me. I fell, and a man helped me up. Our uncle was carrying our bags. It was a bit scary, and I was glad when we got off. That was hard too. Uncle said, "We have quite a long walk." We had been sitting a long time, and it was good walking. We never stopped chatting, telling Uncle all we could think of. It was a long walk before finally we could see in the distance (and I remembered and recognised) that it was the park, and there were trees there. I knew it wasn't long before we would be at Uncle's house. Eventually we reached the park. We ran to the swings. Uncle put his bags down, saying, "I'm glad of the rest." He gave us a push, saying, "Sylvia, you're almost too big for the swings now." We were the only ones there. After a while we made our way to Uncle's. We were so excited, reaching the house. Uncle opened the door, calling out to our aunt, who came hurrying down the hall to meet us, with arms outstretched, saying, "So good to see you again. You both have grown so much." We were all talking nineteen to the dozen. Then Alice said, "Let's get you inside and we will talk in the front room. You must be very tired. Sit down. I will make a drink for you and something to eat." She left the room. Uncle asked, "Are you hungry?"

"Yes. Where are Peter and Marion?" He said, "They must be out. You will see them later." Our aunt came in with a tray of food and drinks, which we enjoyed. Then there was more talking, and she said, "I will show you your room and you can freshen up." We followed her to a room off the hall. It was where we had stayed last time.

"And when you are ready, come to the front room. We'll see you soon." We could hear her talking to Uncle as she walked down the hall. Lydia said, "She has made the room really nice for us."

"Yes, and there is the big bed. We will still be sleeping together." After finding the bathroom and washing our hands, we went to the front room. Then there was more talking, chatting about things, and Alice said, "I've made us a nice lunch, and there will probably be food you haven't seen before." Our uncle said, "Just try some. If you don't like it, leave it on your plate." We were hungry, and watched what our uncle and aunt were doing. Uncle said grace first. "Just put a few things on your plate." Lydia did the same. Alice was asking us more questions. I had something in my mouth. I said, "We have our meals in silence."

"Goodness me!" my aunt said. "You are being brought up prim and proper, like little ladies." My uncle looked at my aunt and said something in another language. "Well, while you're here we all talk together at mealtimes."

"Thank you." It really felt good to be able to join in conversation. I asked about Peter and Marion. "Peter is out playing with a friend and will be home soon, and Marion has gone out with friends. She will be home later. She knows you are here for a few days." We chatted lots and helped ourselves to salad and other cold foods. When we had finished, we helped our aunt by taking dishes to the kitchen. Uncle went to his study. Alice was still asking me about school. What did I like doing? Then she talked to Lydia. When the dishes were finished, we all went back to the front room. Lots more talking. My aunt was so easy to talk with. I asked her all sorts of things, and she asked us lots about Aunty Jean and Uncle Stan, and how we felt about them. I did tell her that I found it really difficult to talk with Aunty Jean. "I don't really like her."

"Have you thought about what you want to do when you leave school?"

"No, I haven't."

"What sort of things do you like doing?"

"You mean, for a job?"

"Yes."

"Well, I'm not old enough to work."

"That's something you need to think about. What interests you, and what would you enjoy doing? You are growing up, and whatever you decide, you'll be doing it for a few years."

"I'm not good at anything, really." Lydia said, "That's not true. You are doing well at school."

"Yes, I am doing better now, but I don't know what I could do for a job." Aunt said, "Just keep it in the back of your mind. What would I like to do? You will be surprised when you have worked it out, and you will be excited about it."

"I still have a couple more years at that school."

"I'm saying, time goes quickly. It's your life, and you want to be happy." I thanked her. Well, I was thinking, I have never thought about that. Alice was talking with Lydia, who said she was looking forward to going to my school. My aunt said, "What I've heard about you, you should sit for an exam to see if you could go to the grammar school. You are bright, and have been able to start school early, and haven't had any interruptions, like your sister, who didn't start school until she was nearly nine."

"Oh. I want to be at school with Sylvia."

"Sylvia will be nearly ready to leave school when you're old enough to start secondary school."

"I hadn't thought it would be like that." Lydia said. We heard the doorbell ring. "That will be Peter coming home." She got up to go to the door. We heard her saying, "Thank you for bringing him home." Then there were footsteps coming down the hall. My aunt said, "Do you remember? These are your cousins. I told you they are staying with us for a few days." We said, "Hello, Peter." He said hello, and said he didn't know us. It had been quite a while since we saw him last. My aunt said, "Why don't you show the girls your room?" He was happy with that, and we followed him down the hall. He showed us all his toys. We spent quite a time playing with him. After a while we were all chatting like we knew each other, and he was happy. It wasn't until much later in the evening that Marion came home. She looked so grown up. She did chat with us for a short time, then went to her room. Aunt Alice said, "You must be tired now. How about getting ready for bed? It has been a big day for you. Do you want to say goodnight to Uncle?"

"Yes," and we walked down the hall to the study. We knocked on the door and opened it. "We are going to bed now and want to say goodnight." He got up from his chair and walked towards us, saying goodnight and giving us hugs. Then Aunt walked back with us to our room. She gave us a hug, saying, "Goodnight. Sleep well."

Chapter 59

In bed, we chatted a long time about things, and wondered what we would be doing next day. We soon fell asleep. We woke up late. Alice didn't wake us. We had breakfast, just the two of us. She wasn't cross with us, and asked, "Were you comfortable?"

"Yes, thank you."

"We have a few things planned to do while you're with us." The most exciting one was we would be taken to the Zoo to see the animals. That would be so good. We said, "Thank you. We would love that."

"Peter will enjoy that too. Now today, later, we will go out walking, just to the park, to get to know one another again."

"That would be good." Alice said for us to relax and try and have fun. We liked her. We could ask her anything. She was so easy to talk to, and we really did love the zoo. We wished we could have stayed longer. Our uncle said, "I must take you back tomorrow, as I have commitments, and you have been away for a week." It went very fast. Saying goodbye to my aunt was hard. I looked on her as a substitute mother. She helped me think about what I wanted to do in the future. Yes, I was growing up, and had more to understand. Uncle and Aunt said what lovely manners we had, and it was a pleasure having us, also what a good job Aunty Jean and Uncle Stan were doing, bringing us up. They really didn't understand what it was like being us, living with them, and how difficult we found it. It was so hard just to have some fun.

After arriving back, our uncle had a few words with A.J. and U.S. Monty was beside himself, so happy to see us. Then we were called in, as our uncle was leaving. It was dramatic saying goodbye. He promised he would be in touch soon. A. J. and U.S. were nicer towards us for a little while. I wondered how long this would last. I caught up with Betty on the vacant block; also, Lydia caught up with her friends. We had just a few days of our holidays left, then it was back to our routine of school again, getting up early, catching the bus. It wasn't easy, and somehow, we were always running late. There was lots of chatter on the bus. Betty mostly managed to save me a seat, and we never stopped talking until we got to school. Saying our goodbyes, we went our separate ways. I could see Angela walking way in front. A few girls started talking with me, asking about the holidays. I felt I had settled in.

We reached the assembly hall. Silence was required, and our headmaster, Mr. Origen, welcomed us all back and had a few announcements. Then we were asked to walk quietly to our classrooms. It wasn't until I reached ours that I spoke to Angela, already sitting at her desk. She asked me about our holiday. "I will tell you later." I had to get to my desk on the other side of the room. We said we would catch up at recess. Our teacher came into the classroom and we all stopped talking. After a few words about the holidays being over, he said, "Now you must all concentrate on your subjects and get good marks for your future." Then it was straight into maths, which I feared most. I said to myself, do your best, which I did.

I talked to Angela at recess. She did try and help me, but we spent most of our time talking about our holidays. Girls were coming up to us, saying, "Come on! Join in!" They were chatting in a group. We did, Angela reluctantly, but I felt happy we were asked, and that they included Angela. I just wished she would want to join in more. Later, when I had a chance to talk with her about it, I said, "You will enjoy it, being part of a group." She felt unsure -- "I'd rather we were on our own all the time." I was hoping eventually she would be happy.

The day went fast, and I saw Betty on the bus and we compared what we had done. No homework, and it was a fairly easy day. It was good to see Lydia and U.S., who had some sweets for me. We really enjoyed them after our break without any. Lydia had had a happy day, and just loved school. She was telling me about another girl whom she had met, and also had a new teacher, who was nice. U.S. said, "Now, no more talking. We are nearly home. Eat up, and remember, this is still our little secret." We told him we hadn't told anybody, even our uncle. He said he was proud of us for keeping our word. We asked him about when we were away. Did he walk Monty? "Of course.", and that he did miss us, and so did Monty. I thought, that was nice. Talking to Lydia later, we agreed that we liked him, but we still couldn't understand how he was about his family.

Since returning from our uncle's, and talking with my aunt, I started thinking what I would like to do when my schooling was finished. Lydia and I talked about it in bed. I really didn't know what I wanted to do. I had another year and a half left at school, then I would be finishing. It was all a bit scary. "Don't worry about it. You will know by then. You have lots of time left." I felt unsure about that. I talked with Betty about things the next day. She said, like Lydia did, "Don't worry. We have plenty of time, and you will have to see how your marks are." I asked, "Do you know what you would like to do?"

"I think I'd like to work in a shop."

"Oh, I wouldn't want to do that."

"Well, we are all different, and at least you know that's something you don't want to do now."

"Yes, but I can't think of anything I would really like to do."

"Just keep trying to get good marks, and enjoy school."

"I am doing that." We chatted a bit more about what jobs I would like to do.

Our first time after being away, we walked to the chapel, passing the house where U.S.'s dad lived. Lydia and I said, "I wonder if he has visited his dad anymore?" We wanted to know. "We must ask him when he is on his own." Lydia agreed, "Dennis is next door. I wonder if we will see him today?" We reached the chapel. There were lots of people outside, talking in a group. A.J. and U.S. said, "We will see you later." Lydia was going to Sunday school and I was following her, going into the side door of the chapel, to sit with the youth group. I saw my friend, Sylvia, with others, already sitting in the chapel. I walked in and could only whisper. It was all very quiet. I gave her a smile. Then a lady started playing the organ. It was lovely music. Everybody was in the chapel now, and the music stopped. The minister was in his pulpit, speaking. Moving along the seat, I was making sure there would be room for Lydia to sit with me when she came in.

I didn't really understand the sermon, and knew that when that was finished there would be a hymn, and the children from Sunday school would come in and sit in front of us. Lydia would always sit with me, and we would whisper to each other. Often, the teacher would give us black looks, and we knew to be quiet. After the minister spoke to the children and youth group, he made announcements of forthcoming events. One was saying he had a date fixed for when the evangelist Billy Graham would be coming to Colchester. If anybody wanted to go and hear him, we needed to let him know what interest there was, and numbers. I whispered to Lydia, "I would love to go and see him." Others in the youth group were also whispering, including my friend Sylvia. We all wanted to go.

When the service finished, and we met A.J. and U.S. outside the chapel, I asked, "Are we going to see Billy Graham?" A.J. said, "We will talk about that when we are home."

"Oh. Why can't you tell us now?" With a cross look, she said, "I have told you. We will talk about it then." A.J. started talking with a lady standing next to her. I said to U.S., "We are going to talk with some of the youth group."

"Don't go too far. We will be leaving soon." I saw Sylvia in the crowd. She had very white hair, and was easy to see in a crowd. I held Lydia's hand. "Come on. Let's talk with Sylvia." When we reached her, there were a few girls all talking together, and we all agreed we wanted to go. It would be exciting. It was at night, in the big concert hall in town, we were told by Sylvia's mum, who was standing there, and seemed to know all about it. She said they would be going. If we were allowed, we could go with them. I said, "Thank you. That would be great. I will tell Aunty Jean. She is going to talk about it when we are home." I could see U.S. coming to find us through the crowd. He spoke to Sylvia's mum, then said, "We are going home now." We found A.J. waiting for us, saying, "Come along. You have kept us waiting. Too much chatter." "But," I said, "We are talking about the evangelist."

"We are discussing it in the front room. No more talking." Lydia said, "We wanted to know what others thought." I said, "Yes, and we can go with Sylvia's mum, if you don't want to go."

A.J. was really cross with me. "You had no right to ask her that."

"I didn't,"

"Interrupting me. Enough. No more on the subject! Now start walking home."

We walked in front, chatting. I said, "I wish A.J. wasn't like she is." Lydia said, "When we are in the front room, I will explain. You won't get into trouble." I squeezed her hand, saying, "Thanks." I thought to myself how nice it would be to have a mum like my friend Sylvia's. You could chat about things any time, and not have to wait to talk until we were in the front room.

On reaching home, Lydia and I went outside to see Monty. U.S. handed us the lead. "You can take him off his chain and walk him in the garden." We could hear them talking, and it sounded as if U.S. was standing up to A.J. We heard him saying, "They were only talking with their friend, and she offered to take the girls. That was very kind of her." I said to Lydia, "That's good. U.S. is telling her about Sylvia's mum. She must have told him that we could go with them." Lydia was pleased, saying, "Now you won't be in trouble. You didn't ask her." We both agreed that we wanted to hear Billy Graham, and hoped she would let us go.

In a short while, we were called in. Lunch was on the table. "Go and wash your hands." A.J. said. When we came through to the kitchen, it was my turn to say grace and then of course there was no talking. I couldn't wait till we were in the front room to hear what A.J. would say about Billy Graham. We helped with the dishes and asked U.S., who said, "You will have to wait to hear about it. I cannot say. Now how about hurrying and putting these dishes away, and then you will find out sooner."

We were all in the front room. A.J. said, "Now. We need to find out more details." I asked, "Do you want to go?" hoping she wouldn't. "Yes. We both would like to hear him." I said, "That's so good. Then we are going."

"It's a matter of finding out how we can get there."

"Well," I said, "We can get a lift from Sylvia's mum." A.J. got cross. "That was rude of you to ask." Lydia interrupted, saying, "It wasn't like that." and explained how it happened. A.J. said, "Well, we all go together, or not at all, so we will have to wait for more details. End of discussion!"

We were allowed to read for a while. It was raining hard. I hoped it would stop, so we could take Monty for his walk, and we could chat together. It was late in the afternoon when we could go out and run in the garden with Monty, as there was not enough time for a walk. Soon we would be leaving for the evening service. We started walking. It had been raining, and we reached the chapel. We went straight inside. There were not many people there. Eventually the minister made his announcement regarding Billy Graham, saying there was a lot of interest, and more details would be announced the next week. When walking home, Lydia and I spoke about it, saying, "That's good. People are wanting to go, but we will have to wait till next week to find out more."

Next morning, on the school bus, I talked with Betty about the evangelist coming. She wasn't very interested and didn't go to Sunday school. She would ask her mother. We arrived at school and were told in the assembly hall what classrooms to go to, as we were all starting a new school year, with a different teacher. I wondered if we would be with the same children again. I soon found out. There were a few changes, but it didn't really affect me much. Betty still wasn't in my class, but Angela was. We had different teachers. It took a while to get used to them. There was no homework for the first week, which was good for me. I was still finding maths difficult and had to stay in class at recess to get help from the teacher. I had a male teacher now, and didn't find it easy to relate to him. I talked with Betty on the bus, comparing our first day. She still had girls in her class from last year, and she had a lady teacher for maths. She said, "You will get used to him."

"I hope so.", and we discussed the situation.

As the bus stopped, I could see U.S. and Lydia walking towards it. Lydia said she had had a good day and was full of chatter, saying that she had made more friends. She liked her teacher and didn't have any homework. U.S. handed me more sweets, asking, "How are things for you?" Also, Lydia was asking me questions. I told them. U.S. said, "It could take a little while for you to get used to a new teacher. Just do your best."

"Thank you. I am trying." We arrived home, having lots to talk about – our first school day after the holidays. When we were in the front room, A.J. listened to Lydia. A.J. was happy with everything except the fact that no homework had been given to her, and it was the same for me. She failed to understand why it hadn't been organised as soon as we were back at school. I didn't tell A.J. I was having maths problems again, and hoping it wouldn't be for long and that it would soon all be good. We were allowed to read in bed. A.J. said she would be up in a while to turn off the light. We ran up the stairs and could see a light shining underneath the door of the little room. I said to Lydia when we reached the landing, "She forgot to turn it off." I tried the door. We couldn't believe it. It opened, and I went in. Lydia stood at the door. There were all these boxes on the floor. Lydia grabbed me, saying, "We'd better close the door quickly and get to bed. We will get caught."

"Let's see what's in a box first.", and went further into the room, to an open box, and pulled out a packet of biscuits, showing them to Lydia, still standing by the door, not wanting to come in. She said, "Put them back. Come on, let's close the door, before we get caught." I put the biscuits back. As I turned to come out of the room, I saw a tin sitting on top of a box. "Come and have a look at this tin." She was really getting cross with me. "We will get caught. Leave it! I don't want to see! Come on. Let's quickly close the door."

"A.J. won't be up for a while. She thinks we're in bed reading." I pulled the lid off, and there were all different kinds of biscuits. I took two out and put the lid on, hurrying out of the door to where Lydia was standing. We quickly closed the door. She said, "What are you doing?"

"I was about to turn the light off."

"Leave it on. Come on, let's get into bed." We hurried into bed. I said, "That was exciting. Now we know what's in there."

"We were so lucky we didn't get caught. And what have you in your other hand?"

"Two biscuits – one each." She was not happy with me. We could hear A.J. coming upstairs, so we quickly grabbed our books. I put the two biscuits under my pillow. A. J. came in. "Time for sleep. Put your books away.", turning off the light, saying "Goodnight." We could hear her stopping at the little room, opening the door. She was in and out fast. She must have just turned the light off, I thought, and locked the door. Lydia said, "She will find out now about the biscuits. We will be in big trouble."

"No, she won't. She wouldn't count the biscuits in the tin. Stop worrying." I grabbed the biscuits from under my pillow. "Come on, we're going to eat them now." Lydia was upset. "What about all the crumbs?"

"Let's get our hankies and hold the biscuits over them. We'll eat them and enjoy them."

So that's what we did, and we really enjoyed them. We talked about what had just happened, saying, "That must be her storage space, but we never get any biscuits."

"Remember when Uncle came, U.S. made him a drink, and he had biscuits on a plate?"

"Well, they must just keep them for themselves. I wonder what's in all the other boxes?" Lydia grabbed me and said, "Promise me you're not going to try and find out."

"I won't, but how about A.J. leaving it unlocked, with the light on?"
"It could have been U.S., but we are not going to find out, are we?"

"I promise I won't. Please don't worry. We know this is where they store stuff."

"We were lucky we didn't get caught," Lydia said. "They still might find out we took biscuits out of the tin." She was very worried about it. I said, "They wouldn't count the biscuits in the tin. Please don't worry." When we were older, we found out there was rationing and you had coupons, and it was a difficult time to buy things. You only bought them on special. The little room was their storage space. I would love to have seen what was in the other boxes and get into the tin of biscuits again. They were yummy, but we never did. A.J. never found out. It was quite a few days before Lydia relaxed and knew we would not get caught.

Chapter 60

I settled into school and found I had more friends. I also joined in at recess playing basketball. Sometimes we played hockey, when it was our sports day. Angela sat and watched. She was not interested in joining in. Other girls were getting used to her being around and were being nicer to her, which made me feel better about playing. When it was wet, we would huddle under the veranda. Angela would help me with my maths. We were not allowed to go into the classroom at recess. Slowly I was getting the hang of maths, and no note was written for A.J. I did still miss my other maths teacher, but we still had the same teacher for history, and we girls all swooned over him. We thought he was great. He made the class fun, and we always ended up having a laugh. A.J. was happy we were now having homework.

After dinner, sitting at the kitchen table once more after the holidays, wasn't easy, and we only ever had maths homework. It was a few days before Lydia joined me. We would talk, and she gave me a little help without A.J. finding out. Later, in the front room, she was pleased with us both, that we were enjoying school, and there were no notes sent home. Things were going smoothly. We were given new readers. A.J. heard us read, and we were allowed to read in bed. We did more talking than reading. We were now getting into a routine, and A.J. was a bit nicer towards me since we came back from our holiday. I was trying not to answer back and only speak when I was spoken to. It wasn't easy.

When walking with U.S. and eating our sweets, we bumped into Mrs. Taylor, who stopped and spoke to us. She was having difficulty walking, and she had a sore foot. U. S. chatted to her for a while, and we talked to the baby, who was called Elizabeth. She was sitting up, strapped into this high pram, and was trying to get out. Mrs. Taylor said, "She has started walking a few steps, and that is what she wants to do." I asked, "Can we see her doing that?"

"Well, it's difficult here on the street." She said to U.S., "Why don't you call in and see me? Elizabeth would like that."

"We are on our way home." U.S. said. "Maybe another time." I said, "Can we make a time now? We would love to, wouldn't we, Lydia?"

She said yes. "Can we?" she asked U.S. Mrs Taylor suggested a Saturday morning, about 10, to U.S., who said, "Yes, that would be good." We said, "Thank you. We must go. Goodbye." We continued walking home, talking to U.S. We asked, "Where does she live? Is it far?"

"Just across the road, and you turn into another street, down the hill a bit. You will see on Saturday." I asked, "Are you going to tell Aunty Jean, or shall we, when we talk in the front room?"

"There is no need for you to mention it. I will let her know. Now we had better hurry home and get your jobs done. We are running late." While we changed, we talked about meeting Mrs. Taylor again, saying, "I wonder if U.S. will let A.J. know, because she will be at work, and we still have to get our jobs done."

We were looking forward to Saturday. Later, in the front room, when talking about our day, we didn't mention Mrs. Taylor, nor did U.S. We thought he would, so he must be going to do it when they were alone, and we wouldn't hear what A.J. would say. We talked about it later in bed. "I hope she will still let us go."

"She knows Mrs. Taylor and talks to her. I'm sure she will be all right about it." "It was good that U.S. decided we could go without checking with A.J. first. That hardly ever happens." We agreed, and we would find out soon about it, and we would not mention it at all. The next morning, in the bathroom, looking out of the window, I saw Dennis cycling past. "We haven't seen him for a while. Wonder if we will see him on Sunday at chapel?" We hurried down the stairs to breakfast. A.J. said, "Your porridge is on the table, ready to eat. Lydia, say grace, please, and eat up." A.J. and U.S. had finished their breakfast and were making our lunches. We quickly finished our porridge. A.J said, "Now take your lunches and put them in your bags. We will be leaving soon." We raced upstairs to finish getting ready. Lydia asked, "When do you have youth group again?"

"I think it's this Friday."

"Do you think I can come too?"

"I will find out. You might be able to."

"That would be so good."

A.J. was calling to us to hurry up. We ran downstairs, calling out goodbye to U.S. A.J. was already out of the front door and at the gate. We caught her up. She said, "Too much talking." We could see the bus arriving. I'm sure it's early, I thought, and hurried to it. Saying goodbye to Lydia, A.J. said, "We are going now. Please learn, and goodbye." She started walking away. There was lots of chatter on the bus. Betty was sitting near the front, and saved me a seat. I told her about Mrs. allowed to Taylor, whom we would see on Saturday. She didn't know her. I asked her about coming to see Billy Graham. She said she was come with us. "That will be good." Her mum wasn't going. "I will talk to U.S. when we see him this afternoon." We arrived at school, saying our goodbyes, and went our separate ways. After assembly, I was walking to the classroom and Angela called me and caught up. "How did you go with your homework?"

"I managed to do it."

"I'll have a look if you like, and see if you did it right."

"Great. Thank you." We went into the classroom. Angela sat at her desk and looked at my homework. "Yes, you have done it right. They are the same answers as mine, and I never get mine wrong." That was true, I thought, she is Little Miss Good Shoes. I said, "I am so pleased. Thank you for checking it."

"That's OK. Go and sit at your desk, before the teacher comes in." More children were all coming in. I quickly went to my desk on the other side of the room. The teacher walked in. All went quiet. After saying good morning, he came round to collect our homework, then back into more new stuff I found hard to follow. I thought, I'll work it out when I'm on my own. When we were given homework on it, we should get our results from the day before. At recess, when chatting to Angela about what we had just been given, she helped me a bit. I thought, I'm so lucky to have a friend who always gets her maths right. Other subjects I had no problems with. I loved sport and gym. I found I had made a few friends, especially when we played netball. I was the shooter, and mostly managed to get the ball through the net. The team I was in would often win. It was a nice feeling, being good at something, and I enjoyed being part of a team.

We were told we would be playing against another school, and they would come and visit us. It would be organised. There was a lot of excitement, and we were told we must practise as much as possible. Nearly every recess, we would play netball. Angela was getting tired of watching me, and other girls started talking to her. Gradually, she was making friends with them, which made me feel better. She said, "It's no fun for me. You're always playing netball."

"I understand, but can we still be friends?"

"Of course." I thought, at last, she is mixing in. It was sort of forced on her, as it turned out, but she was all right about it. That was good.

After school, when waiting for the bus, I was telling Betty about my day. She was pleased that I was in the netball team, and said they had had sports day, and they played rounders. She wasn't keen on it. We spoke a bit more about school. Getting off the bus, we said our goodbyes. Lydia came running towards me, excited, telling me about her day. They had a test in maths, and she received the highest marks. "That's great." I was telling her about being in the netball team, and we would be playing against another school. U.S. handed me my sweets, saying, "It's great that you are both happy and doing well." We were talking together as we walked home about when youth group was on. He felt that it was this Friday, but we would have to check with A.J. Lydia said, "I want to come, and I'm now old enough to start."

We arrived home and got changed, and ran downstairs to the kitchen. U.S. said, "Slow down. What's the hurry?"

"Can we take Monty for a walk?"

"Yes, but you do have your jobs to do, so don't be too long." Monty was jumping up and down, so excited. It was hard to put him on his lead. We ran out of the side gate. All was quiet. Lydia asked, "Which way?"

"To the woods." We loved that walk, taking it turns to hold the lead. Monty was really pulling us all the way and running to the woods. When we got there, I said, "I'm going to let Monty off the lead. He will come to us when we call him."

"Do you think we should?"

"He wants to be free for a while. I'm sure he will come back."

Lydia agreed, but was nervous about doing it. I pulled the lead towards me, and then we talked to Monty and let him off. I don't think he could believe it. He ran between the trees and we could see him stopping, having some sniffs. We started picking bluebells. We had a bunch each and put them together, and then we called Monty. He came running back straight away. That was so good, and we grabbed him, managing to get him on the lead, which he wasn't too happy about. Walking home, we talked about not saying anything. I think both A.J. and U.S. would have been cross about it, and we mightn't be allowed to walk him anymore. We arrived, then put Monty on his chain, and gave him a drink of water. He was really thirsty. We went inside. A.J. was home and in the kitchen. We gave her the bluebells. She said, "Thank you. How about doing your jobs before you have dinner?"

We raced upstairs to change our shoes, and back outside to clean them. It wasn't long before dinner was ready. We were hungry and ate in silence. I was allowed to get Monty's dinner ready, and gave him a little extra. Nobody checked on me now. I went outside. Monty was lying down, asleep, and wasn't in any hurry to get up. I think he was exhausted. We helped with the dishes. A.J. had gone into the front room. I asked U.S., "Can Lydia come to youth group tomorrow, do you know?"

"Lydia must ask Aunty Jean, if she wants to go."

"I do want to go, and I will ask, when we are in the front room." We ran upstairs to get our homework. While chatting, I told Lydia how Monty was asleep when I went out with his dinner. That had never happened before. He really enjoyed his walk. Sitting at the kitchen table, looking at my homework, I was trying to work it out. "Let me see. What are you doing now?"

"New stuff. I didn't really understand what the teacher was telling us." Lydia worked it out and explained it. She was doing her homework when U.S. came in to check on us. He could see we were working, and said, "I'll leave you to it. You're working hard." Lydia said, "We will come in the front room when we have finished." I thanked her. "It was good being able to be together doing our homework." She knew how to work it out. She was so good with maths. She finished before me and went into the front room. When I joined them, A.J. said, "We are waiting for you." Then she asked Lydia about her day. A.J. was happy with her, getting top marks in maths. Then Lydia asked if she could go to youth group with me on Friday. A.J. asked, "Do you really want to?"

"Yes, I'd like to see how it is."

"Very well. You can go tomorrow with Sylvia." Lydia said thank you to A.J. Then it was my turn to say how my day had been. I told how I was in the basketball team, and I was the shooter, and we often won, also how we would be playing against a team from another school. We would need to practise every recess. She said, "As long as you can get your school work done, which is more important than playing basketball."

"But I'm in the school team, and I score the goals. That's helping the school. If we win, we get a trophy."

"As I said, if you are keeping up with your school work, which is more important. Now, how about getting ready for bed?"

We left the front room and ran up the stairs. I said, "A.J. never praises me."

"Don't be upset. You know how she is, and you are doing well – U.S. told you that."

"Yes, it would just be nice if I got a little praise from her, but that's how it is, so I shouldn't expect it."

"I'm coming with you tomorrow night. That will be fun."

"Yes," I agreed. We went down to say goodnight to U.S. As I opened the door, I heard U.S. mention my name. No more was said as we walked in. We said goodnight to U.S. A.J. said, "I'll be up shortly, so you can read for a while." In bed, we talked.

"Maybe U.S. was saying something about how A.J. is towards you." I gave her a hug. "Thank you. At least he is nice to me. I'm coping, mostly."

"Yes, be happy. We are going to Mrs. Taylor's on Saturday. Wonder if U.S. has spoken to A.J.?"

"Let's ask him when he's on his own." We talked a bit more, then we heard A.J. coming upstairs to turn the light off, saying "Goodnight.".

Chapter 61

Next morning, on the bus, I told Betty, "I'm going to youth group tonight, and so is Lydia, for the first time."

"Can anyone join?"

"It's run by the chapel, but I could ask if you could come."

"Yes. Can you let me know about it?"

"Of course." We got off, and I went to my classroom. Angela was sitting at her desk, saying, "You are late."

"I have just got off the bus."

"Well, you had better go and sit down. I have no time to look at your work." I walked to my desk. She was right. Nearly everyone was sitting at their desks. I quickly sat down, as the teacher was coming in behind me. There was silence. "Good morning. I'm coming round to collect your homework. Please have it on your desk." He started walking round to each of us. Pulling mine out from my bag, I thought, that's good. I should know how I went with my other work. After that, there was more talking about what we had learned, and he was using the blackboard, giving us more maths to write in our books. I really didn't know what he was talking about. He was asking questions, and you needed to put your hand up. I didn't. Only a few put their hands up. Of course, Angela did, every time. I was glad when class was finished.

It felt so good, going outside at recess to play netball. Angela followed me, saying, "I can have a look at your new work now, to see how you went yesterday."

"Thank you for helping me." Some girls were calling to me, "Come on. We need to practise!"

I felt a bit bad about just leaving her, but joined the team. I didn't see Angela until another class later in the day. She was rather quiet towards me. I said, "Sorry, but I have to practise all the time now, until we play on Sports Day."

"Nobody would talk with me. Just try and join in with the other girls, like you have been before." I tried to cheer her up, but somehow it didn't work. I was telling her about how I was going to youth group that night, and my sister would be coming for the first time. "You're lucky you have a sister. I'm an only child." We chatted a bit more. She was just lonely, and I felt sorry for her. The rest of the day went all right. On the bus, Betty and I were talking about our day. I told her about Angela. She said, "We all have different circumstances, and I don't have any brothers or sisters either." Betty did have friends she could talk with. She wasn't quiet, like Angela. I said, "It's hard for her. I will try and help her when I can."

"She has to make an effort to mix in, or she will always be on her own." I felt Betty was being hard on her. I thought, I will talk with U.S. and Lydia about it. We said our goodbyes when we got off the bus.

U.S. was standing there, asking me about my day. Lydia said she had had a happy day. I was handed my sweets. I told them about Angela. U.S. said, "It must be hard for her, if she is shy and on her own a lot." Lydia said, "You are doing your best to help." They agreed. I asked, "Can I do anymore?" U.S. said, "Just keep doing what you're doing."

"Can Betty come with us to hear Billy Graham?"

"We don't know what's happening yet with transport. We will find out soon." Lydia was looking forward to youth group. A.J. asked her again in the front room, "Are you sure you want to go?"

"Yes, I want to see what it's like." I had a feeling A.J. didn't want Lydia to come. I think she liked having her on her own, staying behind for company.

We raced and put our coats and shoes on. U.S. walked us there, which wasn't far. "I will be here when you come out." There were many children – lots of talking. We knew a few from the chapel. It wasn't long before somebody called out, "Silence!" He then started speaking, "Welcome to everybody and newcomers." He let us know what we would be doing. There was always a hymn to sing and a prayer to start. We played organised games. Lydia loved it. We saw Dennis with a few boys. He called out to us. We had a lovely yummy supper. As we left the building, a few boys and Dennis were on their bikes riding home. U.S. asked, "How was it?" Lydia said, "It was fun." I agreed, and said, "Did you see Dennis just now? He was riding with some boys. We called out goodnight to him."

"I didn't know who it was you he called out to."

When we were walking home, it was dark, and the street lights were on. We were both asking U.S. about his family again, but didn't find out any more. We reached home and went into the front room. A.J. was reading. Lydia said, "It was fun. I enjoyed it. There were children I knew from Sunday school and youth group."

"Well, it sounds like you want to join."

"Yes. There were a lot there tonight, and some who haven't been before."

"It's the first night, and some have come to see what it's like, and they won't come again."

"I enjoyed it, and it's good that we can go together."

"Well, it's time to get ready for bed." We ran upstairs, asking each other what we thought about it. We could hear A.J. asking U.S. questions. "I'm so glad you liked it."

"What was there not to like? We can do this together."

"Yes, and you can now leave Sunday school, you're old enough, and join the youth group, and sit in the chapel with me."

"Are you sure?"

"Well, there's no reason why you can't. We'll find out on Sunday." We quickly went into the bathroom, had a wash, and got into our night clothes. We ran down the stairs and into the front room. A.J. stopped talking as we went in. We said goodnight to U.S. A.J. said, "I'm coming up with you. I will turn the light off. It's late. Don't forget, you have your jobs tomorrow, and I will be home at lunchtime. We will go and clean the little church." We jumped into bed. "Straight to sleep. Good night." Then she turned off the light and closed the door. We listened, and heard her unlocking the little room. I whispered, "We know what she's doing – getting some biscuits for U.S. and her." It wasn't long before we heard her lock up and go downstairs. Lydia whispered, "We had a nice supper at youth group." I agreed – it was yummy"

"I'm really tired. I'm going to sleep."

"Me too. We have a big day tomorrow. Goodnight."

We woke up late and quickly went down. A.J. had already gone. U.S. was in the kitchen -- "I'll make your breakfast. How about getting dressed as quick as you can, then coming down?" We said thank you. I said, "That was nice of him to let us sleep in. We will have to hurry with our jobs. We are going to Mrs. Taylor's as well." Back in the kitchen, we were eating our breakfast. U. S. said, "Do your jobs as fast as you can. I will tidy up here. No talking – eat up!" That was what we did. When U.S. called us, we were almost finished our jobs. I asked, "Can we take Monty to Mrs. Taylor's? It will be a walk for him." U.S. thought about it for a while, then said, "Yes, that should be all right."

It wasn't long before we were on our way, taking it in turns to hold Monty. We found the house – it was easy. We pushed a button on the door, which U.S. said was the bell, and it would ring. Mrs. Taylor came to the door, saying, "Hello." and for us to come in, but, seeing Monty, she said to U.S., "Would you like to tie him to that tree?"

"I can do that. I thought it would be a walk for him, but maybe we should have left him at home."

"That's all right. I will get a dish of water for him. You girls go inside." We walked in. We saw Elizabeth on the floor and stopped to talk to her. Mrs. Taylor was back, with U.S. She closed the door and picked Elizabeth up, putting her on her lap. She was trying to get down. We were all sitting. Mrs. Taylor let Elizabeth off her lap and onto the floor. She immediately pulled herself up, holding onto my knees, as I was sitting next to Mrs. Taylor. Then she fell down, pulling herself up again, holding onto Lydia this time, making noises. She did walk a few steps. We thought she was like a little doll who could walk. We all talked for a while, then U.S. said, "We must go." Mrs. Taylor said, "You are welcome for a visit any time." Thanking her, we made our way out.

Monty was so good, lying down, waiting for us. We said our goodbyes. Mrs. Taylor, we could see, was still not walking well. On our way home we spoke to U.S. about our time with Elizabeth. I held the lead, saying we had never seen a baby or small child like that. U.S. said, "She will be a handful when she starts walking properly. Poor Mrs. Taylor, with her foot problem."

"Won't it be better soon?"

"It's something she has to live with."

"Does A.J. know we were seeing Mrs. Taylor this morning?"

"I did mention it to her a while ago."

"So, we can talk about it with A.J.?"

"Of course. Now, you have done your jobs this morning?" We said yes. "A.J. will be home soon for lunch. Then you have the little church to clean."

"We are not having any time to play with our friends."

"You have done something different this morning and enjoyed it. You can't fit everything in today." Lydia asked, "When can we visit again?"

"Soon. We will organise it with Mrs. Taylor." We got home before A.J. We ran upstairs to wash our hands. When we reached the kitchen, I put some plates out on the table. U.S. was organised. He had the sandwiches all ready, and we sat down, waiting for A.J. It wasn't long before she came in. She was surprised we were so organised. We ate our lunch in silence, then were told we would be leaving shortly. "Lots to do." After lunch we walked to the church. I said, "We went to see Mrs. Taylor and Elizabeth this morning."

"How did you get on?" We both started talking together. "One at a time, please." I let Lydia do the talking. A.J. said, "Mrs. Taylor is finding it very difficult to get around." I asked about her foot. "It is a condition she has that makes it difficult to walk." We arrived at the church. A.J. got her big bunch of keys out to open the wooden door. It was always so dark in there. She turned the lights on. We knew what to do. We walked to the front. By the altar was a door. We opened it. The room was called a vestry. It had cleaning stuff in. A.J. took the dead flowers out the back. We got into our jobs. It didn't take very long before it was ready for the service next day. We heard a knock on the door. A. J. went up the aisle to open it. We could hear them talking. It was Lena, with some fresh flowers. She didn't come in. We didn't see her, only heard them talking, and the door closing again. A.J. had a lovely bunch of flowers to arrange in a vase for the altar. "Does Lena have these flowers in her garden?" Lydia asked. "Some, and she often buys a bunch to mix in with them."

"That's nice of her." Then I asked, "Why didn't you call us, so we could say hello to her?"

"There was no need to. Now we have finished." She put the flowers on the altar. "Time to go."

"We never meet any of the family."

"Please don't start that again, Sylvia. We have spoken to you on that subject."

"Well, it would have been nice if you called us to say hello. We would have liked that, wouldn't we, Lydia?"

"Yes. We don't get a chance to see anyone."

"Enough on the subject. Come along, we are leaving now." We walked to the door. "Sylvia, you can turn the light off." She closed the door and locked it. We all started walking home in silence. I was thinking, wish it could be different. Nobody was about, and we were almost home. As we turned the corner, we could hear voices. We reached the vacant block. Oh good, I thought. I asked, "Can we join the children for a play, and take Monty?"

"You are almost too old to go and play. You need to act more grown up now."

"But I'm not grown up yet."

"It's about time you started thinking about it." Lydia said, "You are not being very nice to my sister, and I want her to come out and play with me." A.J. was very quiet, not saying a word. We were home now. U.S. met us at the door. "Hello. Monty is looking for a walk." He was holding the lead in his hand. He did not know what had just been said. I asked, "Is it all right for us to walk Monty?" A.J. said abruptly, "Very well, then." U.S. gave us the lead and we quickly ran out of the side gate. It was so good being on our own again. Lydia said, "That was mean of A.J., saying that that to you."

"You were great to talk like that to her. I couldn't believe it, and A.J. didn't say anything. I did expect her to tell you off. I think she was surprised."

We ran to where a group of children were and joined Betty, who was there, and some of Lydia's friends. Betty asked, "Where have you been?" We told her. She asked, "Do you like doing that?" We replied, "It's all right. Just nice now, we can have a play, and have been doing jobs all day."

"Oh, and we went to Mrs. Taylor's," and we told Betty all about it.

"That was good." We ran around with Monty, having to keep him on his lead. He wanted to jump up on everybody. They were giving him lots of pats, which he enjoyed. After a while, U.S. called us and we ran home. We said, "We had fun. Is it dinner time now?"

"Yes, and your program on the radio is after dinner. The one you like to hear." We said, "That's good. Are we to come in now?"

"Yes. I'll put Monty on his chain." We went inside. Lydia said hello to A.J., "What is for dinner?"

"Go and wash your hands. You'll see when you come to eat." We went to the bathroom. I said, "Why couldn't she tell us?"

"Oh well, it will be a surprise, and I'm hungry."

"So am I. We will have to eat it all, whatever it is," looking at Lydia, who said, "I will." We were sitting at the table. A.J. was serving it out, saying to me, "Say grace, please." I looked at Lydia, knowing it was a dish we didn't like. She pulled a face. A.J. saw her. "What's that all about?"

"I just felt like doing it to Sylvia."

"I don't know what that's all about, and I'm sure there is no need for it. Now let's all eat our dinner." No more was said. We ate our dinner, which neither of us liked, and managed to get through it. In the front room, we were able to listen to our program. It was a serial, based on Heidi. It was on every Saturday evening. We really enjoyed that. A.J. would ask us questions about it sometimes. I wished she didn't, as it spoiled my enjoyment. Lydia and I would talk about it afterwards. "Why does she have to do that? What difference does it make how we understand and feel about it?" I said, "We can't really say anything to her, or tell her not to do it." We talked in bed about our day. I said, "Tomorrow we should find out from the minister about what's happening with Billy Graham, and you can come into the chapel with me and sit with the youth group now."

"Are you sure? I might have to check with A.J."

"Well, you're old enough now." After more talking, we said we'd better go to sleep.

In the morning, when we were in the kitchen, after eating our porridge, A.J. said, "Get dressed as quickly as you can. We don't want to be late." Lydia asked, "Can I sit with the youth group now?"

"You need to go to Sunday school. It's up to the teacher to let you know when that happens." I said, "Lydia is old enough now." She said, "We know that, but there is a procedure. You can't just do what you want to do. Now go upstairs and get ready, please." Going up the stairs, I added, "You will be told by the teacher, so it could happen for next week."

"That's all right, and I can say goodbye to the younger ones then." We quickly dressed and did our hair. A.J. and U.S. were at the front door. She called out, "Come along." We arrived at chapel. I followed Lydia down to the side entrance, then we went our separate ways, she to the Sunday school for the last time, I hoped, me to the chapel. Music was playing as I sat with some girls. We whispered to each other about things. When everybody was seated, the music stopped and the service began. The minister spoke a few words and we sang a hymn. I was looking forward to when Lydia came in with the Sunday school class. Eventually it happened. We moved along the bench to make room for Lydia. She came in and whispered to me, "Next week I don't have to go to Sunday school." I squeezed her hand. We listened to the little sermon for us children. Most of us wanted to hear the details about Billy Graham, which would be announced at the end of the sermon. It couldn't come quickly enough for me. After the last hymn, the minister announced that two buses had been arranged, as there had been an overwhelming response from the congregation. "More details will follow."

We started whispering amongst ourselves. "How good is that?" Once we were outside, there was a lot of talk. We girls chatted amongst ourselves. I said, "I'm sure we will have to go on the bus. My friend Sylvia said, "My mum will still want to drive her car. What a shame you can't come with us."

"A.J. wouldn't allow us to go with you, but it's good they'll have buses for lots of people." We were being called, "Time to walk home. We will talk about it in the front room." Lydia and I chatted while walking home in front. Neither of us had seen Dennis. We were walking past where he lived. I said to Lydia, "I wonder why U.S. doesn't call in to see his mum and dad?" Lydia said, "Well, I don't want to go there again." I agreed. "I don't want to, either."

After lunch, in the front room, Lydia said, "I'm not going to Sunday school anymore. The teacher said I can now join the youth group."

"That's great." A.J. said, "Well, now it's been made official, and I'm pleased you're happy about it." I asked about Billy Graham. "Do you think Betty will be able to come with us on the bus?" A.J. immediately said no. "Why did you think she could?"

"She's my friend, and would like to come."

"It's for people who go to chapel, not outsiders."

"How do you know that? There might be room just for her."

"You're not listening to what I'm saying. It's only for the congregation."

"Oh. But are you sure?" A.J. was becoming cross. "I'm quite sure, and it's not going to happen." Lydia said, "She might be able to go with someone else." I said, "Yes. We can ask Sylvia's mum." A.J. was really cross now. "Both of you, please be told. It's not allowed. End of discussion!" When we were on our own, I thanked Lydia for thinking of that, about Betty coming. "If Sylvia's mum is happy to take her, why would it make any difference?" We both agreed – it shouldn't. I said, "Wish we could go with them instead of on the bus."

"So do I."

"We should know the exact date soon, when they work out the numbers." After more talking, we were ready. We were allowed to walk Monty, as it was fine and sunny. Grabbing the lead, A.J. called out, "Only a short walk." We went outside, putting Monty on his lead. Lydia asked, "Where shall we go?"

"We can't go far."

It was all quiet on the vacant block. We decided to go to the allotment, and at the end of the allotments there was a field. On passing our allotment, it looked like there were some vegies ready to pick. We decided we had better leave them. We would let U.S. know when we got home. When walking to the stile and passing the lead to Lydia, I got over when she did. We were now in the field. Nobody was about. "What now?" Lydia asked. "Do you think we had better walk back?"

"We haven't been that long."

"I know we're not supposed to, but shall we let Monty off so he can have a run?" Lydia looked at me. "Do you think we should?"

"He comes when we call him now." With that, I unhooked the lead. Monty looked at us, then ran as fast as he could to the other side of the field. Lydia said, "We'd better call him now. He could go under the hedge, which is at the end of the field, and we won't see where he is."

"All right." We ran and called him. He was in no hurry to come back. We could see him with his nose to the ground, walking near the hedge. "Oh," Lydia said, "He's not going to come back." We ran towards him again, calling him. He looked at us and kept walking, with his nose to the ground. I said, "He's not running away. We will reach him and put him on his lead."

"Hope you're right." Lydia was out of breath. I ran past her and reached Monty, who just stood there, looking at me. I quickly put him on his lead, saying, "You should come when you're called or we can't let you off again." Lydia reached us -- "We'd better not let him off anymore." We made our way home. I said, "Poor Monty. He's always chained up. He loves being free."

"Well, he should come back when he's called." When we reached home, I put him back on his chain. Lydia gave him some water, and we went inside. A.J. said, "You have been away a long time. I said a short walk." I said, "Sorry. We went to the allotment and looked at the vegies. Then I told U.S. some were ready to pick."

"I will have to go there and have a look. Thank you. Now go and wash your hands. Dinner is ready. We have been waiting for you." We said sorry again and ran out of the kitchen, chatting. I said, "Hope it's something nice for dinner." Once we were back in the kitchen, our dinner was on our plates. Lydia was told to say grace. It was our favourite dinner, sausages and mash. I was so happy about that. It wasn't until we had finished that A.J. said, "You both need to get ready for chapel. We are late, and we need to leave very soon." We hurried upstairs. I said, "How good it was that we enjoyed our dinner? I don't really feel like going to chapel again."

"Me neither."

We were both at the front door first. A.J. said, "I'm pleased to see you are ready to leave." Then we were on our way. There were only a few people in the chapel, and it was boring for me. We were never allowed to sit together. I could see no other children. I was having a good look round, and recognised Lena, sitting on the other side of the aisle. I made up my mind. When the service was finished, I would go and talk to her. When the last hymn had been sung and it was time to go, I didn't say anything. I just walked over to where she was. She was still sitting, and said, "Hello." She was surprised, and pleased to see me, and asked, "Are you on your own?"

"No. Everyone is on the other side of the aisle. I wanted to talk to you. You have some lovely flowers in your garden, that you bring for the church."

"Thank you. Would you like to come for a visit?"

"Oh, that would be nice. Can Lydia come too?"

"Yes, well, any time you would like to call in, you would be most welcome. I think you'd better go and find Aunty Jean now." I turned round and could see them walking down the aisle in front. I walked fast and caught up with them. A.J. said, "When we are out of here, I will have words with you, young lady." Lydia whispered, "What happened?"

When walking home, I told her what I did, saying, "Lena is really nice, and we can go any time to see her. She has a lovely garden." On reaching home, A.J. said to me, "Come into the front room." And to Lydia, "Go and get ready for bed." She was really cross, saying I had no right to do that unless she knew about it.

"Why can't I talk to anyone I want to?"

"You need to do as you are told, and not be rude. You are being rude to me."

"Well, I don't understand what all the fuss is about. You see her when she brings the flowers." I asked U.S., who didn't answer. A.J. said I was getting too big for my boots. "Do you understand? Don't speak to me like that again."

"I don't see why I can't talk to whoever I want to," not telling her that we had an invitation to see Lena any time. Later, in bed, we talked about what had happened. I said, "I don't know why she's so cross about it."

"It doesn't make sense really. They talk when she brings the flowers. Why doesn't she want us to talk with her?"

"But they never talk in chapel – nor does U.S."

"That man she was with must be her husband." I said, "Then that must be U.S.'s brother," Lydia said.

"Let's ask him when we see him on his own."

"We had better go to sleep now."

Chapter 62

Next morning, we woke late. A.J. called us, saying, "Breakfast is on the table." We hurried up. It was a rush. U.S. was quiet. A.J. still seemed cross. We said our goodbyes at the bus stop. It was already there. Betty had my seat saved, saying, "You're late again." "Oh," I said, and chatted to her about our weekend. She wanted to know, "Can I come with you to hear Billy Graham?"

"We are going to ask Sylvia's mum if she will take you in her car."

"I would really like to come." We arrived at school and went to assembly. There were a few announcements. One was about the netball team, who would be playing in a few days against Ensleigh School. They would be coming to our school. He also said, "The team are practising very hard. Keep up the good work. I need to mention a note will be sent home so we can get numbers of those who would like to come and support the school. One other thing – some children will be leaving us at the end of the year, and will need to think about what they would like to do. They can get information and advice from a teacher to find out more. A note will be sent home about that too." After more talking, we sang our school hymn, which I enjoyed. Then we all started walking to our classrooms. I reached mine. Angela caught up with me, saying, "I will come and watch you when you play netball, when that other team comes."

"Thanks. We will have our notices to take home, giving the time. Hope my sister and uncle can come."

"What about your mum? Surely, she will come?" I thought, I shouldn't have said that, and quickly changed the subject.

"We only have one more year at school. Do you know what you want to do?"

"Yes, of course I want to be a teacher, like my mum. I'm clever enough to do that."

Everybody was coming into class. Angela said, "We'd better go and sit down." I thought, as I walked across the room to my desk, yes, Angela is clever and she knows it, and has it all worked out. Her mum will help her. I have no idea, I thought, what I will do. Then suddenly there was silence, which took me out of my thoughts, to realise that the teacher had come in. He said, "Good morning, class." We were learning fractions. There was more writing on the board, showing us how to work it out. I really wasn't following, but it didn't worry me like it used to, as I knew Lydia and Angela would help me. But I wouldn't be spending much time with Angela, as I would be practising all the time. We were handed homework before we left for recess. As we walked out, Angela asked, "Do you know how to do it?"

"Not really."

"Well, I do. Are you going out to practise now?"

"Yes, but let's try and talk another time."

"If you want me to help you, you will need to make time. Which is more important?"

I was standing there thinking, well, thanks for that. I was being called by the netball girls, "Come on! We are ready for you!"

"I'm coming." and I ran onto the field. The rest of the day I saw very little of Angela. She was walking way out in front as we were going to our history class. I called to her. She didn't answer. I think she did it on purpose. Oh well, if that how she wants to be, I thought, and kept walking.

Our history class was always fun, and you could sit next to whoever you wanted to. I usually sat with Angela. I went into the classroom, where she was sitting at her desk. Nobody was sitting next to her, so I did. Our teacher came in behind me and started talking. He always made it interesting and fun. He had the class laughing. He would tell a joke in the way he taught us, making everyone laugh. Nearly everyone liked him. He was young, with curly hair, and always happy. We loved him. At the end of class, I spoke to Angela. She didn't want to talk to me. I said, "I'm sorry if I've upset you."

"Yes, you have. You never want to spend time with me. I thought you understood."

"It's only another few days and we'll be playing against Ensleigh. I can spend more time with you then." We spoke as we left the classroom together. We were sort of all right. Then she said, "You need to be fair with me, and not treat me like you have been doing."

On the bus, I told Betty about it, who said, "She needs to grow up. You have already told her that you are committed, and you need to be with the team. Don't worry about her," and started talking about her day. "I will come and watch you."

"Thanks. I'm hoping U.S. and Lydia will be able to come. I am a bit nervous about it."

"You will be fine." When the bus stopped, we jumped off. Betty said, "See you tomorrow." I told U.S. and Lydia about my day. "We play on Saturday. You will come and watch me. We will have a note about it soon." U.S. said, "Well, when you know the time, we can work it out." Lydia said, "I'm coming anyway."

"I'm sure that can be organised."

At home, I said to Lydia. "I won't be able to do any jobs. I wonder what A.J. will say about that?"

"Well, I won't either, as I'm coming to watch you." We changed and ran to the kitchen, asking U.S., "Can we take Monty walking?"

"Yes, but don't be too long." We met the other children on the vacant block and had fun. Everybody said, "We are wanting to come next Saturday to cheer you and our team." I was starting to feel excited.

Later, in the front room, when it was my turn to talk about my day, A.J. said, "I don't know how that's going to work. You still have jobs to do."

"Well, I won't be able to. They will have to be missed, as I am playing for the school."

"You do not make the decisions. When I get the note, I will talk about it then,"

"I can't do any jobs on the Saturday. I need to keep my energy for playing netball, and I will need an early night on the Friday. I thought you would understand that."

"Do not talk to me like that. You are being rude. We will discuss it when we get the note." Lydia said, "I want to watch Sylvia playing."

"Again, we will talk about it when we have the note. End of discussion."

When we were in bed, we talked about it all.

"How unfair is it, if A.J. wants me to do the jobs first?" Lydia agreed. "It won't hurt if they get missed. I guess she won't be coming to watch you."

"I don't want her there. It will make me too nervous. She will find fault with something I do or should have done."

"I will be proud of you."

"Thanks. I hope U.S. and you will come and watch." After a bit more talking, we went to sleep.

Chapter 63

In the morning, when we came down for breakfast, I said, "Good morning." A.J. was serving out the porridge. She did not speak. Only U.S. said good morning to us. She just said, "Lydia, say grace." We ate our breakfast in silence. When I was finished, I put my bowl in the sink and left the kitchen. A.J. didn't say a word. Lydia came up to the bathroom a bit later, saying, "A.J. is not talking. I think that she and U.S. have had words."

"Oh, I thought it was me she is not talking to. Well, it won't last long before she tells us to hurry up, I'm sure." We got ready and went back into the kitchen. Only U.S. was there, and he said, "I will be taking you to school today."

"Oh. What is wrong with A.J.?"

"She's not feeling that well." Lydia asked, "Is she going to the doctor?"

"I'm not sure. Are we ready to leave?" We said yes and started walking to the front door. I called out "Goodbye." There was no answer. I was asking U.S. questions as we walked to the bus. We got there. U.S. said, "Have a good day." Lydia said, "You too.", and I replied, "And you." U.S. started walking Lydia to school. I hopped on the bus and walked towards where Betty was. I told her about A.J., who was not well. She said, "I saw your uncle at the bus stop."

"Yes, it's the first time he has taken us." I told Betty what had happened the night before. She agreed. "You do need to go to bed early Friday night, so you won't be able to go to youth group."

"Oh. That's a shame, but I won't."

"Did you ask for me? Can I come to hear Billy Graham?"

"I have to ask a friend's mum who has a car, and I think she will take you, and I will let you know about the youth group. Would you be allowed to come to chapel?"

She said she would ask her mum. We had reached school and went to assembly, saying, "See you later." When it had finished, I could see Angela walking in front. I hurried and caught her up. We chatted. She said, "I wonder if you've got your homework right, because I didn't get to help you."

"I did find it difficult."

It wasn't long before we were all in class. The teacher was giving out results, and more homework from that morning's lesson. After more talking and using the blackboard, I felt I was beginning to understand it. Looking at my results, I was pleased. I got most of them right. The teacher had written Well Done. As soon as the class was finished, we put our work in our bags. I was walking out of class. Angela followed me. "How did you go?" When I told her, she was surprised. "Do you know how to do it now?"

"Yes, mostly, at last."

"That's good. Well, you would have got them all right if I had helped you." I was thinking, she's such a know-all. She never gets anything wrong. "I have to go and practise now. It's only the end of this week when we will play Ensleigh."

"Well, I will be glad when it's all over, but I will come and watch you."

"Thanks," and I left her, to find the others in the team. Our teacher called us all together to give us a pep talk, and handed us notes, also telling us we would need to get an early night on Friday, and be up bright and early in the morning. We should have a good breakfast and take some water with us. I thought, I hope she's written that in the note, so A.J. can see it. Before we went to the next class, we were all reading our notes. Yes, that's great, I thought, she has put that in the note – bed early, etc. I wonder what A.J. will say about that?

Later, when I was on the bus, I told Betty how A.J. was with me, and showed her my note. She said, "How can she expect you to do jobs before you play against another school?"

"She doesn't think it should make any difference to me." After we had talked a bit more, the bus had arrived. We said our goodbyes, and I ran to where U.S. and Lydia were standing. "I have the note about Saturday, when we play against Ensleigh."

"You need to show it to A.J. when we're in the front room." Lydia asked, "Have you read the note?"

"Yes, all the girls did, and it says we need to have an early night on Friday." I asked U.S., "How is A.J.?"

"She's feeling a little better, but I want you both to be on your best behaviour, and do not upset her."

"Well, she upset me, wanting me to still do my jobs and play well for the school."

"I don't think A.J. realised that you need to keep your energy up for playing."

"I don't understand why not. I don't want to be the one that lets the team down. I feel nervous about it."

"It will be all right. A.J. has been working very hard and doing more than she should, and has overdone it a bit, so please try hard not to answer back and upset her." We both said, "We won't," but I said, "When she sees my note, it will upset her all over again."

"Let me read the note." I gave it to him. "I will have a little word with her about it. I will give her the note."

"You won't be in trouble if you do that."

"No. Now we must hurry home. Just leave it to me. There is no need to worry." Lydia asked, "Will it be all right? Are you sure?"

"Yes. Do not mention it till I have spoken to her about it." We both said we wouldn't. We were almost home. I asked, "Can we walk Monty when we get home, while you show her the note?"

"Yes, that's a good idea. Now don't be noisy. A.J. could be having a rest. Just be as quiet as you can." U.S. unlocked the door and we crept upstairs to our room, and got changed. We went quietly down again. Back in the kitchen, U.S. said, "A.J. is asleep." He handed us the lead. "I am doing dinner tonight. Come back as quietly as you can." We said yes. We quickly left the kitchen and put Monty on his lead. He was wanting to make noises. I grabbed his nose and mouth and we ran out of the side gate. There was nobody about. We ran as fast as we could down the hill to the woods. We both let out a scream. "What do you think of that?"

"It's the first time that's happened with A.J., and U.S. shows that he really cares for her."

"Yes, he does. I hope he can work things out about the note for me." "I'm sure he will. Try not to worry. What time will you be playing on Saturday?"

"Ten thirty, and the school bus will leave at nine thirty, with parents and the girls who want to come and watch."

"Well, I'm coming to watch." We were almost home again and I said, "We had better be as quiet as we can putting Monty on his chain." We went inside with his bowl, to give him fresh water. Nobody was in the kitchen and we could smell dinner cooking. We looked at each other. I whispered, "I'll take the water out. Wait for me, and we will go upstairs together." I came quietly back into the kitchen. No U.S., so we went upstairs together, and we could hear them talking in their bedroom. We went into ours, and quietly closed the door. I whispered, "This has never happened before. What do you think we should do?"

"Let's just stay here until we are called." It wasn't long before we heard the door being opened and U.S. saying, "I had better go and have a look at the dinner. The girls should be back soon." We opened our door. When U.S. saw us, he was surprised, saying, "Come down to the kitchen with me." I closed the door and we followed him down. I asked, "What has happened to A.J.?"

"She is feeling a little better, and I will take her up some dinner. Then we will have ours." Lydia wanted to know, "Has A.J. seen a doctor?"

"We will talk after. I'm going to dish up dinner now."

I set the table for three, got some plates out and we sat down. "You need to get a plate, knife and fork out for A.J." I gave him the plate, and he was putting some vegetables and meat on.

"Now I won't be long. I'm taking this up to her." Lydia opened the door for him. After he left, we started talking. "We will know more when he tells us. I wonder if he has shown my note to her?" It wasn't long before he was back, saying, "A.J. asked for you to be good and helpful to me."

We said, "We will try and do that." After he served dinner, I was asked to say grace, and we ate in silence. As soon as we had all finished, U.S. said, "A.J. needs to take things quietly." We both spoke together: "What has happened?"

"She works very hard and has overdone it. She will need a rest and no upsets." I asked, "Have you shown her my note?"

"No, not yet. I will do that later."

"Oh. Will you be able to come and watch me play this week?"

"I'm sure that can be arranged, but I don't think A.J. will be up to it." I nearly said, "I don't mind," and quickly stopped myself, not saying a word. Lydia said, "I want to go."

"Of course, that can happen." We helped with the dishes, then he said, "I'm going up to see A.J. Can you both quietly go up and get your homework?" We said yes and left the kitchen. Being as quiet as we could, we got our homework out and took it downstairs. Sitting at the kitchen table, we whispered. Lydia did hers. She knew what to do. I sat there and was working it out. Lydia asked, "Tell me, how are you going to do this?"

"Like this."

"Yes, that's right! You can do it."

"It's just that I'm so slow, and not really sure if it's right."

"You need to have more confidence. You're doing well."

"Thank you. I wish I was like you and knew how to do it straight away."

"We are all good at different things." U.S. came in and asked, "How are you going, girls?" Lydia said, "I'm finished, and Sylvia is nearly there."

"Well, come into the front room. I need to talk with you."

We went in and sat down. "Now A.J. will need to rest for a few days, and I need you to help me doing jobs that A.J. normally does." We said, "Yes, we will help you."

"We all need to work together." I asked about the note.

"A.J. is leaving me to make the decisions until she's better."

"That's so good."

"I hope you will make things as easy as possible for us all, and will talk to me about it if you have a problem." We both said yes. I asked, "What are we going to do about our jobs?"

"You will have an early night on Friday – no youth group. The jobs won't get done. We will see how A.J. is for Sunday, regarding the church."

"If you come with us, we can show you what she does, and we can still do our work."

"That might need to happen. We'll see how things are nearer the time. Is there anything else you want to talk about?"

"Are you and Lydia coming to watch me on Saturday?"

"Yes. We will be there, and I'm sure you will make us proud." I went over to him. I wanted to give him a hug, and tried to hug him, and he stopped me, saying, "Thanks. Sit down, please. Now, is there anything else you want to talk about?" I said no, looking at Lydia, who said, "We will help you as much as we can."

"Yes, we can talk to you."

"Thank you, girls. Now, you'd better get ready for bed. I'll come up in a few minutes to turn off the light. Oh, don't forget to be quiet, please." We said, "We won't forget."

We went up the stairs, tiptoeing past A.J.'s room. The door was shut. We got ourselves ready and jumped into bed. I whispered, "We will help U.S. as much as we can. He is really nice to us, not like A.J." We heard him coming up the stairs, and as he turned off the light, he whispered, "Goodnight. I will wake you in the morning, and please remember to be quiet." We said yes, and he closed the door. We heard him go in to see A.J. We whispered, talking about everything for a little while, before we fell asleep.

In the morning, U.S. woke us. "Be as quick and quiet as you can." I whispered, "How is A.J.?" He whispered back, "She is still asleep. We will talk downstairs." When we opened the kitchen door and closed it quietly, U.S. had our porridge all ready, and said, "I will serve it out now that you are here. Lydia, say grace, please. When you have finished your breakfast, we will talk about things." U.S. was making our lunches. He turned around and saw that we had finished eating. He sat down and talked to us. "Now, we are all organised. Any questions?"

"How is A.J.?" Lydia asked. He said, "She was still asleep, so I don't know. Now, both of you, go upstairs to finish getting ready. Quietly is the word, and come back to the kitchen. I will put your lunches in your bags. Then we will be ready to leave." I asked, "Are we all right for time?"

"Yes, but we must keep moving now." We jumped up from the table and left the kitchen, with U.S. opening and closing the door for us. As we went upstairs, one of the steps made a noise. I never noticed that before. We were quiet, and hurried back into the kitchen. U.S. closed the door and put our lunches in our bags. He said, "We must leave now." We all left the kitchen. U.S. opened the front door and let us out, then he closed it quietly. It wasn't till we were walking up the road that anybody spoke. U.S. said, "You have done well. Thank you, girls."

We could see the bus arriving. I said, "I'm not late. Have a good day."

"You too." U.S. said, "I will be here when you get off the bus." They watched me get on. I waved as it was leaving. I could see them walking away. Betty said, "Wow. You are on time for a change," and wanted to know all about things. We were still chatting when the bus stopped. "I'm allowed to go to chapel with you, so I can join the youth group now."

"That's great. We will talk about things later." I walked into assembly. The headmaster mentioned our notes, the ones we had been given, and they needed to be returned, with the numbers of those coming on Saturday. They would have to be handed to our teachers. I thought, did U.S. put the note in my bag, and write on it how many would be coming? I'd better check when I can. If not, I will have to ask him to do it for tomorrow. I walked into the classroom. Angela was sitting at her desk, asking me questions. I said, "I will talk later. I had better go and sit down." I was feeling pleased with myself, knowing I was at last understanding maths. I guessed it would be more new stuff.

The teacher came in and started asking us to have our homework out. He was coming round to collect it. "Today we will be doing revision of what we have learned over the last few weeks." I was looking in my bag, pulling my homework out, and saw U.S. had put the note in my bag. I read it. There would be two coming on Saturday to watch the netball match. I was really pleased. A.J. wouldn't be coming. I knew I would be more on edge if she was. There would be bound to be something that wasn't right. U.S. was good to remember the note. The teacher was coming towards me and collected my homework. I was given more stuff. Then he spoke and wrote on the blackboard what we had learned. At the end of the class he asked, "If anybody has their notes to return, hand them to me." I was able to do this. I hurried out of the class with some of the girls from our team, to practise. In our break, we all chatted, asking each other, "Who is coming to watch you?" Oh, I thought, I will have to say my uncle and my sister, and then I will be asked, "Why isn't your mum coming?" I was still thinking, I will have to say my mum died when I was young. It always upset me to talk about her. I often think about how it happened.

Chapter 64

The teacher blew a whistle and we were told, "Enough talking!" He had the ball and threw it. "Now start playing." We had a good practice. The bell went, and it was time to go into class again. My day went well. I didn't see Angela. I had a feeling she was still upset with me. I spoke to Betty later, on the bus. She had handed her note in, and would be coming with her mum. "Lydia and our uncle will be coming."

"They can talk about things together." I explained about Billy Graham. "I am going to ask Sylvia's mum. Don't mention it till I have spoken to her." She said she wouldn't. The bus stopped. I jumped off. We said our goodbyes. Lydia and U.S. walked up to meet me. I asked, "How is Aunty Jean?"

"She is feeling better and is still staying in bed resting. So, I still need you both to be quiet." We said we would. I thanked U.S. for putting the note in my bag. "Did you hand it in to the teacher?"

"Yes, and we will find out the details soon." He gave me some sweets. Lydia had already finished hers. When walking home we saw Mrs. Taylor on the other side of the road and waved. She waved back. She called out, "Let me know when you want to come round again." U.S. said, "It won't be for a little while," telling her I was playing netball for the school that Saturday. She wished me good luck. We came home. U.S. said, "Now go and get changed quietly, then you can walk Monty while I get dinner organised." We changed and came down to the kitchen. He had a drink ready for us, and said, "Just make it a short walk," handing us the lead. I said, "We won't be long." We put Monty on his lead. He made a lot of happy noises and ran out of the side gate. Lydia asked, "Where to?"

"This way." We ran up the road and round the corner, to where Lena lived. I said, "Let's just have a look at her front garden, because when we clean the little church, we are always walking on the other side of the road."

"She has some lovely colourful flowers," Lydia said, "We had better not go in."

"I would like to, but maybe another time. U.S. wants us back soon." So, we walked home again, wondering how things were. I said, "Well, we have seen her front garden. It is nice." U.S. was pleased when we were back that we hadn't been long. Dinner was ready. He said, "You'd better go to the bathroom and wash your hands quietly. After dinner you will have your jobs to do."

"Is A.J. having any?"

"I will go up and see how she feels." It was so good – just the three of us having dinner again. It was much nicer when that happened. After dinner, we did our jobs, cleaning our shoes for school. We could talk in the kitchen without waiting till we were in the front room. U.S. wasn't as strict with us. He managed well. It was almost a week that A.J. spent in bed. We had no upsets, and liked helping him. I asked, "When do you think A.J. will be coming downstairs?"

"It shouldn't be much longer now. That's what I want to talk to both of you about. Can you try very hard not to upset Aunty Jean?" I replied, "It's difficult, because it's how she speaks to me." Lydia said, "We don't mean to upset her."

"Sometimes it just happens. We don't do it on purpose."

"I'm sure you don't, but how about thinking really hard before you speak? Is that going to be upsetting?" We both said, "We will try and do that."

"Now I'm going upstairs to talk to her. Oh, first, can you go quietly and get your homework?" That's what we did, and we sat at the kitchen table doing it, while U.S. was up talking with her. Lydia asked, "How are you going to do this?" Often, I was going about it all right. Other times, she would show me a quicker way. She was so good with her maths, and helped me heaps.

When U.S. returned, we were finished. I asked, "Before we talk about our day, please can we let Monty in?"

"It's not raining, but it's really cold, and it would be a nice treat for him." Lydia said, "That would be so good." U.S. asked, "Has he been fed?"

"All right. You can let him in, and bring his dish in." We both thanked him and ran outside to undo the chain. He was so excited and made noises. We patted and fussed over him. U.S. said, "Let's keep the noise down." I got Monty's dinner ready and gave him a bit extra. I think U.S. saw and pretended not to. He never said a thing. That was something that didn't happen often. I always felt sorry for Monty, and when it was time for him to be put on his chain again, his tail went down between his legs. He looked so sad. I would manage to grab a handful of dog biscuits and throw them in his kennel before I ran inside. U.S. said, "It's time for bed. Please do it quietly, and I will be up in a little while to turn off the light." In bed, I whispered to Lydia, "I am surprised A.J. is still unwell."

"We will have to try hard not to upset her."

"Hope she will be nicer to me." We could hear U.S. coming upstairs. He whispered, "Goodnight. Go to sleep." He turned off the light and closed the door. We heard him go into their bedroom. We talked about what had been happening and then fell asleep. U.S. came to wake us in the morning. "Get dressed. Come down as soon as you can." We hurried. He had our breakfast all ready. We sat and ate while he made our lunches. He said, "Go and get your bags. We are nearly ready to leave." We didn't talk until we were out in the road. We could see the bus coming. He said, "Sorry, girls. We are a bit later today." We quickly said our goodbyes and I hopped on the bus. I was talking to Betty. "It's been nearly a week, and U.S. has been doing everything. We haven't even seen her."

"It's only two days until Saturday, and you will be playing netball." I told her, "We had Monty inside last night. I like it with U.S. looking after us. It's so much nicer. He has asked us not to upset her by how we talk."

"Well, you don't need any upsets before you play." We chatted a bit more before we reached school. I only saw Angela briefly to talk to. I was really busy those last two days. I was managing well with the homework. U.S. was still doing everything, and we had a routine without A.J. I was really hoping it would stay like that until after I played. U.S. told us that A.J. could be well enough by the weekend. On the Friday night, after school, we had a really early dinner, then, U.S. told us to have a wash, get into our night clothes and come into the front room. We would be able to listen to our serial. We were not to worry about homework or jobs. They could be done over the weekend, and we would be going to bed early. After we had listened to our serial, he said we should go straight to bed. It was hard to get to sleep. I was nervous and excited. We talked in bed. Lydia said, "It's going to be all right. Just try and get to sleep."

"U.S. has been really understanding, and it is great having no jobs or homework." We talked a bit more and finally fell asleep.

U.S. woke us in the morning, and whispered, "Come down in your night clothes. I will have breakfast ready for you," and he went downstairs. We quickly went to the bathroom, had a bit of a wash, and went down to the kitchen. He said, "Sit down. I will serve the porridge out." He asked me, "How do you feel?"

"A bit nervous, and I'm hungry."

"You will be fine once you start playing, and I'll give you a large helping for breakfast. Lydia, say grace, please." We ate our porridge. As soon as we had finished, he said, "Go and get dressed and ready. We will be leaving in half an hour." We ran upstairs and closed the door. I had my sports gear to wear. Lydia said, "You look great." She had never seen me in it. She had to work out what to wear – no A.J. to get the clothes out. We walked quietly past A.J.'s door to the bathroom. Lydia whispered, "Do you have to wear a hat?" I laughed. "No."

"Shh! I wonder if A.J.'s still asleep, or if she heard us?" We had a wash, did our hair, and went back to our bedroom. Lydia said, "We'd better make the bed. I can do it – you don't have to help." She did most of it. "We are ready. Let's go down to the kitchen." U.S. said, "You have done well. I think we will head off now, taking our time. We don't want to rush to catch the bus." He was opening the front door when A.J. called out, leaning over the banister, "I hope you do well, Sylvia."

"Oh, thank you." Lydia asked, "Are you feeling better now?" She answered, "I will be up and about now." U.S. said, "We will see you later. Goodbye." We said goodbye too. When walking up the road, I asked, "Does that mean A.J. will be in charge again?"

"Now, no more talking about that. You have a big morning and we are all behind you. Just do your best – that's all anybody can do." "Thanks." We saw the bus coming, and there was quite a crowd waiting. We joined them. Betty came up to us and introduced her mother to U.S., who said, "Pleased to meet you." Everybody was chatting, and the driver had a list in his hand, and asked for our names as we got on. We managed to sit close together. U.S. spent his time talking to Betty's mother. We girls all chatted together. The bus stopped. We could hear someone talking on a loudspeaker, directing visitors where to go. I knew where I had to go. I said goodbye to everybody. Lydia gave me a hug. "Good luck." U.S. said, "Just do your best."

"I will." Some called out, "Do well. You can do it!" I ran to the netball courts. Our teacher was there, giving us a pep talk. All our team arrived. We were lucky with the weather – it was fine and cold.

The teacher asked, "Any questions?" Somebody asked about a drink. "At half time we can drink our water. Now, there are ten minutes left. If anybody needs to use the toilet, go now." A few left. When we were all together, he said, "This is what we have been practising for. Do your best. Good luck!" We called out, "Thank you!" It was time, and we walked to the court. We saw the Ensleigh team at the other end, and beyond, a mass of people, all sitting further back, on the field. I was thinking, out there are U.S. and Lydia. An announcement was made and then there was a lot of clapping. Then the game began with the blowing of a whistle. I was so nervous. When the ball came to me to shoot a goal, I missed it. I thought, this is awful. I must concentrate next time. It took me a while to settle, and Ensleigh were in front at half time. We ran to where our teacher was. He was really nice, and encouraged us all. "Don't look at the people. Just play like you do at recess." I drank some water. Some of the team said, "You can do it."

"I will try to do better. I'm a bit nervous."

Chapter 65

In the second half of the game, we played better, but they were still in front. I managed to score and we caught up. I could hear a lot of shouting and cheering. I was doing better when the ball came to me, and scored each time. When the game finished, we were in front by one goal. We had won! It was so close. There was a lot of shouting and excitement, lots of patting on the back. We were so happy. Our teacher congratulated us. We all joined hands and made a circle, shouting with excitement. An announcement was made and we had to line up with the other team. There was a speech on the loudspeaker and we were presented with a trophy, which would go in the assembly hall. I was walking towards the people and wondering where U.S. and Lydia were. There were people everywhere. I saw them eventually.

Lydia came running over to me, saying, "Well done. You were great." Betty and her mum were talking to U.S., and then saw me, saying to me, "Congratulations. We enjoyed the game." We all stood talking. There were refreshments you could buy. U.S. said, "How about we go and have a look at what there is?'" We all wandered to where there were two queues, one for coffees and teas and the other for ice cream and food. Lydia, Betty and I ended up with ice cream, U.S. and Betty's mum bought drinks. I could see Angela coming towards me with her mum. She introduced me, and they said, "You did well."

"Thank you. This is my sister, Lydia, and my friend, Betty. My uncle is talking over there."

"Oh," Angela said. "Where is your mum?" Lydia said, "We don't have one now." There was silence. Angela's mum said, "Sorry to hear that." I said, "It's harder sometimes more than others."

"But we have each other," Lydia said. There was a bit more talking, and they left to join the queue. We could hear an announcement on the loudspeaker. "Those who caught the bus – it will be leaving in ten minutes." We walked down to where the bus was. Betty's mum was getting on well with U.S., which was good. We didn't see Angela or her mum anymore. I was still feeling excited that we won. It wasn't till we got off the bus that we could talk to U.S. on his own. He said he really enjoyed watching me play, and thought I did well. I told him I was so nervous. "Well, that's natural. It's a big thing, playing in front of a crowd."

"I don't know if I could do that," Lydia said. We chatted till we reached home. I asked, "Do you think A.J. will be up?"

"She could well be, now. Please, both of you, be on your best behaviour." He opened the door, and we could smell dinner cooking. We looked at each other. I whispered, "She's up." U.S. said, "Let's go into the kitchen." He opened the door. A.J. asked, "How did it go?"

"Our team won by one goal. It was a close game." Lydia said, "Sylvia did really well." U.S. said he enjoyed it and it was well organised. He asked, "How are you feeling?"

"Much better, thank you, and I have dinner almost ready. Now, girls, go and wash your hands." I asked, "Can we just go and see Monty and pat him? Do we have time to run him in the garden?"

"Very well. Just a few minutes." We said thank you and grabbed the lead. When we were outside, Lydia said, "I couldn't believe you asked that. I didn't think she would let us."

"Me either. Maybe she will be a bit nicer now."

"We'd better hurry." We ran up and down the garden a few times with Monty. We could hear U.S. knocking on the window – time to come in, so we did. We went upstairs to wash our hands. I was asked to say grace. Dinner was served, and it was something we both liked. I was really hungry. We ate in silence. After dinner, A.J. said, "Come into the front room when you have helped with the dishes." After she left, I asked, "Is A.J. back doing her work again?"

"Yes, and you both need to be helpful, and careful how you talk." "How long do I need to be careful for?"

"Sylvia, you should be doing that all the time."

"Well, I find it so difficult to do that with A.J., and I don't have to do that with you. We can talk with you, and mostly you understand us, where we are coming from."

"Now, no upsets. We are ready to go into the front room."

A.J. was reading, and asked Lydia to talk with her. "How have you been managing the last few days?"

"Everything has been fine. U.S. has done really well." I asked, "Can I talk?"

"Yes. Have you had problems?"

"No. It's been really good. We haven't had any upsets, and I enjoyed today. We got a trophy for winning, and it will be placed in the assembly hall."

"I'm pleased everything has gone smoothly while I was unwell. Now I'm back, and I will take over."

"Oh. Do you think that's a good idea? Maybe you should let U.S. do more." As soon as I said it, I knew I shouldn't have. I saw U.S.'s face. He gave me a look. I thought, he just sits there, not saying a word. He must have known what I meant. A.J. became cross. "I don't need you to speak to me like that. I am quite capable now."

"Can I explain? I was just thinking, that if ---" A.J. interrupted, "No more. You have said quite enough. I'd like you to leave now and get ready for bed."

"I'm sure Sylvia thought it might be too much for you, and U.S. could help you more."

"I know you are just sticking up for your sister, but I won't be spoken to like that. You can now go and get ready for bed. Come down to say goodnight to U.S." We talked about it in the bathroom. I said, "I was only trying to help, so she didn't have to do so much, and we could have U.S. doing more, which is much nicer for us."

"I tried to explain that you were thinking of her, that it might be too much, but you know how she is."

"Thanks. Why doesn't U.S. say something? I'm sure he knew what I meant. Now he's upset with me, because I've upset her."

"Don't worry. We can talk to him when he's on his own and explain it."

"Yes. How about A.J., who never said a thing about me winning? She never says anything nice to me."

"Try not to let it upset you. It's just the way she is." We went downstairs to say goodnight to U.S. He only said goodnight. I could tell he was cross with me. A.J. said, "I'll be up in a while." We spoke more about how A.J. was towards me. I was still feeling upset and tired. It wasn't long before we heard A.J. come up and turn off the light. "Goodnight," and closed the door.

"She's never nice to me. Oh, don't forget, we have chapel tomorrow."

"Let's get to sleep. She might be nicer tomorrow."

Chapter 66

In the morning, when we went down for breakfast, it was being served. I was asked to say grace. We always ate in silence. As soon as we were finished, we were told to hurry. Our clothes were on the chair for chapel. When we were walking, I said to Lydia, "We must ask Sylvia's mum if she will take Betty in her car. She wants to come and hear Billy Graham. I said I'd let her know."

"We should find out today when we are going."

"Yes, and Betty is allowed to come to chapel too, and she wants to join the youth group."

"That will be good."

We were passing Dennis's house and he was coming down the drive on his bike. He hopped off and walked with us, talking. U.S. and A.J. were walking behind. He didn't speak with them. Dennis asked me, "Why weren't you at youth group? I looked for you." I told him I was playing netball for our school and had to have an early night, because I was playing on the Saturday. He told us that he worked at the hospital. It was a long time since we had had a talk with him. He was asking me questions. A.J. called out, "You had better get on your bike now and go! There isn't enough room on the pavement for three and a bike."

"I know when I'm not wanted," and hopped on his bike. I said, "Sorry."

"That's not your fault," he said quietly, "See you on Friday night." Before he rode off, he called out to U.S., "How are you going, Uncle?" U.S. answered, "Well, thank you." We talked between ourselves the rest of the way.

"It's good he spoke with us. Maybe we will find out more about the family. He might tell us something on Friday night at youth group." We had reached chapel and said to them, "See you after the service," and we walked through the side gate into the chapel, joining the youth group. Some of the girls were whispering to me about the netball win, "You did well," which was nice. We listened to the service and then the announcements came. There was now a date, and we were asked to put our names down for the bus at the end of the service. I whispered to Lydia, "We must look for Sylvia, to see if she is here." We hadn't seen her. When I stood up, I looked around and saw her on the other side of the aisle. We walked up to her, asking, "Do you think your mum would take a school friend, Betty, to hear Billy Graham? Do you think there would be room?"

"We can ask her when we get outside." We made our way slowly down the aisle and out of the chapel. We followed Sylvia to where her mum was standing, talking in a group. When she saw us, she said, "Hello, girls." I asked, "Do you mind taking a school friend in your car to hear Billy Graham?"

"I'm sure we can squeeze one more in."

"Oh, thank you so much. Her name is Betty, and she will be coming to chapel soon." We could see U.S. walking towards us, coming to find us. "We are waiting for you."

"When can we talk to you on your own?"

"I don't know. Not now. Please don't upset A.J. anymore." Lydia said, "It wasn't said on purpose." We reached A.J., who was talking with people. We just stood there, waiting. Eventually we were asked to start walking home.

"I wonder if they've put our names down for the bus."

"We will find out in the front room." I said, "You ask, Lydia." She said she would. We could see Mrs. Taylor, walking way in front, coming towards us. I said, "We must find out where she goes." She was really hobbling when we reached her. I asked her about her foot.

"It's really sore today." A.J. and U.S. spoke with her then. Elizabeth was trying to get out of her straps again, and wanting to get out of the pram. We spoke to her. Mrs. Taylor asked, "Would you like to visit again soon?"

"Yes, please." Then I asked U.S., "When can we do that?"

"After school, if that suits Mrs. Taylor." She said, "Any time."

"We will do that on a day when the bus comes in early." After more talking, we said our goodbyes. We reached home and were allowed to walk Monty while lunch was organised. We ran to the woods, saying, "A.J. doesn't mind us seeing Mrs. Taylor, which is good. I wonder if Elizabeth is walking on her own?"

"We might be able to walk her. That will be fun." There was nobody around, so I let Monty off to have a run. Lydia was always nervous about that. I was a bit, but knew Monty really enjoyed it. I felt sorry for him, on his chain all the time. He came back to us mostly, when we called him, but sometimes it took a few calls. We talked about Monty while walking through the woods. He enjoyed his freedom. The bluebells were finishing now. Lydia said, "We'd better get back. We don't want to be in trouble." I called Monty, and he came running straight back. How good was that! We patted him, but we had no food. We agreed we would save him titbits from dinner. After running home, I put Monty on his chain. Lydia went in to get Monty some fresh water and came out with it, saying, "A.J. said we're just in time for lunch and to go and wash our hands, so be careful how you talk."

"I will really try. It's hard for me – it just comes out." We went inside. I said, "Dinner smells nice." We ran upstairs to the bathroom. Lydia said, "Nobody answered, which means it's a bit rocky. Just be careful, please."

"I will, thanks." and I gave her a big hug. She rolled her eyes at me. Lunch was served and Lydia was asked to say grace. We ate in silence. I managed to put a piece of meat in my pocket for Monty. A. J. left to go into the front room. We helped U.S. with the dishes. I asked, "Is there any gravy over? I can give it to Monty."

"See what you can get out of the saucepan." I put some water in and stirred it.

"Is it all right if I take it out to him now?"

"Yes. Don't be long." I looked at Lydia --- did she manage to save anything for him? As I went past her, she put something in the saucepan. I took it out and used the spoon, getting as much as I could out of the pan. He so enjoyed it. I went inside. U.S. said, when I put the pan in the sink, "You did well. There's not much to see." Everything was tidy again.

"Before we go in, please behave."

"I'm really trying. That's what I wanted to explain to you."

"Not now. Another time." He opened the door to the front room. A.J. was reading, and asked, "Is everything done?" We said yes and sat down. A.J. asked Lydia, "Is there anything you want to talk about?"

"Yes. Did you put our names down for the bus to hear Billy Graham?"

"Yes. Our names have been added." I asked, "What time will we be leaving?"

"Seven o'clock, so it will be a late night."

"Oh," I said, "That's next Friday." A.J. said, "Yes."

"So that's another night we will miss youth group."

"I expect most of the youth group will be going." Lydia said, "That will be good."

"We might all be able to sit together." A.J. said, "No. You will sit with us."

"I thought it would be like chapel and youth group and we all do it together."

"I don't feel that's necessary. Does Dennis go to the youth group?" We both said yes.

"I wasn't aware of that."

"So, he is family," I said.

"What makes you say that?"

"Well, he called out to U.S., asking, "How are you, Uncle?"

"Well, that's as may be. We don't have any contact with him."

"Can I ask why not?" I saw Lydia first, then U.S. gave me a look. He was rolling his thumbs.

"We won't go into that."

"Why not? He seems nice, and is friendly."

"It's something I don't wish to discuss. I don't approve of him walking with you both and wheeling his bike."

"He just happened to come out of his drive as we were passing, and said hello."

"As long as it doesn't happen again. That's enough on the subject." Lydia asked, "Are we able to go for a walk with Monty now?"

"Yes, that's a good idea. Don't be too long." We both got up quickly and left, grabbing the lead and hurrying out of the side gate. Lydia said, "I was so worried you would get into big trouble and upset her again, when you were talking about Dennis."

"I was hoping we could find out more about family, and U.S. doesn't say anything. I wish we could all talk about things together, and they would tell us stuff."

"Well, we might find out more from Dennis."

"Yes, you're right. Let's ask him when we see him."

"I wonder if he's going to see Billy Graham?" Lydia asked, "Where to?" We were on the vacant block.

"Let's just go round the corner and see if we can call on Lena."

"Do you think we should?"

"Come on. She said we could call in any time."

When we reached her house, I said, "Let's open the gate and go into the garden." We walked up the path, and a man came walking towards us. "Can I help you?" he asked.

"We want to see Lena. She told us we could call in."

"I will call her. Just stay here." We were looking at flowers when Lena and the man walked over to us. I said, "Your garden is really lovely."

"Thank you," they both said. "It's nice to see you," and she introduced the man to us. "His name is Dennis, my husband, and he is working in the garden." Lena asked, "How did you enjoy your netball? I heard your team won."

"Yes, it was a close game. Did A.J. tell you?"

"I heard from your uncle, as A.J. wasn't well enough to clean the church, so I did it last week, and put some fresh flowers on the altar."

"That was nice of you."

"Is she feeling better?"

"Yes, she is, thank you."

"Would you like to come round the back?" We said yes, and followed her. There was a garden seat, and we sat down.

"It's nice of you to come and visit me." I asked, "Can I ask you a question?"

"Yes, of course."

"Is Dennis U.S.'s brother?" She replied, "Yes. Why?"

"I wondered, because they don't talk in chapel or outside, I mean."

"You are observant. It's been like that for a long time." Lydia said, "That must be hard. We don't mean to be rude." I said, "It would be nice for us to see family."

"I can understand that, and it was brave of you to come round and see me."

"Oh, A.J. doesn't know we are here. We just wanted to meet you and see your lovely garden." I stood up. "We'd better go now."

"Nice of you to call in, and please come again." She walked with us through to the front garden. Dennis was digging and called out, "Goodbye." We replied, "Goodbye." Lena opened the gate. "Come again, girls." Monty was glad to be going – he was pulling us along. Walking back, we talked about everything. I said, "I wonder what happened, and how is it going to come right?"

"Do you think she will tell A.J.?"

"No, I don't think so, and we're not going to say anything, are we? We would be in big trouble if they found out." We put Monty back on his chain and went inside. A.J. said, "You have been a long time." I said, "Sorry."

"Please go and wash your hands. Dinner is ready." We raced upstairs. Lydia said, "I thought she was going to ask you where have you been?"

"Well, it might still happen. We won't mention about Lena. All right?" We agreed. Dinner was served when we got back to the kitchen. I was told to say grace. It was not our favourite dinner, but we got through it. Then we helped with the dishes and got ready to walk to chapel again. There were never many people at the evening service. I was wondering if Lena would be there. When everyone was coming in, I was turning around to see, and was told to stop doing that, "It is rude." A.J. always had her same seat at the front. I thought, I will have a look when it is time to leave. The service wasn't as long as the morning one, which I was glad about. Eventually it finished, and I was the first to get out of the pew, as I was sitting at the end. I could see Lena and Dennis there, a few pews behind. I put my hand up, and she saw me and did the same. They were out of the chapel way before us, so I couldn't say hello. I didn't see them anymore. It was dark. The street lights were on when we were walking home. Lydia and I walked in front together. We were always separated in the evening service, so we couldn't talk.

Chapter 67

On Sunday night we got to sleep easily, as we did a lot of walking. A.J. woke us in the morning. We were always told to hurry up. I said, "It sounds like A.J. is back to her normal self."

"Yes, but try not to upset her."

"I won't do it on purpose." We raced to the kitchen. Our porridge was already on the table, getting cold. Lydia was told to say grace, and we started eating. A.J. walked us to school. We said our goodbyes. The bus was there, and I got on. Betty called out, "Come down to the front. I have a seat here for you." "Well." She said, when I reached her, "Did you ask about me coming to hear Billy Graham?" "Yes, and Sylvia's mum will take you in her car." She was so pleased, and wanted to know what time. We told her, "The bus goes at seven o'clock, so it will be around that time."

"Can I go to chapel with you, and join the youth group?" We talked about it until the bus reached school. The girls were saying, "You did well with your netball." At assembly, the headmaster made an announcement, saying those who were in the netball team should come up to the stage. I wasn't expecting that, and felt nervous. We walked up to the stage. When all the team were there, he gave a little speech to us and presented to each one of us a small trophy. We thanked him. He said we did well. I went back to my seat and had a look at my trophy. It had my name and the date on. I thought, that's nice. I will show it to Lydia and U.S. I wonder what A.J. will say?

When we walked to class, some girls wanted to have a look at the trophy. The girls from the team said, "We are still playing at recess. See you then." As I walked into the classroom, Angela called out. She was behind me. "Let me have a look. What have you got for playing netball?" I showed her, and she said, "That's nice to keep."

"Yes."

"Well, I'll see you at recess. Hooray! No more netball!"

"I won't have to practise anymore, but the team still want me to play sometimes. Sorry, I'm playing at recess. How about lunchtime? We can spend time together." She was really cross with me. "I thought you were not going to play anymore, and spend time with me now." She walked away. I thought, it's difficult, but I enjoy playing. I wanted to spend some time with her also. I wished things were different, and that she would understand. For the rest of the morning, Angela had nothing to do with me. When lunchtime came, I found her standing on her own. I said, "Let's talk."

"You just don't want to be my friend." I tried hard to explain that I couldn't simply never play again, but I wouldn't be doing it as much. It wasn't good enough for her. She said I was being selfish, and walked away, leaving me on my own. I went out to the playing field. Girls were sitting on the grass. I joined them. One said, "Thought you were having a break from us." I explained. They said, "Well, let's play, then." So, we did, and had fun. I was sad about Angela and felt I had lost a friend. I thought, I must ask what U.S. says. Am I being selfish? I didn't think I was. I tried again to talk with her at the afternoon break. She was on her own again. I walked over to her and said, "Let's be friends. I'm not playing this recess."

"You can't do that when you want to. What about what I want? I want you to be with me, and you still go out and play. Well, you just want your own way." She walked away. I could not fix it. I said, "Let's talk," but I don't think she heard me. I was left standing on my own. More girls were talking with me, because of netball. I wasn't lonely, but it would have been nice to have her as my friend still. At the end of the day, catching the bus, more girls wanted to look at my trophy. I showed it to Betty. She said, "You're famous now!"

"Not at all," and I told her about Angela.

"Honestly, she is the one being childish, to expect you never to play again, and no, you're not being selfish. You need to have more confidence in yourself as a person." Betty was so grown-up, and always made me feel she knew what she was talking about. "I'm sure your uncle will say the same, when you ask him." Then we chatted about other things until the bus stopped. We said our goodbyes, and Lydia came running up to us.

"Did you get anything for winning at netball?"

"Yes," and pulled out my trophy from my bag, showing her and U.S., who said that was nice, and something to keep and remember. U.S. handed me some sweets and said, "I thought we might call at Mrs. Taylor's, as you are here a bit early."

"That would be nice, and I can show her my trophy." Lydia was saying she had had a good day, telling me she had another friend now, who had joined their group. She asked, "How about your netball?" I was then able to let her know about my day. U.S. said exactly what Betty had told me – no, I was not being selfish, and Angela was asking too much of me not to play again. If I enjoyed and was good at it, why would I not want to play? Lydia said, "She is the one being selfish, wanting you all to herself, and she doesn't want to mix in with others."

"I just wish she would understand that I could still be her friend. I feel sad that it is this way."

"She will think about things, and might talk to her mum, and it could all change by tomorrow."

"Well, it would be good if that happened."

"You have friends, because you joined in with others, and now she is the one alone." We had reached Mrs. Taylor's house. U.S. rang the bell. It was a long time before she came to the door, as she could not walk well. She was pleased to see us. "Do come in." Elizabeth was crawling towards us, on the floor. We bent down and each held her hand. We helped her pull herself up and she walked a few steps with Lydia and me, and seemed to like it. Mrs. Taylor chatted away to U.S. We enjoyed our time with Elizabeth. Just before it was time to leave, I showed her my trophy. She thought it was a nice keepsake, and thanked us for coming. "Come again any time." We said thank you and made our goodbyes. We talked to U.S. about Mrs. Taylor, who would be happy if we called in more often, as she was on her own a lot and finding things difficult. I asked, "Does she live by herself?"

"She has a husband who works long hours, so I told her, when the bus comes in early, we can call in."

"That's good. I asked her if we can do anything to help her."

"We could do that. I think she would appreciate it." Lydia said, "I'm sure that we can help her." I asked U.S., "Was A.J. working today?"

"Yes, for a few hours. Remember, please – no answering back." We got home. A.J. was still at work. U.S. said he would start the dinner and told us to get changed. We hurried as quickly as we could, back down to the kitchen. "Can we quickly walk Monty?"

"Yes," and I grabbed the lead. We ran out of the door. Monty was excited to see us. It wasn't easy to get him on his lead. All was quiet on the vacant block. We ran down the hill to the woods.

Lydia said, "We must try hard not to upset A.J." We talked about her.

"It should be fine. There's nothing she can be cross about. I will show her my trophy."

"Well, we have a problem. We can't do our jobs again on Friday night, and it will be hard getting up early on Saturday."

"Yes, you're right. It will be a very late night. If it was U.S. making that decision, we would just not do them."

"Don't bring it up. It's still two days away, and we can ask U.S. about it."

"What if she brings it up?"

"Well, don't argue with her. Go along with it, and we can talk with U.S. when he's on his own." So, we agreed that was what we would do. There was nobody about in the woods. I let Monty off for a run. Lydia was nervous about that. He had a lovely time, and when I called him, he came flying back.

"See – he is so good now, and enjoys being off the lead."

"Well, we are taking a risk." Putting Monty on the lead, who didn't want to be put on, we hurried home.

A.J. was at the window, calling us to come in. We said, "Hello."

"Dinner is ready. Go and wash your hands." We did as we were told.

"She sounds a bit cross."

"Maybe we were a bit long. Let's be careful." I was asked to say grace. Not a word was spoken. When dinner was finished, we helped with the dishes. We were asked to go and get our homework. I was coming downstairs. U.S. was on his own.

"Do your homework and come to the front room." We quickly asked about Friday night and our jobs.

"Don't mention it. We will talk about that another time," and he left to go into the front room. We were doing our homework. I whispered, "Can you check this, please?" Lydia grabbed my work and had a look. "You're fine. Just keep on doing what you're doing." She had finished, and said, "I'd better go in the front room." I still had a lot to do, and worked away at it. U.S. came out and asked, "How are you going?"

"I'm nearly finished. I had a lot to do today." I hurried, and went into the front room. A.J. said, "We have been waiting for you again."

"I was given a lot today." She gave a big sigh.

"Lydia first. How was your day?"

"I had a nice day. I have another new friend. I enjoy school, and all is going well." It was my turn, and I told them what had happened at assembly. "Each of us was presented on the stage with a small trophy, for winning at netball. Can I go and get it to show you?"

"Yes, but what about the rest of your work?"

"I am doing well."

"I am pleased to hear it." I left the room and got my trophy to show her.

"That's nice to have."

"Thank you."

"Now you know you only have one more year at school, and you need to work on your subjects, which are more important than your netball."

"We still have sport as a subject."

"I am aware of that, and yes, you have shown you are good at it, but that won't help as far as a job goes. Now, I'd like you to get ready for bed and come down to say goodnight to Uncle Stan."

We left the room. Lydia said, "It was good Billy Graham didn't get mentioned."

"At least she thought I did well with my netball, and liked my trophy. It's hard for me to believe I only have one more year, and what will I do after that?"

"I only have one more year at my school, too. Let's talk about things when we're on our own."

We got ready for bed, and said goodnight to U.S. A.J. said, "I will be up soon to turn the light off." In bed, we talked about what was said in the front room. Lydia said, "I want to go to your school, but you won't be there then."

"No, and where will I be, I wonder?"

"Don't worry about it now. You will know closer to the time. It is still a long way off." We heard A.J. coming up the stairs.

"Goodnight. Straight to sleep." It took me a long time to get to sleep, thinking about what sort of job I would like to do.

In the morning, Lydia was awake before me and woke me up, saying, "A.J. has called out. Time to get up!"

"We are coming."

"I'm so tired. I didn't sleep that well."

"Stop worrying about when you leave school. It will work out all right. Just keep doing the best you can."

"I will." And I jumped out of bed to start our day. We were running late, and just caught the bus. A.J. was almost back to her normal self, saying, "The bus will go without you one of these days." After saying our goodbyes, Betty said, "I really thought you weren't going to make it today. What happened?" So, I told her I hadn't slept much, as A.J. was saying I only had one year left at school, and to work hard on my subjects, not my netball. I had been worrying about what I wanted to do after that. Betty said, "That's ages away. Lots can happen before then. Anyway, you can always work in a shop, like me. That's what I want to do."

"I don't want to work in a shop."

"Well, if you get stuck, you can always try it for a while and see."

"I wonder if Angela's talking to me today?" We said our goodbyes. Betty said, "I'll see you later." I walked into assembly. Only a few announcements were made, but one was telling us about a teacher who was leaving, and it happened to be my maths teacher. I thought, I was just getting used to him. Wonder if he will tell us anything when we're in class? Lots of girls were walking, and I joined them to go into class. They were all talking about our maths teacher leaving. One girl said, "We can ask him, if he doesn't say anything." We all agreed. We thought he was O.K. Angela was sitting at her desk when I walked in. I said, "Hello." She was looking down, and didn't answer me. I just walked to my desk and thought, it's like that again.

When our teacher came in and said, "Good morning. You would have heard at assembly that I will be leaving at the end of this term, for personal reasons." One girl asked, "Is that in three weeks?" He said, "Yes." Some girls called out, "We are sorry you are leaving."

"Thank you, class. It was nice of you to say that. Well, we'd better get into doing some maths now." It was more new stuff, which I really wasn't following, and we were given homework. At the end of class, I could see Angela walking out. Her desk was right near the door. I was sitting at the other end of the room. Oh, I thought, she doesn't want to see me. I'll join the others and go onto the field. They were sitting on the grass. One girl asked, "Why aren't you friends with Angela?"

"I am. It's just that she doesn't want me to play netball and she wants me to spend all my time with her. I enjoy netball. She is not interested in seeing me sometimes." There was a discussion with the girls about it. I said, "I hope she changes her mind, and we can still be friends."

"Well," some girls from the team said, "Let's play at lunchtime. We need you."

"I won't let you down, but if she wants me to be with her sometimes, I'll let you know when."

"OK, that's fine. So, we are playing at lunchtime."

"Yes," I said.

At each lesson that day, Angela didn't speak to me. She looked miserable. I tried talking to her and she just walked away.

At the end of the day, I talked to Betty, then Lydia and U.S. They all said, "You haven't done anything wrong. She will realise, if she wants your friendship, she will have to accept how it is." We were visiting Mrs. Taylor after getting off the bus. U.S. said, "We will ask her if we can help her with anything."

"That will make it easier for her. That's good." We rang the bell again and waited. Eventually she opened the door. "Sorry it has taken me so long." She could hardly walk. "Come in." U.S. asked, "What can I do to help? Are there any little jobs that need doing?" I asked, "Where is Elizabeth?"

"She is in her playpen. She is getting into cupboards now."

We walked into the lounge, and she was making noises, with her hands up, wanting out. Mrs Taylor lifted her out. We tried holding her hand and walking her. U.S. said, "Tell me what you would like me to do."

"That's very kind of you," and walked into the kitchen. U.S. started doing some dishes. Mrs. Taylor was chatting to him.

"Who is going to look after Elizabeth?"

"My husband will be taking time off work. You're still welcome to call round, and it will be lovely for Elizabeth to see the girls."

"Yes, we will do that." After more chatting, he said, "We had better get going now. Oh, when are you going into hospital?"

"Next week."

"We will call in before you go, if we can." She thanked him and said, "Elizabeth will be tired now, which is good, and will sleep well." As we were walking home, I said, "It must be really hard for her, not being able to walk far or to do things." U.S. agreed. Lydia said, "Elizabeth is lovely."

"Yes, and she is getting to know us now, so can we go more often?" "We will try and do that."

We reached home and quickly got changed. A.J. still wasn't home, and we were allowed to walk Monty. "Just a short one." We stayed on the vacant block. A few children were there, and we ran with Monty. He was full of energy. We saw A.J. walking past. We knew we had better get home quickly. I put Monty on his chain and Lydia took his dish in to give him some fresh water. She came out with it, saying, "U.S. has dinner going and A.J. isn't very talkative."

"I know. Be careful what I say!"

"I'm only trying to help you."

"I know, and thank you. It's not easy for me, you know. What's for dinner?"

"It smells good and I'm hungry." A.J. was knocking on the window for us to come inside. I said, "Hello."

"Please go and wash your hands. Dinner is ready." We left the kitchen and ran upstairs. Lydia asked, "Do you have much homework?"

"It's new stuff. I hope you can help me."

"I don't have that much. I don't mind. I find it easy."

"I'm glad I have a clever sister who can help me."

We ran down to the kitchen. I was asked to say grace. Dinner was on the table. I ate most of it and saved a little piece of meat for Monty. I looked at Lydia, who knew what I was doing. Her plate was empty. We both liked our dinner.

"Now go and get your homework." She left to go into the front room. After the dishes were done, we chatted at the kitchen table. Lydia said, "Show me quickly what you want me to help you with." She explained it to me. She did her homework and I did mine. U.S. came out to check on us. Lydia said, "I'm just about finished," and I was left on my own. After a while, I went into the front room. A.J. said, "We've been waiting for you." We were asked about our day, Lydia first. She said, "I've had a good day, and then we went to see Mrs. Taylor, and she will be having an operation on her foot. We are going to see her more, and help her."

"That will be a nice thing to do, and her husband will be grateful. It's going to be difficult for them." I thought, that's good. A.J. is happy about us doing that. Then I was asked about my day at school. "Our maths teacher is leaving at the end of term. It will be sad. We all liked him."

"I haven't had a note saying you have a problem. Are you doing well?"

"Yes, thank you, and he wrote on my work --Well done."

"You will just have to get used to the next teacher. Now, time to get ready for bed. Say goodnight to Uncle Stan, and I will be up soon. You can read for a while."

In bed, we talked, "Oh, we haven't said anything to U.S. about Billy Graham and our jobs."

"It's only two more sleeps. I can hear A.J. coming up the stairs."

A.J. said, "Goodnight. Go straight to sleep," as she turned off the light.

The next morning, on the bus, there was a lot of chatter about who was going to hear Billy Graham. Quite a few said they would be going. I was asked, "What night are you going?" There was more talk about it at school. It was a huge thing. I found out that a lot of the girls didn't go to any church, but were going with their parents. I thought, I'll ask Angela if she is going to hear him, if she is talking to me. It was even mentioned at the assembly, "We are having a visit from the evangelist, Billy Graham, from the U.S.A. He will be speaking at the Town Hall. Those who want to hear him need to check to see if there are any seats left." I walked to class with a group of girls, and was asked, "Are you going?" I said yes, and said it was through the chapel I went to. I could see Angela in front, and said, "I'm going to talk with her." I ran and caught up with her. I said, "Hello. How are you? Do you want to be friends?"

"Of course. Let's meet at recess."

"All right." I thought, that's good. Let's see how it goes. I was really pleased. My homework was correct, my maths, and had Well Done written on it again. We had more given to us. Walking out from maths, Angela and I went to recess together. After a lot of talking, we sorted it out, in a way, and I said, "I'll play at lunchtimes and see you at morning and afternoon recess." We were going to try that. Then I asked her, was she going to hear Billy Graham? She said yes, with her mum, and it was on Friday night, too. We had lots to talk about. She was surprised I was doing so well with my maths, as she hadn't been helping me. "Well, at last, it's sinking in. I'm not quick at working it out, though, but I'm getting there." She was impressed.

I had had a good day at school, and chatted to Betty on the bus. She said all was going well for her. I got off the bus, and saw Lydia and U.S. waiting. They asked me about my day. "Angela and I are talking, and we have worked out when we are going to see each other. The team was happy with that, so I hope that works out."

"I told you she would think about things and want to be friends, as she is the lonely one, not you."

"Yes, you did. You were right. I do feel sorry for her, as she doesn't mix at all. She just likes doing school stuff. She is top of the class in most subjects." U.S. said, "You need friends as well, otherwise you can be very lonely."

"I think she has realised that." We were walking home, and I had just remembered to ask U.S. about Friday night, when we were going to hear Billy Graham. "We won't be able to do our jobs." Lydia said, "Or on Saturday morning. We will be too tired, and it will be a late night." U.S. said, "I will talk with A.J. Now, don't mention it.

"We won't." I told U.S. that Betty was coming, and Sylvia's mum was taking her. "She can come to chapel now, and join the youth group." He was surprised we had organised it. "We want Betty to sit with us and join our friends, so we can all sit together." I asked, "Can you talk with A.J. about that?" Lydia said, "You will still see us if we are in front, with our friends. It shouldn't make any difference." U.S. said, "I can understand how you feel, and it would be nicer for you. I will speak with A.J. regarding that." We thanked him, and we had reached home. "Do not mention anything, please, and no answering back," as he turned to me.

"I will really try not to say anything that will make A.J. cross. I just wish she was like you, and we could talk like we can to you."

"We are all different, and A.J. is bringing you up in what she feels is the correct way. You need to understand that." As he opened the gate, he said, "Not another word, please."

"Can we walk Monty?"

"That should be all right. Go and get changed, and Sylvia, you really do like to have the last word." A.J. wasn't home, so we hurried and changed, ran down to the kitchen, and grabbed the lead.

"Don't be long, please."

"We won't." Monty was always excited to see us. We put him on the lead and ran. Lydia asked, "Which way?" We ran to the allotment, and it was all quiet on the vacant block. Lydia said, "Glad you remembered to ask about Friday night. It's good that he understands how we both feel and will talk to A.J."

"I wonder if she will let us sit with our friends? Anyway, we are growing up now. We shouldn't have to sit with them all the time. It's harder for me, as I'm that much older." She agreed. "Let me do the talking if it comes up."

"Are you sure? You don't want to get into trouble."

"If I do, it wouldn't be as much as you."

"You're right there. You get on better with her than I do."

"She is nicer to me, and not so strict." So, we made a pact. I was to keep quiet and let Lydia do the talking. She said, laughing, "That is going to be a hard thing for you to do."

"I will just leave it to you to do the talking. We had better get home." We arrived home and all was quiet. We ran upstairs to wash our hands. I was asked to say grace. We ate dinner in silence. After dinner, in the front room, A.J. was asking about our day. Lydia was always first. Everything was going well for her, and there was a lot of talk about Billy Graham at school. A.J. said, "There has never as far as I can remember been an evangelist coming from overseas and giving a talk in our town." Lydia said, "My friends are all going to sit together. Can I join them, please?"

"Well, I don't know if that's such a good thing. You need to sit still and listen to what's being said."

"I'm sure I will. I'm interested to hear him. I'm growing up now, and I feel I should be able to sit with my friends."

"Well, do you now? I will think about it."

"Sylvia, what do you think?"

"We are both growing up, me more, as I'm older, and I would like to be able to do that. I'm really looking forward to hearing him. He is young, and I think it will be more interesting for me than chapel." A.J. said, "It will be different – not necessarily what I go along with, but I want to hear what he has to say."

"Will you let us know?" She answered yes, and then asked me about my day. I mentioned again about my maths teacher leaving, and feeling sad about it. "He put Well Done on my work again and I am understanding it better."

"I am pleased to hear it. You need to think about what you want to do when you have finished school."

"I still have one more year."

"I am well aware of that. I am just saying, you need to start thinking about it."

"Yes, I will."

Chapter 68

When we were in bed, we discussed A.J., and how she said she would let us know. Lydia said, "I think she will let us, and don't forget, U.S. said he would talk to her too. She was all right about it, I think."

"She didn't get cross about it." So, we decided we wouldn't mention it until another day. We only had two days left. The next day, on the bus, there was excitement. Only one day left! There were a lot of us going to hear Billy Graham. After assembly you could feel a general buzz about it and everyone was talking about going. I was walking with a group of girls into class. The room was empty, except for Angela, who was sitting at her desk. She looked up when we came in. "See you at recess."

"Yes, we'll talk then." It wasn't long before the teacher came in. He asked for silence, and we went straight into maths. At last, I was understanding it better. I felt happy, now that Angela and I were friends again, and we were getting into a routine, when we would see each other. I was managing all right with the rest of my subjects, some better than others, and had no real problems. My day went really well.

I caught the bus with Betty. We always had things to talk about. Our bus came in. U.S. and Lydia were standing there. He said, "You are early. We can fit in a visit to Mrs. Taylor, the last one before she goes into hospital. Let's see if she needs any help." We were happy about that. Again, there was a long time before she came to the door. When she finally opened it, she said, "Come in." We could hear and see Elizabeth, who was in her playpen. She was wanting out. Mrs. Taylor said that I was allowed to lift her out. Lydia and I held her hands and walked her. She loved that U.S. was doing some tidying up and chatting to Mrs. Taylor. She was telling him the date when she would be going into hospital. "My husband will be pleased that you will be able to call in." She thanked us and said she hoped she would be able to walk better after her operation. Mrs. Taylor and Elizabeth were waving goodbye. Elizabeth was starting to say a few words. We gave her a hug before we left. As we were walking home, U.S. said, "She is really getting to know us. We can visit again next week." I said, "I hope they can get Mrs. Taylor walking better."

"Were you able to talk with A.J. about sitting with our friends?"

"Yes. I think she will allow you to do that." We wanted to show our affection, trying to give him a hug. He stepped back. "There's no need for that. You must wait till A.J. tells you."

"Why can't you make the decision? Why is it always her?"

"You ask too many questions. This is how it is." Lydia asked, "When are we going to be told?"

"I'm not sure." I asked, "What about our homework and jobs? It will be hard getting up early in the morning."

"I will talk with A.J. about that, and do not mention it." We thanked him again. A.J. wasn't home yet. We quickly got changed and were allowed to walk Monty. We were told not to be too long. We went to the woods. It was all quiet. I let Monty off. Lydia was always worried about that. She put on a brave face. I said, "Isn't it good that we will be sitting with our friends? We only have one night left. Betty asked me if she could sit with us.

"Leave it to me. I will find out. All right? Just don't say anything."

"I'll try not to."

"Just don't." I called Monty and he came straight back. We hurried home. We could see A.J. was in the kitchen. "Hope she's in a good mood," I said.

"So do I." After putting Monty on his chain, we went inside. A.J. and U.S. were in deep conversation. She turned round. We said, "Hello."

"Go and do your jobs now." We ran upstairs and took our shoes off, then put on our slippers. We went outside to clean our shoes. A.J. and U.S. were still in deep conversation. We talked outside, saying, "U.S. is probably talking about Friday night and homework."

"Yes --he really tries for us." We came inside with our clean shoes. We just walked through the kitchen and took them upstairs. They were still talking, and nobody said a word to us. Lydia said, "Let's wash our hands. Don't forget – leave it to me to do the talking." We opened the kitchen door. We were told to sit down. I was asked to say grace. Dinner was served and we ate in silence. After dinner, A.J. said, "When you have helped with the dishes and homework is done, then come straight to the front room." As soon as we were on our own, I asked U.S., "Did you ask A.J. for us?"

"Yes, and it has all been sorted." Lydia asked, "Is A.J. going to let us?"

"You will be told, one way or the other." We thanked him. "Please do not answer back." We said we would be careful.

"Go to your room and get your homework, then come into the front room." We ran upstairs. Lydia said, "I think I will be asking about it."

"Well, you never know. She might just tell us." We sat at the kitchen table. Lydia did hers so fast and was ready to go to the front room. She asked me, "Can you do yours?"

"I think so, but I have to work it out."

"Show me. You're doing it right. Keep going! Leave it to me to do the talking. I'm going into the front room now." I kept going with my homework, wishing I was like Lydia and could do it fast. I was thinking, at least I'm doing it right. I finished at last and went into the front room. A.J. said, "We are waiting for you."

"I had a lot to do tonight."

"Well, now that you are both here, I will tell you what's happening tomorrow night." I thought, that's good, and I hope it's what we want.

"U.S. and I have decided you can sit with the young people." We jumped up.

"Thank you."

"We are trusting you to behave, and not spend your time talking to each other." Lydia said, "We won't. We are really interested to hear him." I said, "Yes. There is a lot of talk at school about him coming. We want to listen to him."

"Very well, then. You will do your homework over the weekend, and I will still be up early on Saturday to go to work. When you wake, U.S. will organise you, and, depending on when you wake, what jobs are left to do." I said, "Thank you. That sounds fair." A.J. gave me a look and said, "Glad you approve. Now, Lydia first: how has your day been at school?"

"Good. I'm enjoying it, and not having any problems."

"That's good to hear. How about you?"

"I am managing, thank you."

"That is also good to hear. Well now, have you anything else you want to talk about?" We both said no. "We are looking forward to tomorrow." We were allowed to read for a short time in bed. We talked about the decision they had made. I said, "That is really good. We can sit with the youth group, and Betty will be able to sit with us."

"We must thank U.S. when he is on his own." We could hear A.J. coming up the stairs. "Straight to sleep!" as she turned off the light.

We listened. No going into the little room tonight. We whispered for a little while and then went to sleep.

Chapter 69

A.J. woke us, saying, "Time to be up and get moving. I will have breakfast ready. Come down as quickly as you can." We hurried, saying, "It's tonight. We will be getting the bus and hearing Billy Graham. It's going to be a late night, and it's so good we can sit with our friends." Lydia agreed. We ran into the kitchen. Our breakfast was on the table, ready to eat.

"Lydia, say grace, please." We started eating. When we had finished, we were told, "No time for chatter. Please go and get yourselves ready for school." We raced upstairs and hurried. A.J. was surprised when we were back in the kitchen, ready for school. "Well, this is good," putting our lunches in our bags. "It shows you can do it if you put your minds to it, and no chatter." We said goodbye to U.S. and were on our way. A.J. was telling us that we would be having dinner early, as we would be walking to chapel to get on the bus, and needed to be on time. "U.S. will be at the bus stop this afternoon. Come straight home." We said, "Yes, we will do that." We had reached the bus and said our goodbyes. "Be good and learn." She took Lydia by the hand. I called out, "Goodbye." She answered, "Goodbye and have a good day."

I got on the bus. Betty called out, "I have a seat for you," and started talking about after school. "Can I come around to your house and walk with you to chapel?"

"Oh. When we see U.S., we will ask him. That should be all right. Then we will have to find Sylvia's mum, who is taking you in her car. Nobody knows anything about it." Betty said, "I will stay with you while you ask." We talked about it. I felt excited. We reached school and walked into assembly. There was a buzz. After we sang our anthem, our headmaster made a few announcements and mentioned Billy Graham. "Those that are going to hear him will be enlightened, I'm sure. I'm looking forward to hearing him." Well, I thought, I wonder if we will see him. I walked to my classroom with a group of girls. We were all talking about hearing him.

Angela was sitting at her desk when I walked in. "See you at recess."

"Yes. Talk then." I had just got to my desk. The teacher was right behind me. He said, "Good morning, class. We are going to be doing revision this morning. After looking at some of your homework, there are a number of you who do not know how to work things out. We will go through it step by step." I thought, that's good. No more new stuff, and I wondered if I had got my homework right. After our lesson, I did feel I understood it better. I thought, I will miss him. We were given more homework on the same subject. He handed us our results, as we left to go to recess. Angela waited for me. She asked, "How did you go?"

"I've only had a quick look at it." She grabbed my work out of my hand and had a look. "Yes, I can see where you went wrong. Do you understand it now?"

"I think so."

"I will help you." Our whole recess was spent with Angela showing me where I went wrong. She, of course, got everything correct, and was so good at all her work. She was always letting you know that. This was one of the reasons why she had few friends. I thought, nobody wants to hear that all the time. She did help me, and I thanked her. We got on well and I didn't let it upset me. We were going to our next lesson, talking about what we were going to be doing. "I'm playing netball at lunchtime."

"I know. See you at recess." I thought, she is accepting that now. "We might see each other tonight, when we see Billy Graham. Talk soon."

At last! I was so glad that Angela had accepted that I played at lunchtime, and we got into a routine. Things were going smoothly. I really didn't have any problems with other subjects. I was enjoying school.

Later, on the bus, there was a lot of chatter about hearing him. We could hardly hear each other talk. I was so glad to get off. Betty stayed with me while we walked to where Lydia and U.S. were standing. He said hello to Betty. "Is everything all right?"

"Yes, but Betty wants to walk with us to chapel, as Sylvia's mum is taking her in her car." Lydia said, "Hello. Does A.J. know?" I said, "No. That's why we were asking. Can you let her know, and that she can walk with us, if we tell her what time to come round?"

"Well, that should be all right, and we will be leaving about 6.30." "Thank you, and you will explain it to A.J." We said our goodbyes to Betty, who said, "I'll come around then. Thank you."

After she had left, U.S. said to me, "You have put me in an awkward situation, explaining to A.J. that you have organised this by yourself, which won't go down well, without letting A.J. know."

"Sorry. It just sort of happened, and A.J. wasn't around to ask." He said he would sort it out, "But in future, please don't commit to something until you have asked if it's all right."

Lydia said, "I hope A.J. isn't going to get upset about it and be cross with you, Sylvia."

"I will do my best to explain it. Just don't do this again, either of you."

"Sorry." We were walking quickly home. I knew U.S. was cross with me and I really felt sorry for him. I could now see that I shouldn't have done it. Just as we reached the gate, he said, "Please, Sylvia, think before you speak. Check with me first." I said I would, and said sorry again.

As I opened the door, A.J. called out, "I'm upstairs." We raced up. "I have your clothes out for you to wear and dinner is organised. Now I will go down to talk to U.S." We got changed. Lydia said, "U.S. will have to tell A.J. now about Betty. I hope you won't be in trouble."

"Oh, I wish it wasn't so hard. I didn't mean it to be difficult."

"Well, we will soon find out when we go downstairs." We could hear raised voices, and I thought, I'm going to be in trouble. We walked downstairs into the kitchen, and A.J. asked Lydia to say grace. A.J. didn't speak to me. We ate our dinner in silence. When we had finished, A.J. went into the front room, asking me to go with her. I closed the door. "Now why did you make plans before asking me first?"

"I'm sorry --it just sort of happened, when Betty asked me. I didn't think it would make any difference if she walked with us. She wanted to know the time when we would be leaving." A.J. said, "That's the problem, Sylvia. You don't think. You make decisions. It's not your place to do that. Do you understand?"

"Yes. I'm really sorry. I can see that now. I was excited that Betty was wanting to come with us, and that's how it happened."

"I am pleased you can see that now. It's not the way to do things. I hope you have learned from this."

"Yes, I have."

"Well, Betty will be here soon. We will say no more on this matter. Now go and get ready. We will be leaving shortly." I left the front room and ran upstairs. Lydia was putting her coat on and asked, "What happened? Are you being punished?" I told her quickly and went to the bathroom. As I was putting my coat on, we heard the bell ring and knew it would be Betty. A.J. called us to come down, "Betty is here." After a bit of talking, we were on our way to chapel.

We made it

It was a bit squashy, with three of us walking on the pavement. U.S. and A.J. walked behind. On arriving, we could see the buses, and people standing everywhere. I said to Betty and Lydia, "I had better ask A.J. if we can come with you to find Sylvia's mum." With that, I turned and asked, "Can we go and find Sylvia's mum, as she is taking Betty in her car?" Betty said, "Thank you for letting me come and walk with you." A.J. and U.S. said, "That's all right. Yes, do that and come back here, and we will wait for you to find out which bus we are on." We hurried through the crowds. I could see Sylvia. She had that almost white hair that stood out in a crowd.

We all buzzing with excitement, and I introduced Betty to Sylvia's mum. She said, "Nice to see you, girls." Sylvia said, "When we get there, we will save you a seat, because we all want to sit together." I said, "That will be good. We are allowed to, but we must try not to talk too much, otherwise we will be in big trouble." We said our goodbyes and hurried back to the buses, where we found A.J. and U.S. in a line waiting to get on. We could hear a voice over the loudspeaker calling out names. U.S. asked, "Did you find Sylvia's mum all right?"

"Yes." A.J. said, "Now we stay together while we get on the bus." We ended up sitting at the front, and A.J. and U.S. were sitting behind us. It was exciting being out late, and now it was dark. The street lights were on. On arrival, we could hear a voice on the loudspeaker telling us where to go. A.J. said, "We still need to stay together until we're inside. Then, if you see your friends, you can sit with them." We said thank you. There was a man at the door as we went inside, showing us where to sit. I said, "We are sitting in front with our friends." He replied, "That might not be possible, unless you can see them." We looked around, and Lydia said, "I can see Sylvia down the front." She turned around and stood up, beckoning us to come down. The man said, "I will take you down." A.J. said, "When the service is over, we will see you at the door and wait for you. Please behave, and no chatting." We said yes, and followed the man, who took us to Sylvia and Betty.

Sylvia had saved us two seats. That was so good. Sylvia's mum was sitting there, too. There was a real buzz and music was playing. I turned around and could see the hall was filling up. I couldn't see A.J. and U.S., which I thought was good. I thought, that meant they couldn't see us. We were whispering and looking around to see if there was anybody we knew. Betty said, "I can't see Angela. I wonder where she is sitting?" Eventually the music stopped, and it was all quiet. A man was walking onto the stage, and more people followed him. I whispered to Lydia, "That's Billy Graham over there."

A man stood up and welcomed everybody. He then said, "We are opening the evening with a hymn." It was one we knew, and everyone stood up and sang. We joined in, and then, I listened. It sounded amazing. So many people all singing. After everybody had sung, we all sat down. Then the man talked some more, and eventually, Billy Graham was introduced. We girls all whispered, "He is so young and good-looking." He had an accent, as he was American. Then he started preaching. It was so different from what we had heard at chapel. He was explaining how you can do good in the world by your actions and what you say and do with your life, by giving yourself to God. I didn't understand that part, but I had this overwhelming feeling I would like to do that. I wasn't sure how one goes about it.

While he was talking, we girls just listened. Nobody whispered. There was this hush, and he said, "We will sing this hymn, and if you want to give yourself to God, you can walk down to the front, and I will lay my hands on you." I turned and looked at Lydia, and Sylvia whispered to me, "I'm going to do that." Lydia whispered to me, "What do you think?"

"Yes, I'm going to."

"I'll come with you." I thought, I wonder how it will feel? Betty said, "I'm coming too." There were a lot of people getting up from their seats and walking to the front. We followed. When the music finished, he said a few words, asking if anyone else wanted to give themselves to God. A few more people came to join us. More music was played. Then he came down from the stage and said a prayer. I could see he was putting his hands on a person in the line in front of me, and continued to do that with each person, then it was me. I couldn't believe it. My whole body started to tremble. I had never had that experience before or since, and I watched and wondered whether others were feeling like me. I was looking forward to going back to my seat. Lydia was holding my hand.

The music stopped and we were asked to go back to our seats. I saw a few girls from my school as I was walking back, but didn't see Angela. Everybody was seated and Billy Graham started talking again. We all listened. Nobody whispered. We were in awe. He introduced a young lady, who sang. She had a lovely voice. There was also a choir, all young, who sang. Then he spoke, giving a sermon – more about how you can live your life, and what you can do to help one another: "We all have choices to make, and it is by making the right choice that you enter the Kingdom of Heaven."

Chapter 70

I had never heard anybody speaking like that, explaining in the way he had done. I felt I could understand what he was saying. I was looking forward to talking to the others at the end of the service. After the last hymn, we started talking about it all. Lydia said she understood what he said, and Betty and Sylvia agreed. We all thought he was good. Sylvia's mum said he made it easy for all ages to understand the Word of God.

People were leaving their seats and walking up the aisle. Sylvia's mum said we had better follow. "Your aunt will be waiting for you." As we were walking, I thought, I wish we could all talk about it more with Sylvia's mum. I could see A.J. and U.S. near the door, waiting. Sylvia's mum introduced herself to them and said how much she had enjoyed it. We girls were talking amongst ourselves. A.J. said, "Thank you. Nice to meet you. We had better go outside, to where the buses are. We need to get on one." I asked, "What did you think of the service?"

"We will talk about that later," and she started to walk outside. We said our goodbyes to Betty and thanked Sylvia's mum. She said, "See you soon." Once we were on the bus, Lydia and I talked about the experience. I told her how I felt when Billy Graham put his hands on me. She said she had a funny feeling too. "I wonder what A.J. and U.S. thought about it? Hope we can talk about it when we get home." We got off the bus and had to walk home. We were both tired, and it was so strange walking back from chapel. It was late, and very dark. We were still discussing it, and were glad that we had gone. We really wanted to find out what A.J. and U.S. thought.

On reaching home, we were told, "No talking. It's late. Go to the bathroom, have a wash, and into bed. I will be up to turn the light off." We said goodnight to U.S., and did as we were told. After A.J. turned the light off, we were both so tired that we fell asleep. It seemed no time before we were woken again. We were running late. It was nearly lunch time. U.S. said, "This is breakfast and lunch together." He had it all ready when we came into the kitchen. Then he sat down with us and asked what we thought of the service. We both said we could understand what he was saying. I asked, "Did you see Lydia and me going to the front, and Betty and Sylvia too? And did you see Billy Graham put his hands on us?"

"Yes, we saw you walk to the front."

"It was a strange feeling when he did that." Lydia said, "It happened to me too. We talked about it afterwards with Betty and Sylvia, and it was the same for them." U.S. said, "That was the power of the Lord."

"I don't understand that, how it can happen."

"It is difficult to explain." I asked, "What did you think of the service?"

"He speaks from the heart, and I can understand how so many people want to come and hear him. Now, I'm going outside. Finish your breakfast, tidy your room, then Monty could do with a walk."

"We will do that."

After U.S. had gone outside, we talked together. I said, "I think U.S. enjoyed the service and he's so nice when A.J.'s not around."

"I wonder what A.J. will say about it?" We hurried and tidied our room, and got ready to walk Monty. U.S. was in his greenhouse when we had Monty on his lead. He said, "Now don't be too long. A.J. will be home, and you will be helping her with cleaning the chapel."

"We won't," we said. Once we were outside the gate, I said to Lydia, "Let's go and visit Lena."

"Do you think we should?"

"Well, nobody is on the vacant block to play with, so let's run with Monty just round the corner." We reached Lena's gate and opened it. Nobody was about. I said, "I will knock on the door, and say we have just come to say hello. She did ask us to visit again."

"Yes, she did, but she might not want to see us now."

"Oh well, we're at the front door," and I saw a bell, and pressed it. Lena came to the door.

"Hello, girls." I said, "We've just come to visit."

"Oh, that's nice. I'll come out the back to see you. Just walk around to the back." Lydia said, "It's because we have Monty. She won't invite us in. "

"She's all right with us coming." As we were walking, Lena came to meet us. There was a garden seat there and we sat down. She asked us if we would like a drink. I said, "That would be nice, thank you. We are only allowed to do short walks, and thought we'd come and say hello."

"I'll get you a drink, and you can tell me what you have been doing." With that, she got up and went inside. Lydia said, "Monty could do with a drink too. We will ask Lena for some water." She came out with a tray and had a drink for each of us. I asked if Monty could have a drink of water. She showed us a tap, not far from where we were sitting. I turned it on and Monty drank, then lay down by our feet. We spoke to Lena about the service, "Did you go?"

"I will be going to hear him tonight." We told her that Billy Graham had put his hands on us, and how we felt. "Yes, that happened to me, many years ago, when I gave myself to the Lord, and it changed my life."

"Well, it was only last night, and nothing has happened to us yet." Lena explained, "It's how you live your life as a person, and how you act towards other people. Not so ready to find fault with others, and how you treat them." After more talking, I said, "We had better get back before we are in trouble."

"A good idea. Just remember to do your best, and we can keep your visits as our little secret. They wouldn't go down well, unfortunately. That's the way it is." We thanked her. "Come again any time." We said our goodbyes and ran all the way home. We put Monty on his chain. I said to Lydia, "Did you understand what Lena meant?"

"I think so. Let's talk about it when we are on our own."

Chapter 71

A.J. was home, and said, "Just in time. We have the chapel to clean." It wasn't long before we were walking past Lena's house to chapel, on the other side of the road. Then I asked A.J., "What did you think about last night?"

"Well, Billy Graham certainly gets the crowds. I don't really agree with how he goes about it."

"I thought he was good, and I enjoyed it." Lydia said, "So did I."

"We saw you girls go out to the front. Do you understand the meaning of what you did?" I said, "I think so. It only happened last night, so I haven't been able to see any difference." A. J. looked at me. "It would be good if your behaviour improves. No more talking." We had arrived. "We have work to do." She got her bunch of keys out and opened the wooden door. I was asked to put the light on. It was very dark inside. We walked to the vestry and got our rags out, which were our dusters, and started dusting the seats. A.J. was taking the dead flowers out. We heard a knock on the door. A.J. said, "I will go." It was Lena – we heard her voice, giving A.J. some fresh flowers. She called out, "Hello girls." We answered, "Hello," then we heard A.J. close the door with a bang. We kept doing our jobs.

While walking home, I was thinking about things. Does that mean I have to like A.J.? I don't feel any different about her. I was looking forward to the time when Lydia and I would be on our own, so we could talk. U.S. was in the kitchen, making dinner. We were having an early one, due to our late night. We ran upstairs to wash our hands, talking. I asked, "How are you feeling about things?"

"No different. Do you?"

"Do you think it means we have to like A.J.?"

"No, but maybe we should try not to answer back or make her cross."

"I know it's me who does that. I will try to be different. You don't have anything to change."

"I do, but not as much as you. It will be good when we can talk to our friends about things." A.J. was calling, "Too much chatter. Dinner is on the table." We ran downstairs. I said, "Sorry." She gave me a look. "Sylvia, will you please say grace?" We ate in silence. A.J. said, "When you have helped with the dishes, come into the front room." We said yes, and she left. I asked U.S., "Can I see Monty?", as I was clearing the plates. There wasn't anything left on them. There was some gravy in the saucepan, I could see.

"Yes, you can put that with Monty's dinner." I looked into the pantry for something else I could put with his dinner, but couldn't find anything. Neither of us had managed to save any meat, as it was mince and it was too difficult. I went outside. Monty was in his kennel. It was raining. I came back inside, saying, "It's raining. Can I get Monty's rug and put it under the kitchen table, and let him inside?"

"Is it heavy?"

"It is getting heavy. I think he needs to come in."

"Very well. You can do that, and settle him, so he just stays on his rug." I quickly did it. Monty was so happy, and I gave him his dinner, which he ate under the kitchen table. We had the kitchen all tidy, and were ready to go into the front room. The door opened and A.J. came into the kitchen. She heard me let Monty in. "It's not raining that much. He has a kennel to go into."

"It was, when I was outside giving Monty his food." Monty was settled, and just lying on his rug.

"There is no need for him to be inside now."

"Why are you like that?" I asked. "He is happy and not doing anything wrong." A.J. was really cross.

"Go to your room. You do not speak to me like that." U.S. said, "I made the decision, and he has settled down now." I left to go up to my bedroom. I could hear them talking, and Lydia's voice too. I sat on the bed and thought, what did I really do wrong? I only asked why A.J. was like that. She really didn't have anything to do with Monty. I had never seen her giving him a pat. She never walks with us. She really didn't like him, I thought. I must remember to ask U.S. how it came about that they had Monty.

I heard Lydia coming upstairs. She came in, saying, "A.J. said you can come down now. Why did you say that?"

"Well, it just came out. Why is she so against Monty being inside? He doesn't move -- he just stays on his rug."

"I know that, but you shouldn't talk to her like that. You must try harder not to. It upsets me, how A.J. is with you." A.J. called out,

"Girls, come down now. Enough chatter!" Lydia squeezed my hand. "Be careful."

When we were in the front room, I said, "Sorry. I didn't mean to be rude."

"It's not for you to question me on my decision. We will say no more on the subject. Lydia, is there anything you would like to talk about?"

"Yes. Can we talk about last night, and explain what it means, giving yourself to God?"

"Well, you live your life doing the best you can, the Christian way, helping others who are less fortunate than you." Lydia asked, "Why did Sylvia and I have a strange feeling when Billy Graham laid his hands on us?"

"That can happen, but doesn't always. It's a gift some ministers have. It's called the Holy Spirit."

"It's hard to understand."

She asked me, "Do you have any questions?"

"Yes. So, nothing is going to happen to us after that?"

"It's up to you how you see things. If you want them to change or not, and that hasn't happened to you yet."

"It was only last night that Billy Graham laid his hands on us."

"That is true."

"I enjoyed it much more than chapel, and I don't understand what the minister says." Lydia agreed. "It's how he talks, and the way he explains it makes it easy for us to understand." A.J. said, "I think what he's doing has made it become sensational, which I don't agree with."

"But lots of people can hear him, and he is young, and that makes a difference to us." U.S. didn't say a word, just sat there rolling his thumbs. I looked at him and asked, "What do you think?" A.J. gave me a look. U.S. spoke, "I feel he speaks convincingly and it comes from the heart, and that draws the crowds."

"Yes, you're right," we said together. A.J. just looked at us. I think she couldn't believe what just happened. She was taken aback that U.S. had spoken. He hardly ever did – always sat there without a word. It all went very quiet. Then A.J. got her composure back, saying, "I think it's time for bed. I will be up shortly." We said goodnight to U.S. and left the room. Climbing the stairs, I asked, "What do you think of that?"

"I thought you were going to be in trouble yet again." We had never seen that happen – U.S. giving an opinion. We wished we could hear what was being said now. It was a while before A.J. came up to say goodnight. She said nothing else, turned the light off and left. We talked about what had happened with U.S.

Chapter 72

When we awoke, we knew it was Sunday, so we didn't have to rush, and our breakfast was different – we could have toast and dripping or jam, if we chose. "I wonder how it will be when we go down for breakfast?" We were discussing A.J.'s mood and heard her opening our door. "Good, you're awake. I will get your clothes out. Time to get up. Bathroom first, then come down for breakfast." We knew on Sundays we put our best clothes on just before we left for chapel, so no food could get on our clothes.

U.S. was very quiet when we walked to chapel, and we didn't hear them talking, which meant we had to be careful what we were saying, because we didn't want to be overheard. When we arrived, we saw Betty with Sylvia and her mum outside the chapel, waiting for us. I said, "That's nice. We can all sit together, with the youth group."

"You need to listen to the service. No talking."

"I will." We walked in together, and Betty whispered, "You will talk, or you will listen to the service."

"Oh, that's funny. I didn't mean it like that." After we had sung our first hymn, the minister spoke, and mentioned about hearing Billy Graham. He found it very enlightening, and went on, "Some of you have committed yourselves to the Lord, which was wonderful to see. Billy Graham is doing amazing work, and people are listening. I feel it is becoming a revival in religion, which is a good thing." He spoke more about Billy Graham and his life. I found it interesting. It wasn't boring this Sunday.

After the service, outside, we girls all chatted together, away from the adults. I would be seeing Betty next day at school, but I only saw my friend Sylvia on a Sunday, except sometimes in the school holidays. We were being called, so we had to say our goodbyes. Lydia and I, when walking home, started to talk. I said, "Listen. They are talking now.

That's good, so we can." Lydia agreed, "How good it was to hear more about Billy Graham."

"I wonder what A.J. will say when we talk in the front room?" We were passing Dennis's house when he called out. He was coming down the drive on his bike. "Did you go to hear Billy Graham?"

"Yes. Did you?"

"I went last night. It was really good." We had stopped walking now. I said, "We went on Friday." A.J. had caught up with us and stopped. She could now see we were talking to Dennis, "We need to keep walking." Dennis said, "What's the hurry? Hello, Uncle." U.S. said, "Hello. How are you?"

"I was talking about Billy Graham." A.J. interrupted, "Yes, well, we need to keep walking. We need to get home." U.S. said, "Sorry. We had better go." We said our goodbyes. Dennis said, "I'll see you at youth group."

"Yes, see you then." We started walking and heard A.J. and U.S. talking. I said, "I wish we could hear what they are saying." I also wished we could have talked longer with Dennis, and found out what he thought.

"Well, he said he will see us at youth group, so that will be good."

We had reached home, and did what we always did – got changed, and were told we could take Monty up and down the garden while lunch was being prepared. I grabbed the lead and ran outside. I took him off. He was in a hurry and managed to get away. He ran down the garden before I could put his lead on. We ran after him. He thought that was fun, and it was quite a while before we caught him. He ran to the gate and sat waiting, panting. We said, "No walking! Only in the garden!" He should have been on the lead. A.J. was knocking on the window, "Lunch is ready!" We put Monty on his lead and took him to his kennel. Lydia said, "He's looking for a walk."

"We should be able to later, after lunch." In the front room, A.J. asked Lydia first, "What would you like to talk about?"

"I enjoyed the service today, finding out more about Billy Graham." A.J. asked, "How about you, Sylvia?"

"I agree. It wasn't boring, and the minister feels it's a good thing, what he is doing."

"Yes, well, we all have our opinions."

"Why couldn't we talk longer to Dennis?"

"Because we had lunch to organise."

"But he is family, and we don't get to talk to anyone who is family."

"Well, that's just the way it is, and you have to accept it. You have been told before, and this is how it is."

"Why can't it get changed? We have hardly any family. Why don't you want it changed?"

"This is how it is."

"It just came out. I really didn't know I was going to say that. It wasn't planned." A.J. was getting cross. "How many times do you need to be told? It's not going to happen. End of discussion! Do you want to spend time in your room?"

"I just want you to explain why it can't happen." Lydia said, "It would be nice if you could explain it to us, and we could understand the reason why you say this can't happen."

"Girls, there will be no more talk about this. Do not mention this again. Is there anything else you would like to talk about?" I said, "I think you're being unfair." Lydia quickly said, "Can we go and walk Monty?"

"Yes, you can." We jumped up fast from our chairs and left the room. I grabbed the lead. Lydia was holding Monty still so I could put the lead on, and we hurried out of the side gate. "You choose,"

"Let's go past the allotment. Well, why won't they tell us anything?"

"I really thought you would be punished." We talked more about it. Nobody was about as we passed our plot. There was lots of green stuff growing. I wasn't sure what it was. "We must tell U.S. when we get back." We went over the stile into the big field. It was still all quiet there. I let Monty off, and he raced to where there were trees in the distance. We chatted about the situation more. I said, "It looks like we are not going to find out more from A.J., and U.S. won't tell us anything when we see him on his own."

"Well, when we are at youth group, let's ask Dennis. You can do that. He talks to you more." So, we made a pact. "He must know something," I said. We called Monty. He didn't come. Then we sat on the grass, talking some more. I asked, "Why don't we write to our uncle and tell him about Billy Graham? I still don't feel any different. Do you?"

"Yes, but it takes so long to hear from Uncle." We stood up and called Monty again. This time, he came running back. I managed to get him on his lead. As we walked closer to home, we could hear voices from the vacant lot. We hurried back and saw a group of children. Lydia saw some of her friends, but no older ones were there. We talked for a while, and I said, "We'd better go now."

Chapter 73

We opened the gate. U.S. was in the garden, and asked, "Where did you go? You have been a long time." I told him we passed the allotments, and saw all this green stuff growing. "Oh, that's good. It's the lettuces I planted. We will go. They must be ready to come out."

"Are we going now?"

"Well, I will go and check with A.J." He went inside. We just waited. Monty had a drink from his bowl.

U.S. said, "Yes, we have time to go straight there and pull some out." He had a bag. We went out the gate again. Monty was surprised. We talked to U.S. "It is hard for us to understand why we can't see any of your family."

"Please, no more talking about it now."

We reached the allotment, and U.S. was happy, pulling out some lettuces. There were also some carrots. When walking home, he said, "Girls, I think you will need a rest before we walk to chapel again."

"Yes, thank you. Can we go and read?"

"I'm sure that will be all right. I'll attend to Monty. You go in and have a rest." We said thank you.

A.J. was in the kitchen, and I told her, "We are going to go and read in our room."

"Well, yes. It will be some time before we eat." Sitting on the bed, we mostly talked, saying we wished we didn't have to go to chapel again. "It's so boring, and there are hardly any young people at the evening service, and we have to sit with them." This was the routine we had, and I found, as I was getting older that I didn't want to do this anymore. It was becoming more difficult for me. None of my friends were going to the evening service. I said, "When we talk in the front room, I will ask, "When can we stay at home?"

"Oh. You know that won't be allowed and she will get cross with you, and you will be in trouble. Please don't!" After more talking, I said, "I won't say anything, but surely, when I'm fifteen, I will be grown up, and she can't make me."

"Well, maybe that's the right time then, to say something."

"Let's hope we can see Uncle soon, and talk with him about everything. I will ask A.J. if she has heard from him and say we would like to see him." We decided that was a great idea.

In the front room, I was asked if I had anything I wanted to talk about.

"Yes. Have you heard from our uncle?"

"He said he was going overseas, and would be in touch when he gets back. You were told that."

"But that was a long time ago. Can you please write to him? We would like to see him. We want to ask him something."

"You can ask me. Do you have any problems?"

"We just want to see our uncle and talk with him."

"Well, I'm sure he will contact me when he gets back."

"Can you please write and let him know we want to see him?"

"There is no need to. He is a busy man, and he knows you like seeing him, and he will write when he is back. Now, it's time to get ready for chapel."

"Can you please write to him?"

"Sylvia, you have been told – I will wait until he contacts me. Now, enough! Please go and get ready. We will be late." Lydia said, "It would be nice if you could let him know we really miss him and want to see him, and if you could ask when he will be back."

"Well, if I don't hear from him for a while, I will make contact. Now please, both of you, go upstairs and get ready for chapel. We will have to hurry. I don't like being late for the service." When walking to chapel, I said, "It was good that you said something too, about our uncle. She might contact him and find out when he is coming."

"Yes, I thought she was starting to get cross with you. Let's write a letter, just to say, we hope we can see you soon, and we'll have to ask A.J. to put it in with her letter, and see if he answers it."

"A good idea."

There were only a few people at the evening service and we both found it boring. I was asked a few times to sit still. We stood up to sing a hymn. I was looking around to see if Lena was there, but I couldn't see her. I thought, when we leave, I will have a good look. I was glad when the service finished, and I walked to the aisle and looked around. I saw her. She was sitting with her husband at the back. She put her hand up, and I did the same. A.J. was behind me, and said, "You can start walking out now." Walking past Lena, I put my hand up again. A.J. just walked past. Lydia caught up and whispered, "Did you see Lena put her hand up?"

"I know. I did that too." U.S. caught up with A.J. and we were way behind. I slowed down, hoping we could have a word with Lena, but it didn't happen. There were more people behind us. Once we were outside, A.J. said, "You girls need to stay behind us, so we can all get out together. Now, we need to start walking home." So that's what we did.

On Sunday night we were really tired, as we had done a lot of walking, and it never took us long to fall asleep. A.J. had to wake us, even though we had not talked for long in bed. She said, "Your clothes are ready. Please don't take long. I will get breakfast." We hurried to dress.

Chapter 74

"It will be good being back at school and finding out what others thought of Billy Graham." We said our goodbyes. A.J. walked Lydia to school. She had told me she was going to tell A.J. she didn't want her to do that anymore. There were children, her friends, whom she could walk to school with. She wouldn't be doing it on her own, and felt she was grown-up enough now. I wondered how she would go with that. I hopped on the bus. It was noisy. Everybody was talking about Billy Graham. One girl said, "We saw you walk out to the front, and you were asked, "Do you feel any different?"

"No." Betty had a seat for me, and we talked about it. In assembly, it was mentioned by our headmaster, who said he was pleased to see so many of us there, and felt it was an enlightening evening. He closed with a few more announcements. I hurried, walking to the classroom. I still hadn't seen Angela. I was looking forward to hearing what she thought about Billy Graham.

She was sitting at her desk when I walked in, and said, "See you at recess."

"Yes, talk then." There was lots of noise, with everybody talking, as I walked to my seat. Our teacher entered. There was silence. He spoke, and mentioned Billy Graham. He had heard him, and felt he was helping a lot of people. We were fortunate to have him in our town. Then he went straight into maths. At the end of the class, he said we had one more week with him. Everybody said, "Ohhh!" We really liked him. There was lots of chatter, saying that we wished he wasn't leaving.

At recess, Angela and I walked onto the field by ourselves. I asked, "What did you think of Billy Graham? I didn't see you on Friday night." She said she didn't see me, as it was very crowded, and she didn't know I went out the front. We spoke about it all. Angela didn't feel she needed to go out the front and have Billy Graham lay his hands on her. I thought, she is a strong person, and confident in herself. She said to me, "If you feel it helped you to do that, then you did the right thing." We talked more about our maths teacher leaving, "I am at last better with my maths."

"That is good, and I can always help you. I know it all." The bell rang. It was time to go to our next lesson. "Are you still going to play netball?"

"Yes. See you at afternoon recess." I thought, as I walked to my English lesson, Angela really wants me to give up netball. That wasn't going to happen. I had no problems with English, and loved reading, which we had to do aloud. I always got good marks.

At lunch recess, I got together with the girls. We played netball and it was fun. Afterwards we sat chatted about the game while we ate lunch. Of course, the talk was more about Billy Graham. Most of us did go out the front, and we discussed the meaning of our experience. It was agreed, it meant we needed to be a nicer person, depending on what we were like now, I said, and how we could improve. I felt it was good, getting other points of view, and knew what I needed to improve on. I thought, I must try harder.

On the bus, Betty and I talked about our day. It had helped her, hearing Billy Graham, because it made her think what sort of person she wanted to be. I told her what Angela had said to me, about not going out the front. Betty said, "Oh well. Angela is a very confident person. She feels she hasn't any problems."

"If she did have, she has her mum to ask. She is a school teacher and can help her. I guess that makes a difference." We said yes. The bus had stopped. Everybody was getting off. We said our goodbyes. U.S. and Lydia walked towards me. She said, "We are going to visit Mr. Taylor, to find out how Mrs. Taylor is."

"That's good," and we started walking and talking about our day. Lydia told me her day was really good. She got high marks on all her subjects, and just loved school. I said, "That's great." U.S. said, "Well done." He asked me how I was going.

"I'm doing all right and enjoying school." We told him what we had discussed with Betty and the girls at netball, regarding Billy Graham, and what Angela had said. "The really good thing that is happening is, everybody is talking about it, and it is making people think how they feel about their life." I said, "You are right." We had reached the house. U.S. rang the bell. Mr. Taylor opened the door quickly. He was pleased to see us. "Come in." We could see Elizabeth, who was standing up, holding onto a chair. We ran over to her and each held her hand, walking her. Mr. Taylor spoke with U.S. I heard him say she had had the operation and was doing well, and hoping to come home later in the week. Mr. Taylor had the place tidy, and there were no dishes. He and U.S. sat and talked. We had fun with Elizabeth, who could do a few steps and then fall down. She was also saying a few words, like "No." and "Bye."

It was time to leave. U.S. said, "We will visit again next week. Can you send our best wishes from all of us? I hope she'll be home soon."

"Yes, I will do that. Thank you for coming." When walking home, I asked, "Do you know if A.J. has written to our uncle? We really want to see him." He didn't think so. "Can you please ask her to write? I really want to see and talk with him. Do you think that, if we write, A.J. will post it with her letter?"

"Can you tell me? I might be able to help. I'm sure she will be writing."

"Thank you, but no. It's our uncle we want to spend time with and talk about things."

"I will speak with A.J. about it." We thanked him. Once we got home, we knew our routine and said how nice U.S. was. "We should hear news soon. Let's write a letter and give it to A.J. to post with hers. That might make her write to him quicker." We tore some plain pages from our notebooks, and managed to write a few lines each, telling him we wanted to see him soon. Lydia said she would give it to A.J. when we were in the front room. "That's a good idea. She won't get cross with you."

"Leave it to me to do the talking."

"Yes, I will." We had it all organised. After dinner, we were sent to get our homework. Lydia put the letter in her pocket. We were left on our own at the kitchen table, and chatted. When it was her turn to talk, she would give A.J. the letter. I found my homework much easier, as it was revision. Lydia did hers with no trouble, and we were ready to go into the front room together. A.J. was surprised, as that rarely happened, and wanted to know, asking me, "Have you done it properly? And Lydia, have you been waiting for Sylvia to finish?" I said, "No. Mine was revision, and I found I could do it easily."

"Well, that's good to hear. Now, Lydia first. How was your day?"

"I had a good day, thank you, and everything is going well." Then she pulled out the letter from her pocket. I could see A.J.'s face. She was wondering what it was all about. U.S. was just sitting rolling his thumbs. Lydia said, "We have written a letter for our uncle, hoping he will be able to see us soon. Can you please post it with yours?"

"I have not written to your uncle. He will write when he is back, like he always does. We don't need to worry him."

"Can you please post it for us? We just want to see him." A.J. turned to me. "You have put Lydia up to this. This is not necessary. When your uncle feels he has time, he will make contact."

"We both want to see him and tell him about Billy Graham." Lydia said, "I want to see Uncle too. It's been a long time. Can you post it, please?" She was still holding the letter. A.J. grabbed it and asked me, "How was your day?"

"It's been good, thank you. I'm not having any problems and I am enjoying school." She gave me a look. "I hope you're learning. You need to start thinking about what job you want to do. It's not that long until you will be leaving school."

"How will I know what I want to do?" A.J. thought I was being rude, but I wasn't – I just didn't understand what my choices were, and how I would go about it. She said, "Don't be smart with me." I tried to explain, but was told, "Enough! Time to get ready for bed."

We said goodnight to U.S. I just wished he would say something. I felt he knew what I meant. When he is on his own, I will ask him about it. In bed, we talked about the whole thing. Lydia said, "I hope she posts the letter. Don't start worrying about what job you will do when you leave school. I think the teachers help when the time comes."

"Yes. They might suggest, but it's hard to know what you would like to do."

"Yes, but by the time it comes to leave, you might know what you want to do anyway. Oh, I didn't tell you – I told A.J. I didn't want her to walk me to school anymore."

"Did you really? What did she say?

"She said, of course I will be walking you to school. I can walk with my friends. They have been asking me to join them. She is not happy about this, but will think about it." We didn't hear A.J. come up the stairs. She was standing at the door. "Time for sleep. Good night." She turned off the light. We whispered, saying we'd better get to sleep. I asked, "Do you think she heard us?"

We were awake before A.J. called us. Lydia said, "I wonder how she will be when I say I'm walking with my friends to school now?"

"If she allows you to. Then there is no need for her to come out. I can walk to the bus by myself."

"Yes, you are right. We can just walk together, and I can say goodbye when you get on the bus, and keep walking with my friends."

A.J. was calling, "Breakfast is on the table!" I asked Lydia, "When are you going to say something?"

"After she puts our lunches in our bags." We quickly dressed and ran down for breakfast. A.J. said, "Lydia, say grace, please." Our porridge was on the table, and we ate in silence. When we were finished, we were told to go and get ready for school. "Come down. I will have your lunches ready for you." We hurried upstairs to the bathroom, and I was cleaning my teeth when I saw Dennis cycling past. I called out to Lydia and told her. "It will be good when we talk to him at the youth group."

"Yes. Are you really going to say something to A.J. about walking to school with your friends?"

"Yes."

"Hope she will let you." A.J. had our lunches ready and put them in our bags. Lydia asked, "I want to walk to school with my friends. I did talk with you about it."

"Well, I don't know if that's such a good idea."

"All the other girls walk without an adult, and I want to join them."

"I am aware of that, but I like to see you arrive at school." I said, "I can walk with Lydia and see she joins her friends, before I get the bus. That means you don't need to come out. I'm way old enough to walk to school on my own."

"You are, but your sister – I'm not sure about that. I feel I need to walk with you still."

"Why, when other children of the same age are doing it?"

"Now, that's enough talking. You will be late. I'm coming today, and will think about it. Now we had better leave. Say goodbye to U.S." We left. I could see Lydia wasn't happy, and felt for her. She is growing up, I thought, I would discuss it with U.S. when he meets us from the bus. We were at the bus stop. I said my goodbyes to Lydia. "Have a good day," and gave her a hug. A.J. said, "Come along. You will be late." She turned round to me, saying, "Goodbye, and learn."

PART 2

Chapter 75

Betty was calling out as I got on the bus, "I have a seat for you!" We talked until we reached school about Lydia wanting to walk with her friends. We walked to assembly. It was nearly the holidays. It was announced that our maths teacher would be leaving that week, and we would be having a lady next term. I thought that might be good. I went into the classroom with a lot of girls. Angela was already sitting at her desk alone. Our teacher came in behind us. The room fell silent. He said, "Now, class, this will be my last lesson with you."

"Oh!" voices called out. Somebody said, "Sorry you are leaving."

"It has been enjoyable, teaching you all. Now, we will be doing something different for our last lesson. I will ask questions. Put your hand up if you know the answer." That was how we spent the last lesson. We said goodbye to him as we left the classroom. At recess, Angela and I talked about him. She agreed that he was a good teacher. I said he had helped me lots. We talked about the holidays. I told her that we were waiting to hear from our uncle to know what we were doing. 'I might be going away too."

The rest of my day went well. I saw Betty in the bus on the way home. We talked about the holidays. She said, "I hope we can get together some days." We had arrived. I could see Lydia and U.S. waiting and talking. I said goodbye to Betty. I walked to where they were standing. Lydia was talking to U.S. about walking to school with her friends. He said, "I will have a word with A.J. If you are walking in a group, that should be all right." He told us that Mrs. Taylor should be home, "We will make a quick visit and see how she is." We were happy.

We rang the bell. Mr. Taylor came to the door quickly. He said, "Come in." Mrs. Taylor stood up and came to meet us. She was so pleased to be home, and was still in a bit of pain, but that should go soon. She could walk better. We couldn't see Elizabeth. We were told she was having a nap. U.S. said, "We won't stay. We are pleased you are home. Take it easy." Mr. Taylor said he would be back at work the next week. U.S. arranged for us to visit and help. He was pleased about that and said thank you, and that he would make sure Elizabeth was up to see us next time. We said our goodbyes. While walking home, U.S. said we might be able to visit more in the school holidays. I asked, "Has A.J. heard from our uncle?"

"Not yet." We spoke more about it, and had now reached home. U.S. opened the front door. There were some letters on the mat. I ran and picked them up and went through them. I could see there was one from our uncle. I turned to ask, "Can you open it, please?"

"Now you know, Sylvia, it's for A.J. to open, and you will know what it says after that."

"Yes, but when will she tell us?"

"After she has read it."

"Oh. It all takes so long. We want to know now." I was told I was being impatient. "You will find out soon." We ran upstairs to change, talking, "We will find out soon."

"I wonder what it says?" We were excited, and couldn't wait to hear what A.J. would tell us. We could hear children's voices and ran downstairs. U.S. said, "You can take Monty to the vacant block for a few minutes. Don't be long." We were chatting to our friends, and could see A.J. walking home, so we ran to her, telling her there was a letter from our uncle. "Well, I will read it, and you will be told when we are in the front room. Have you done your jobs?"

"Not yet."

"Come home in a few minutes, please." We said yes, and ran back to have a short play. We knew we must get home to do our jobs, such as cleaning our shoes, before dinner. I put Monty on his chain and we went inside. Nobody was about. Dinner smelt good. I was hungry. I hoped it was something I liked. Lydia and I raced upstairs. A.J. was in the front room with U.S. We heard them talking as we ran past. She opened the door and called out, "No running in the house!" We took our shoes off and sat on the bed. I said, "I think A.J. and U.S. have read the letter." Lydia agreed, "Well, we will soon find out." We carried our shoes to go outside and clean them. As we walked through the kitchen, dinner was burning, I thought, and they were still in the front room, talking. I said, "I'd better open the door and let them know. Dinner is really burning!" We could see U.S. was upset, and A.J. was saying she was sorry to hear it. She hurried out to the kitchen -- "Thank you, girls."

I asked what had happened. "I think it's for U.S. to tell you. Go and clean your shoes." We went outside talking. After we had cleaned our shoes, we went into the kitchen. A.J. said, "Wash your hands. We will have dinner when you come down." U.S. still wasn't in the kitchen. We were worried. I said, "I hope he is all right and will have dinner with us." Hurrying, we washed our hands and went downstairs. This time, U.S. was sitting at the table. He looked upset and didn't speak. I was asked to say grace, and of course we ate in silence. After dinner, U.S. started tidying the kitchen. He was getting ready to start the washing up. A.J. asked, "Would you like me to do them?" I thought, that's the first time I've heard her ask that. "No, you go into the front room. The girls will help me." I couldn't wait for A.J. to leave, so I could ask U.S. what had happened, --- he looked upset.

As soon as A.J. had left the kitchen, I asked, "Can you tell us what has happened?"

"Yes. My brother has had an accident and has died." We both said, "Oh. We're sorry that happened." I asked, "Have we met him?"

"I don't think you have."

"What was his name?" Lydia asked.

"Dennis." I said, "We have met him, and he is Lena's husband.

U.S. was surprised, and asked, "How did you know that, and where did you meet him?" We both started talking. U.S. said, "One at a time, please!" I said, "We met him in Lena's lovely garden, and visited them." U.S. didn't know anything about that, and I asked, "Please don't tell A.J."

"I won't mention it." Lydia asked, "How did it happen?"

"It was a car accident. He was alone in the car."

"I wish we could have got to know him. He was nice to us when we visited, and oh, he was sort of family, wasn't he?"

"I don't feel like talking anymore. Hope you understand." We said yes. We left the kitchen and ran upstairs to get our homework. I really didn't have any, but Lydia did. I watched her. She was so fast. "I'm going to ask A.J. if I can walk with my friends tomorrow."

"Oh, be careful. With U.S. being upset, he might not have spoken to A.J. about it. I really want to ask. My friends want me to join them. You can help me." "Of course I will, but you might have to wait a while longer before she lets you."

We went into the front room. They were talking, but stopped when we came in. A J. asked, "Have your both finished your homework together?" I said quickly, "I really didn't have any. We are having a new maths teacher."

"Lydia first. How was your day?"

"It went well, thank you, but I want to ask you something. Please, can I walk with my friends to school tomorrow, on my own?"

"I have given it some thought, and I feel you are responsible enough, and will allow you to."

"Thank you. I will say goodbye to Sylvia at the bus stop, then walk with my friends to school, like we do every day. The only difference will be that you won't be there."

"Yes, that's exactly what you need to do. Is there anything else you want to talk about?"

"Yes, it's about the letter from our uncle."

"We will discuss that soon. Sylvia, how was your day?"

"It went well, only I will miss our maths teacher, who has now left, and we will be having a lady teacher."

"I'm sure you will get used to her. Is that all?"

"Yes."

"Now, your uncle has written, and wants to see you both." We said together, "That's so good." I asked, "When?"

"I am about to tell you. It will be in the second week of the school holidays, and you will be able to stay with him for a few days."

"That is the best news," I said. Lydia asked, "How long before that happens?"

"Well, you finish school this week, and spend one week of holidays here, and it will be the next." I asked, "Did he write a letter to us?"

"No. He sends his love and will see you soon. Now, please go and say goodnight to U.S. You can read for a while." We walked over to U.S. and said, "We are sorry your brother has died."

"Thank you, girls, and goodnight." We left the room and ran upstairs. I said to Lydia, "Wonder when they saw each other last?"

"Well, you never saw them talking when we were at chapel. Let's try and visit Lena when we can." After more talking, it was quite a while before A.J. came up and turned off the light, saying, "Goodnight."

The next morning, Lydia was excited, "We are going to walk on our own today." After breakfast, A.J. was putting our lunches in our bags. Lydia said, "We are ready to leave."

"Yes. You'd better go now, or, Sylvia, you will miss your bus, and Lydia, your friends will be waiting for you." We said goodbye. It seemed strange that A.J. was hurrying us out of the door, then going back inside. I walked with Lydia, talking. We were on our own. It was so good. We could see the bus pulling in. Betty was waving to me. Lydia said, "Goodbye," and we gave each other a hug. She ran to where her friends were waiting. I watched from the bus, and she was walking and waving to me, very happy. Betty asked, "Are you walking on your own now?"

"Yes. We will be walking together, and Lydia can walk with her friends every day, by ourselves." I told her how sad it was that U.S.'s brother had died in a car accident.

"That must be awful for him."

After more talking, we had arrived at school and walked to assembly. It was mentioned that we were nearing the end of the year. I thought, I only had one more year left. I would talk with other girls and find out what they wanted to do when it happened to them. Walking to the classroom, I joined the girls. We were having maths. We would be having a lady teacher. I wondered what she would be like. We would soon find out, as we entered the classroom. Oh, only Angela was sitting at her desk. Then more girls came in, with lots of chatter. It was quite a while before a young lady walked in. Still, everybody kept talking. She had to shout, "Silence, please!" Eventually, the room was quiet. She introduced herself as Miss Thompson. "I will be teaching you, and it will take a little while to get to know you all. If you have any problems, you can come and see me." I didn't understand any of the maths she talked about, and knew I would have to ask for help.

At the end of class, I wasn't on my own. There were a few of us. She had us sitting down and explained how to go about it. It was like another lesson. Other children went to recess, and Angela was waiting for me outside the door. She was not happy that I had stayed behind. "I could have helped you. I could have shown you what to do." She had no problems, of course. "You need to ask me for help." I thanked her, "It might just take me a little while," and it did. It was the last week before the holidays. We had no homework. At lunchtime I played netball, and a few girls were talking about what they were going to do when they left school, what sort of jobs they wanted to do. Most were happy to work in shops. One girl wanted to be a teacher, but she had not got good marks, like Angela. There were a few of us who had no idea what we would like to do. I wasn't on my own, so that made me feel better.

I thought, I would talk with Uncle and Alice when I saw them. There was more talk about the holidays, and excitement. Our lessons were winding up. We were told that next year would be an important one. It was a bit scary, I thought, and after that it would be the unknown. What would I be doing? Our last day came, and we said our goodbyes. There were some hugs and general chatter. Angela said, "Well, I hope you will know what you would like to do when I see you next."

"If not, the teacher will help me."

"I don't have that problem."

"You are lucky to have a mum who is a teacher."

"Yes. See you when school starts."

I told Betty on the bus what Angela had said. "Oh, she is so sure of herself. I'll see you in the holidays."

"Yes. And don't forget to come to youth group on Friday. It's our last one."

"Oh. See you then." U.S. and Lydia were waiting. She handed me a large bag of sweets. She was eating hers. "We are visiting Mrs. Taylor."

"That's good."

"I had a fun day." We talked as we walked. U.S. was very quiet. We reached her house. He pressed the bell. Again, it was a while before Mrs. Taylor came to the door. She was still finding walking difficult. Elizabeth was walking towards us, before she fell down. She picked herself up, saying words we couldn't understand. U.S. asked, "Can I help you with any jobs?"

"That would be lovely. There are a few dishes still to do." She took him into the kitchen. We had fun with Elizabeth, who was really getting to know us. Mrs Taylor asked, "Would you like to come in the holidays? I'm sure there is someone who would like to see you, and I'd be very grateful."

"We are going away in the second week." I asked U.S., "Can we come in the first week?" He thought that would be all right. We said our goodbyes and gave Elizabeth a hug. She kept saying, "Bye bye!" and waved to us until we were out of sight. U.S. said, "It's a shame Mrs. Taylor is still having problems walking."

"Will she get better?"

"Hope so. They are unable to do any more for her." After more talking, we reached home. We quickly changed and took Monty for a walk. He made lots of noises and was excited to see us. We ran to the woods, our favourite place. After a while, I let Monty off the lead. We talked about our last day. I told Lydia what Angela had said. "She knows exactly what she will be doing. She has it all planned."

"Well, don't worry. I'm sure, when the time comes, you will know."

"Hope so."

"I have a letter for A.J. about my year at school."

"Yes. I have, too. I nearly left it behind. I wanted to have a look, but it's all sealed down, so I couldn't read it."

"We will have to give it to A.J. in the front room. I am sure yours will be a good one. You are doing all right now."

"Yes, I think I am."

After dinner, in the front room, A.J. asked Lydia how her day was.

"It's so good, walking on my own, with my friends, and I have no problems. I love school. I have an envelope to give you. It must be my school report. Can you tell me what it says, please?"

"Yes, of course." She took the envelope, read it and said, "Lydia, you have an outstanding report. You are top of class!"

"Oh. Am I? It's easy for me, and I love school. Everybody is nice."

"Well done. I am proud of you." U.S. said, "Yes, that's very good to hear." I gave Lydia a hug. "I have a clever sister."

"I don't find it hard. School is fun." A.J. asked for my report. I was nervous. What would it say? She opened it and looked at me. "Well, you have improved. That's something." Lydia said, "That's great." U.S. commented, "That's good to hear." I said, "Thank you. I am enjoying school too." A.J. said, "Well, you have one year of schooling left. You need to know what job you can do or want to do."

"The teacher will help and talk with the class."

"Well, you still need to think about it."

In bed, I said to Lydia, "When we see our uncle, I am sure he will help me."

"Yes, and Alice. Don't worry about it." After more talking, we eventually went to sleep. In the school holidays, A.J. went to work and U.S. looked after us. We were allowed to sleep in and make our own breakfast. U.S. was in his little greenhouse. He was a lot quieter and more sad-looking; he had changed. He let us do more of what we wanted. So, we took Monty for a walk and went to see Lena. She was pleased. We found out a little more about the family. U.S. had three brothers and one sister. Dennis was the youngest of the four boys. They were not close, since there had been a family disagreement many years ago, which caused a rift. We were never able to find out what it was about.

Chapter 76

One day in the holidays, U.S. took us to visit Mrs. Taylor, who still had problems walking. She needed some shopping done. She was happy for U.S. to do it. He took Monty, and Elizabeth was strapped into her pram, which was a high one. I was doing the pushing, with Lydia's help. We enjoyed that, and Mrs. Taylor thanked us very much.

We were counting the days until Uncle would come. Only two days left. A.J. said, "We must sort out what clothes you are taking." She eventually worked it out, and made two piles ready to be packed. We were told not to touch them. At last, the day arrived, and we were so excited. We had our bags packed, all ready at the front door, way before time. I asked, "Can we walk Monty? We have time."

"Yes. Only a short one." We grabbed the lead and ran out of the side gate. Monty was so happy to get off his chain and go. We saw U.S. in his greenhouse as we ran to the gate. We told him we were doing a short walk. I said, "Then we will be leaving."

"I will be inside when you get back. I will miss you, girls." He still looked so sad. We raced past the allotment and over the stile. There was nobody about and I let Monty off. I knew how he loved to be free. It would be a while before he could do that again. Lydia and I talked about leaving. When I called Monty, he came running straight back. That was good. We were walking back. We could see our uncle walking past the vacant block. We called out and ran to meet him. We were so happy. He came with us through the side gate into the garden, and watched. I think he was surprised, as I put Monty on his chain. Lydia gave him fresh water. We opened the door and went into the kitchen. No-one was there, so we went into the front room. A.J. and U.S. couldn't believe our uncle was with us. They were waiting for the bell at the front door. After some talking, we said our goodbyes.

At last, we were on our way. We were talking excitedly to him. He said, "One at a time, please." On the train we were able to have a proper talk, telling him how things were. Nobody came into our carriage and we had him all to ourselves. When we reached the house, Alice opened the door, looking just the same. She gave us big hugs and said how we had grown, especially me. "Take the bags to your room and then come to the sitting room." It was so good being able to talk together, saying what we wanted to say, feeling free and not restricted in any way. Alice said, "You are here for a few days to relax, and we can all enjoy ourselves while you are here." She had made a lovely lunch. Neither of us had to say grace. I did notice Uncle bowed his head and closed his eyes for a moment. We all talked about how good it was to be together.

Later in the day, Marion came home. She was so grown-up. She had a friend, a girl, with her. We sort of talked, and she left, saying they were going out again. Uncle spent time in his study. He said, "We will all go for a walk later." Alice was asking us questions and told us A.J. had given Uncle our school reports. He hadn't spoken to us about them yet. Alice hadn't seen them. She said, "So that's something to look forward to." She didn't want to hear anything until she had seen them. I asked about Peter. Would he be home for dinner? "Yes."

"So, we will all be together then." She took us into a small room, and on a table, she had jigsaw puzzle pieces laid out. There was a box standing up with the picture of what it was. She had been working on it. "Would you girls like to help me?" We said yes, and that is what we did until Uncle called, "Let's go and get some fresh air!" We ran to get our coats, and were ready to leave. It was fun, all walking together. We saw the swings in the distance. There was nobody about, so Lydia and I ran to them. I guessed I was too big for them, but I still fitted on and got the swing moving. I said to Lydia, "Do you remember the first time we came, and Uncle gave us a push?"

"I do." Then we did more walking, until it was time to head back home.

We helped Alice prepare dinner. It wasn't long before we heard Peter coming home. He had been at a friend's place. We were all a bit strange at first, before we started chatting, and he was pleased to see us. We put dishes of food on the table, so I thought we would be helping ourselves. Marion called out, "I'm home! Sounds like you have plenty of help. You don't need me." Then she went to her room. Alice said, "It will take time until you get to know one another again." She talked continuously, asking us what foods we ate, naming some we had never heard of, "What foods do you like? Try them. If you don't like them, that's fine. Just leave it on the side of your plate." That's what we did. There were some I really liked. We all talked together. It felt really good.

After dinner, we all went into the sitting room. Uncle had our school reports, and passed them to Alice, who said, after reading them, "You have both done well. Lydia, my goodness – top of the class! Such good marks. Well done," and to me, "You have done well to be where you are, and catch up after such a late start with your schooling. Don't you agree?" – asking Uncle. "Yes. I am pleased with how you are both getting on." Afterwards we all played a board game, which was fun, and we were all talking to one another by the end of the evening. It was time for bed. After saying our goodnights, Alice said, "Come into the kitchen in the morning, when you are awake. No rush."

In bed, I just remembered that we hadn't told Uncle about Billy Graham. I still didn't feel any different. I chatted to Lydia. She didn't either. We talked a bit more. "We must tell him tomorrow," Lydia answered, "Yes. We are having a lovely time. We'd better try and get some sleep."

We woke up and had no idea of time. We quickly got dressed. Alice was in the kitchen. "Come and sit down. You have had a good sleep. How are you?"

"We are well, thank you." She made us brunch, as it was late morning. She was chatting away to us, asking what we felt like doing, and made some suggestions.

I decided to tell her about my not knowing what I wanted to do when I left school. "Don't worry about it. You will know, closer to the time." We then had a discussion. "What do you like doing?"

"Walking, reading. That can't get me a job!"

"What else, after school?" Lydia said, "We have homework and walk our dog, Monty. We like doing that."

"Oh, and we go to youth group one night a week, and we have to walk to chapel morning and night on a Sunday. I find it boring." Alice laughed. "So would I."

"But I'm growing up. I shouldn't have to, if I don't want to."

"Well, you are not an adult yet, and are still under A.J.'s care, but that won't go on much longer. Things will change."

"When?"

"After you leave school, you will have a job."

"But I don't know what I want to do."

"Like I said, as the time gets closer, you will know."

"What if I don't then?"

"Do not worry about it. Just have a think from time to time about what you would like to do. There will be suggestions from your teachers during the year, and you will be able to get help with it." I thanked her. She was so easy to talk to.

She said to us, "Keep up the good work, and Lydia, with your marks, I feel you will end up going to a grammar school." After more talking, and helping her to tidy up, she said, "We're going on a bus ride to the city." We had fun. Alice bought us some clothes each and a present. We came home and spent time with Uncle, telling him all about it. Then I said, "We haven't told you that we went hear to Billy Graham, the evangelist, when he came to Colchester." Lydia said, "He was really interesting."

"After he spoke, he invited anybody to come to the front of the stage and he would lay his hands on them, if they wanted Jesus to come into their life. A lot of people walked to the front, so I thought, why not?" Lydia said, "All our friends did too, and older people. When he put his hands on us, I had a funny feeling."

"My body sort of trembled, and I understood we would feel different after that, but I don't."

"Nor do I." Uncle explained that at that time, the experience we had was the power of the Holy Spirit, and he was amazed that we both felt that. "It is something that can help you in life, your decisions and what you do, and what sort of life you want to live." I said, "It's hard to understand. So, we are just the same as before?" "Yes, but that experience can help you." Lydia said, "He was easy for me to understand." I agreed, "It was very moving, not boring, like we have to listen to in chapel." He said, "Yes, it's an entirely different experience when you have a large crowd, and an evangelist speaking." After some more talking, I thought I sort of understood it.

Chapter 77

Our time with them was coming to an end. It was time to pack our things and the gifts and clothes Alice had bought for us. Neither of us wanted to leave. We had really enjoyed our time. Saying goodbye to Alice and family was hard. On the train, we talked about our stay with Uncle, who said he was proud of us, and to keep doing well at school. We told him about U.S. and his brother, who had died in a car accident. I said, "He seems so sad. He's not like he used to be with us."

"It will take time. One never gets over something like that."

"I wonder if they will be pleased to see us?" Lydia said, "Monty will, for sure."

"Yes, you are right." I asked, "Are you staying for a while?"

"If I'm invited, I will stay for lunch."

"That would be good, and you might be able to come for a walk with us."

"Yes, we will have to wait and see what happens."

We had now reached the bus stop. We walked towards the house, past the vacant block. Nobody was about. I opened the gate and ran in front, pushing the bell hard. U.S. opened the door and said, "I'm pleased to see you, girls." We were all talking together for a while at the door and then followed U.S. into the kitchen. A.J. said, "Hello. I could hear you were back." Monty was making lots of noises. Our uncle asked, "Have you had a nice quiet time?"

"Yes, thank you."

"Girls, please take your things to the bedroom." We ran upstairs, dropped our bags on the floor and sat on the bed.

"Well," I said, "Let's go down and find out if Uncle is staying." We raced down. I asked, "Is Uncle staying?" A.J. said, "Sylvia, we are talking."

"Can we go and walk Monty?" She gave me one of her looks. "Yes. I have invited Uncle to stay for lunch, and you can go for a short walk."

"Oh, that's good." I grabbed Uncle's hand. Lydia had the lead. I said to Uncle, "You said you would walk with us if you were staying for lunch." A.J. gave me another look. Uncle said, "Sorry," He turned to A.J. "Yes, I did. We can finish our conversation after lunch. I will have time, as I will be getting a later train back." Monty was jumping up and down, making lots of noises. Our uncle helped us put him on the lead. He was so excited. We ran to the side gate. Lydia said, "We haven't time to go far." Our uncle spoke, "We mustn't upset Aunty Jean, and Sylvia, it was rude of you to interrupt while we were talking." I said, "Sorry." Monty was pulling me really hard. I said, "We will have to walk to the allotment. It's the shortest walk." We showed him our allotment. We passed some more allotments. When we reached the stile, we all climbed over into a big field, with trees at the far end.

I thought, Good. Nobody was about. I let Monty off. My hands were really sore. He ran to the big trees, away in the distance. Uncle asked, "Should you be doing that?" Lydia said, "Not really, but we do sometimes." I said, "You saw how he has been pulling me. Please don't say anything. We have trained him to come back when we call him."

"Sylvia, you are making a decision. If something goes wrong, there will be a consequence. At some stage, when Uncle Stan walks with you, you must tell him, and let him see how Monty is when you call him." I crossed my fingers, and called him. He came running straight back. "See, we have trained him." It was time to walk back. I said, "I think it's not right that Monty has to be on the chain all the time."

"Sylvia, I understand how you feel, but one has to respect other people's decisions. I am pleased to see how you both have compassion." He gave us both hugs.

"I really don't like A.J. and how she is with me. I feel sorry for U.S." Lydia said, "Sometimes A.J. is not that nice to Sylvia, and she's not that understanding."

"Well, I am pleased how you girls are developing."

"So, I have to put up with that?"

"Sylvia, you will find that is part of life, but you are strong and are dealing with it." Lydia said, "It doesn't seem fair."

"As you grow older, you will understand." We had now reached home. Uncle helped us put Monty back on his chain, before going inside. Later in the afternoon, we had to say our goodbyes, which was always hard. He said he was proud of us both and would keep in touch.

We settled into our routine that we had to have. School was starting very soon. A.J. had to buy school books and other necessities. I was thinking, it was going to be an important year for me, so I must really try hard with everything, and it would be nice to see my friends again. It was also Lydia's last year at primary school, and she was really looking forward to being back. I think A.J. was looking forward to it too. It was often difficult for us. Some days, whatever we did was not quite right.

U.S. took us to see Mrs. Taylor, who was still having difficulty walking. He helped by doing some jobs. We had fun with Elizabeth. Mrs. Taylor asked if we would visit when we could, to help. He said, "Yes, we will call in next week."

The next day was Sunday, and we would be going to chapel. It had been a while. A few people said it was nice to see us. Sylvia, my friend, walked over to see us, and we chatted. She asked, "Are you coming to sit with the youth group?" I said, "Yes," and left, saying goodbye to A.J. As we went into the chapel, walking down the aisle, I saw Lena, sitting with some ladies. She put her hand up to us. I did the same. We listened to the sermon. Nothing had changed. I still found it boring. I spoke to Lydia about it. She agreed. We saw Dennis sitting at the back. As we were leaving, he came over, asking us where we had been, so we told him we had been away. He said he had missed us.

Later, in the front room, A.J. asked, "What did Dennis have to say?" She had seen him talking to us.

"He just wanted to know where we had been. He said he missed us."

"Did he, indeed?" After more talking about the service, we told A.J. we found it hard to understand and uninteresting. This didn't go down well. U.S. didn't say a word.

School would be starting the next day. We were happy. A.J. had our uniforms all ready for the morning, and I think she was looking forward to us going back. We really found it difficult to settle since coming back from our uncle's.

The next morning, we were up bright and early, and ready to go. A.J. was surprised, "This is a good start," putting our lunches in our bags. Saying our goodbyes, we hurried out. It felt so good being on our own, walking, chatting and wondering who would be in our class. We could see my bus pulling in. We ran, saying our goodbyes. We hugged, saying, "Enjoy your day."

Betty was at the bus stop. There was lots of chatter. We were pleased to see each other. "It's good you are on time." We were the first to get on, and didn't stop talking until we arrived. We walked into assembly together. What a surprise we had, when it was announced who was going to be in which classes. We found out Betty was in the same class as me and Angela again. There were a few girls I didn't know. It was no surprise when we reached our classroom. Angela was sitting there all on her own. We chatted, and I introduced Betty to her. "See you at recess," she said. Betty came over to sit where I was. I thought, I wonder how it will go, now Betty is in my class? Maths was our first lesson. We had the same teacher as last year.

At the beginning of class, she said, "We have some new pupils, who are now with us. This lesson, we will do some revision, and I can assess you all," and that was what we did. When class finished and we walked out to recess, Angela was waiting. We talked. She asked, "Do you know what you want to do yet?"

"No, but I will get some help as the year goes along."

"You need to have an idea." Betty joined us. We all went out into the field and sat down, before chatting. It went quite well, getting to know each other. We talked about what we had done in the holidays, and it was good having Betty in my class.

On the bus, Betty told me she knew most of what the teacher was talking about. U.S. was waiting. Lydia ran towards me, full of excitement, telling me she had had a great day. Most of her friends were in her class, and she was happy being back at school. I told her my news about Betty being in my class. She thought that was great. U.S. said, "It sounds as if you both had a good day." He still had some sweets for us, which we ate while walking home.

Chapter 78

Lydia and I settled into school well, and I found, if I was unsure about anything, Betty or Angela would help me. I was surprised how well they got on. Angela knew everything and would always let you know it. Betty was able to stand up to her, and they would have discussions and compete with each other. Listening, I found it interesting, and learned a lot from this. Both were wanting to help me if I had any problems. It was really good for me, and I benefitted so much.

Doing homework after dinner with Lydia at the kitchen table, she noticed I wasn't having any problems, and was not asking her for help. She wanted to have a look at what I was doing. After a minute or two, she said, "I know how to do that." We then spoke about it. At last, I was understanding. Lydia said, "You have got on better since Betty has been in your class." I agreed.

I felt so much better about school. I still played netball sometimes, at lunch recess. Angela was happy she had Betty for company, and we were all getting on really well.

Youth group was starting on Friday. This was the first time since we had returned. We were allowed to walk by ourselves now. It was only a block away, and A.J. told me, "You are old enough to be responsible now, as you will be leaving school at the end of the year. You will need to know what job you want to do, and be capable of doing it." I still had no idea, but I knew I didn't want to work in a shop. Talking with others, I found I wasn't on my own, and that made me feel better.

Youth group was fun. Lydia and I mixed in with the others. We knew a few teenagers, and Dennis was there with a group of boys. Lydia said, "We should talk to him and see what we can find out about the family." It wasn't until the end of the evening that he came over to us. We talked about the family. There were other boys with him, and it was difficult to ask him anything. He did ask us questions about U.S.: how was he since his brother had died? I said, "He is very sad and quiet." Lydia added, "We would like to know more about the family." She gave me a nudge. I said, "Yes. That would be good, if you could tell us why it is this way." Other boys were becoming restless, and wanting to leave. Dennis said, "I will talk to you when I see you again." They all left, got on their bikes and rode away. We walked home. Lydia said, "I thought you weren't going to say anything."

"I didn't want to, with all the boys there. We will have to wait till next Friday now, before we see him again."

"You're right. Hope he can tell us more, and will be on his own."

"I don't think he wants to talk with his friends there." We reached home. A.J. said, "You are late back. You were told to come straight home."

"Well, it didn't finish on time, and it isn't easy to leave if somebody is talking to you. It's rude if you do. You have told us that."

"Sylvia, you always have an answer for everything." Lydia said, "It was our first time back. Everybody was chatting. There were a lot there."

"Very well, then." U.S. didn't say a word. I asked him, "Was it nice, not having to walk with us?"

"It felt strange. I caught up with some reading." A.J. said, "Go and get ready for bed. I'll be up shortly." We said goodnight to him and ran upstairs, chatting. I said, "I thought she'd ask who we were talking to."

"Don't mention Dennis. You know that upsets her." We agreed we wouldn't.

A.J. went to her job the next day, and we were allowed to make our own breakfast. U.S. was always in the garden or the greenhouse. If he saw us in the kitchen, he would come in and often make breakfast. He would sit and have something to eat with us. We were able to chat with him. He was so different then, when it was just the three of us. That was the nicest time. Even though we had our jobs to do, like the dusting and polishing the stairs, and having to tidy our rooms, we would rush through our jobs and then walk Monty, and often go with U.S. to the allotment. "When you have finished your jobs, just let me know," he would say.

Left on our own, inside, we enjoyed that. I would still try the door of the little room. It was always locked. We never did find the key. Then we would go into their bedroom, and Lydia would move the mirrors and look at herself at different angles. I was looking at A.J.'s jewellery on the dressing table. On this particular day, U.S. called out, "Have you nearly finished? We need to do a different walk." We said yes and hurried up. "I wonder where we will be going? If we walk somewhere that we can let Monty off, we had better show U.S., like our uncle said, so he can see how he is off the lead, and comes back."

"You know, there are times when he doesn't come when you call him."

"Yes, but it doesn't happen often, and we always get him back after a few more calls."

"Let's just see what happens, and how he is with us."

"You could be in big trouble. Be careful!"

U.S. had Monty on the lead when we came outside. I asked, "Where are we going?"

"A.J. needs me to take a letter to a lady's house for her, and it's quite a long walk." We left, and reached Lena's house, and stopped. I was looking at all the lovely flowers in the front garden. I said to U.S., "It must be hard for Lena. Who will do the garden now?"

"I don't know, but I'm sure she will organise somebody to help her."

"Why can't we call in and say hello?" U.S. was taken aback, "Oh, I don't know if we should do that."

"She will be pleased to see us. She always is, when we see her, and it would be a nice thing to do, I'm sure." We were still stopped at the gate. I opened it. Lydia looked at me. We walked down the path. U.S. was following. We walked down to the back. Lena was outside, "Nice to see you, girls," then, seeing U.S., she was surprised. After a bit of talking, they were getting on well. He said, "We'd better get going now."

"It was lovely of you to call in. Please do it again." We said yes, then our goodbyes and kept walking down the straight road, passing the little chapel that we would be helping A.J. to clean after lunch.

"Thank you, girls. I am pleased we did that."

"I think that Lena was happy to see us."

"Yes, it was nice to see her, as she is on her own now." Lydia asked, "Maybe you could help her."

"Well, I don't know about that, but I would like to keep in touch."

"That's so good," we both said, "We really like Lena." U.S. looked at us. "I think there's something you haven't told me. Never mind, you don't need to say any more." We said, "Thank you. We don't want to be in trouble."

"We will say no more about it, girls."

We were still walking, almost at the end of Straight Road, which was like its name. We reached the number on the gate and saw the letter box. Lydia asked, "Can I put it in?" He said yes. I asked, "Are we walking back the same way, or is there another way back?"

"We can go a different way, and it is shorter. We need to keep walking a bit further, and there is a lane which will take us to where the allotments are." Monty was pulling me so hard, and I knew he was wanting off. I was thinking, if we come to the field and nobody's there, will I be brave enough to show him, and let Monty off? How would he be with me?

We were all talking. Lydia squeezed my hand. She knew what I was thinking, and wasn't sure what I was going to do. We had reached the lane and were walking down it. U.S. asked, "Do you know where you are now, girls?"

"Yes, I think so." Nobody was there. I saw the big trees, and I thought, we were at the far end of the field. There was a small gate that we opened. I was looking around. Again, nobody. I asked, "If we show you something, please don't get cross." Then I let Monty off. He ran everywhere, round and round the trees. U.S. was shocked and amazed, "Why did you do that?" Lydia said, "He is good. Nobody is about, and we let him off for a run. Sylvia calls him and he comes back to her."

"I have trained him, and he's so good. He can have a run, and not be on a lead or chain all the time." U.S. was cross. "What if someone comes along?"

"I will call him."

"Well, call him now, please." I held my breath and called Monty. He stopped and looked at me. I called him again. Then he came running back. I put him on the lead. U.S. asked, "How long has this been going on for?"

"Quite a time. He's so happy, and we have trained him."

"You have been taking a big risk, and I trusted you to walk him. I'm not happy, knowing what you are doing."

"Monty loves it, and he knows to come back when I call him. We always make sure nobody is about. It must be awful, always being on a lead or a chain, and never being free." We had now reached the allotment. There were a lot of things growing. U.S. said, "I will just give them some water." We stood and watched. Monty was wanting to get wet. I had to hold him tight. Lydia whispered to me, "We could be in big trouble."

"I will ask him not to tell A.J. when he has finished." We were walking now, and nearly home. U.S. was quiet. I asked, "Can you not tell A.J.?"

"Sylvia, I'm finding it hard to decide, now I know what you have been doing. I need time to think about what should be done." I became upset. I didn't understand what that meant. Lydia said, "We still want to walk Monty."

"Yes, Monty does need walking. We will say no more about it for now, girls." He took Monty and put him on his chain. We went inside and ran upstairs. "Well," Lydia said, "It is out in the open now. I wonder what will happen?"

"Our uncle wanted us to tell him, and we have, so we have done the right thing.'

"Yes. Let's hope he doesn't tell A.J." We agreed we wouldn't mention it. We washed our hands and ran down for lunch. We heard the door closing, and A.J. was home. We were having sandwiches for lunch. She asked U.S., "Did you take my letter?" He said yes. Lydia said, "I put it in the letterbox."

"Thank you." We ate our sandwiches in silence and were told we would be leaving shortly to clean the chapel. "Go and put your shoes on." We left the kitchen and could hear them talking.

"I wonder if U.S. will say anything?"

"Also, about seeing Lena." We hurried downstairs, not knowing if we were in trouble. A.J. was her usual self, so, I thought; nothing was mentioned.

We were in the chapel, dusting. There was a knock on the door. A.J. called, "I will go." It was Lena. We heard her voice. She had flowers for the altar. They really didn't speak. She just said thank you. Lena called out, "Hello, girls." We answered "Hello." I said, "The flowers are lovely." A.J. closed the door and walked back to the vestry, and was busy arranging the flowers. We talked between ourselves. "We have to just wait and see what happens, if anything gets said."

Chapter 79

A few days passed. We didn't walk Monty on our own, only with U.S. A whole week went by. When U.S. had Monty on the lead, we came out and were walking together. I asked, "Can I hold the lead?" He said yes, and he wanted to talk to us. We were walking to the allotment. Monty was different when I held the lead. He wanted to go fast, so I ran with him. U.S. said, "He knows the difference, who is holding the lead." We had reached the allotment. He had a bag with him, 'On our way back you can help me pick some vegies." Lydia asked, "Where are we going?" He looked at us. "To the field. I think Monty would love a run." We ran up to him to try and give him a hug. He just stood there, still not knowing how to react. We said, "Thank you. He will love that."

"We will need to make sure nobody is about." I said, "We always do that. And wouldn't it be nice if he came back for you, when you call him?" Lydia said, "Yes. You could do that when you are on your own, when walking him."

"I have been giving it a lot of thought, and have come to this decision. It would be good for Monty to have a run, as long as he comes back when he is called."

"Yes, you must try it and call him. You haven't done that before, and he needs to know you are happy with it."

"You are right. We will try it." We had climbed over the stile and reached the field. It was all quiet. Nobody was about. Monty was looking at me. I said, "He knows. Is it all right if I let him off?"

"Yes." Monty ran fast to the trees. He had missed that so much. U.S. said, "You are right. He is enjoying it." After a little while, U.S. called him, and Monty took no notice. He tried a few times. He said to me, "We need to leave. Can you call him, please?" I did. Monty stopped running and looked at me. I had to call him again. He was still undecided whether to come or not, so I kept calling him, "Come on, Monty!" and he came running back. "Well," U. S. said, "I will need to call him on our walks, so he knows to come back to me."

"Yes, he hasn't been off the lead for a few days, so he will need to get into a routine again." Lydia said, "He needs to know when you call him that he should come back, too. I never call him. It's only Sylvia."

We were so happy U.S. was all right with us and wanted to do it for himself. I asked, "Does A.J. know?"

"There is no need for this to be mentioned." We looked at each other and agreed.

School was going well for me, and it was so good that Betty was in my class. I was mostly managing my homework and had only a few problems. There was a discussion in our English class on careers, and what some of the choices were. This depended on our marks, what we would be suited for. We were asked to put our hands up. Those who had no idea what they wanted to do. I put my hand up. There were a few of us, when I looked around the room. The teacher went through some careers and made some suggestions. We were also asked to have a talk with our parents, to get their help. I thought, I can't talk to A.J. about that.

At recess, the first thing Angela said to me was, "You really should have an idea by now." She wasn't being nice about it, and was being critical, as she could be sometimes. She knew everything, and always let you know it. That side of her could upset me, but I had made my mind up. I wasn't going to let it anymore. I said, "I will work it out." Betty said, "Anyway, you can always work in a shop, like me." Angela said, "You should be wanting to do something better than that. You are clever enough for it." Betty was cross with her, "If that's what I want to do, and there's nothing wrong with it, that's what I'll do. Stop trying to be above everybody. You can be such a snob." It all got very heated. Then, Angela apologised, saying, "I'm so lucky to have a mother who is a teacher and helps me." We both said, "Yes, you are, and we don't need to hear it all the time." We were sort of being friends again, when it was time to go back into class.

I got off the school bus and thought, I would mention to U.S. what my English teacher had said about jobs. Lydia was full of chatter and, handing me my sweets, wanted to know about my day. "We had a discussion on what we want to do when we leave school. There are only a few of us who have no idea, like me. It's so hard." U.S. started telling us that when he was young, he took an interest in plants, and eventually became one of the gardeners who worked looking after the grounds and gardens at Colchester Castle. Roses were his speciality and he really enjoyed it. We didn't know about that. He said, "You need to think about what you really like doing." We had now reached home. I thanked him. Lydia said, "I will help you work it out." I gave her a hug. We got changed, and she said to me, "I have to do an exam, like you did, to see what school I will go to. I will have to tell A.J." We got into our routine. After dinner in the front room, A. J. said, "Lydia first. How was your day?"

"I'm enjoying school, and will be having to do an exam, and there will be questions to answer, like you did," turning to me. "Will you still be at your school?" A.J. said, "Sylvia will have left school then. You need to do your best. You could go to the grammar school. I think you're clever enough."

"Oh. I'm happy to go to Sylvia's school.'

"Well, like I said, Sylvia won't be there then." I knew it was my turn, but before I could say anything, she said, "You do realise, if you don't have a job to go to when you leave school, you will be doing all the jobs around the house."

"Oh, I don't want to do that. '

"Well, that will happen."

"My marks have been a lot better.'

"You only have a few weeks left at school." I thought, I will tell A.J. Then, I said, "We had a discussion with our English teacher, and she asked for us all to talk to our parents, to see if they could help." A.J. said, "That is the only suggestion I can give. You will be old enough to do more jobs." Lydia added, "The teacher will help you."

"Oh, I hope so."

"Please go and get ready for bed. I will be up shortly to turn off your light." We said our goodnights to U.S. and ran upstairs. Lydia said, "That wasn't nice of A.J. to say that to you."

"She doesn't like me. I must get a job. It would be awful if I had to do all the jobs and be at home all the time." We talked about it, even after A.J. had turned off the light. Lydia said, "We had better try and get some sleep. Try not to worry." I thought, what am I going to do? I couldn't get to sleep. I felt so unhappy.

In the morning, Lydia had a job to wake me. She said, "Please, try not to worry. See if you can ask the teacher for help."

"Yes. I will talk to the other girls like me, who don't know what they're going to do."

"And you might get some ideas." On the bus I told Betty what had happened. She said A.J. was being unkind to me. "Just be like me and work in a shop. That would solve everything." I thanked her, but I didn't feel I would be happy doing that. "I might have to. It would be awful doing jobs at home all the time." How would I ever get a job? These thoughts were playing on my mind.

At recess, I discussed with other girls like me what their parents had said about finding a job. Angela and Betty were sympathetic. One or two said they were going to ask friends, to see if they knew anyone who could help, or knew of a job. Angela started to say how lucky she was, but Betty told her to shut up, "That's not helping!" Immediately, she stopped talking and said sorry.

We walked back into class. I said, "They will get help from their parents, not like me." Betty said, "Don't give up. When we have our next English class, see if you can talk to the teacher."

"Thanks. I will. That's what Lydia said."

The rest of the day went well, and it wasn't till the next day that we had English. The teacher said she would spend time helping those who needed it. There was a small group of us. She spoke about different jobs and careers, saying what they entailed. Office work was mentioned, or you could do more studies and go to college to get a higher degree. "That would get you into nursing." I suddenly thought that was something I would like to do, helping people, but how would I be able to do it? At the end of class, I asked the teacher if I could talk with her. She said yes. When it was recess, after everyone had left the room, I stayed behind. Angela and Betty gave me a look and went out. I said, "I will see you later."

The teacher asked me to close the door. Then I explained about myself and living with A.J. I told her, "When you mentioned nursing, I thought, that's what I would like to do."

"You would have to do a lot of study, and more schooling. You would have to go to college."

"Oh. Is there anything else I could do, helping people?" I became upset, and asked, "Can you help me with anything?" I think she felt sorry for me. I even told her what A.J. said, that I would have to do all the jobs around the house if didn't have a job to go to. She was nice to me, and said she would think about my situation and that it was good that I had a talk with her. "Try not to worry." We heard the bell go. Recess had finished. The teacher said, "You had better go to your next class." We left the room together.

I knew I had History next. I was the last to go in and sit down. The teacher was already there, but didn't say anything to me. I enjoyed History, and it wasn't long before he had the class relaxed, and would say something funny, in what and how he said it. Everybody liked Mr. Turner.

I walked out. Betty and Angela came to talk to me, wanting to know what had happened. I explained how things were at home. "And I know now what I want to do." Angela said, "At last! What?" When I said, "Nursing," she said, "You can't do that. You don't have high enough marks. I could do that if I wanted to, but I don't." Betty said, "You're not helping,", then, to me, "What made you want to do that?"

"As soon as the teacher mentioned nursing, I suddenly thought, that's what I want to do, helping people." Betty asked, "What are you going to do now?"

"The teacher is going to help me." Angela said, "Well, you can't do nursing, unless you want to do more schooling, and you wouldn't manage that."

"Thanks for that. You are right. I do need to think of something else. I still would like to do something to do with helping people."

It was time to get the bus. I said goodbye to Angela. Betty and I walked together. She said, "It's good the teacher knows about you. I would hate to have to do more study." I agreed, "I don't think I could manage it." We kept talking till it was time to get off the bus. We said our goodbyes. Lydia walked up to me, wanting to know how I got on. "She mentioned nursing as a career, and suddenly I felt that's what I want to do. She explained, my marks are not good enough, and I would have to do more study, and go to college." Lydia said, "That is a shame."

"I would like to do something that involves helping people."

"You would be good at that."

"Do you think so?" Lydia said, "Yes. You have helped me heaps."

"And you have helped me with my homework." We talked about it while walking home. U.S. was very quiet, listening to our conversation. "Well," I said, "I have to get a job, or else A.J. will make me do all the jobs around the house. I would hate that." Lydia said, "That wasn't nice of her." She turned to U.S., "Don't you agree?"

"It is a difficult situation. If you don't have a job, you need to do something. You can't just sit in your room." I said, "But she could try and help me. That's what other parents are doing." Lydia asked, "Are you able to help?"

"I will put my thinking cap on."

"I know now what that means." I said thank you.

Later, in the front room, no more was mentioned about me finding a job. I didn't tell A.J. that I had spoken to the teacher on my own. The next few days went all right – no real upsets. On Friday night, at youth group, Betty came for the first time and loved it. She said she would be coming to chapel and sit with the youth group. We saw Dennis with his friends, and he spoke to us. I asked him, "Can we talk with you on your own later?"

"All right." When it was time to leave, he came over to where we girls were standing, and asked me, "What do you want to say?" Lydia said, "Go outside and talk with him on your own."

"Oh, all right." So, I went outside. He followed me.

"I just want to know more about the family, and U.S. and what he could tell us."

"Well, nobody likes A.J., and U.S. doesn't come to see us now." He wanted to know how I got on with her.

"Not that well." More people were coming out of the hall. He said, "Things changed when they got together." His friends were coming out. I said, "I'd better go and find Lydia now." He said he liked me, then tried to give me a kiss. I ran inside fast to where Lydia and Betty were standing. Lydia asked, "Is everything all right?"

"I didn't find out that much." Betty said, "I think my mum might be here." We walked out to the porch, and she could see her mum. She said goodbye. We started walking home. Lydia asked, "Tell me what happened. Why did you come running in? Your face was red."

"I couldn't believe that happened, and I had no idea." Lydia asked, "What happened? You haven't told me yet."

"Oh. He said he liked me and tried to give me a kiss."

"Really? What did you do?"

"I left and ran to find you."

"How do you feel?"

"I don't know now. Well, I can't talk to him on my own any more. We only wanted to find out about the family."

"Did you find out anything?"

"It all changed a long time ago, when they got together, and U.S. stopped seeing his family then." We had reached home. I said, "Before we go inside, we won't say anything about things."

"No. Just don't mention Dennis."

"I won't."

A.J. called out, "You are late home again."

Lydia said, "It seems to go a bit longer now."

"Are you walking straight home?" We said yes together. We were asked a few more questions. Dennis wasn't mentioned.

Chapter 80

In my next English lesson, there was more talk about jobs, and the aim was to give us information. I sat listening and thinking, I wonder if my marks are good enough for helping people in another job? At the end of class, my teacher called my name, and asked to have a word with me. The room was empty. I closed the door and she asked, "How are you? Has anything more been said at home?"

"No, but my uncle said he would put his thinking cap on." She smiled at that. "How would you feel about working in an office?"

"Are my marks good enough?" She felt that was a possibility, and would be looking into it further. I thanked her. I was then told to go out to recess before the bell rang.

I was feeling so much better, knowing I was getting help, and glad I was brave enough to talk to her about it. I didn't talk with Betty or Angela until the end of the day. I played netball at lunchtime. Both came running up to me, asking, "What did Miss Jones have to say?" When I told them, Angela asked, "Do you think you can do that?"

"Well, Miss Jones feels that I could. She is going to find out more. I think I'd like to try it."

Betty said, "That's so good. I hope it works for you."

I told Lydia and U.S. how Miss Jones was helping me. They were pleased. Lydia said she did her exam, and thought it was quite easy. There was only one question she found hard. She would find out next week. U.S. said, "It will be just the three of us for dinner tonight and you've got time for a walk." I said, "That's good." He gave me a look. I quickly said, "It's good that we can walk Monty before dinner. Can we go to the woods?"

"Yes, that is all right."

Later, when walking, and talking amongst ourselves, I said, "I'm not going to tell A.J. that the teacher is helping me about a job, unless she asks."

"Well, we won't be doing it tonight, and A.J. is out."

"Maybe we can find out more about the family."

"Yes, that's a good idea." U.S. had made our favourite dinner. I asked, "Can Monty come inside? It is really cold."

"It's not raining."

"But it would be a treat for him and us."

"All right, for a little while, then he will have to go outside." We thanked him and walked over to him to show our thanks, and were told, "There is no need for that. Just get his rug out, and don't get him too excited." Those times were special to us.

After dinner, we asked more questions about the family, but U.S. didn't tell us anything different to what we knew.

I asked, "Why don't you call in to see your mum and dad and sisters?"

"There is no need to."

"But why wouldn't you want to see your family?"

"Well, that's just the way it is." Lydia said, "It's hard for us to understand, because that's what we would want to do." I asked, "They are sort of family to us, aren't they?"

"When you put it like that, yes, they are." Lydia asked, "Can you change it, so that we can meet them?"

"I don't think that's possible."

"Why?" I asked.

"Well, it's because of circumstances."

"Oh. What are those circumstances?" He then said, "Enough. Too many questions, and what you know already is all you need to know."

"Why won't you tell us more?" He was becoming cross with us, and said, "There are some things children don't need to know, and you have to accept that."

"Are we ever going to meet the family?" He didn't know, "And please, no more talking about it." We knew we couldn't say any more, and were told to get ready for bed. We chatted. We really had tried, and just couldn't find out anything more. Then, I remembered we had let Monty in. He was so quiet, and asleep. We knew that if A.J. came home, she would be really cross. It wasn't even raining. We ran downstairs. I said, "Monty is inside still, asleep. When will A.J. be home?" He said, "A bit later. Girls, he hasn't been fed." So, I ran outside to get his dish, and was allowed to put his dinner in it, and took Monty outside and put him on his chain. I asked, "Why does Monty have to be on a chain all the time?"

"Sylvia, you ask too many questions." Lydia said, "He can't get out of our garden." We were told, "Get into bed. It's late." He followed us up to turn the light off, saying, "Goodnight." We chatted for a while, and eventually fell asleep, not hearing A.J. come in.

Schooldays were going well for both of us. It was getting closer to me leaving school. A few weeks had passed. It was the end of a week. I got off the school bus. Lydia ran to me, telling me she had her exam results, and had a letter for A.J. We walked to where U.S. was standing. He asked, "Are you going to tell us?" I said, "You sound happy."

"I am."

"Well, tell us."

"I got really good marks, and can go to the grammar school if I want to, and A.J. won't have to pay for books and stuff. I've got a scholarship."

"Really?" I gave her a big hug. U.S. said, "You have done really well, and I'm happy for you."

I said, "That is so good." We were walking home, talking. I said, "Lots is going to change." I thought, I wonder what I will be doing? She was telling me that a few of her friends got good marks and would be going to the grammar school with her. I was really proud of her. My little sister loved school, and was so clever.

Later, in the front room, when Lydia was asked about her day, she showed A.J. her letter, telling her about her exam results. She was so pleased, and said how proud she was. She would be writing to tell our uncle. When it was my turn, I hadn't heard anything about myself. I just said everything was going well. "You haven't got much longer at school now. You need to get a job."

"I know." In bed, we spent a long time talking about things, and eventually went to sleep.

After a few more days, our English teacher spoke to us, saying that spending time in different employment places would be organised, and I was told I would be going to an office to see what went on there, and to see what I thought of it. I was excited and nervous. Angela and Betty said that was so good. Neither of them needed help from the teacher. Their parents were going to organise work for them.

I told U.S. and Lydia, who were pleased for me. "Hope you will like it," Lydia said.

"So do I." I told A.J. She said, "We will see how you go, if you can do it."

"I hope so." I thought, at least I will be doing a job. Talking with Lydia in bed, she said, "I am sure you will be fine with it."

"I wonder what sort of things I will be doing?" We talked for quite a while before Lydia said, "We'd better try and get to sleep." It took me a long time, thinking about things, but eventually I fell asleep.

In the morning, we said goodbye to each other. Lydia gave me a hug. "Hope it works out well for you, and you like it." I thanked her, then jumped on the bus. I chatted to Betty, who said, "You will be going this morning. How do you feel?"

"A bit nervous."

We walked into class. It was organised for a few of us to go on a bus with another teacher, and we would be taken to various places. The bus took me to an office in town, where I was introduced to a lady. I would be there for the day, she told me. She then took me over to a younger lady, who said I would be with her, and she would show me what happens, and what I would be doing. Phones were ringing and people were walking around. It was busy. I was shown to her desk and sat down on a chair beside her. She explained how to answer the phone and what to say. She had a typewriter on her desk and said she had to type some letters. I could put the letters in the envelopes and put the stamps on. She then showed me how to do some filing, which, I was told, I managed well. The day went fast and I enjoyed it. I was picked up by the teacher and got the bus back to school. There were others on the bus who had been picked up. There was lots of talking, and I was asked how I got on. "I liked it."

"What did you do?" I told them. We arrived back at school, and it was time for me to get my bus home. Betty was on the bus and asked how it went. I told her it was good. "I wonder what happens now?"

"Well, you will find out in English class." After more talking, the bus had arrived. We said our goodbyes. Lydia and U.S. were waiting to meet me. Both asked me, "How did it go?" I replied, "I liked it." Lydia asked, "What did you do?"

"Filing and being shown how to answer the phone. I did it once, and just being shown what goes on in an office. Now, I have to find out what happens next." U.S. said he was pleased for me.

In the front room, when we were asked about our day, I told A.J. all about it. "I am pleased for you, but you need to get a job."

"I know. The teacher will tell me what happens next."

On our own in bed, we talked about the situation. Lydia said, "It's good A.J. said she's pleased with you."

"Yes, that was nice of her, but I must get a job, so I hope I can. I might find out more soon." After some more talking, we got to sleep.

Another few weeks went by, and I hadn't heard any more. After our English lesson, Miss Jones spoke, saying she was still waiting to hear what positions were vacant. There were only a limited number. I decided to see if I could talk with her. When our class was finished, I waited until everyone had left, and asked if I could talk with her. "Yes, just a few minutes, though." I quickly closed the door. She said, "It's not going to be easy, because of where you're living. With distance and transport connections, and there could be a walk as well. It would be an early start. Living in town or close to it would be an advantage." She then asked me, "Do you still want to live at home?"

I was thinking, I hadn't considered not living with A.J. any more. I asked, "Where would I live? I have never thought of not living where I am."

"Well, from what you have told me, I wonder, are you happy to continue living there? These are things you need to think about."

"But, how could I find somewhere else to live?" I was becoming upset. Miss Jones said, "I don't want to upset you, but you need to think about what you want. It's a big decision. I will help you as much as I can. Now, I must go, and you need to go to recess." I walked out of the room to the field, and sat down, thinking, I really don't know what I should do. I must talk with Lydia. How can I do any of this? The rest of the day was hard for me. I had a lot on my mind. It wasn't until I was in the bus that Betty asked me, "What's wrong? You're quiet. What happened with Miss Jones?"

"I hope you don't mind, but I need to talk to my sister on her own first. I've got lots to work out."

"Oh, all right. When I've sorted it out, we will talk." She replied, "That's fine." I couldn't wait to talk to Lydia on her own, and it wasn't until we had changed and were walking Monty, that I could tell her everything Miss Jones said. "That is hard. We knew lots would be changing, but we didn't know it would be like this, with you being able to get a job." We chatted away. I asked, "How would you feel, being on your own with A.J.?"

"I would miss you heaps, but we won't be able to be like this for ever. Miss Jones feels it's going to be difficult for me to get a job unless I'm closer to town. If I live here, I would need to be up really early to get a bus, and I could have quite a walk before I get to work. Well, I could ask her to try and see what happens.'

"But what would happen if you had left school and you didn't have a job?"

"I know -- I would be doing all the stuff around the house, jobs and more jobs. Well, I could ask Miss Jones to try and get me a job soon, before I leave school, and I will know if that works out. If not, she can still help me."

"Yes, do that. It's a good idea."

"All right, I will. I won't mention it to A.J. or U.S. Let's just see what happens."

I felt a bit better after we had talked. We knew our lives would be changing, but decided to make the most of our time together.

The next day, when walking to school, Lydia asked, "Are you going to talk with Miss Jones today, and see what she thinks you should do?"

"Yes, I will, and if I get the job, A.J. might be nicer to me. She should be happy then." We had reached the bus stop. We hugged each other goodbye and I jumped on the bus. Betty ran to me straight away, wanting to know how I was. "Tell me everything."

"All right. I have a lot on my mind."

"I know that. You said that." I told her what Miss Jones had said about me having a job. "I'm going to speak with Miss Jones again in English."

In assembly it was announced that Year 12s would be leaving in four weeks.

I felt quite sad. I really did enjoy my school, and would miss it. I talked to Betty and Angela. They were happy to be leaving, and were looking forward to their jobs. Later in the morning, we had English, and I started thinking, not many more classes. At the end of this lesson, when everyone was leaving, I stayed behind and asked the teacher if I could talk with her. "Yes, very quickly, though. Have you decided already?" I asked if she could help me find a job and still live at home.

"Of course, I will do my best, but it would be a very long day for you."

"I want to try, please."

"It's good you have let me know straight away. I will get back to you when I know something." I thanked her and went out to recess.

I walked onto the field and found Betty and Angela. They wanted to know how I got on. Angela said, "I have heard them saying that you are a teacher's pet, always staying behind to talk to her." I explained. "Well, that's what they're saying." Betty said, "Don't worry about it. They don't know the circumstances."

"Thank you for your understanding. I just hope it works out." Angela started to say, "I'm glad I don't have that problem." Betty jumped on her, "We don't want to hear it. Have some feeling." Then the two of them had a disagreement. The bell went, and we walked back to our next lesson. It was all sorted out by the time they got to class, and they were friends again.

At the end of the day, Lydia and U.S. were waiting when I got off the bus. U.S. said, "We will visit Mrs. Taylor and tell her the news." As we walked and talked, Lydia said, "We will be finishing school in four weeks."

"Yes. It was announced at assembly that we would be too." U.S. said, "Goodness, that isn't long," as he handed me some sweets. I asked, "Has A.J. written to our uncle?"

"Yes. And have you any news to tell?"

"Not yet. I hope, soon."

We had reached Mrs. Taylor's. She was pleased to see us, and still having problems walking. Elizabeth was now walking a few steps, holding onto furniture. We all chatted, telling her about Lydia going to grammar school, and that I hoped to get a job soon. She said, "Any time you want to call in, please do." We said thank you. U.S. and she went into the kitchen, and we could hear the noise of some dishes being done. We played with Elizabeth. She was growing up and could say more words. We loved being with her. U.S. said, "Time to go." We said our goodbyes and gave Elizabeth a hug. They watched us leaving. They waved, calling out, "Bye bye. Come in the holidays, if you want to."

"Thank you." U.S said, "Well, we won't be doing this much longer. I will miss you, girls." Lydia said, "I'll still get on a bus for school, but I will be able to walk by myself."

"We will have to see about that. There will be a lot of changes, that's for sure." We arrived home and got changed. I said, "I can't believe there's only four weeks left." Lydia asked, "Tell me, how did you go with your English teacher?"

"I asked if she could find me a job where I can still live at home. I have to wait and see what happens."

"You're not going to mention it, are you?"

"No. If I'm asked, I will say I haven't heard yet, and that's the truth – I haven't." We raced downstairs and asked if we could walk Monty. "Yes. Please don't take long. A.J. will be home soon." We ran onto the vacant block. A few children were there, and we chatted. We decided to walk to the allotment. Monty was really pulling me very hard. "Let's see if we can hurry, and let him off at the field."

"Hope nobody's about. We'd better not be long. A.J. will be home soon." We ran to the stile. As we climbed over, we could see people walking in the distance. I said, "We will have to wait for them to go." We walked slowly, waiting for them to disappear. It wasn't long. I let Monty off the lead. He raced towards the trees. Lydia said, "We need to get back."

"I know. He so enjoys having a run." I called him, and he came racing back. "That was good. Come on, let's run! We could be in trouble." We got back and put Monty on his chain. A.J. was at the window, knocking. We hurried in.

"We have been waiting for you."

"Sorry. We passed the allotment. There are vegies growing." U.S. said, "I will go tomorrow and have a look." We ran upstairs to wash our hands. Lydia asked, "Have you any homework?"

"No. I don't think I'll get any more now."

"I have only a little."

"That means I'll be the first to go into the front room. That hasn't happened much, so I'm going to try and wait for you to finish."

"I won't be long," as we were running down the stairs.

Dinner was served, and of course, we ate in silence. A.J. said, when we had finished, "Come into the front room as soon as you can." After we had done the dishes, I sat with Lydia while she did her homework, which didn't take very long. We went into the front room together.

"Lydia first. How was your day?"

"Oh, good, thank you. I have some friends who will be going to the grammar school with me."

"As I have said before to Sylvia, it doesn't mean they will be in your class."

"I know that, but they will be on the bus with me, so I will know someone." When I was asked, I said, "I haven't heard anything yet."

"It's taking a long time. You haven't much longer before you will be leaving."

"Yes, I know that. I hope to hear soon." I was told I was being rude in the way I spoke. I said, "Sorry. I didn't mean to be rude."

Later, when we were talking about it in bed, Lydia said, "She really picks on you."

"I know. I wish she wouldn't. I do hope I hear something very soon." After more discussion, we went to sleep. It was a week later, in English, when my teacher asked me to stay behind. She wanted to talk to me.

"There is a job in the town centre, in an office, and you can go along for an interview. See what you think, and what they think of you." I thanked her. I was to go the next day, after school. I asked, "How will I get there?" She offered to take me and bring me home. She was so kind to me. I felt I wanted to give her a hug, but stopped myself. It wasn't the right thing, I thought. After I had thanked her again, she said she would organise it. I went out to recess, and told Betty and Angela, who were pleased for me. Angela asked, "Why would she do that for you?"

"She knows my aunt couldn't do that. I just hope it works out, and I get the job, in the time before I leave."

For the rest of the day, I couldn't concentrate. I could only think about the next day. Later, when I got off the bus, I told Lydia and U.S., who were pleased for me. He said, "That is kind of your teacher. And she will bring you home?"

"Yes. If I get the job, I will have to find out how early the bus leaves." We were walking home and talking. U.S. said, "It will be a long day for you."

"I know. I will have to get used to it, won't I?" Lydia said, "As long as you like doing it."

We had reached home, and ran to get changed. We were allowed to walk Monty, so we went to the woods. Lydia asked, "I wonder how late you will get home?"

"I will find out everything tomorrow, if I get the job." I let Monty off. He was so good now, and would come straight back when called. We talked about everything as we walked home. Neither of us had any homework. In less than two weeks we would be finishing. Lydia said, "I wonder if A.J. has heard from our uncle? I will ask in the front room."

"I wonder what she will say when I tell her my news?" We had reached home. I put Monty on his chain and we went inside. A.J. said, "Dinner is ready to be served. Please hurry up." We ran upstairs. I said, "She doesn't sound very happy."

"Just be careful how you talk."

"I will, thanks." I was asked to say grace. Dinner was on the table. We ate in silence again. As soon as it was over, A.J. got up and went to the front room. We tidied up. I asked U.S., "Is everything all right with A.J.?"

"Nothing for you to worry about."

"Can you please tell us?"

"Just let's hurry and tidy up. You can feed Monty." So that's what I did, always giving him a bit extra, because we hadn't saved anything for him.

We walked into the front room. A.J. asked, "Now, Lydia, how was your day?"

"Good, thank you. Have you heard from our uncle?"

"No. I will let you know when I do." Then I was asked, and said, "Miss Jones, my English teacher, is taking me tomorrow after school to see about a job that is available."

"At last. Something is getting done!"

"Miss Jones is being kind, taking me and bringing me home."

"It's all part of her job."

"I'm not sure what time I will be home."

"Well, we will know where you are." Lydia said, "I hope it works out for you."

"Thank you." A.J. said, "You have very little time left. You need to get this job."

"I will do my best." U. S. said, "That's all anybody can ask for." U.S. hardly ever said anything. A.J. looked surprised. "Now, it's time to get ready for bed. You have a big day tomorrow."

We got up and left the front room. We chatted as we ran up the stairs. "I hope it works out. I will be thinking of you." We hurried and got into bed. A.J. came up to turn off the light. "Straight to sleep – no talking!" She closed the door. Lydia said, "We'd better try and get to sleep." It took me a long time. I kept thinking about things. I was nervous.

Chapter 81

In the morning, as we were leaving for school, A.J. said, "Now, I hope you get this job." U.S. said, "I hope it all works out for you." We said our goodbyes. Lydia was walking to school and I to the bus stop. She asked me, "Do you think you'll like doing this job?"

"I think so. I hope I can get there on time. Once I find out more about it and do it for a while, I should be all right. It's just going to be a bit hard at first."

"I wonder how long a holiday you'll have?"

"I don't know." The bus was there. We hugged each other and she said, "Good luck. You will be fine." I jumped on the bus.

Betty called out, "How did you go?" We chatted till we reached school. We walked to assembly. I saw Angela sitting in front. There were a few notices read out, then we sang our anthem. Angela turned around and saw Betty and me. I said to them, "I'm feeling nervous about going to see about the job." Angela said, "Well, it's like when you did your job experience."

"It's more important. It's the job I need to get. It's not at the same place."

"Well, we will be thinking of you, and you can tell us all about it tomorrow."

It wasn't easy to concentrate. Lunchtime came, and I was asked to play netball. That relaxed me, and I enjoyed it. After lunch, back in class, there was a feeling that school was finishing. We were more at ease. We were just going over work we should have known, doing revision. We were not given any homework. Each class I went to was the same – an easier feeling, just checking what we knew, or didn't, often having questions thrown at us on the spot, to see what we knew.

It was the end of the day, and I was to meet Miss Jones in our classroom. I said goodbye to Betty and Angela. Betty said, "It will be strange that you won't be on the bus to go home." They both said, "Goodbye. See you tomorrow." Miss Jones was waiting for me, and we walked to her car. She drove into the town. I was asking her about the job. "You will find out all about it soon." As we drove along and got closer, we passed a bus stop, where I would have to get off if I was going to the job. There was a bit of a drive. She showed me where the offices were before she parked the car. "You would be walking that distance, and would need to allow time for that." We got out of the car and had a short walk to the office, which was up on the second floor. We climbed the stairs. There was a lift, but Miss Jones said it would be quicker to run up the stairs, so that's what we did. I was introduced to a lady who showed me around the office. My job would be filing. She had heard I was quite good at it, and taking letters to the post box. Also, anything else that was asked of me. I was told I could work my way up, over time, and do a typing course. There were girls sitting typing. I was asked, "How do you feel about that?"

"Good, thank you." She walked me back to where Miss Jones was sitting, and said that I had the job, and would be on trial for four weeks, to see how I got on. I was to start at the beginning of the year. I couldn't believe it. I was so happy. After I said goodbye, we went downstairs. Miss Jones said, "Congratulations. You have done well."

"Oh. Thank you for helping me." I still couldn't believe it. I felt so relieved. "I think I can do it, and the lady said I could do a typing course if I get on all right."

We walked back to the car. Miss Jones said, "Yes. Now, I feel the hardest thing will be getting you to the office on time. It's an 8.30 start. We will find out about the bus timetable, and you will need to allow time for the walk to the office. You finish at 4.30."

"How do I know how long it will take me to walk to the office? Will I find it all right?" We were driving home. Miss Jones said, "Leave it with me. I will let you know. Now, your aunt should be pleased with you. You have a job to go to next year!"

"She will. She has been saying to me that I must get a job. Thank you for helping me. I have been so worried about it."

"Now you can relax. I will be in touch when I have found out all the details." She was now driving up my street. I asked, "Do you want to come in?"

"No, thank you. I won't do that. Well, I'll see you in class." She stopped the car. I got out. "See you tomorrow. Thank you for helping me again."

"You're welcome." She watched me as I opened the gate and walked up the path. She then drove off. I walked around to the back of the house.

Monty was so excited to see me. After giving him some pats, I opened the kitchen door. The room was empty, so I walked to the front room and opened the door. Lydia jumped up to meet me. "How did you go?"

"I got the job!"

"That's great." U.S. said, "Well done." A.J. said, "That is good. It's sorted." She asked for more details. "My teacher will give me those. I will find out all about it, and also when my bus leaves. I have a bit of a walk before I get there.

"Well, you will have to be up and organised really early."

"I know." Lydia asked, "Can I go and get Sylvia's dinner, and make it hot?" U.S. got up, saying he would do that. I followed him into the kitchen and Lydia came too, leaving A.J. alone in the front room. We chatted while U.S. was getting my dinner organised. He then went into the front room, and we were on our own. Lydia was asking me lots of questions. I answered in between mouthfuls. I had finished dinner, and we went into the front room. I asked, "Have you heard from our uncle?" A.J. said, "Not yet."

"There will be a lot of news to tell him." Lydia said, "Lots of changes happening to both of us."

A.J said, "Well, yes. Please go and get ready for bed." We left the room and ran up the stairs, talking.

"I'm so glad you got the job."

"So am I." We could hear A.J. coming up the stairs to turn the light off and say goodnight.

"I'm so tired. I didn't get much sleep last night."

"Let's go to sleep now, then." So that's what we did.

In the morning, we were walking to school. Lydia asked, "I wonder how long a holiday you will have?"

"Miss Jones is going to find out all the details. I hope we hear from our uncle soon." We had reached the bus stop, and said goodbye to each other. Betty called out, "I have saved you a seat. Tell me, how did you go?"

"I got the job." Everybody on the bus said, "Hooray! You got the job!" I started telling her all about it. We had lots to talk about, until we reached school. We walked into assembly. I could see Angela sitting at the front. There were a few announcements, then we sang our anthem. We then walked to class. Angela saw us, and asked, "How did you go about the job?" I told her I got it and told her all about it. "That's great." Her mum had a job for her already, teaching at the same school she was at. She was really looking forward to it, and it was maths, teaching younger children. I replied, "That's good." Betty said her mum was still looking for a position working in a shop. Betty wasn't worried if she didn't get a job straight away. "It will be nice not to have to do anything, and no school anymore."

Well, I thought, it's only me feeling a bit sad to be leaving. I still played netball at lunchtimes, which I really enjoyed. I wasn't looking forward to the unknown for me. I would miss what I had now. A few days passed, before Miss Jones asked me to stay behind. She gave me a bus timetable and the number of the stop to get off. Then there was the walk to the office. She had written it down for me, telling me how long I would need to allow. I thanked her, and she said she would find out how I went. She hoped it would all work out for me. "It is a really early start."

"I will do my best and will have to get used to getting up early." "It will take you a little time to get into a routine." I thanked her again.

"I will hear how you get on."

We only had one week of school left after this weekend. It was Friday. Betty said, "See you at youth group."

"Yes, I am looking forward to it." We continued chatting. We were getting off the bus. U.S. and Lydia were standing at the stop. Betty called out to Lydia, "See you tonight at youth group."

"Oh yes. See you then." We walked home. Lydia said, "I am finishing school next week."

"Yes, so will I. One week left, and I won't be going to school anymore. I feel a bit sad."

U.S. said, "It's hard to believe. You both have big things happening to you."

We had reached home, and changed out of our uniforms. We were allowed to walk Monty. We ran to the woods. I let Monty off the lead. He had a great time. We talked about how things were going to change. Lydia was looking forward to going to the grammar school with her friends. I wasn't sure how I felt about working. "I hope A.J. has heard from our uncle and we get to see him. You call Monty. See if he comes back for you."

"Oh, all right," so she did. Monty came running straight back. We both gave him pats.

"See how good he is? He comes straight back when he is called. We must ask U.S., does he take Monty off the lead, and does he come back for him?" We hurried home. A.J. was in the kitchen. We quickly put Monty on his chain and went inside. "Dinner is ready." We ran straight up the stairs and washed our hands. "I wish we could find out now if A.J. has had a letter from our uncle."

"Well, we'll have to wait till after youth group, when we go into the front room." Dinner was served, and of course, we ate in silence.

We helped with the dishes. I was allowed to give Monty his dinner. No titbits tonight. I gave him a bit extra, and took it out to him.

It was time to leave for youth group. We said goodbye. A.J. told us to come straight home. As we were walking to the hall, we could see a lot of children outside, talking. It was our breakup, our last youth group for the year, and more turned up, because of that. There were games organised, and we had a speaker. There was a lovely supper. Betty was already there. We could see Dennis with his friends. He came over and spoke to us, asking what was happening next year. We told him Lydia was going to grammar school. He said, "Oh, you're a clever one."

"I have a job in town."

It wasn't long before we were asked to be silent, and were told what the program was. We had a lovely night and nice things to eat that we didn't have at home. It finished later than usual. We said our goodbyes to Betty. Her mum picked her up. We were walking home, when Dennis called out to us. He was riding his bike with his friends. "See you at chapel." We said yes. We got home and went into the front room. A.J. said, "You are late. You were told to come straight home." I whispered, "We knew she would say that. It's because it was our last night, and there were extra activities." Lydia said, "We did come straight home."

"Very well then. Sit down. I have something to tell you. I have a letter from your uncle, and he will be making a quick visit when school finishes." We asked, "How long, and will we be going to his house?"

"No. It is a quick stopover, and he will be going overseas again."

"Oh," I was disappointed. Lydia said, "That's a shame. It's only for a short time."

"I was hoping we could stay with him again."

"He is a busy man, and you will see him in the holidays. Now, I think it is time for bed. It is late, and you will have your jobs to do in the morning, and then when I get home, we will clean the little chapel." We said goodnight to U.S. and ran upstairs. Lydia said, "It's good that we will see Uncle."

"But we are disappointed that we're not going to his house." We talked for a long time in bed.

Chapter 82

It was my last week at school. I felt sad. It was announced at assembly that Year 12s would be leaving at the end of the week. We would be given a school report to take home. I had made up my mind that I wanted to enjoy my last few days. Most girls I talked to were happy to be leaving and had jobs to go to. At each recess, we talked about the jobs different ones had, and said we might get to see each other sometime. Angela said, "I will be at another school, teaching. It is on the other side of town, so I don't think I'll see you."

"Well, you never know," I said. "It would be nice to find out how you like it."

"Oh. I will like it. I am really looking forward to it. Besides, my mum is working at the same school, in the senior classes. When we get our reports, mine will be the best, because I've had the top marks in most of my subjects." That's true, I thought. She knew just about everything, and would let you know it – confidence plus. I thanked her for helping me. I hoped we would see each other sometime. She said, "I hope you get on well and like your job."

"Thanks." Betty said, "We can get together in the holidays, and I will see you at chapel and youth group." Angela said, "Hope you find work soon." Betty said, "Oh, I don't mind. Something will turn up. I'm in no rush."

"That's not the right attitude." She was Little Goody Two Shoes. Then it got a bit heated between them, but it never lasted long, and they were friends again in no time. I thought, I will miss these disagreements and discussions.

Our last day came. I was walking with Lydia to school. "This is it," I said.

"It doesn't feel any different to any other day."

"No, but it is. I won't be catching the bus to school anymore, and you won't be going to that school again." I said, "I will really miss school."

"Yes, it's for ever for you. Have a fun day."

"Thank you. You too." We said our goodbyes. Betty called out from the bus, "I have a seat in the front for you." We chatted some more. I said, "We will get our reports to take home." Betty said, "Yes. Mine will say "You could try better."

"I'm not sure what mine will say. We will soon find out." We talked more. "Of course, Angela's will only say good things."

When we arrived at school, and were at assembly, those who were leaving were asked to come onto the stage. The headmaster gave his little speech that we had heard before, for those who were going out into the world to remember their school grounding. He wished us every success in what we did with our lives. We were then asked to leave the stage. He called out our names one at a time, and everybody clapped.

Back in class, the teacher asked if anybody had any questions. That was how we spent most of our last day – questions and answers. Lunchtime was my last game of netball. We said our goodbyes, hoping to see each other around. In the afternoon, back in class, we were handed our reports. They were in an envelope, all sealed up. We were disappointed, as we couldn't read them. Angela said, "I'm not worried. I know mine will be good. I was hoping to read it out to you."

"I wish we could have a look and see what it says." The bell rang. It was time to go home. My schooldays were over. There were goodbyes and hugs. Some were happy – I was sad. Betty and I caught the bus home. It was very noisy. There was lots of chatter and calling out, and happiness: "No more school!"

I got off the bus for the last time. U.S. and Lydia were waiting. Betty called out, "I will see you around. Enjoy the holidays." U.S. had a large bag of sweets. "Let's visit Mrs. Taylor and let her know you have now left school. You might be able to visit in the holidays." We were chatting about our last day. Lydia, like me, felt a bit sad to be leaving that school. We were comparing what our last day was like. U.S. was holding the sweets, and helping us eat them. "I will miss this,"

"This has been our little secret, and you have enjoyed it. Everything has an ending, and you both will have a new beginning, so look forward to that." I tried to give him a hug. He just stepped away, and could never respond. I said, "I hadn't thought of it like that," and he went on to say, "There is sadness and there is joy." Lydia said, "You are right, but at the moment, we feel sad to be leaving what we have done and enjoyed for a long time." U.S. said, "I do understand that." We had now reached Mrs.

Taylor's. I pressed the bell. It was a while before the door opened. Mrs. Taylor was pleased to see us. I said, "I have left school now."

"Goodness me. Come in." Elizabeth came to meet us, walking two or three steps before she fell down again. We gave her a hug, each of us holding her hand and walking with her. She loved that. We all chatted, telling Mrs. Taylor our news, that Lydia was going to the grammar school and that I had a job. She was happy for us and asked if we could visit her in the holidays. Then U.S. and she went into the kitchen, and we could hear dishes being done. After a while, we said our goodbyes. We would try and come in the holidays.

Chapter 83

At home, after we changed our clothes, I said, "No more school uniform for me! I will need clothes for work now. I won't be wearing this uniform again." We were allowed to walk Monty, who was excited. We walked past the allotments, over the stile into the field. A few people were walking. We sat on the grass, talking, holding Monty tight. He wanted to get going. After a little while, nobody was about. I let Monty off. We walked to the trees, where Monty had run to. We had lots to talk about. I had three weeks' holiday before I started my job, and Lydia had a lot longer. I said, "You might have to walk Monty on your own sometimes. Not sure how late home I'll be, so you call him and see. He needs to come back to you." She agreed. "But I won't always let him off."

"Oh. He will miss that." After more talking, we said we were going to mention it to U.S. "Call him and see if he comes running back," and she did. He came running straight back. "Now you can hold the lead on the way home. You can do it if I'm not around."

"I will miss you."

"So will I, but we will check with U.S. that you can do it by yourself."

After dinner, when we were helping with the dishes, and A.J. was in the front room, I asked U.S., "If I'm not home, may Lydia take Moty for a walk on her own?"

"Yes, but only a shorter walk." Then I asked, "Are you still letting Monty off the lead for a run when you walk him?"

"Yes. He is very good for me." Lydia said, "He's good for me too."

"We will have to see how things work out, with the changes to you both. Remember, this is our little secret, what we do." We agreed, "Yes."

We all went into the front room together. That hardly ever happened. No homework! A.J. was reading our reports. She looked up. "All finished?" We said yes.

"Lydia, how was your day at school?"

"I will miss that school."

"You have an outstanding report." Lydia asked if she could read it.

"Yes. I will give it to you in a little while. Sylvia, I have read your report. It shows you have improved, so that's something, and you have a job to go to." I was asked about my day. "Well, it was sad for me, saying goodbye to school and friends."

"You are no longer a schoolgirl. You are an adult."

"Because I have left school?'

"Yes, and you need to behave like one."

"I will try. When is our uncle coming?"

"He will be here next week, and will be staying in town. There is a lot to talk about and sort out with you both. I think an early night for you. I will be up shortly to turn off the light." We said goodnight to U.S. and ran upstairs.

In bed, we talked about leaving school and how sad we were. I said, "Just because I have left school, I'm now an adult. I only took my uniform off a few hours ago. How can that change me into an adult?"

"I know what she means. A.J. is hard on you, though. You are a young lady, and you can still be like you are, I think. We will talk with our uncle when we see him, and see what he says." After more talking, A.J. came upstairs to turn off the light and say goodnight.

Saturday mornings were good. A.J. went to her job. We never did find out what she did, or where she went. We could get up late, and U.S. often made us breakfast, and sometimes he would sit with us and have a cuppa, and we would all chat. We still had our jobs to do, and would rush through them. Then we would take Monty walking, which we enjoyed, or play on the vacant block with those who were there. We still did this, even though I had left school. Sundays were more difficult for me. I didn't mind going to the morning service, but the evening service I really didn't want to attend. I asked if I could stay at home, and was told, "Unless you're sick, you will attend." I felt I was in some ways treated like a child, whereas in others, like a grown up. It was difficult and confusing for me. My relationship with A.J. was becoming even more strained. I was counting the days until Uncle would arrive. I really needed to talk to him. We both wished we could stay with him again.

At last, the day arrived when Uncle would visit. It was early morning. We were so excited. After breakfast, we were told we could walk Monty. "When you get back, Uncle will be here. I need to speak with him and U.S. alone." We were told we could stay away for an hour. We ran to our favourite place, the woods. I said, "I hope we can talk with him on our own. I wonder where we can go to do that?"

"Maybe he will take us to town."

"That would be nice." We talked between ourselves. I had a watch now, and felt important. We would be checking it every so often, to know when we were allowed to come back home. Sometimes, it seemed that it didn't move, and it was hard to wait. Eventually, it was time to go home. We ran back quickly and put Monty on his chain. We went inside, through the kitchen. Nobody was there. We opened the door of the front room. Our uncle was sitting down, talking with A.J. We ran to him and gave him a hug. He said, "Hello, girls. That's nice. We are nearly finished here." A.J. said, "That outburst wasn't called for." Our uncle replied, "Oh. I think we can make an exception under the circumstances. I have been hearing and seeing your school reports. Lydia, you have really outshone yourself, and winning a scholarship will certainly help with fees at the grammar school. Sylvia, congratulations on your school report, which shows improvement. You have done well to get a job." We both said, "Thank you."

"We will only be a few minutes, and then we will catch the bus and go into town."

"That will be good," we both said. "Please go to your room." A.J. said, "And we will call you when we are finished." Uncle said, "See you soon." We left the room, and ran upstairs. I said, "I'm glad our uncle is taking us into town."

"So am I." We sat on the bed and wondered what they were saying about us. "Uncle is pleased with you too," Lydia said. "Yes. That was nice of him, saying congratulations to me, and you have done so well to win a scholarship."

"I don't find it hard, and I'm glad I have some friends coming with me."

It was a while before we were called to come down. Uncle said, "We will leave now, to get the bus, and will go out for dinner." We said goodbye and ran down the path. Uncle said, "We have time to catch the bus. I just want to leave so we can talk." We were each holding his hand. Uncle said, "Slow down! Sorry, this is a quick visit. You were told I'm going overseas soon." I asked, "When are you coming back?"

"That hasn't been decided." We were chatting. As we walked, we could see the bus coming, and hurried. Uncle said, "It's early. We will have to stay at the shops until it's time to leave." He asked Lydia, "How are you getting on with A.J. and U.S.?"

"All right. I don't mind her, and U.S. is nice on his own. Otherwise, he doesn't say much. He just agrees with A.J. She is nicer to me than to Sylvia."

"You have said that before." We were now on the bus. There were only two people in there. He said, "We will talk about things when we are off the bus. I thought we could go to the park and have a walk, and find a seat and talk about things."

"That sounds good," I said. He started telling us about his travels. He would go home for a short while, and then fly out from London. It was so good being with him. We got off the bus and walked to the park. We had a look in the castle. He hadn't been there before. We told him that U.S. used to be a gardener in the grounds. There were lovely roses in bloom. We found a seat, and I was asked how I felt about things. "Well, I've been told I'm an adult now, but I only took my school uniform off a little while before then, and I don't feel any different." He said, "A.J. is right. You are no longer a schoolgirl." Lydia said, "Sylvia is a young lady." He laughed. "Yes, that is true, but she is also an adult. You are growing up and you need to show that as a person."

"How can I do that? A.J. makes the decisions. What can I do if I don't want to?"

"It is a difficult situation, and not an easy one, but maybe you can ask in a way that shows how you feel, without upsetting her." Then he asked me about my job, and heard that I would have to be up really early, because of the distance to work. "Yes, that is true, but I will have to get used to it, won't I?"

"I hope you won't be putting too much pressure on yourself." Lydia said, "We still want to stay together. If it works out, it will be good."

"Yes, I can understand that, but there is going to be a time when you will have to go your separate ways. You can still see each other and meet, but you won't be living together."

"I know. My teacher thought it was too far for me, but I want to try it, and anyway, where would I live? How would I manage on my own?"

"Yes. These are hard decisions." After asking when I was starting work, Uncle said he was going to find out from A.J. how I was going. I told him my teacher was going to inquire how I was going too, and had offered to find me somewhere to live, but I wanted to try and see if I could do it. I said, "I didn't tell A.J. any of this."

"I understand, as long as you both realise there will be a time when you won't be living together. Lydia, with more schooling, it will be a while before you move out, but you, Sylvia, have a choice. You need to be happy in work and home life. Where is the job?" I told him the street and the number of the bus stop where I had to get off. Then I had to walk.

"Well, how about we go on the bus and have a look where it is?"

"Oh, that would be good, and you can see what you think. I will show you the building where I will be working." Lydia said, "And I will get to see it too,"

"Let's go now. We will have time, and then we will find a place to eat." We had quite a walk before we caught the right bus. We got off at the right number bus stop. Then we started walking. Uncle said, "Look at your watch, and we will time it." That's what we did. After a while, I could see the building. It took nearly fifteen minutes. He said, "That's not too bad. How do you feel about it?"

"I can do that. It's just that it is such an early start."

"I will work out what time you need to catch the bus. There is a lot to work out, and how much A.J. will help you with breakfast and lunch. You might be expected to do it all, or maybe A.J. will still make your lunch. You may have to do that too." I hadn't thought of that. "Do you think A.J. won't make my breakfast?"

"I will have a talk with her about how she feels, and what she will do or not do. First, we need to work out what time you need to be up by."

"Thank you. A.J. hasn't asked me anything about my job or how I will get there."

"You will need to try harder to get on with her, as you will need her help. You are now an adult, and a working one, and as such, she might see that you need to fend for yourself. That will make it difficult for you." Lydia asked, "Why would she be like that?"

"Well, A.J. doesn't have to help, now that Sylvia is working. She is no longer a child, and that is the law. She will be expected to give A.J. part of her wages she earns, for food and board."

"That seems unfair. Just because I'm working, she won't do anything for me." We were on the bus, which was empty now. I asked, "How will I manage?"

"I will find out what she is prepared to do, and her feelings about things. I am pleased I am here and am able to see your situation. I will let you know what she is thinking, and what she is prepared to do." I said thank you. "I didn't know it would be like that. I thought A.J. would still be doing everything, like she does. It's hard for me to understand."

"A.J. can make things easier or harder for you. That's why I'm saying, try and get on with her, if you really want to continue as you are."

"I really don't like her. I can't take to her. I don't know how I can get on with her better, when she is how she is with me." Lydia said, "She has always been hard on Sylvia." We were getting off the bus now. We walked and talked, looking for a place to have dinner. Uncle stopped outside a place that looked as if it would cater for us. There were not many people inside. It had small, round tables. He asked for a table, which we got. I told him about my friend Betty, who was in no rush for a job, and her mum was going to find her a job in a shop. He said, "They have different circumstances."

"Yes, but the main one is, they have a mum."

"That is true. It makes a big difference."

"I remember you telling us when we first met A.J., that she would be like a mum to us, but she hasn't really." Lydia said, "They have looked after us."

"Yes, but not with love. We have never been given any, and we are not allowed to show it."

"That is true." Uncle said, "Some people are unable to show or feel love."

"When I first saw A.J., I remember I felt she wasn't like a mum, because I still remember my mum, and thought she was just another lady to look after us."

"Both A.J. and U.S. have done a good job bringing you up, under the circumstances, and you both know what love is, as you have had the closeness of each other, through what you have experienced. Now, let's choose what you would like to eat."

After our dinner, which we enjoyed, there was more talking. Uncle said it was time to go back. He was going to talk to A.J., and would see us again the next day for a short time before he had to leave. We really enjoyed our time with him. We said our goodbyes and hugged him. He spoke briefly with A.J. and left. He said, "I'll see you all tomorrow."

In bed, we talked about our day. I said, "I'm glad Uncle saw where I'll be working, and will find out things for me from A.J. I had no idea how different things would be." Lydia said, "Yes, you really need to try and get on with her a bit better."

"I will. It's just not easy for me."

"We'd better go to sleep now."

In the morning, after breakfast, A.J. said, "Your uncle will be here shortly. We have lots to discuss, so no interruptions."

"Can we take Monty for a walk?"

"Yes, and I will tell you when we have finished."

"How long can we be? What happens if we get back, and you are still talking?"

"Just wait, and I will let you know when we are finished." We said yes, and ran up the stairs to put our coats on. We grabbed the lead, put Monty on, and ran down the garden. U.S. was in his greenhouse. He called out, "Where are you off to?" We told him Uncle would be here for a talk soon, and we needed to stay away till A.J. called us. U.S. said, "Oh, I had better go inside now. See you later, girls."

A few children on the vacant lot called out to us. We ran and had a play. Then we saw Uncle walking to our house. We ran to him and said, "We have been told to stay away for about an hour."

"Yes, it will take that long, or even longer, and I will then take you back into town for lunch." We said together, "That will be so good. Thank you."

"Now, I had better go inside. See you soon." We ran to the woods, taking it in turns to hold Monty. We were looking forward to lunch. I said, "I wonder how Uncle will get on, and if A.J. will be helpful? I hope so." We did a longer walk before going into the woods. I checked my watch. It was nearly time to go back. Lydia said, "It won't matter if we're away longer, will it?"

"But we don't want to keep Uncle waiting."

"You're right. We will walk back now. It will be nice seeing him alone again and going out for lunch."

We reached home, put Monty on his chain, and got him some fresh water. There was nobody in the kitchen, so I gave him something to eat. We walked past the front room. We could hear them talking. We sat at the top of the stairs and tried to listen, but really couldn't hear what was being said. We sat on the bed and played a game. I looked at my watch and said, "They should be finished now."

"We will just have to stay here till A.J. calls us. Hope it works out well for you."

"So do I."

After we had talked some more, we could hear the door open, and listened. Uncle was saying, "I'll take the girls into town again for some lunch." A.J. said, "There is no need to. I can make something to eat here." We looked at each other. We wanted to go into town. Uncle said, "I told the girls that we would do that and I could have some more time with them. Thank you, that is kind of you." I jumped off the bed and stood up. Lydia grabbed me. "Just sit here till she calls us!" We sat on the bed again and heard them go into the kitchen. A.J. said, "Monty is back. They can't be far away." She called out, "Are you in your room, girls?" Lydia answered, "We are playing a game."

"You can come down now." We said thank you and quickly put our game away. We ran downstairs. A.J. said, "Your uncle is taking you out for lunch."

Thank you." We went to Uncle and each held his hand. I asked, "Can we leave now?" It didn't happen straight away. There was more talking. We were taking Uncle to the front door, and said, "Goodbye." Uncle said, "You know, that's a bit rude."

"How did your talk go?"

"We will talk soon." We were still walking to the bus. He said, "Mostly, well, but there are changes that you will need to accept, and not make a fuss about. You will need to adjust. I will be in contact to find out how it is all working out."

We were on the bus. There were lots of people about. He said, "I think it might be a good idea to go to the gardens again, and find a seat and talk. It will be too difficult in the restaurant. We'll have lunch after our talk." That's what we did. Even in the gardens, there were lots of people – it was a sunny day. We eventually found an empty seat, then Uncle told us what was going to happen. "You will need clothes for work. A.J. will take you shopping. We worked out what time you need to be up by. It seems U.S. is an early riser, and is happy to make your breakfast, and he will help you after dinner to make lunch for you to take to work the next day." I said, "That's really nice of him."

"Yes, it is. You need to be responsible, to get up and dressed in time for work, to catch the 7.30 bus. If you miss that, you will be late for work." I thanked him for finding that out for me. He said, "You still need to help with jobs around the house, and at weekends. You will need to give A.J. something towards your board."

"What is board?"

"It is money for living with A.J. We will work out how much. The rest you will save, and you will need to look after yourself." I had not realised how much would be changing with me. "You are no longer at school. It is all different now, as you will be earning money, and anything you need you will spend out of your wages. You will have money for the bus, and the rest you can save. How do you feel about that?"

"All right. I didn't know it was going to be like that. I will get used to it, won't I?"

"You will. You are now a working girl." Lydia said, "A young lady." He said, "Yes, that too."

"It's a lot to take in suddenly. I feel I'm a different person."

"I can understand that. It will take you a while to get into a routine. Just try and get on better with A.J."

"I will do my best." He gave me a hug. "Let's go and find somewhere to have some lunch."

We walked into town. It was crowded. We managed to find a little restaurant and went inside. They had little round tables. We sat down and ordered our lunch. Uncle spoiled us. We had a lovely lunch. We were all hungry. We so enjoyed our time together. We caught the bus home. He said, "I will keep in touch, to find out how you are getting on." I asked, "Can you send me a letter, so I can write back?"

"Yes, I will try and do that, and Lydia can write a few lines to tell me how she's getting on. I am proud of you, winning that scholarship. It will certainly help with the school fees." Lydia said, "I didn't find the work hard, and loved school."

"That might change. It could become more difficult now." We were walking home. He said he wouldn't be able to stay, and would have to leave almost at once. We thanked him again. A.J. opened the door. Lydia said, "We've had a lovely time." I said, "Yes, and a lovely lunch."

"That's good. Come inside." Uncle said, "I really can't stay, or I will miss my plane." After a bit more talking at the door, he said goodbye to us and whispered to me, "Try hard." I asked, "Can we walk to the bus stop and see Uncle off?" Before A.J. could answer, Uncle said, "That would be nice." So, we both held his hands and started walking back to the bus stop, saying we wished he could stay longer. He told me, "Enjoy the rest of your holidays, before you start work. I hope you will like your job. And Lydia, you have lots of holidays. Enjoy your new school." We said goodbye to Uncle as he got on the bus. We waved till it was out of sight.

"Well, lots of changes for me."

"Yes. We must make the most of our time together, as you will be working, and I will still be on holiday."

"I agree. I guess we will have jobs to do now."

"Let's see how A.J. is with us. Don't forget to try to be better with her." I gave her a hug. "Yes, I will try harder."

"It will be better for you. It will help you."

"I know you are right."

Chapter 84

The time went fast in those weeks I had before starting work. A.J. took me shopping for work clothes. Lydia came, and said I looked so grown up now. A.J. agreed, saying, "You need to act grown up now."

"I will try." I also needed shoes and another haircut, which I really didn't want. I decided not to make a fuss, but just go along with it. I was really trying not to have any disagreements with her. We were now on our own, "You're doing really well. I think A.J. was surprised you didn't answer back."

"I'm just trying to go along with things."

It was Sunday night, and we were walking home from chapel. "I'm starting my job tomorrow."

"How do you feel?"

"I'll have to get up really early, and it's tomorrow. It's hard to believe."

"Yes, you will need to get your clothes out ready, and be organised, and get to sleep as soon as you get to bed. No chatting." We had reached home. A.J. said, "Now, you need to organise your clothes and get ready for bed." I said yes, and asked U.S., "Are you going to wake me up?"

"Yes. I will have breakfast ready for you."

"Thank you." I said goodnight to him. A.J. said, "I will be up shortly." Lydia said, "That's good, U.S. will wake you." We quickly got ready for bed. "I hope you will get on well with your jobs, and get there on time. I might still be asleep when you leave."

"Thanks. I won't wake you." We could hear A.J. coming up the stairs to say goodnight.

"I hope you get on well with your job."

"Thank you."

"Sylvia, please don't wake Lydia, and I don't need to be woken up that early, either."

"I will be as quiet as I can."

"Goodnight," and she turned off the light. I whispered, "I am going to try and get to sleep."

"Yes, you should, and you can tell me all about it when you get home." We said goodnight.

U.S. woke me. I found it difficult to get up, and knew I had to hurry. This is my first day working, I thought. Lydia was sound asleep. I took my clothes to the bathroom and got dressed. I went downstairs to the kitchen. U.S. was stirring my porridge. "Sit down. I will serve it out. I'm going to have some with you." He sat down.

"Thank you."

"I'll say grace." We ate breakfast together. He handed me my lunchbox. He had made my lunch the night before. "Oh, thank you for doing that. Am I doing all right for time?"

"Yes, you're doing well. Try to be quiet when you go to the bathroom."

"Yes, I will." I walked upstairs quickly and checked on Lydia, who was still sound asleep, and went to the bathroom. I was back down after a short time in the kitchen. "Goodbye. I'd better go, hadn't I?"

"Yes. Hope you get on well." He came with me to the front door and opened it. "Goodbye. Go well," and quietly closed the door behind me. I hurried down the path, opening the gate and closing it quietly. I ran to the bus stop, and got there before the bus. There was only one person there. I seemed to be on it for a long time. Looking out of the window, I knew what stop I needed to get off at. My stop came at last, and I got off. Now the walk. I looked at my watch and thought, I am going to have to hurry, so I did. It seemed a long time before I could see the building. I went up the stairs. I was out of breath. I looked at my watch – I had five minutes to spare. A lady walked towards me and said, "I'm Margaret. We are expecting you." She took me to a desk and said, "You have done well. You are on time. I'll show you what needs to be done." There was a big pile of folders on the desk that needed filing. She showed me where the cabinet was.

More people were coming into the office. Margaret said, "I'll introduce you." I didn't remember their names, only the girl I would be working with, whose name was Sarah. It was her desk I was standing at. Margaret said, "I'll see you later." Sarah said, "Tell me about yourself. Why do you want to work here?" Oh, I thought, I didn't expect that. I chatted with her, telling her how I got the job, and felt I could do it. "As long as you can file these folders. We need to get them out quickly and put them away correctly."

"I was told I did a good job when I did work experience."

"That's good. We had better make a start. Now, all these folders need to be put away." She showed me where they went.

"I will be typing and answering the phone, and will write down the number of the folder I need. You will go and get it out for me. Now, this pile needs to be put away." Phones were ringing and typewriters were going. It was noisy. I had a little trolley to put the folders on, and would then walk to the other side of the room and file them.

Time went quickly for me. I was kept busy putting away and getting out what was needed. Lunchtime came at last, and there was a room that people went to, where there were tables and chairs. I took my lunchbox. I had half an hour, and could make a drink if I wanted one. I was glad to sit down. More people came in and told me their names. The room became crowded and there was lots of chatter. It was time for me to go back. Sarah said, "I'm going to lunch now." There was another piece of paper with more numbers on it – more files to get out. I was kept busy all day, and when it was time for me to go home, I was glad. "See you tomorrow," Sarah said.

"Goodbye." I had this walk to do before I could catch the bus. I finally reached the bus stop, and had a wait before it came. I was so glad when I saw it coming, and I could sit down on my way home. I was really tired. I will have to get used to it, I thought. I looked out of the window, watching the numbers of the bus stops. At last, I was at the right stop, and jumped off to walk home. I looked at my watch. It was nearly 5.30. It had taken me nearly an hour. I went in by the side gate. Monty was on his chain, making lots of noises. I walked over to him and gave him pats. A.J. was at the window. Lydia came out the door and gave me a hug. "How was it?"

"Come inside," A.J. called, which we did. I sat down. U.S. asked, "Your first day working. What was it like?"

"I'm so tired." A.J. said, "That is something you will have to get used to. Now, please go upstairs and get ready for dinner, and we will talk in the front room." Lydia came up with me, chatting. "I walked Monty – only a short one. Are you all right? Did you like it? You do look tired."

"I'm sorry. Let's talk after dinner. I hope I will feel better then." We ate in silence. I was really hungry. A.J. went into the front room, and I was going to help with the dishes. Lydia said, "Sit down. I can do this." U.S. said, "It's been a big day for you."

"Yes, it has."

"You can tell us all about it in the front room."

It wasn't long before we all went together into the front room. A.J. said, "Well, Sylvia, you'd better tell us about your day." So, I went through it all from the beginning. A.J. asked, "How do you think you went?"

"All right. When I left, Sarah said I had done well. It was a busy day. Mondays usually are."

"Well, that's good to hear. You will get used to working. It does take time." Lydia talked about her day. She had fun with friends, and did walk Monty, who was good. "I missed you, and I think he did. He kept looking around, waiting for you to come."

"Oh. I won't be able to walk Monty until the weekend." U.S. said, "We'll see what we can organise." A.J. said, "I think an early night is what you need."

"Yes. Thank you," and said goodnight to U.S. Lydia came upstairs with me. She kept asking me, "Are you all right?"

"Yes. Sorry, I'm so tired. We will talk tomorrow." I jumped into bed and was asleep in no time. That was my first day of work. It took me the whole week to get used to doing what I did. I was so glad when Friday night came. We walked Monty and went to the woods. I felt so happy, and we sat on the grass. Lydia and I had our first big discussion about how I felt in my job. I said, "It's all right, but I'm finding it a bit boring."

"Well, they did say you can work your way up."

"Yes. I don't know how long that takes. I never sit, only for lunch and on the bus."

"That would be a bit hard, when you're not used to doing that."

"But I will have to, won't I? And it's only my first week."

"It will take time for you, and I hope you get to like it."

"So do I. Everybody is busy. I'm glad I finish at 4.30. I'm the first to leave." After more chatting, we walked home. I said, "I'm glad tomorrow is Saturday, and we don't have to be up early." It was the best day for both of us, and we could relax, not having to be up at a set time.

The weekend went so fast for me, and it seemed no time before I was back at my job. I made the most of my time on the bus, sitting and looking out of the window, relaxing a bit more, knowing that if I walked fast, I would not be late. I knew now what was expected of me, and I wasn't so nervous. U.S. had made my lunch, which I enjoyed. I was getting into a routine by the end of the second week, and was not quite so tired. Margaret came to the desk and said I was doing well, and handed me an envelope which had money in it. It was my pay for working the two weeks. I thought, I know our uncle said that after working for two weeks I would be paid, and I need to give it to A.J., and she will take out some for my board. She will also put some in an account for me. I felt important – I had money. I wondered how much would I get for myself?

I must ask when I give It to A.J. It feels heavy. I will look at it when I get home, before I give it her.

I got off the bus and was walking home. I could hear children's voices as they played on the vacant block. Then I saw Lydia walking towards me with Monty. That's nice, I thought. Monty was so excited to see me. I grabbed the lead and held it till we got home. Lydia said, "I wanted to tell you, A.J. is out at one of her meetings, and it will only be the three of us."

"That's good." She told me she now had a school uniform and books ready, and would be starting school next week. She was looking forward to it.

We hurried home. I told her, "I got paid today, and I want to have a look to see how much it is, before I give it to A.J."

"That's a good idea." We put Monty on his chain and ran inside. U.S. asked, "How are you? Dinner won't be long." We ran upstairs. I opened the envelope on the bed, and the money fell out. There were eight silver two-shilling pieces and a piece of paper telling me how many hours I had worked, and the total. Lydia asked, "Are you going to keep any?"

"I'll have to show A.J., and she will know if I do. It will be on the piece of paper." I put it back in the envelope. Lydia helped me. She picked a coin up and said, "It's quite heavy."

"I will show it to U.S." I quickly got changed, and we went down to the kitchen. U.S. said, "Dinner is ready. I was about to call you." He started serving it out. I was really hungry, but managed to save some meat for Monty. Lydia was asked to say grace, and we did eat in silence. As soon as we had finished, I said, "Thank you. I really enjoyed my dinner."

"It is nice of you to say that. Let's hurry and get these dishes done. I want to hear all about your day in the front room." I fed Monty, and added the piece of meat. I asked, "What time will A.J. be home?"

"It will be quite late." I thought, that's good. It wasn't long before we were in the front room. I told him about my day.

"I'm getting used to it, but I can't say I enjoy it. It's all right."

"With time, you might enjoy it, and progress with other things."

"I wonder how long that will be? I got paid today," and showed him the envelope. I took out the shilling coins again.

"That is good. Your first wage!"

"But I don't understand. Is it very much?"

"It's quite good for your age and the job you're doing. A.J. will put some in an account for you each week, and it will grow."

"Yes, I know that, but will she take some out for the food I eat, and living here?"

"Yes. It was worked out with your uncle and A.J., so it will be taken care of." He couldn't tell me how much, or any details. We talked about Lydia starting at the grammar school the next Monday.

"You will have to be organised, although you don't need to be up as early as Sylvia." Lydia said, "You didn't wake me when you left. That's good. A.J. was pleased that she wasn't woken either." U.S. said, "So we did well, Sylvia." I thanked him for helping me, and said I did enjoy the lunches that he made. Those times were relaxed, talking without A.J. around.

"We should try and see Mrs. Taylor tomorrow, after you get your jobs done. She will be interested to hear about your job." We agreed. It was time to get ready for bed. He would be up shortly. We ran upstairs, saying how nice it was without A.J. around. It wasn't long before U.S. came to turn the light off, saying goodnight. We chatted, then I said, "Let's get to sleep. I'm really tired. Hooray. Tomorrow is Saturday, our favourite day." We said goodnight, and we didn't hear A.J. come home.

We woke up late, and A.J. had already left. In the kitchen, U.S. was having a cuppa. He looked up. "I'll make your breakfast – hot toast and dripping. How does that sound?"

"That would be good, thank you," we said together. "Now I have a message from A.J." We looked at each other. "To do your jobs well and be organised, and ready to clean the chapel when she gets home."

"Oh. That's what we always do."

"When you have done those jobs, we can walk to Mrs. Taylor's, and I will come with you to see if she needs any help."

We enjoyed our breakfast and got through our jobs as quickly as we could, then put our coats on and grabbed the lead. U.S. was in his greenhouse and asked, "Have you finished already?"

"Yes."

"Hope you have done them properly."

"We have just hurried."

"Give me a few minutes." I asked, "Can we wait for you on the vacant block?" We could hear voices.

"Yes, I'll see you there." We ran through the side gate. There were a few children playing whom Lydia knew. None of the older ones were there, though. It wasn't long before U.S. came out, and we all walked to Mrs. Taylor's. She opened the door after a little while, and was really pleased to see us. We tied Monty to a tree. Elizabeth was walking towards us, wobbly, but doing more steps, before she fell down. Mrs. Taylor wanted to know all about my job. We all chatted for a while, before she and U.S. went into the kitchen. After a short time, U. S. said, "We had better go, as you girls have a busy afternoon." We said our goodbyes. "You are welcome any time," she said. We gave Elizabeth hugs and left, waving goodbye.

U.S. told us as we were walking home, that if we had time one day, we could take Elizabeth for a walk in her pram. She would love that. "Mrs. Taylor is still having problems with her foot."

"Well, will A.J. allow that?"

"I will talk with her about it." We were pleased, "We would like to do that. Thank you." We talked on the way home. I asked, "Have we time to call in to see Lena for a few minutes? I want to tell her about me working now."

"We haven't long before A.J. will be home."

"Please, please!" I asked.

"All right. I'll take Monty home and make lunch. You girls can go, but don't be long!" We thanked him and ran ahead to Lena's. Lydia said, "He is being really nice."

"Yes, he has helped me in the mornings before work. I just wish A.J. was nicer to me."

We had reached Lena's house and knocked on the front door. When she opened it, she was pleased to see us. "Come inside. No Monty!" We told her why. We had never been inside before. It was really nice. I said, "I am now working," and quickly told her about it. Lydia said she was going to the grammar school. Lena made us a drink. I said, "We can't stay. U.S. is making lunch, and A.J. will be home soon. Then we have the little chapel to clean."

It's so nice of you to call in. I will be bringing the flowers over later on."

"We never get to talk to you."

"I know. I wish things were different, but you'd better go now. You don't want to be in trouble." She opened the door and said, "Goodbye. Thank you for coming." We ran all the way home. We got inside and ran up the stairs, took our coats off, and were washing our hands, when we heard the front door open. A.J. was home. "We just made it," I whispered. Lydia whispered, "Be careful how you talk." We went downstairs. A.J. asked, "What have you been doing?" Lydia replied, "We were just washing our hands."

U.S. said, "Lunch is ready." He said grace. We ate in silence. We were then told to get ready for cleaning the chapel. We ran upstairs, talking. It wasn't long before we left. We walked to the chapel and passed Lena's house. I said to A.J., "Aren't the flowers lovely?" She didn't answer. We were now at the chapel, and ready to do our jobs. It wasn't long before we heard the knock on the door. We knew it was Lena, with the flowers. A.J. hurried up the aisle and opened the door. I waved, and Lena waved back. "Thank you for the flowers." A.J. said, and closed the door. I said, "They are lovely flowers. She has such a lovely garden. Can we talk with her sometime?"

"There is no need for that." I was asked to take the dead flowers outside. I tried to talk with her and be nice, but I found, either I was asked to do something, or there was no conversation with me.

Later, when we were on our own, I talked to Lydia about it.

"I know what you mean, but just keep trying, and don't upset her, that's the main thing."

The days went by, and Lydia had started at the grammar school, which, she said, was so different, and new to her, but she was getting used to it. She now had homework, and seemed to be managing it. I was settling in to my job, but finding it a long day, and a bit boring. After I had been there for four weeks, I asked, "Can you show me something else I can do now?" I was told I was doing well, and would be given other jobs as time went by. I missed my friends and school, and knew I must get used to how things were. U.S. helped me in the mornings.

Chapter 85

It was Friday night, and youth group. I was really looking forward to seeing my friends. I knew Betty would be there. Lydia said, "I don't have much homework. It won't take me long." A.J. said, "I'd like you to do it now. It will be a while before dinner." I helped get the veggies ready. U.S. asked me how my day was. "I found it a long day."

"We will talk in the front room," giving U.S. a look. Not another word was spoken. It wasn't long before Lydia came into the kitchen. A. J. said, "Goodness. Have you finished already?"

"Yes. I didn't have much to do."

"Dinner will be a few minutes." We went outside in the garden and walked Monty. I asked, "How are you going with your homework?"

"I'm doing all right, and it's not very hard, and it's good – I have one friend in my class."

"How was work?"

"I'm finding it easier, but I wish I had something new to do. It's a long day and I'm finding it boring." There was a tap on the window – come inside for dinner. I was really hungry, but still managed to save a piece of sausage for Monty, and I knew I was giving him his dinner before we left for youth group.

It was really good to see Betty again, and we enjoyed our time with the others, whom we hadn't seen since school. Betty still hadn't got a job, and was enjoying being at home with her mum. Dennis came over for a chat, asking me about my job. We had a good time and a lovely supper. When it had finished, and Lydia and I were walking home, she said, "Leave it to me to do the talking." We were late finishing. I said, "I'm happy with that."

It was my week to get paid, and when it was my turn to speak in the front room, I gave A.J. my envelope with the money in. I asked, "How much have I saved now in my account?" She became cross with me, and handed me my bus fare. "You have been told what happens to the money."

"Yes, I know that. I just want to know how much is in my account, that I have saved."

"There will be no more talking on the subject." I could see Lydia had looked worried. I decided to say no more.

When we were in bed, and could talk, Lydia asked, "Why did you ask about your money?"

"I just wanted to know what I have saved."

"You were told how it was going to be."

"I know that, but I want to know how much is in my account."

"I can understand that, but A.J. puts it in an account. She wouldn't know how much is in there straight away."

"Maybe not, but she could say she would let me know."

"Yes, you're right there, but you need to be careful how you talk to her. She can make things difficult for you."

"I know. Sometimes I feel I'm treated like a child. Other times, I'm a grown up. It's difficult for me. What do you think I should do?"

"Wait till she's in a good mood with you."

"That hardly ever happens. I wish I could talk with her like I can with U.S."

"I know what you mean."

"I'm doing my best. I have been really trying."

"I know you have."

"I just want to know what I have in my account."

I had now been working for a few months. I found the days long, and the job monotonous. I asked Sarah, "Can you show me some other work as well, that I can do?" Sometimes, I would have to stand and wait for more files. Sarah said, "I can show you how to do the mail, and you can walk out and post it." She showed me, and that made it more interesting for me, and broke the monotony.

A few more weeks passed. I was in the same situation with A.J., regarding my wage. I would give her the envelope, and was given the money for my bus fare. I didn't bring the subject up again. I really wanted to, but wasn't sure how she would be with me. A.J. was polite to me, but unapproachable on the subject of my wages. I could talk with U. S., but he didn't know any details. I felt I should know what I was working for, and the amount I was saving. Lydia agreed that A.J. should tell me. "But don't worry about it. You will know one day." She was worried that there could be a big upset that would make things difficult for me. I was finding it hard to be constantly careful how I spoke, and not answer back.

We both wrote to our uncle and gave the letters to A.J. to post. Of course, I couldn't put my problem in the letter. We knew she would read them before posting. We wondered how long it would be before we heard from him, and asked in the letter: When can we see you again?

Lydia was settling in well at the grammar school and making new friends. She had more homework, and I was helping more with the dishes. Monty was always pleased to see me, and if dinner wasn't ready, I would walk him on my own. I noticed he was slowing down when I walked him. When I was on my own with U.S., I asked, "How old is Monty?" It took him a while to work it out. "Now, how long have you been with us, you girls?" We told him, and eventually he worked out that Monty was thirteen, or a little bit older. He said, "That's quite old, for a dog."

"Oh. When it is cold, can he not come inside more?" I tried really hard for him. When A.J. was out, he would allow it, otherwise A.J. would say, "He has a kennel to go to." Then I would say, "He stays on his rug. He doesn't move." Lydia gave me a look. If it was really wet, he could come in. Lydia and I would spoil him with titbits from our dinner, and it was easier now, as I always fed him.

The following Friday evening, before we left home, A.J. told us, "You have time to walk Elizabeth in her pram tomorrow. Mrs. Taylor has a doctor's appointment." We were walking and chatting about it. I said, "We still have to do our jobs first," but we were looking forward to seeing Mrs. Taylor and Elizabeth. We arrived at the hall. Betty was already there, full of chatter and excited, saying she now had a job, starting on Monday, and her mum would be driving her. She didn't have to start until nine o'clock. It was good seeing her and talking about our week. The hall was full. They had a speaker there, and there was a text to learn for the next week. One person would be asked what it was. If you got it wrong, the next person would be asked, until someone came up with the right answer. There was a message to be learned from it each week, and the evening ended with a nice supper. When it was time to leave, we would stay with Betty till her mother arrived. Sometimes she would pick us up too.

That Saturday morning, we got up quickly, enjoyed our breakfast with U.S., and rushed through our jobs. He said, "Let me know when you have finished." Lydia replied, "We want to be able to walk Monty, and Sylvia's pushing the pram." I said, "You're right, but U.S. can take Monty. We will ask him. It won't feel right, leaving him behind." We talked about whether Monty was coming as we ran down the garden, telling U.S. we had finished. "That was quick," he said, looking up as he worked in the garden. "Yes, we hurried. We have done them properly."

"Glad to hear it."

"Can we take Monty too?"

"I will come to Mrs. Taylor's, and you can walk him there. I will take over while you push the pram."

"That's good. I don't want him to miss out." We were ready to leave, and reached Mrs. Taylor's. The pram was outside the front door. I rang the bell, and after a little while Mrs. Taylor came out, carrying Elizabeth, and put her in her pram, strapping her in.

She was pleased to see us, saying, "This is kind of you. It makes it easier for me, not having to take her." She had a chat to U.S. Then we were ready to leave. I ran to get Monty. U.S. was pushing the pram, until we got onto the pavement. We took it in turns. Elizabeth was excited, making lots of noises and waving her hands around. We enjoyed pushing. It was hard to get used to. U.S. helped us up the kerbs. Monty still got his walk, and we ended up at the entrance to the field. No one was about, so we let Monty off. He had a walk. We made our way back to Mrs. Taylor's. She was already home, and pleased that it had gone well. She thanked us. We said we enjoyed it and it was time to say goodbye. We hurried home to organise lunch. A.J. would be home soon. We helped, and had just got it ready when A.J. came in, saying, "I'm home. How did the walk go with Elizabeth in the pram?" We both started talking at once. I said, "It went well." I was going to say more, but A.J. stopped me. "We will talk about it in the front room." I was asked to say grace, and of course, we ate in silence. After lunch, our routine would all start again, walking to the little chapel and cleaning it, getting it ready for the Sunday service. I found the weekends went fast for me. Then it was Monday – back to work.

Chapter 86

A few weeks passed before we saw Mrs. Taylor again. She was feeling a bit better, but still had difficulty with her walking, and wanted to know if we were happy to take Elizabeth in the pram again. We said yes. U.S. arranged it, after helping her in the kitchen. We spent time walking and talking with Elizabeth, helping her to say new words. We enjoyed our time. Mrs. Taylor told U.S. (and we overheard), that her doctor wanted to know where Elizabeth was. She told her about us helping when we could. She mentioned that she was looking for a young girl to work as a nanny, but it was out of town. I was listening in. I said, "What a shame."

"You couldn't fit any more in your weekend, and you will need some rest before you start your job on Monday."

After saying our goodbyes, we were walking and talking on our way home. I asked U.S., "I wonder where the job was, and what time you would have to start?"

"You already have a job." Lydia said, "Sylvia would be good at that."

"I don't think you can do anything about it. You are settled in the job you have."

"I'm just interested to find out more." Nothing else was said. We reached home.

When we were alone, Lydia and I chatted about what Mrs. Taylor had told us about the job working with a family. I said, "I think I'd like to do that, but it's too late now, and I have a job."

"Well, we could ask Mrs. Taylor if she can find out more before we see her next."

"Yes, you're right. Let's do that."

The weekend was over. Lydia was back at her new school and had settled in. She had homework as well. It was work for me. U.S. was still helping me with breakfast in the mornings, and made lunch for me. I'm sure I wouldn't have managed it all on my own, leaving so early. I hurried to catch the bus, then waited at the bus stop. It arrived late, which it often did. I now knew what stop to get off at. I would have to walk really fast, I said to myself, or even run, to be on time. That's how it was that morning. Sarah was working at her desk when I entered. "You're late!"

"Oh, sorry. The bus was late, and I walked as fast as I could."

"Never mind. Can you get these files out as quick as you can?" She sounded cross. I picked up the list of numbers and pulled out the files. It was a busy day, and I was on the move all day. I was glad when it was time to go home. Then I had to walk to the bus stop. I was standing waiting for the bus. I felt really tired. Good. I could see the bus coming. I would be able to sit down. I sat and thought about my day. I hardly spoke with anyone at work, and really didn't enjoy what I was doing. I knew Mondays were always busy, and hoped tomorrow would be a better day. I had arrived, and jumped off the bus. I was glad to be walking home. I could hear children's voices, the closer I got to home. I wondered if there would be anybody on the vacant block whom I knew. A voice called out to me. I said hello and waved. I kept walking to the side gate and opened it. Monty gave me a big welcome. Lydia came out, full of chatter, asking, "Have you had a good day, and are you happy? Dinner is ready."

"We are waiting for you." A.J. said. I hurried upstairs, took off my shoes, and quickly went to the bathroom. I ran downstairs. A.J. was serving dinner. I was asked to say grace. I managed to save some meat. I gave Lydia a look, so she could do the same. When dinner was finished, Lydia had to do her homework. She was getting more and more. So, it was me helping with the dishes. A.J. would go in the front room. I found that during the time doing the dishes I could talk to U.S. and open up to him. I told him I was finding it difficult with the bus, which had been late that day. "Sarah was cross." He asked me if I liked the job. "It's all right, but even if the bus is on time, I have to hurry, and I'm standing for most of the day. I'm really tired. I only sit when I'm on the bus."

"So, you say the job is all right."

"Well, not really, but I know I have to keep doing it. Maybe it will get better." He didn't say anything. I asked, "Is it all right for me to feed Monty?"

"Yes, you do that."

I got Monty's food ready and added my titbits of meat from dinner to it. Then, later, in the front room, I was asked about my day. I mentioned that the bus was late, which made me late. A.J. asked, "Did you apologise?"

"Yes, I did, and Sarah replied, "Never mind," but sounded cross."

"Well, these things happen sometimes. You will just have to hurry as much as you can."

"I already do that." A.J. gave me a look and said I was being rude. I didn't think I was -- just saying how it was. She said nothing.

Lydia and I talked about my job when we were on our own. She understood how difficult it was. We were hoping we would have heard from our uncle, and I could talk with him about things. That would be so good. "Just do your best. That's all you can do."

Chapter 87

It was a few weeks before we saw Mrs. Taylor again. U.S. was helping her, and we spent time with Elizabeth. When it was time to leave, I asked Mrs. Taylor if she had heard anything about the job the doctor had mentioned. "No, but I have an appointment in the week, and I can ask about it."

"I just wondered where the job is, and if it is still available."

"I will let you know." I thanked her. U.S. didn't say a word. We were walking home, talking. I was holding Monty. I noticed he had slowed down a lot, and was still limping. I said to U.S., "He could be in pain."

"We could get him checked. We are going past the shops, where the vet is. Yes, you're right. We had better get him looked at." We found the vet's rooms. U.S. held Monty and we all went inside. There was a lady sitting with a cat on her lap. Monty started barking and pulled on his lead, trying to reach the cat. A man was coming out of the room with another dog, who started to bark at Monty. U.S had a real job to hold onto him. I tried to help. It wasn't easy. The lady with the cat was called to go into the surgery. The man with the dog left, and then it was just us, waiting to see the vet.

U.S. managed to get Monty to lie down. He said for us to sit and wait. He would go in by himself. This was a new experience for us, and we hoped Monty would be all right. It was a little while before the lady came out, without her cat. She walked straight out of the door. The vet called Monty and it was his turn. He was really limping. I said to Lydia, "Yes, he hasn't been wanting to run like he used to." Then we spoke about the lady who had the cat, sitting very quietly on her lap, and she came out without it. "I wonder if it's still alive?" Lydia asked. I said, "I wonder how Monty will be? I wish we could have gone in too." It seemed a long wait, before Monty and U.S. came out. Monty was pulling him, and he was excited to see us.

We left the surgery, and I asked, "What's wrong with him?"

"He has arthritis, and has been given some tablets to help. We cannot take him on long walks now, and the warmer weather will be better for him, too." It was still quite a way to walk home. U.S. said, "A.J. will be home, wondering where we are."

"Yes. She will make lunch for us. That never happens. Hope she's not cross." Lydia said, "Leave it to me to do the talking." U.S. said, "Girls, I will explain that Monty had to be looked at. Please do as you're told and don't make any upsets."

"We will do what is asked of us." We reached home. I put Monty on his chain. U.S. went inside. Lydia gave Monty some fresh water. We heard raised voices from inside. I gave Monty a pat and he went into his kennel and lay down.

Lydia and I went inside together, walking through the kitchen and straight up the stairs. They were in deep conversation, not saying anything to us. We went to the bathroom and washed our hands, then came downstairs. Lunch was ready. A.J. said, "Lydia, say grace, please." Nothing else was said until we had finished. "Girls, we are over an hour late. We need to hurry." We left the table, not saying a word, and ran upstairs. I said, "So far, so good."

"Just don't upset her."

"I'm not going to say another word."

A.J. was waiting at the front door. "Are you ready, girls?"

We said yes, and started walking out of the door, to clean the little chapel. We met Lena, walking back from the chapel, with flowers in her hands. Nobody answered the door. She reached us. A.J. said, "I'll take the flowers," and grabbed them out of her hands and started walking towards the chapel. I said, "Sorry." to Lena. A.J. was walking fast in front, saying, "Come along." to us. We ran and caught up with her. I turned round and saw Lena, just standing there, watching us. Lydia gave me a look, "Don't say a word." I really wanted to say, "That was so rude. How could she do that?", but I didn't open my mouth. Inside the chapel, A.J. said, "Get your jobs done as quick as you can." We said yes, and ran to the vestry to get our rags, to dust the pews. A.J. was really busy with the flowers. Nobody spoke. We had finished. A.J. locked the chapel and said, "Thank you, girls." We were now walking home. She asked Lydia, "Do you have much homework?"

"Yes, I do have a bit."

"Well, I'd like you to do it when we get home." I wasn't spoken to.

We reached home. Monty came out of his kennel, limping badly. I went over and patted him. I stayed outside and sat with him. Lydia and A.J. went inside. It wasn't long before I was called.

It was about another week, when U.S. said, "We will call in at the vet's to get Monty looked at again." He hadn't really improved. We hadn't walked him. He still enjoyed his food, though. We missed taking him on our walks, and we would go out of the front door, so Monty couldn't see us. So, I said to Lydia, "How can Monty possibly walk all that way to the vet's?"

"I don't know what else we can do."

"I know. Let's talk to U.S. We could put him in the wheelbarrow, and put a rug in the bottom, to make it soft for him to lie on. We don't want to upset Monty, when he can hardly walk. It will make his leg worse." We ran down the garden to talk to U.S. We told him our suggestion. He said, "That might be a good idea. We will be ready to leave shortly." We went down the garden to get the wheelbarrow. "How will he get in there?" asked Lydia. "He can hardly walk."

"We'll just have to try, all of us, to put him in there." We went to see Monty and waited for U.S., who pushed the wheelbarrow up to the kennel. "I'm afraid he is getting worse. It's harder for him to stand. These tablets are not helping him."

"Will the vet give him something else?" I asked.

"I hope so." Monty was still wagging his tail. I got the rug out of the kennel and put it in the wheelbarrow. U.S. took Monty off his chain and lifted him into the wheelbarrow. We girls took it in turns to walk beside him, patting him, as he was trying to get out all the time. We held him to try and get him to lie down. Lydia fetched his lead. Monty was becoming excited. He tried to walk, but couldn't. We could see he was in pain. I ran to the kitchen to get a dog biscuit, which he ate very quickly. We arrived at the vet's. This time, the room was empty. It wasn't long before the vet called U.S. to come through. We had to wait, as we had before. It did seem a long time before U.S. came out on his own, saying he had some sad news. "The vet can't do any more for Monty. You can go in to say goodbye to him."

"Why can't he do any more for him, and what will happen?"

"He won't be in any pain. He will give him something to go to sleep." Lydia said, "And he won't wake up." We became upset. We went into the room. Monty was lying on the bed, still wagging his tail when he saw us. We walked over to him and said our goodbyes. It was so sad. We cried and gave him a hug. Then we went back into the waiting room and waited for U.S. We walked to Mrs. Taylor's. "It's hard to see, but Monty was in pain, and crippled, and could no longer walk. We will all miss him."

Chapter 88

We arrived at Mrs. Taylor's. She could see that we were all upset and sad. She was so sorry about Monty. Elizabeth walked towards us. We played with her while U.S. helped Mrs. Taylor. We didn't stay long. U.S. made another time to help her. She had made and appointment to see the doctor. I asked, "Do you know if the job has been taken?" She said she would ask. We walked home. We were tired and sad. We helped to make lunch. Neither of us wanted to eat. U.S. said, "You need to eat something." We could hear A.J. coming, and U.S. told her about Monty. She said, turning to us, "Yes, it is sad, but that's part of life, and it's hard. It's your first experience." I said, "We will miss him so much." It felt strange without Monty.

It was another two weeks before we saw Mrs. Taylor again. Lydia and I were taking it in turns to push the pram. I said, "I hope Mrs. Taylor remembers to ask if the job is still available."

"Well, we'll find out when Elizabeth's home. I will be told whether I got the job or not." We missed Monty terribly. U.S. had now removed the kennel and chain. There was this empty space. Elizabeth came out to see us.

"What do you think I should do?"

"It's a big decision. Would you really change jobs?"

"I think so. I feel I'd enjoy it more than the job I've got."

We arrived home, and U.S. asked, "Where have you been?" He had lunch ready for us. I told him what had happened. He asked, "Do you think you would like that?"

"I'm really not sure, and I might not hear anything, although they did say they would let me know."

"Well then, they will. You must have a big think. It is a huge decision." We could hear A.J. come in. "I'm late. It's been a full morning." We ate our lunch in silence, and had to hurry to leave to clean the chapel. No more was said about anything. I knew when I would be able to talk -- in the front room, later.

We had finished helping at the chapel. Lydia and I went for a walk to the woods, without Monty. We were still missing him. We could have a talk about things. I felt I was being pulled. In a way I wanted to do it, but I didn't want to leave Lydia. She said, "I understand, and would be all right on my own, as long as we still see each other some weekends." She knew I wasn't happy living with A.J., and missing Monty had changed things. I was still being treated as a child, having to do what she wanted me to do. I was finding it difficult to constantly be aware I must conform and go along with her rules. I was really not enjoying my job.

Lydia asked, "Well, are you going to tell A.J. about the interview you had this morning?"

"Yes, I think I should. I wonder if U.S. will tell her?"

"I think he will, but it's best you tell her yourself."

"Yes, you're right." After more talking about what I should do, we had reached home. It was so different without Monty, and we were feeling sad. The vacant block was quiet. There was nobody about. We went inside. Both A.J. and U.S. were in the front room. A.J. said, "Hello, girls. Are you ready to talk about things? Lydia first." Then it was me. I explained what had happened that morning, and about my interview. "I thought I might like to do the job. I'm not really happy in the job I've got, and I'm finding the travelling very hard."

"Whatever you do, there could be some part of it that you won't like. You need to think long and hard about this. You can't expect to go through life enjoying everything. Do you understand?"

"I like helping people, and know I would be good at it. I would like one day to do nursing, when I am old enough."

"Well, I don't know how that would happen. You needed to have better marks at school."

"I'd still like to try when I'm older."

"You will have to work hard to achieve that."

"Yes, I know. Have you heard from our uncle yet? We did write, and you said you posted the letter."

"No, I would tell you. He is a very busy man." Lydia asked, "Have you written to him again?"

"No, I'm waiting for him to reply."

"Can you write again, telling him I have a situation and need his help, please?"

"Sylvia, he will tell you the same as I am doing, to think hard about what you want to do."

"I think my uncle should know I need his advice. Please write to him again." Lydia said, "Please. This is important." I asked, "If I write, will you post it?"

"Girls! You can write, and I will post the letter."

"Thank you," we both said. Then I spoke. "We miss Monty lots."

"I do know that. He was an old dog. He did well for his age."

"You really didn't really like him, did you?" I didn't stop to think – it just came out.

"That sort of talk is uncalled for. We will say no more on the subject. Now, is there anything else you would like to talk about?"

"No, thank you. Can I have some writing paper, so we can write to our uncle?"

"Lydia, have you anything else to say?"

"Only, I need some paper too." A.J. asked Lydia, "How would you feel if your sister gets the job?"

"I will miss her, of course, but she has to do what she thinks is best for her. We hope to see each other at weekends."

"Well, that might not always work out. And Sylvia, what if you don't like working and living away? You can't keep changing jobs."

"I know that, but I think I'd like to do it."

"Well, I think you should stay at your job, and you will get used to it and come to like it." She got up to get us some writing paper. U.S. didn't say a word. We followed her. She gave us the paper, then we went upstairs to our room, talking. We sat on the bed. I asked Lydia, "Are you really all right with it, that is, if I hear, and get the job?"

"If you're sure that's what you want to do. A.J.'s right. You won't be able to change jobs. If you don't like it, it will be hard to get another job."

"I know. I don't want to upset you. If you want me to keep doing my job, I will."

"Don't be silly. I can manage A.J. I will miss you, but you need to be happy, and we will see each other at weekends, I hope." After more talking, we went downstairs and sat at the kitchen table, writing to our uncle. We gave it to A.J., who said, "Goodness. That is quick." I said, "Can you post it, please?"

"Yes." We ran down to U.S., and I asked him, "How would you feel if I got the job?"

"It's a big thing. You have to be really sure."

"I know. I haven't got the job yet. I wonder when they will let me know?"

"It will probably be in a week. That gives you time to think hard about things." We chatted to him while he was working with his seedlings. A week had passed, and I hadn't heard anything. It was Friday night, and

I was going to youth group. I told Betty, who said, "It sounds exciting for you. Are you sure that's what you want to do?"

"Oh, I just know I don't really like my job, and the travelling I'm finding hard."

"And you're not really happy at home, are you?"

"No, and I'll miss my sister. It's so difficult for me."

"I'm lucky. I love my job, and I have a mum I love."

"Yes, you are." We chatted more. Lydia said, "I'll still see Sylvia at weekends, and now, after school, I'm having more homework. We don't have that much time together." We enjoyed our Friday nights at youth group.

Chapter 89

It was another two weeks before I heard about the job. Could I come in again? Lydia asked me, "I wonder if you have the job?"

"Well, they haven't said so."

"You have had a long time to think about it."

"I know. I would like to try it."

"Well, you'd have to make it work. You can't go back to your job once you have left it."

"I know that."

"It's a big decision. You will have to decide when you get there."

It was Saturday morning. A.J. was leaving for her job. We never did find out what it was. She asked, "What have you decided if you do get the job?"

"I will say yes. I feel I can do it and would enjoy it."

"Well, you have had plenty of time to think about it. Remember, you can't go through life enjoying everything. You have a job that you are settled in. I don't think that is the right decision." She said this as she went out the door. Lydia said, "I don't think she wants you to leave."

"I wish I could talk to our uncle."

"It's only you who can decide."

I walked to the surgery. Lydia came with me. We sat, waiting to be called. I had butterflies in my stomach. Was I doing the right thing? I really wanted to try it and see how I liked it, but I would have to stick with it. These thoughts were going through my head. The door opened and I was called to go through. A lady asked me to sit down and asked me questions, "How do you feel about leaving home?"

"I think I should be all right." I was asked to talk about myself, which I did. Then, I was told I would be shown the place the next day, and to see how I felt. I was given a time. She said, "I will see you in the morning." I walked out. Lydia was waiting. She jumped up, asking "What happened?" We left. She asked me, "Did you get the job or not?"

"I don't know. I'm going to have a look at the place tomorrow." I was excited, but nervous. We hurried home and told U.S. all about it. He asked, "How do you feel?"

"I think I would like it."

"You will have to be sure when you go tomorrow. It's a big thing you are doing, and you will have to make it work."

"I know that."

"What sort of questions did they ask you?"

"He asked me how I felt when I helped with Elizabeth."

"I said I enjoyed helping to look after her. Mrs. Taylor had already told them about me. I was asked about living away from home. I said I didn't think I'd mind too much, but I would like to come back at weekends, and I would miss my sister."

"You really don't know how you'd feel until it happens. I know it is a hard decision."

It wasn't till later, in the front room, that I was able to talk about my day. A.J. was surprised to hear that I would have a look at the place the next day, and be shown what the job consisted of.

"I might be getting the job."

"I feel you should stay in the job you have."

I didn't sleep much. I wasn't sure I was doing the right thing. I really wanted to try it. If they liked me, and I could manage the children, it would be nice to have a week's trial. Lydia said, "If you really want to do it, it's all right with me." She understood I wasn't happy, and how hard it was for me with A.J.

The next morning, I walked to the doctor's rooms. I was taken in the car to Aldham. It seemed a long way and took about twenty minutes. I was told there was a bus that went there. It was in the country. We went through this small town, then over a bridge and turned into a long drive, with a huge house at the end. I got out of the car and was shown inside. I remember this so well. We went through the front door. To the left there was a spiral staircase. This whole floor was the children's quarters. My job would be looking after two children, aged three and one. I would have my own bedroom close to the children's room. I was introduced to the children, Catherine and Luke. Then I was left with the children on my own for a while, to see how we got on. Catherine, the older child, was full of chatter, holding my hand and taking me to her bedroom. Luke was shy and quiet. I found them easy to talk and play with.

The doctor came in, and said, "I will introduce you to our maid, Ethel, who cooks our meals and looks after us." At the bottom of the stairs there was a huge kitchen. I met Ethel. She asked, "Are you coming back here to stay?"

"I don't know."

"Come, and I'll show you the garden." There was a river flowing beside the grounds, and there were locked gates further down the property. I just loved the place, and the doctor was easy to talk to. His wife's name was Margaret. She said she had heard from Mrs. Taylor how well I had got on with Elizabeth. She had a talk with me, asking, "How do you feel about coming to live with us? You will be the children's nanny."

"I think I'd like it," and thanked her. Margaret wanted me to start as soon as I could. She knew I had a job, and I would have to let them know. She also knew my circumstances. I was taken upstairs again, to say goodbye to the children. Then I was driven back home. I was so happy, and couldn't wait to tell Lydia all about it. I told her that I thought I had the job and was happy about it. I would tell her more later.

In the front room, when A.J. asked me, I said, "I am going to let work know I will be leaving."

"I hope you won't regret this. I am not sure your uncle would approve."

"I wish I could have talked with him about it, but I'm nearly sixteen, and I think he would say I need to make my own decisions."

"What about your sister? Have you thought about her, how she feels, or others, how they feel?"

"Lydia and I have talked about it, and I will miss her a lot, but I can still see her on some weekends." Lydia was asked, "What have you got to say?"

"Sylvia must be happy doing what she wants to do. Of course I will miss her, but will look forward to the weekends, when we can see each other."

"You will have jobs to do, all by yourself."

"I know, but I want to spend time with my sister too. I will help you when I come to stay."

Lydia said, "That would be good. Thank you."

"We will have to see how things work out." U.S. didn't say a word. We were told to get ready for bed. We talked about everything in bed. She said, "It sounds a lovely place."

"It is. It is huge, and it's because of what Mrs. Taylor said about me, how well I got on with Elizabeth. I think that's how I got the job. I must thank her."

"I will go and see Elizabeth still."

"Yes, and if I get some time off, I will visit too. I will miss our chats. Oh, I will have to tell Sarah at work that I am leaving at the end of the week."

"I wonder what she will say?" We could hear A.J. coming up the stairs. She said goodnight and turned off the light. We still kept chatting in the dark. Eventually I said, "We'd better try and get some sleep."

The next morning, U.S. had to wake me. It took me so long to get to sleep. It was a rush. He had my breakfast ready. He said, "Just eat. No talking. You have a big day in front of you., and you don't want to miss the bus."

"Thank you." I just managed to catch it. The bus was a bit early, so I ran. I caught my breath. I was thinking, it was not going to be easy. I was a bit nervous, but I really felt sure this was what I wanted to do. I arrived at work early. Sarah was there, and said, "Good morning. Nice to see you on time."

"Well, the bus was early. Can I talk with you?"

"Yes. Is it urgent? We are going to have a busy day, so you can start straight away."

"It is urgent." She looked surprised, and took me into the office. More people were coming in. Sarah asked, "What is so urgent?"

"Well, I want to leave at the end of the week."

"Why? I thought you were happy here." I told her how it was, and about my new job. I think it was a shock.

"I will be sorry to lose you. I hope you will be happy in what you do. Well, we'd better get into working." It was a big day, and I was kept busy. I was glad when it was time to go home. I was standing at the bus stop. This time, the bus was late. I was so happy when it came, and I was able to sit down. Now, it was all looking forward. I got off the bus, and Lydia was waiting for me, asking, "Did you tell her? What did she say?"

"Yes," and went into details about it. Lydia said, "It's all happening."

"Are you sure you are all right about it all?"

"Yes, but I'm going to miss you a lot."

"Me too. I feel I'm going to be happier than in the job I am doing. We will see each other at weekends."

After dinner, in the front room, A.J. asked, "Well, what have you to tell us, Sylvia?" I told her about my day from the beginning to the end.

"You do realise there is no turning back."

"Yes. I feel it is the right decision."

"I hope you won't regret this."

"I don't think I will."

"Time will tell." U.S. spoke, "I hope you will be happy, Sylvia."

"Thank you." A.J. asked Lydia, "What do you think?"

"I will miss my sister, of course, and will look forward to seeing her at weekends."

Chapter 90

My last week of working in the office was really noisy and busy. Time went fast. Everybody was nice to me, and said that they were sorry I was leaving. On my last day, Sarah made a nice afternoon tea for me, and I had a reference to take with me. Then it was time to say goodbye. I was surprised how nice everybody was to me, and it made me think I might miss it just a little.

Friday night came, and I told everyone at youth group, as I didn't think I'd be able to come all the time. Betty said, "I will miss you."

"Lydia will still be coming." I enjoyed our time, and so many children wished me good luck.

My last weekend with A.J. and U.S came. On Saturday morning, A.J. went to her work. We did our jobs. Lydia said, "I'll have to do them on my own next time."

"Sorry."

"Don't be silly. I'll manage, and on the weekends when I see you, I'll be able to help you."

"I will have to find out what my hours are. I will need to get the case down, so I can pack my things. I am leaving tomorrow." Lydia helped me pack. I said, "Let's walk round to Lena's so I can tell her the news." She was surprised and pleased for me. Then we visited Mrs. Taylor, who knew, and was also thrilled to hear it. She wished me all the best. Then we walked home. Lydia said she would still call in sometimes to see Mrs. Taylor. "That would be good, and I will visit when I can."

Once we got home, we went down the garden to talk to U.S., who was working in his greenhouse. He asked, "What have you been up to?" We told him that I had said my goodbyes. I was nearly packed. This was my last night living at home. I was catching the late afternoon bus to Aldham. U.S. asked, "How are you feeling about it?"

"Excited, but nervous."

"That is to be expected. I hope you will be happy there."

"Thank you. I will come and see you when I get time off. I will miss you." I went to give him a hug, but he stepped back. I said, "Thank you for what you have done for me." He was taken aback. "That's nice of you to say that." We all went inside to help make lunch. He said, "A.J. will be home soon."

We walked to the little chapel to help clean it. I thought, I won't be doing this again. I might help if I come to see Lydia. A.J. was very quiet, and hardly spoke to me. We did our jobs, and afterwards, she just said, "Thank you, girls." We now had time to do whatever we wanted. We walked to the woods. Our lives were changing, now that Monty had gone. Lydia said, "I will be fine, and will be studying to get good marks. Not sure what I will do when I leave school, but something to do with health."

"I would still like to do nursing, but I have to be 18. I am not sure if I can do it, with the schooling I have done."

"Oh well, you will be looking after children for a doctor's family now." We talked between ourselves. We started walking home. I would be catching the bus after dinner. I was packed and organised. I asked, "I wonder how A.J. will be with me?"

"Well, you won't have to wait long to find out." After arriving back, we ran upstairs. Nobody was about. When we came down, they were both in the kitchen, and dinner was all prepared. A.J. asked, "Sylvia, would you like to say grace?", which I did. We ate in silence. A.J. went to the front room, and Lydia and I helped with the dishes. I spoke with U.S. "I'm leaving in an hour to catch the bus, and it feels like everything is just the same." Lydia replied, "It will be, till you're gone. We will miss you, won't we?" U.S. said to her, "Yes, we will."

"I'm walking with Sylvia to the bus."

"I will come to help carry the bags."

"Thank you." It was time to go into the front room. A.J. was reading, and looked up, asking, "Are you organised?"

"Yes. I have everything at the front door." Lydia said, "I'm walking to the bus and seeing Sylvia off." U.S. said, "I'm helping to carry the bags."

"Well, you have chosen to do this. I still feel you should have stayed with your job."

"I was finding the travelling difficult."

"Yes, I know that, but you will learn, there will always be something that will be difficult."

"Have you heard from our uncle?"

"No. I would have told you if I had, and I'm not sure he would agree with what you have done."

"Well, I'd better say goodbye. I'm hoping I can come next weekend to see Lydia."

"Well, you will have to fit in with what we are doing."

"I will, and I want to see my sister."

"She has lots of study to do. She will be busy." Lydia said, "I will always find time to see my sister, and will look forward to her coming next weekend." U.S. said, "We'd better go. You're going to miss the bus." I turned to say goodbye, and said, "Thank you for taking me in, and sorry we don't really get on." A.J. was very surprised, and said, "What I have done has been for your own good, and I hope you'll come to realise that." I got up and said goodbye. U.S. and Lydia followed me out of the room. I ran upstairs to get my last-minute things I had left on the bed. Lydia came up with me, and said, "You did well, what you said to A.J. "

"Thanks." We gave each other a hug.

"This is it! I'll see you next week." U.S. was calling us. "You will miss this bus. Let's get moving." We walked fast and could see the bus coming. Another hug for Lydia, and I said goodbye to U.S. I said to Lydia, "I will see you next week." I whispered, "I hope I've done the right thing." I jumped on the bus. I waved goodbye as it moved away. I sat down, thinking, this is it. My new life is starting, and I'm on my own.

The bus stopped at Aldham. I got off, and there was a lady there to meet me. It was Margaret, the doctor's wife. She had her car. "It's not far, but too far to walk with your bags," she said. We drove down the long driveway, to the front door. Catherine ran to meet me. I really didn't understand what she was saying. Luke was sitting on the ground. Margaret came and picked him up. Doctor Tom took my bags upstairs. Margaret showed me my bedroom. She said, "We'll leave you to unpack and settle in. I'll take the children downstairs for a while. If there's anything you need, let me know."

"Thank you." She left. I emptied everything on the bed and started putting things in drawers and hanging things in the wardrobe. I looked out of the window. It was a lovely view of the back garden, and I could see the river alongside it. I finished my unpacking and walked to the main room, which had the bedrooms running off it. I wondered, should I go down now? I had finished. I opened the door and went down the winding staircase, to the huge kitchen. The maid, Ethel, talked with me, saying she would bring breakfast up for me and the children at 7.30. She was telling me what she cooked for breakfast. I only needed to tell her if I didn't like anything. I said, "Thank you, and I would." She also told me that she had been with the family for years. "I'm sure you'll like it here. They are easy to get on with." I could hear the children. It wasn't long before the door opened, and Catherine came out, grabbing my hand and chatting.

Margaret said, "You have met Ethel," and she introduced me properly. "The children need to go to bed now, so I'll help you get them settled, then you will take over after that."

"Yes, thank you." I was shown where their things were, and watched what happened. She was easy to talk with, and I was told to ask if I wanted to know anything. She had a programme written out for me, showing times, and what had to be done. This was stuck to a board on the wall. This was my routine that I needed to stick to. If I had any questions, I could contact her. She would come to see the children every night to say goodnight.

In a few days, I would be asked whether I wanted to stay, because I was to wear a uniform and get fitted for that. I noticed, when I saw Ethel, that she had a uniform on. I watched Margaret put the children to bed. They had to be bathed first. I was shown where their things were. I did ask some questions, and was answered. Eventually, the children were in bed. Margaret said I could call her Margaret, but in front of anyone else she was Mrs. Brady. I would be having meals with the children, and after they were in bed, Ethel would make me supper and bring it up. Margaret said, "It's a lot to take in. I hope you will be happy living with us."

"Yes, thank you. I think I will."

"Now, I think you need to get an early night. The children wake up early. Ethel will bring breakfast up at 7.30. So, I'll say goodnight. See you tomorrow."

"Thank you. Good night." I was on my own. So much had happened. I checked on the children. They were sound asleep. I walked into my room. I still had some things on the bed I needed to put away. I thought, I wonder what Lydia is doing? Has she started missing me? It was all strange. I quickly finished unpacking and went into the bathroom, taking some of my things in. I thought, I'd like to have a bath. I turned on the taps, and had one. It wasn't long before I got into bed. I was feeling really tired. I had another look in the children's rooms. They were still sound asleep. I went into my bedroom and got into bed. I couldn't believe it – I had slept really well, and only woke when I heard Luke crying.

I quickly got up and went to him. I took him out of his cot, and he stopped crying. I got some toys out and played with him. Catherine was still asleep. After a while I got him dressed, and dressed myself. It was only seven a.m. It would be another half an hour before Ethel would bring breakfast up. I had a look on the notice board to see what my jobs were. Catherine was now up and walking towards me. She asked, "Where is my mummy?" She didn't seem to know me. I talked with her and got her dressed. I told her my name was Syl. Then she remembered, and was full of chatter, showing me different toys. There was a knock on the door, and Ethel came in with breakfast. She said she would be up later to collect the tray.

The children had two small chairs and a table. There were a larger table and chair for me. I got them organised, and helped feed Luke. He was a really good eater. Catherine was full of chatter, independent, and not really eating. I tried to stop her talking. It wasn't easy. "Eat your breakfast!" When we had all finished, I put the tray at the top of the stairs. Then it was off to the bathroom, to clean teeth. Catherine showed me her toothbrush. She could do it by herself. I needed to put the toothpaste on. Then I brushed her long hair and tied it back. Luke had curly hair, which was easy to do. I looked at the notice board. Margaret was coming up at 10 a.m. to see the children and me. I was to get measured for a uniform. I quickly made the beds and tidied up. Settling the children with their toys, I got it all done before Margaret came in. She asked, "How did you manage?"

"It went well." The children were playing with their toys. Catherine ran to her mother. Luke was still playing happily on the rug. Margaret stayed about an hour, and had a look at the bedrooms. She asked me some questions. She also checked my measurements. She said, "I will give it a week before sending it off, to see how you like it here. We'll go for a walk and I'll show you the garden. The children will need coats on, and so will you. It is quite cold outside." Margaret carried Luke and I held Catherine's hand. We went outside into the garden. It was huge, with big trees and flowers, and extensive lawns. There was a path to walk along, by the river. On the other side of the garden there was a hedge, with a path going into a small gate. We walked along by the river. There were lock gates. The water was rushing through. It was lovely to see. Margaret said, "Don't go there with the children. You can on your own. I'm just showing you if you wanted to do a walk by yourself."

"Thank you. I have never seen anything like this before." Then we walked to the hedge through the gate. There was a gardener working in the vegetable garden. "That's where we get our vegies." We closed the gate. "Well, you have had a tour of the grounds. I will take you to the village later. We have a few shops and a pub. It's only small, but it's enough, without having to go into the town."

"Thank you."

"Now it's time to go inside. Ethel will be bringing the lunch up soon. I will see you later in the day."

I was thinking, I really am enjoying being here. Lunch was brought up by Ethel. I looked at the roster. Luke had to have a sleep after lunch. I could spend time with Catherine to do whatever activity I chose. She was easy to bond with, a real chatterbox, and loved books. I would read to her, or we would play a game. She called me Syl. Later, when Luke was awake, Margaret came up to see how I was faring. I found it easy and enjoyable. I did miss Lydia, though. I wondered whether she was missing me. I was looking forward to having time off on Friday and Saturday that week. Margaret told me it wouldn't be the same every week. She would make a roster, showing when my days off were. Sometimes, I had days off in the week. Then I would just meet Lydia off the school bus, and only have a bit of time with her. I would visit Lena and Mrs. Taylor, and spend some time with U.S. when A.J. wasn't around.

Chapter 91

Margaret said she had something to tell me. She was expecting a baby in a few months. She would need my help then, and Catherine would be starting school the next year. She asked, "How do you feel about that?" I said it was exciting, and I would like to help. "It will get very busy. You will have settled in here by then, and the children will know you. I feel we can work together, and you will get a rise in your wage then. Have a big think about it. Talk with your family when you get home at the weekend."

"I will. Thank you."

Luke was awake. Margaret said, "We will walk to the village. Put him in his pram." Catherine wanted to push the pram, and was excited to be going out. It was just a short walk to the village, and I was introduced as we went into each shop. They all knew Margaret well. Her husband was the doctor for the village, and in Lexton too. We bought a few groceries and all had an ice cream. We sat on a seat in a grassy area. Margaret was asking me a few questions, saying I had been recommended by Mrs. Taylor, who had been a patient for many years. I told her a bit about my life with A.J. and my sister. "We have never been apart, and I am really missing her."

"I am sorry. She could come and visit you here, and stay over one night." I thanked her. "That would be lovely. She would love to see the river and your lovely garden."

"We will work on that." The children were getting to know me. Catherine wouldn't leave my side. Luke started to cry, though. Margaret said he was teething. She was pleased how I was managing and settling in. We started walking home, and this little red car passed us and slowed down. Catherine said, "That's my daddy," and wanted to run to the car. It stopped. Margaret held Catherine's hand and walked over to it. Catherine jumped in. Margaret came back and we walked home. "Catherine is very much a Daddy's girl. You met Tom when you had your interview."

"Yes, and other times, I saw you."

"Yes, that's right. When we get back, you can meet him again."

We went through the front door. I hadn't done that before. It was the back entrance last time. This was a huge entrance hall, with rooms going off it. There were a lounge and staircase to the right. Catherine came out of one of the rooms, calling, "Come this way, Mummy. Syl, you can come too." We all followed her. Doctor Tom was sitting behind a desk. He got up and said, "Hello. I have met you once."

"Yes. I have shown Sylvia the village. We have had a nice afternoon." He said to Margaret, "You now need to have a rest."

"Yes, I will do that." Turning to me, she asked, "Do you know your way back to the rooms?" Catherine said, "I will show Syl." She held my hand. Margaret lifted Luke out of the pram. He could walk a bit. We said our goodbyes, and followed Catherine to the staircase. I carried Luke upstairs. It wasn't very long before teatime. I was settling in and enjoying my job. Catherine really helped me. She was so friendly, and bright for her age. Luke cried a lot. It wasn't easy for me to manage him, but he was teething. It would just take a bit longer for him to get used to me.

Friday morning came, and I was really excited. I would be seeing Lydia that day. I had a small bag packed, and was ready to catch the bus in the village. Catherine said, "I don't want you to go."

"It's only two nights, and I will be back." Margaret came in and said, "Have a nice time. We will see you on Sunday." Catherine gave me a hug. Luke waved. He could have been glad I was leaving -- I wasn't sure.

I caught the bus. It was still early in the morning. I thought, I'll call in and see Mrs. Taylor. It was close to the bus stop. She was really pleased, and Elizabeth was walking on her own, not falling down. "How are you finding the job?" I told her all about it. I spent a little bit of time there, and then I went to see Lena. It did feel strange doing this. Lena was home, and surprised to see me. She welcomed me in. I had something to eat with her, and a good chat. She told me that A.J. was still cleaning the chapel, and Lydia was helping. I said, "I will be spending part of the weekend with A.J., but have to be back on Saturday night. I hope it will be all right. I just want to see Lydia." I knew the times the school bus got in, and I would be there by then.

That's what I did. I wondered if she would be expecting me. I was standing, watching the bus come in. When it stopped, a few girls got off. Then I saw Lydia coming, running towards me. "I wasn't sure if you would be here." She had this heavy bag. She threw it on the ground and gave me a hug. "I'm so pleased to see you!" We chatted so much. She had missed me heaps. "Are you happy? What's it like? Are you glad you left your job?" We walked and talked until we reached the vacant block. We opened the side gate. U.S. was in his greenhouse and was pleased to see me. He asked me some questions. "We were sort of expecting you."

"How is A.J.?"

"Just the same."

"Oh. When will she be home?"

"It won't be that long."

We ran through the kitchen and upstairs to the bedroom. We sat on the bed. Lydia was filling me in about how her week had been. "Hurry up and get changed. Let's go for a walk to the woods." We heard the front door open. A.J. was home. She called out to Lydia, "Come down when you've changed." "Sylvia is here. I am getting changed." She whispered to me, "Be nice to her."

"Of course. I wonder how she'll be with me?"

"We will soon find out." We ran downstairs to the kitchen. I said, "Hello. How are you?" She looked at me. "You have never asked me that before, how are you?"

"Well, thank you."

"We will talk after dinner in the front room."

"I'd like that, thank you."

"Can we go for a walk while you make dinner?"

"Yes. You have half an hour."

"Thank you," and we went out the back door, down the garden and through the side gate. A few children were playing, and called out, "Hello." Lydia knew them, and waved. It was so good being on our own, and able to talk about anything and everything. Lydia asked, "Are you really happy?"

"Yes. It's so different," and I went into detail. Lydia was telling me how things were at school. She was managing, doing jobs and studying. "A.J. is OK. I get on mostly with her. Sometimes I find her a bit much, and ask her to leave me alone, and she respects that. U.S. is just the same. He doesn't say much, only when we do the dishes, and he talks then."

We were walking home. I asked, "I wonder what we'll have for dinner?"

"Don't forget it's Friday night, and youth group."

"It will be so good to be back. I'm not going to get every weekend off. I think it will be every other one, and might be in the middle of the week." We got home. A.J. had dinner ready. It was one of our favourites, toad in the hole (sausages in batter). I was asked to say grace. Nothing had really changed. We ate in silence. I helped with the dishes and was able to chat with U.S. He said I looked well, and asked if I enjoyed my job. "Yes, it's a lovely place by the river."

"When you're in the front room, you must tell us all about it." It wasn't long before we were in there. I was asked to talk first. I went into detail about where the place was, by the river, underneath a bridge. "The house is called Bridge House. It is huge. I have my own area, with the children,

Catherine and Luke. I have a roster showing what is to be done. Lydia has an invitation to come and see where I am. It is such a lovely place."

"It will have to be in the holidays. You know she is studying hard."

"Yes. I'm proud of my sister."

"It's good that Sylvia is happy. It sounds a lovely place."

"It is, and I have been measured for a uniform. They have a maid who wears a uniform, and she brings meals up for the children and me. Catherine, who is four, is a real chatterbox, and will start school next year. She loves books and wants me to read to her. Luke is shy and quiet. I hope he will get used to me."

"Well," A.J. said, "Sounds like you are happy working for the doctor. Mrs. Taylor feels he is a good doctor."

"Yes, Mrs. Brady is nice and easy to get on with, and she told me she is having another baby next year. She will need me to help her. It will be very busy, she said."

"That will be a big family."

"I will get every other weekend off, and one day in the week."

"Well, everybody will be at work or at school, so that's not much good."

"I can spend time with Mrs. Taylor and U.S. I can still come."

"Lydia has to study after dinner. I don't know if that will work." Lydia said, "I still want my sister to come. I will manage with my schoolwork."

"I can do any jobs, and do the dishes, to give you time."

"We can give it a try, and see how it works out."

"Thank you," Lydia said, "It's time for youth group. Is it all right if we go now?"

"Very well. We will see you later." We said good goodbye and left the front room.

We walked and talked on our way to youth group. I said, "U.S. still doesn't say anything. He is very quiet. Do you get on all right with A.J.? She seems a bit better towards me." We had now reached the hall.

"So nice, being with you again." Betty was already there, with a few friends. My friend Sylvia was there too. We all gave each other hugs, and they asked how I was getting on, and where was I living? I really enjoyed youth group. The boys were there. Lydia said Dennis wanted to know where I was, and I told him. He'd never heard of the place. When we said our goodbyes, I said I hoped I would come back in two weeks. I asked Lydia, "Do you walk home by yourself when I'm not here?"

"Well, Dennis walks me home."

"What about when you go to chapel?"

"I walk behind U.S. and A.J."

We reached home. A.J. asked, "How was it? You're late."

"It just lasts longer now, and people want to talk to Sylvia."

"Well, I think it's time for bed. Don't forget, you have your jobs to do in the morning."

"I will help Lydia with those jobs." In bed, we chatted.

"I feel I've made the right decision to leave."

"Yes, I'm glad you're happy. I think we'd better try and get some sleep."

We woke up late. A.J. had left. We went down to the kitchen. U.S. was having a cuppa, and said, "Good morning, girls. I'll make you some breakfast."

"That would be great," I said. He was asking me more about my job. He said, "I'm pleased it has turned out well for you and that you are happy."

"Thank you. I am kept busy, and I'm helping, which I enjoy. It's such a lovely place. I wish you could see it. I think I am fortunate to have the job. It was Mrs. Taylor who recommended me."

"Yes, she has known the doctor for a long time, and told him how good you were with Elizabeth." We chatted while he made breakfast. I then helped Lydia with the jobs. U.S. said, "I'll do the dishes. You don't have to help." We ran upstairs and got dressed. Then we had the rest of the jobs to do upstairs. It didn't take us long. We chatted all the time. I asked, "What time does A.J. get home?"

"We've got about an hour and a half. Let's have some time to ourselves." So, we went outside, where we could hear children playing. There were some older ones whom I knew. We joined in a game of cricket. We could see A.J. coming home. Lydia said, "It will be sandwiches for lunch. Then I have the chapel to clean. Are you helping me with that?"

"Of course I will." We went inside. A.J. asked, "What have you been doing?" Lydia said, "We've just been playing cricket."

"I thought you'd be too big for that," she said to me. "It was a bit of fun." We went upstairs and tidied up before lunch. We came downstairs. I went down the garden to let U.S. know that our sandwiches were ready. I was asked to say grace, and we ate in silence. "It is now time to clean the chapel, girls."

"I'm coming to help." I didn't mind doing it. A.J. was slower in walking. I didn't think she was that well. I asked Lydia, and she hadn't noticed anything. "She does get very tired, and needs to rest more." I asked, "What is her job?"

"She says, it's not for me to say. I try and help where I can."

"We are doing that."

Chapter 92

When we got home, I visited the allotment with U.S. and pulled out vegies that were ready to eat. We had to take the wheelbarrow to carry them. It brought back memories of Monty, whom we loved. He used to jump around when we watered the vegies. We did our walk over the stile to the field. I really missed Monty now. I asked Lydia, "If I wasn't here, what would you be doing?"

"I spend a lot of time studying and doing homework. My marks are OK, but they could be better."

"Are you sure?"

"Yes. There are two in my class that have higher marks than me. I want to get top marks. That's my aim."

"Well, don't overdo it. You will have to help A.J. more."

"I know. It's good you're here and are giving me a break for a while."

"Wish I could come every weekend, but it's every fortnight. I can help then."

"I hope you don't mind."

"I just want to be with you. That's fine."

On Sunday morning, I walked with Lydia and sat with the youth group. Sylvia and Betty were there. It was so good to see them again. We whispered together, and were getting looks from some people. After the service, we walked out together, chatting. I would have to leave at four to catch the bus back. I said, "See you in two weeks," to my friends. I was feeling sad at leaving, but Lydia knew I wouldn't want to be living with A.J. full time and doing my old job. I said goodbye to U.S. and A.J. "Thank you for having me. I hope you feel better soon."

"Thank you. I see I have brought you up well." Lydia came with me to the bus stop. We gave each other a hug. We just made it – we could see the bus coming. I said, "See you soon. Take care," and I jumped on the bus, waving till she was out of sight. I got off and walked to Bridge House and down the drive. Catherine ran towards me, saying," So good you're back!" She gave me a big welcome. I could see Margaret with Luke at the door. She asked me, "Did you have a happy time?"

"Yes, it was good seeing my sister again."

"Catherine has really taken to you, asking me all the time when you would be back." She had been holding my hand the whole time, chattering. "Let Sylvia settle in and take her things to her room. We will come up in an hour, and you can take over then. "

"Thank you." I didn't expect such a welcome, I thought, as I went upstairs to my room. I'd better unpack and be organised. It didn't take me long. I tidied up a bit, putting toys away. When Margaret came in, I could see she was pleased I had the place tidy. She sat down and had a talk with me. Catherine asked, "You're not going away for a long while, are you?"

"No, I won't be."

"Because I like it when you're here."

"Thank you," and I gave her a hug. Margaret smiled. "She's really taken to you, which is good." Luke didn't like being left with me, and cried when Margaret left. "Don't let it upset you. It will take longer before he gets used to you." I asked, "What do you think I should do?"

"Just get his attention with a toy or a game. It will take time. He will eventually get to know you. Ethel will bring up tea soon. I will see you tomorrow." Catherine said, "Goodbye." And "Stop crying!" to Luke. She held his hand and took him to the other side of the room. She showed him his car that he could sit in. It had a horn that he could press. That got him to stop crying. Catherine asked, "Can you read to me?" She ran to get a book. I started reading.

I settled into the job and enjoyed it. Margaret asked me, after a few weeks, "How are you feeling about things? Are you happy to stay?"

"Yes, thank you."

"How are you managing with the children?"

"Catherine is really good. I think I'm managing Luke."

"Well, I want you to wear the uniform, so we'll get that sorted, and it will be official that you are the children's nanny." In a few days, I had my uniform. It felt strange. It took me a while to get used to it. Margaret and I got Catherine ready for school. Margaret showed me where the school was. Of course, I was in my uniform, showing I was with the children. The school wasn't far away. Catherine was excited, and wanted to go there. I thought, I will miss her chatter. Luke wasn't crying quite as much. He was getting used to me slowly. He was a quieter child.

The day arrived for Catherine to start school. She was ready, with her uniform on. She just wouldn't stop talking. "When are we going to get there?" Margaret took her in the car. We went in with her. A teacher spoke to Margaret, then it was time to say goodbye. "I will see you when

I've finished," Catherine said. "Yes, we will be here." She spoke to a teacher, "I hope she won't be disappointed, say she's had enough and want to come home."

"We will have to wait and see till later this later this afternoon." It was so quiet without Catherine, until it was time to pick her up. We walked to the classroom. Lots of children were coming out. Then we saw her. She was so pleased to see us, full of chatter, telling us what she had been doing. "What a relief!" Margaret said. Catherine asked, "When do I go back again?"

After a few weeks, Margaret came to see me, to tell me she was going into hospital to have her baby, and Tom would be checking with me to see how I was going. I would get in touch with him if I had any problems. Margaret said, "I will be kept busy when the baby comes." It was an education for me to learn about childbirth. Margaret had another little boy, and Tom took me in with the children to visit. Catherine wanted to hold the baby. She was very excited, asking, "When are you coming home?" It was nearly two weeks. She came to the nursery, and I was shown how to bath and dress the baby, and even bottle feed. Tom would take Catherine to school before going to the surgery.

My life became really busy. I got on really well with Margaret. They named the baby Mark. When he was two months old, Margaret said he would be staying in the nursery with Catherine and Luke. Margaret would come over to help me. I still saw Lydia, and arranged for her to visit, staying over. Tom would pick Lydia up after surgery in Lexton. It didn't go well with A.J., but somehow, Lydia talked her round. It was so good having her stay. Catherine enjoyed meeting her. We showed her the village and the walks by the river. She loved the place, and helped me with the children. Margaret said she must come again. We all got on so well. Lydia said she could understand why I liked my job, and the place was so lovely.

As the children grew older, I would go with them to their various interests. We went on a holiday to the seaside. Tom had a yacht, and I was shown how the sails worked. It was fun. I was being part of their family. I had now settled in my job, and Tom spoke with me, saying, "When the children are old enough, and are all at school, you really won't be needed any more. Have you thought about what you would like to do?" He wanted me to know this, so I could have a think. "You can stay with us until you find what you want to do next."

"Thank you. I've always wanted to do nursing, but my marks at school were not good enough."

"We'll have a little talk about things later."

Chapter 93

A few days passed, then Tom spoke with me again. He said he had enquired at the hospital, and I could do a three-year course in Colchester. "It will be hard work for you, but you could live in the nurses' quarters while you do your training."

"Oh. I would like that."

"I will talk with Matron and see what I can arrange." Margaret came to see me. "We will be sorry to lose you, but you understand, the children are all at school and growing up." I was there for nearly four years.

"I understand. I will be sorry to go." Tom said, "You must keep in touch, and we know Catherine will really miss you." I felt close to her, too.

Another few days passed, and it was finalised. Margaret said, "We will have to tell the children." Nothing had been mentioned before. "I have enjoyed my job and being here, and will miss you all."

"It's been a pleasure to know you. I hope it all works out for you. I know the children will miss you, and I will too." So, we had organised to have a talk and let them know. Catherine was very upset. "I don't see why you have to go." Tom explained, "You are all at school and growing up. Sylvia is not needed. She can come and visit us and we will keep in touch." Margaret spoke with me later that day, saying she was happy that Tom could help me with the details of when I could start at the hospital. It was amazing how it all happened so quickly. Margaret said, "I am glad Tom can do this for you."

After the children were asleep, I was reading, when there was a knock on the door. It was Tom, to say, "I have got you into the course, and you have a room at the hospital. It starts next week."

"Oh, that is quick."

"There is a room vacant for you." It was hard to believe. I asked, "Does Margaret know?"

"Yes. I have told her, and she says we should tell the children tomorrow. We will do it all together, and then you can decide when you want to go. We will talk tomorrow about it." I thanked him very much.

I couldn't sleep. How quickly things had changed! I hadn't told Lydia, but should be seeing her at the weekend. I eventually fell asleep.

The next morning, I went with the children to school, thinking, they will know tonight I will be leaving. After getting back, I put my things on one shelf and tidied everywhere. Margaret came in and helped me to pick up the toys. Later in the day, Tom was home, and we all went into the study. Catherine asked, "Why are we here?" "We have something to tell you all." He told them. Catherine said, "We don't want Sylvia to leave." She turned around and asked me, "Do you want to leave?" I explained, "Now you are all at school, I am not needed."

"But we do, when we get home." Margaret said, "I will be there for you."

"I want Sylvia to stay." The boys said, "Yes, she can stay." Tom said, "Sylvia needs the job. There really isn't one now you are all at school. She will come and visit us." Catherine asked, "Do you really want to go?"

"I will miss you, but I have to have work, and like your dad said, you are all at school now. I have nothing to do in the day. I am going to do nursing," I told them, "And when I get some time off, I can come and see you."

"Oh, if you really have to leave. You promise you will come back to see us?"

"Yes, I will."

"We will organise that when Sylvia gets some time off."

"I still don't want you to go, Syl." Margaret said, "It has to be. We will all miss her, but we will keep in touch." Catherine gave me a hug. "When is this happening?"

"At the end of the week. The course is starting on Monday, and there is a room at the hospital for me." Catherine said, "That is quick."

"But I have to be there when the course starts." Margaret said, "We will get Ethel to make us a nice picnic, and we will have it down by the river, when you get home from school tomorrow."

"That will be nice. I still don't want you to go, Syl." Margaret said, "I know, but we have to keep moving forward."

There was lots of chatter as we all went up to the children's area. The next day, when the children came home, they raced to their rooms and got changed. Ethel had made a lovely picnic, and wheeled it on her trolley with all the food, and a picnic rug was spread out on the grass by the river. It was a lovely day, with lots of nice food, and everybody loved it. It was so nice that they did this for me. I thanked them very much. I would miss them, and I now had to start looking forward to my next job. Margaret said, "I think you should go and see Lydia, and let her know all your news."

The next morning, I caught the bus and visited Mrs. Taylor. She was pleased to see me. Elizabeth was at school. Then I called to see Lena. I stayed a while and told her my news. She was happy for me. Then I went to see U.S., who was working in his greenhouse. He was surprised to see me, and pleased. He hoped I would get on well. I met Lydia off the school bus. She asked, "Why are you here now?" She was surprised. She found it hard to believe that I would be doing nursing. "How good is that? The doctor has really helped you."

"They have been so good to me." We talked. "The children don't want me to leave. Catherine is a bit upset about it."

"I wondered what would happen when all the children would be at school, and you would have nothing to do."

"I just read until it is time to pick them up."

"Well, I guess they can't keep paying you when there is no work for you to do."

"Tom is going to take me to the nurses' quarters, where my room is, with all my stuff, tomorrow. I don't know what time I will have off to visit you. I hope I get some weekends."

"You will have to study hard."

"I know. I hope I can do it."

"I will help you when I can."

"That would be good. I can ask you if I don't know things."

"You will get to know some of the girls in time, and they will help, I'm sure."

"It's a bit scary right now, but I'm going to try my hardest."

"Good for you. Do your best, that's all you can do."

"Thanks." We hugged. We had walked home. A.J. asked, "What has happened? We weren't expecting you. Are you staying for dinner?"

"Yes, please."

"Well, I'm not sure if we will have enough food." Lydia said, "She can have some of mine." U.S. came in. "Girls, let's go to the allotment and see if we can get some vegies." That's what we did. We took a bag, and U.S. took a spade. We went to the allotment. He dug up some potatoes, pulled out some carrots, and there were peas ready to be picked. We hurried back and got the vegies ready. I said, "I'll do the peas."

"Well, don't start eating them all, like you usually do." We were all busy getting dinner organised. A.J. said, "We will talk in the front room, after dinner. I do hope you haven't lost your job." I went to speak, and was told, "After dinner, in the front room." It wasn't very long before dinner was cooking, and we ran up to the bedroom, chatting, sitting on the bed. Lydia told me she was managing with the jobs and studying, and getting good marks. She and A.J. were getting on better now that I had left. U.S. was just the same.

We enjoyed dinner and helped with the dishes. I was able to talk with U.S. He said, "I am glad you have done well, and how it is all turning out for you." The dishes were done and put away. "Let's go into the front room and tell A.J." We sat down. "Well, Sylvia, what have you got to tell us?" She listened. "Goodness me! Now you don't have a job."

"Not at the moment. I will be doing nursing. I have a room at the nurses' quarters."

"So, how are you going to get money to look after yourself?" Oh, I thought, that's something I hadn't thought about.

"Doctor Tom has organised it for me. I need to check with him what the arrangements are."

"I think you do, and your school marks weren't good enough for you to go into nursing. How do you think you will manage?"

"I'm going to study hard."

"Well, you will need to. Now, if you had kept your job from school, you wouldn't be in this situation."

"I have been really happy working at Bridge House, but all the children are at school, and I'm no longer needed."

"Like I say, you wouldn't be in this situation if you had listened to me."

"Sorry you don't see things this way for me, but I'm looking forward to doing my nursing. I will work hard and do my best with it."

"I'm proud of my sister, and I will help her where I can."

"Well, we shall see what happens." U.S. just sat there, not saying a word. Lydia asked, "When does this start?"

"Doctor Tom is taking me in on Friday. I'm only staying here tonight because I wanted to let you hear my news. I'll catch the bus in the morning." A.J. said, "Thank you for letting us know, and no doubt we will hear how you get on." Lydia said, "It's kind of Doctor Tom to do this."

"I do appreciate it. I get on well with him and Margaret and the children. They want me to keep in touch with them."

"That is good. You have been brought up well. I am pleased to hear you are putting it into practice."

"Thank you, and for having me for dinner."

"That's nice to hear."

"I'm getting the early bus. I will walk with Lydia in the morning."

A.J. said to Lydia, "I think it's time for you to go to bed."

"I'll go too. Goodnight and goodbye." U.S. said, "I'll see you in the morning," and we left the room. We ran upstairs.

"Well, she didn't really say anything nice to me."

"I know. I'm sorry. That's how she is with you. Don't get upset about it."

"U.S. was nice." We talked about what was going on. It was quite late when we heard A.J. call out -- "You'd better get to sleep. You need to be up early."

"We will, now." In the morning, A.J. had already left. U.S. had breakfast ready, which was nice. Then it was time to leave. I said my goodbyes to him. "I will come and see you when I'm settled."

"That would be nice. Hope it works out for you."

"So do I." Lydia said, "Come on! We will miss the bus!" We ran to the bus stop. Lydia's bus was first. We gave each other a hug.

"Good luck."

"Thanks. See you soon." I could see my bus coming. I jumped on, and sat, thinking.

When I got back, the children were pleased to see me. Catherine helped me put my things into bags. I was leaving in the morning! We all had dinner together. Tom asked me, "Are you organised? We will be leaving early in the morning. We will take the children to school first, and then we will take you, before surgery." It was time to say goodnight. "I will miss living here. Goodnight."

Everybody was up early. Ethel brought up the breakfast on a tray. Lots of chatter amongst the children. They were eating breakfast while I was getting their schoolbags organised. Catherine said, "I am feeling sad." I gave her a hug. The boys said, "We will miss you too."

"I will miss you all, and promise to come when I can to see you." Margaret helped me put my bags into the car. She gave me a hug. "Hope all goes well for you. Please keep in touch."

"I will." Tom got in his car. "Come on, children." He said to Margaret, "Goodbye. See you soon." We reached the school and the children said goodbye and wanted to keep talking. Tom said, "We have to go, and you need to get into class." We all shouted, "Goodbye!" We were in the car for a little while. Tom asked, "Are you all right?" I was quiet, and feeling nervous. "It's a big thing, what you are doing. I'm sure it won't take you long to make friends and get into a routine."

"Hope you're right. Thank you for your help."

"You have been part of our family. It's the least we could do. I will come and see how you are when I'm at the hospital."

"Oh, that would be good, and you can tell me how the children are going."

"Yes. We will keep in touch." We had arrived. Tom took me to the office and saw Matron. They had a chat, and I was introduced, "This is the young lady I was telling you about." After more talking, Tom said, "I must be off. Mind you look after her, Matron. Goodbye, Sylvia. See you soon." Then he was gone. Matron said, "I'll show you your room." I followed her down the corridors with all my stuff. She stopped outside a door. A girl came out of the room next door. Matron introduced her, "This is Rosalind."

"Nice to meet you. I'll see you later." She walked away. Matron unlocked the door and gave me a key. "Now, get yourself unpacked, and I will ask Rosalind to show you around."

"Thank you, Matron." She closed the door. Well, this is it, I thought. Looking around, I put my things on the bed. I could see a wardrobe with drawers at the bottom. I quickly got into the unpacking, and had nearly finished, when I heard a knock on the door. It was Rosalind. "Matron asked me to show you around. I only moved in yesterday. We start lectures next week." We could see Matron coming along. "Girls, you need to move yourselves. You have to book yourselves in."

"Thank you." Rosalind was nice and friendly, and helped me settle in. I met a lot of girls in my first week, but Rosalind and I became firm friends.

Chapter 94

At the end of the week, the nursing quarters were full, and we all went to a meeting, where we were given timetables. We would also be getting uniforms, and eventually, doing practical duty on the wards. I was looking forward to that. I had been there two weeks before I got any time off. I slowly got my bearings and was able to take a bus to Lexton, where I arrived at the bus stop and waited for Lydia. She was so pleased to see me, and wanted to know everything. We chattered nineteen to the dozen. I asked, "How do you think A.J. will be if I stay two nights?"

"I think she'll be OK. I can talk to her and get round her. She's all right with me." We were home before A.J. U.S. was in the garden, and pleased to see me. He asked me questions. I said, "Do you think A.J. will be all right with me?"

"I'm sure she will be." We heard the front door. A.J. walked into the kitchen. Lydia said, "Look who's here!"

"Yes, I can see. How are you? Are you staying for dinner?"

"Yes, thank you. That would be nice."

"Well, you can talk later, in the front room, after dinner."

"Yes, I will."

"Lydia, have you organised dinner?"

"Yes," U.S. said. "We can get more vegies from the garden." I said, "I can help you," and went out with U.S.

"Do we need to go to the allotment?"

"I think we should be all right." He dug up some potatoes and pulled out some carrots. There was a marrow growing. "I think it will be ripe enough." Lydia put them on the stove, and A.J. said, "I will let you know when dinner is ready."

"Thank you. We are going up to the bedroom."

"You are getting on better with A.J. now I've left."

"Yes, she is easier to get on with, and my marks are improving. I did find it hard for a while. Tell me everything about you." There was a lot to tell since I saw her last, and she had much to tell me. We chatted away, until we heard A.J. call us for dinner. I was asked to say grace, and we ate in silence. In the front room, A.J. asked me, "Tell me what's been happening to you." She showed surprise at how Doctor Tom had helped me move into the nurses' quarters.

"I know it's going to be hard for me, but I'm going to give it the best I can."

"Well, you should have done that when you were at school." I didn't say another word. I just let her go on with more of the same, how I didn't listen to her. When she stopped talking, she was surprised I didn't say anything – I didn't interrupt or contradict her. She asked more questions, which I answered. "You have grown up a bit more. I am pleased to see that some of my upbringing came through."

"Thank you." I was asked when I was going back. "Can I stay tomorrow night as well, and then leave the next morning?"

"Very well." After Lydia spoke about her day, we said goodnight. It was so good being together again. We left in the morning to see Mrs. Taylor. She was happy to see me and wanted to know all about what I was doing. Elizabeth was now at school. Then, we called in to see Lena, who was interested to know what was happening to me. She said I had done well, and wished me all the best with my studies, and the same for Lydia. We walked back together. "I have a bit of homework to do."

"Okay. What can I do to help with dinner?" U.S. was in the kitchen getting things started, and I helped. He chatted to me. He was so different when A.J. wasn't around. She came home, and was pleased to see that Lydia was doing her homework. It wasn't long before we had dinner. A.J. asked me again to say grace. After dinner, we were back in the front room. I was asked first, "What have you been doing today?" She was interested to hear about it, and surprised that I had visited Lena. Mrs. Taylor, she understood, but couldn't quite understand why I saw Lena. "Well, she has a lovely garden, and I like to walk around and look at it." She seemed happy about that.

It was my last night with Lydia, before I went back. I had some textbooks with me, and showed them to Lydia, who was interested to see what I was studying. I didn't do any while I was with her. I said, "I'll have a look at them on the bus." We chatted for a short time in bed, before going to sleep.

U.S. had breakfast ready, and said it had been nice to see me again.

"Not sure when you will see me again."

"Well, all the best with your studies."

"Thanks." We hurried upstairs and got our things. We called out, "Goodbye." We walked to the bus stop. Lydia said, "Hope all goes well for you."

"With you too."

"It's been good being together, and you are managing A.J., and getting on all right."

"Yes. I know how to treat her. Still miss you, though."

"Me too."

"It's good that she lets me stay, and I can see you." The bus had arrived. We were able to give each other a goodbye hug. It wasn't very long before my bus came. I opened my books. I tried to concentrate, but couldn't.

Back in my room, I unpacked and had a look at the roster. I thought, I must study. I walked to the desk, sat down, opened the books, and managed to do a little bit, before Rosalind called to see me. She wanted to know about my weekend. She told me what she had been up to. We became good friends, and we found that if we studied together, we could ask each other questions that really helped us. I settled in quite quickly and was really starting to enjoy what I was doing. I hoped I would pass my first exam.

We walked to the dining room, passing Matron walking the opposite way. She asked me how I was settling in. "Well, thank you." We walked along a bit further, to the dining room. Rosalind said, "I was never asked how I was settling in. How come?"

I explained about myself and Doctor Tom. "Oh," she said, "I guess he might ask her when he is here next." It wasn't long before we had uniforms to wear, and we would be going on the wards with a senior nurse, who would show and tell us what to do. I really enjoyed helping and learning. By the end of the day, I was tired, and went to bed. It did take me some time to adjust. It was a full day. We had lectures to attend. I did find it hard. Sometimes, Rosalind and I would talk about it, which helped us. It was so good to have that friendship. We both gained from it. Our first exam came. Rosalind got through easily. I passed, but only just. I was so happy. I enjoyed the practical side, but found the theory hard. But I was managing. Doctor Tom came to see me and asked how I was getting on. He gave me an update on the children. Catherine had written me a letter, which I treasured. They sent their love, and said I must come and visit. I made a time when I was next off. He congratulated me on passing my first exam. Things were going really well for me. We had a routine that had to be adhered to. It was a bit like being at school. Up at a certain time and in bed by eight o'clock. Lights were turned off. That's how it was then.

We really enjoyed our time off, but we had to be back by a certain time. We had to clock on and clock off. I did organise a visit to Bridge House and waited outside the school. I met Margaret, to pick up the children in her car. She was pleased to see me and wanted to know how I was getting on. She told me how the children were. It was so good seeing them walking towards the car. They were so excited. They were all chatting at once. I managed to squeeze into the car with everyone to travel home. I would always have good memories of the place. Catherine couldn't stop talking, asking me questions and chatting about what she was doing. The boys finally got a word in when Catherine stopped. I had a lovely dinner with the family, and afterwards we walked in the garden by the river, to the floodgates. It was lovely, but it was time for me to say goodbye. The children gave me big hugs, and Catherine wanted to come with Tom to drive me home, which she did.

Chapter 95

It was Friday night, and Lydia would be going to youth group. I thanked Dr. Tom, gave Catherine another hug, and said goodbye. "I will keep in touch." I got out of the car. I opened the front gate and knocked on the door. A.J. opened it, asking, "Why didn't you go round the back?"

"Dr. Tom just dropped me at the gate, and I had my bags."

"Well, you have missed your sister. She has already gone."

"I will still go to youth group. I will just run up to the bedroom with my things."

"It is not a good idea, you arriving late. Maybe you ought not to go."

"Oh. I'm going. I'll hurry, and apologise when I get there." I quickly said goodbye. I didn't see U.S. A.J. just stood there, watching me as I ran out of the house. I was out of breath when I arrived. The door was closed. I managed to open it. It was heavy. They were playing a noisy game. I just joined in. It was a little while before I saw Lydia, and a bit longer before she saw me. She looked so pleased. As soon as the game was finished, she walked over to me. We whispered to each other. "It's so good to see you," she said. At suppertime, we all sat in a circle. Betty came over and asked, "When did you come in?" I told her and Lydia about my day: "It was so good to see Dr. Tom and the children. He drove me here." There was a lot of chatter while food was passed around. Lydia was telling me, "A few people are asking where you are, and why you're not at chapel, and Dennis has been too. He is here, over there." She pointed to the other side of the room. "Oh. What did you tell them about me?"

"I couldn't say when you're coming, if they asked."

"Well, it sometimes changes. I don't know myself." After supper, we had another game, then sang a hymn and said a prayer, before it was time to leave. A few people came to talk with me, the ladies who ran the group. "I'm sorry I came in late." The lady said, "It's just nice to see you.

Come when you can." Then the boys came over to talk to us. Dennis was asking lots of questions, and wanted to know if I would go out with him. I said, "Oh, all right." He then told me he had a motor bike and asked, "Will you be all right to be a pillion passenger?" I said I wasn't sure, and asked, "Would I have to wear a helmet?"

"We should, but I don't yet."

"Can we leave it for another time?"

"All right. How long are you back for?"

"I have to go home tomorrow. I want to spend time with Lydia."

"When are you off again?"

"It will be in two weeks."

"Well, can we go out then?"

"Oh, all right." We said goodbye. Lydia said, after he left, "I knew he liked you." Betty said, "I've been out with two different boys. One is OK."

"Oh, It's Dennis. I sort of know him." We walked out of the hall, chatting. Betty's mum had a word with me, asking how I was getting on. After more talking, we were late home. Lydia said, "I'll do the talking."

"Thanks." We walked into the front room. U.S. was there, and said, "Nice to see you, Sylvia." A.J. gave him a look, and said, "You are really late home." Lydia said, "Yes. People were pleased to see Sylvia, and have been talking with her." A.J. asked, "Did you apologise for your late entrance?"

"I did. The lady just said she was pleased to see me."

"I would have thought you coming in late was disruptive."

"They understood."

"Well, it's late. Have you anything else to discuss?"

"Yes. I spent my day with the children at Bridge House and had dinner with the family. It was so good to see them all, and Dr. Tom drove me here. Oh, and I passed my first exam." U.S. said, "Well done!" A.J. said, "That's one of many, with more to come."

"I know that." Lydia said, "You're doing well."

"Thank you." A.J. said, "Now, Sylvia, you will help Lydia with her jobs. She has a lot of study to do."

"Of course I will."

"Well, I think it's time for both of you to go to bed." We said goodnight and left the room.

In bed, we spoke about everything. Lydia said, "It's good you have settled into nursing."

"I am enjoying it. I do find studying hard. It's nice that I have a friend. We can help each other.

"That's important, to have friends."

"Yes," I agreed. Lydia told me about school and about herself. She was doing well. I was proud of her. We didn't say much more, because we decided we had better get some sleep. "U.S. doesn't say much. He's a lot quieter since you left."

"I think he would be missing Monty. Does he go out walking?"

"Only to Mrs. Taylor's. He still does what he can to help her, and to the allotment, of course."

"Let's see if we can call into Mrs. Taylor's tomorrow. I haven't seen Elizabeth for quite a while. She has been at school." We agreed that's what we would do. I said, "We'd better get some sleep. We have all day together tomorrow."

We woke up late and went down to the kitchen. U.S. was sitting at the table having a cuppa. "Morning, girls. I'll make you some breakfast."

"That would be nice. Do you need us to help?"

"No, you sit there and chat. I'm fine." We chatted to him while he was cooking our breakfast. He was so pleased that I was doing well. I thanked him and got up to walk towards him, wanting to give him a hug, but he just walked towards the sink. That was something we were never able to do. We were never given any affection, and we couldn't show any. We missed out on love while growing up, but Lydia and I always had that together, from an early age, all our lives. We enjoyed our breakfast. We got through our jobs as fast as we could and ran to tell U.S. we were going to see Mrs. Taylor. "I'll come with you." It wasn't long before we were on our way.

She was pleased to see us. Elizabeth came to the door and called out, "Look who's here." Mrs. Taylor was really pleased to see us, and wanted to know how I was getting on with my nursing. When she saw Dr. Tom, she asked about me. Elizabeth asked, "Can we go to the park?" It had been a while since I had seen her. She liked school. She enjoyed the slide and the swings. Lydia sat on a swing. She was really too big for it. We all chatted. Then it was time to walk home. "We had better get home," U.S. said, when we arrived. So, we said our goodbyes and walked home. We had the rest of the day before I had to catch the bus back. It was good to know that Lydia was happy and doing well. She had no problems with that. Lydia walked with me to the bus stop, chatting, and said, "Don't forget, when you're off next, you're going out with Dennis."

"Yes, I'll see him at youth group and let him know then."

"How do you feel about it?"

"A bit nervous."

We saw the bus coming. We quickly said our goodbyes and hugged. I waved at the window until Lydia was out of sight. I picked up my books and had a look at them, trying to encourage myself to study. I managed to do a little. I got off the bus and walked to the nurses' quarters and clocked in. I walked into my room and closed the door. I heard the door of the next room close, and knew Rosalind was back. I decided to go and see her. She had had a lovely time, and told me all about it. She asked me what I had been doing. I told her, and also said that Dennis wanted to take me out next time I was off. "This will be my first time going out with a boy." She said she had been going out with boys for quite a while, "Paul is the boy I'm going out with now. It is serious. When I finish my nursing, we will be getting married, and you can come to my wedding."

"Thank you. I'd like that."

"How did you meet this boy? What's he like?"

"I sort of know him through family. His name is Dennis."

"You'll be fine."

"I am nervous, though."

"Well, it's not for another two weeks, so don't think about it. We have to study, and get so much more done before then."

"Yes, you're right. I'll try not to."

"Just don't, or you won't get through your next exam. Matron doesn't want us to go out with boys, you know that."

"I haven't told anybody."

"We'll keep it a secret," and I agreed. We studied together. She really helped me. I thought, I'm so lucky to have her as my friend. We had to be up early. It was full on, with lectures and study, and sometimes on the wards, which I enjoyed, over those two weeks. Lights out at 8 p.m. – a very strict regime. Matron did her rounds. Our days off came. I had the Friday and the Saturday off. Rosalind wished me all the best. "Tell me all about it when we're back here again."

Chapter 96

I met Lydia off the school bus. She was full of chatter and pleased to see me. It was good catching up with her. When we got home, U.S. was in the kitchen. He was also pleased to see me, saying, "It's only the three of us for dinner. A.J. won't be home till late." I wanted to say, "That's good," Instead, I said, "Oh." We ran upstairs. Lydia asked, "When are you going out with Dennis?"

"I think, after youth group. Do you think I should tell U.S.?"

"Well, it's late when we get back. It might be better to go out on Saturday afternoon, then you can go straight back to the nurses' quarters."

"Yes, you're right. Then I don't have the problem of coming in really late."

"That wouldn't go well with A.J." We came downstairs and helped to make dinner. U.S. was really interested in how I was getting on. After we had helped with the dishes, we went into the front room. Lydia spoke about her day, and she had some homework. I chatted about my nursing friend, Rosalind, until it was time to go to youth group. U.S. said, "A.J. will be home soon."

"We will see her when she gets back." Lydia said, "We had better go." We ran upstairs to get ready, and called out, "Goodbye!" as we left.

As we were walking to the hall, the boys were riding their bikes down the street, and called out to us. They got there before we did, waiting until we arrived. Dennis came up to me and asked, "What time do you have to be back tomorrow?"

"Five p.m."

"How about the afternoon? I'll come around for you."

"Oh. Can I meet you?"

"Tell me, where?"

"I won't say anything to A.J. yet." We worked out that we would meet at the bus stop, and we went inside the hall. "I'll see you tomorrow." It wasn't long before our evening started. It was good catching up with Betty, and we enjoyed our supper. She was telling me about her boyfriend. She really enjoyed working at the dress shop. "Enjoy your time with Dennis."

"Thanks." When we got home and walked into the front room, A.J. was home, saying, "Late again!"

"It is lasting longer, and people are pleased to see Sylvia and chat."

"Everybody is so nice, and I enjoy the evening."

"Lydia, do you have a lot of homework?"

"I have done some, and will do the rest tomorrow."

"Very well. Glad you're organised. Now, Sylvia, you will help Lydia with her jobs."

"I always do."

"Have you anything else to tell us?"

"Only, I'm doing quite well and I'm enjoying what I'm doing."

"Pleased to hear it. I think it's time for bed." We said goodnight and left the room. We were in bed, chatting. I said, "After we have cleaned the chapel, and when we get back, I'll just have to tell A.J. I have to leave early." Lydia asked, "Are you catching the early bus into town with Dennis?"

"Yes. You can still walk with me to the bus stop."

"I will. I wonder what you'll do in town?" We talked more about things.

It was good catching up with my sister, hearing what she had been up to, and knowing she had settled into the routine of seeing me once a fortnight. As she said, after dinner it was homework and bed. We wouldn't really be able to chat for long.

I was a bit nervous about meeting Dennis at the bus stop. Lydia did come with me, and we chatted to Dennis as we waited for the bus. It arrived late. I said goodbye to Lydia and hopped on. Dennis was asking me questions: "Do you really have to be back at a certain time?"

"Yes, I do. Matron doesn't want us to even go out with boys. It's all about getting through our exams. No distractions!" Dennis, of course, didn't agree. "That's ridiculous. I want to take you out every time you have days off." The bus had now stopped. We were in town. I asked, "Where are we going?"

"We really don't have that much time. Let's go and have a drink in a café, and talk." He seemed to know where to go, to a particular cafe. There were a few people in there, and he started talking about himself. He was working at the hospital, in the old section. He was a plumber. I was surprised. "So now I can come and see you."

"I don't think you should. I really don't want to be late back. Please don't. It would make it difficult for me and cause a problem." I was getting upset.

"All right, I won't." I asked him to promise not to, which he did. After a while, I kept looking at my watch. "I really don't want to be late."

"I'll walk you to the hospital. Don't you really get time off for another two weeks?"

"No, I don't. It's Friday and Saturday again, in two weeks."

"Well, I'll see you on the Friday, at youth group."

"Yes, see you then." I hurried through the gate. I didn't turn around. I kept walking until I reached my room. I didn't know how I felt about Dennis. I just knew I wanted to be back on time.

Later, when Rosalind and I got together, she was telling me about her time off. She asked, "How do you feel about Dennis?"

"He is nice enough, but it's going to be difficult to see more of him, which is what he wants."

"If you really like him, you'll find a way. Now, don't think any more about him. We have to study, remember? You must switch off, or you won't get through our next exam." Rosalind helped me heaps, and we never talked about boys until it was our days off again. I'm sure I wouldn't have managed without her. We would ask each other questions, which helped me, and would give ourselves tests. She was so focused, and I was managing, with her help.

It was two days before our time off. Rosalind came to my room. We were walking to lunch, and she told me, "I'm going away on my days off, with Paul, and this is the first time I'll have done that. Mum and Dad have got to know him, and get on well with him, and they want to know that I'm doing the right thing." I was surprised, and found it hard to believe. I said, "Really, they don't mind you doing that?"

"They feel it's better we know each other really well before we get married and make a mistake."

"Oh. How do you feel about it?"

"I'm looking forward to going away with Paul, but the rest, I'm a bit nervous. What will be will be, and I will be prepared." Rosalind was so matter of fact about things. I thought, A.J. would be horrified. "I haven't told anyone else but you." We had become close friends, and she knew a lot about me that I hadn't told anyone, either. We had now reached the dining room. We had our lunch, then we had a lecture. We had to go back and get our books and notepaper. After this, Rosalind said, "It's time to pack for our days off."

"You have a lovely time."

"Just do what you want to do, and enjoy." I was getting my things together, thinking how different my life was from Rosalind's. I made a plan, about what I would do. I would if see if Lena was home, and have a chat to her about things. I got off the bus and walked up the straight road. Lena was in the garden. She hadn't seen me yet. I opened the gate. She turned round and said, "Hello. This is a nice surprise." I was invited in. She was very pleased to see me. I asked, "Can I talk with you about things?"

"Yes." She had heard Dennis was sweet on me, then I disappeared. "A.J. won't be happy about you going out with him."

"I know. It's going to cause a problem. What do you think I should do?"

"Well, I think you should tell her. It's better coming from you than if she hears it from someone else."

"Yes, you're right. Thank you, but I know it won't go down well. I might go and talk with U.S. now, then I want to meet Lydia off the school bus."

"Yes, that's a good idea."

"Thank you for your help."

"You're welcome. Come by any time," and she gave me a hug.

U.S. was pruning his roses in the front garden. He was pleased to see me. "I need to talk with you about something."

"All right," and I went straight into it, telling him about Dennis. He said, "Goodness! That will cause a problem with A.J." I asked, "How do you feel about it?"

"Well, it's all right with me." Again, I wanted to give him a hug, but knew what would happen. I just said, "Thank you. I will go now and meet Lydia off the bus, and I'll tell A.J. tonight."

"Oh dear, but you're right. It has to be said."

The bus was early, and Lydia was walking home. When I saw her, she said, "Oh. I thought maybe you weren't coming, when you weren't at the bus stop." I told her everything about my day.

"A.J. is not going to like it."

"U.S. said that."

"Well, he's right, and he is OK with me seeing Dennis."

"That is nice. Wish we could find out why A.J. is the way she is about family."

"Are you going to see Dennis tonight?"

"Yes, at youth group. Then he wants to take me out from there, and it will be really late."

"A.J. won't like it. That will cause more problems, so I'll have to tell Dennis I can't."

"I think that might be better. She will already be cross you are seeing him."

"Just do like you did last time."

"What did you do?"

"I told her we just went to the café and had a coffee and a talk. Also, I told him I can't be late back. We have to clock in and clock out."

We had now reached home. Lydia got changed. We told U.S., "We are going on our favourite walk, to the woods." We had lots to talk about. Lydia was getting good marks and enjoying school. She had made a lot of friends, and was managing all right with A.J. "I wish it was easier for me with her."

"I know, but it hadn't been that bad lately, and now I have to tell her about Dennis."

"Well, it's better she hears about it from you than if she finds out another way."

"You are right, but I'm not looking forward to it." We walked back and helped U.S. with the dinner. We heard A.J. come in. "Hello. It's been a big day for me."

"Hello," I was going to say a bit more, but she stopped me. "We will talk in the front room." U.S. served dinner. Lydia got into her homework. I helped with the dishes. A.J. went into the front room. "I'm not looking forward to telling A.J. about Dennis."

"I understand, but you must, before she hears it from anybody else."

"I will." Lydia was still doing homework when U.S. and I passed her. "I won't be long." We walked into the front room. "We will wait for Lydia." There was silence. Lydia came in, saying, "I'm finished."

"Very good. How was your day?"

"I'm keeping on top of my subjects."

"I'm pleased to hear it. Now, how about you, Sylvia?"

"I'm doing well. I'm studying as hard as I can, for our next exam. I need to tell you something."

"Well, what is it? Out with it!"

"Dennis has asked me to go out with him."

"Well, really! He would know I wouldn't want that."

"Why not?"

"I don't need to go into it, but I don't want you going out with him. Understood?"

"I've already said yes. He seems quite nice. Can you please tell me the reason?"

A.J. was becoming cross, "It should be enough, when I say I don't want you to go out with him."

"Please. I would like to know the reason."

"I am not going into it."

"I don't think that's fair."

"Well, you will have to accept it. That's enough on the subject."

U.S. never said a word. Lydia said, "We'd better get ready to go to youth group, or we will be late." She got up, and I followed. Once we were upstairs, I asked, "Well, what do you think of that? I wish we could find out."

"You need to ask Dennis. Are you still going to see him?"

"Yes. I'll ask him at youth group. It will be the early bus, as before." We ran downstairs. We could hear raised voices in the front room. We opened the front door and called out, "Goodbye!"

Chapter 97

As we walked to youth group, we could see a crowd at the hall door. Betty came out to meet us. She said, "There's a special supper tonight. I saved you a seat." Dennis was sitting with the boys across the room. He waved. It was a good evening, with a speaker, and an amazing supper. Dennis came over and said, "We are going out from here. Don't forget!"

"It will have to be another time. Can we do what we did last time, and I can catch the early bus?" He was not happy, and walked back to where he was sitting. Lydia said, "He'll get over it. When you get to see him, you can explain, and find out what the problem is with A.J."

"You're right." Betty wanted to know what it was all about, and I quickly told her. Supper was all finished. We sang a hymn, after which there was a prayer. Then we walked towards the door to go out. A few people came to talk with me. The leader of the group said, "It's nice to see you. Come when you can. All the best with your studies." Dennis was waiting outside. He asked, "Why the change?" I told him about A.J. He called her a name, which I said wasn't nice. Lydia said, "We want to know why she doesn't want Sylvia to see you."

"Oh. It goes back a long way with family. I don't really know the details. So, what are you going to do?"

"I will see you. I'll get the early bus and meet you, like we did before."

"I had it all planned for a late night tonight."

"Sorry. It's a difficult situation."

"Do you have to be back so early?"

"Yes. That's how it is!"

"All right. I'll see you at the bus stop, at the same time." We started walking home. He walked with us. He didn't have his bike with him, because we were going to do what he had planned. He was cross, saying goodbye at the gate. Then he had a long walk home. We were really late. Lydia said, "I will do the talking."

"That's good." A.J. wasn't happy. "It's only when Sylvia is here that you come home this late."

"Yes. Everybody wants to talk with her."

"We will talk tomorrow about the situation." We all said goodnight.

When were in bed, we talked. Lydia asked, "What will you do with Dennis this time?"

"I don't know."

"A.J. could make things difficult for you, not being able to see me."

"Can you try with her, to find out more?"

"I could try. Sometimes she's all right with me, other times I can't get through to her. We'd better try and get to sleep."

In the morning, when we woke up, A.J. had gone. "That's good." We ran to the kitchen. U.S. was sitting at the table. "Morning, girls. I'll make you breakfast. What would you like?" We told him, eggs and bacon. I said, "I would like to talk to you about Dennis, and get to know him."

"I can understand that. A.J. is very upset about it."

"What can I do?"

"I will put my thinking cap on." He started making breakfast, and we helped.

"After your jobs, what are your plans, girls?"

"We want to see Mrs. Taylor."

"Well, I'll come with you, to see if she needs any help." So, we ran up to do our jobs. It didn't take us long. We were ready to leave. We ran down to tell U.S. I said, "We are ready to leave!"

"That was quick. Have you done all the jobs?"

"It doesn't take us long, with two of us."

"All right. I'm ready. I'll come." We arrived at Mrs. Taylor's. She was really pleased to see us, and asked me about my job. Elizabeth came out of her bedroom, full of chatter. "Can we go to the park?" Mrs. Taylor said, "Yes, for a little while." Elizabeth really enjoyed it. Then we walked home with U.S. I asked, "Has A.J. heard from our uncle? It's been so long since we heard from him?"

"I think you need to ask her. I thought she did, but it was quite a while ago." Lydia said, "I have been meaning to ask, but I've been very busy."

"Well, I'm not here much. We need to find out." We arrived home and helped make lunch. We heard A.J. come in, and I called out, "Lunch is ready!"

"Thank you." I was asked to say grace, and of course, we ate in silence. After lunch, I asked, "Have you heard from our uncle?"

"Yes. That was a while ago. You haven't been here to be told." Lydia said, "I have, and you didn't tell me."

"It had slipped my mind." I asked, "Is he coming to see us?"

"Girls, we will talk in the front room. Now we have the chapel to clean."

We ran upstairs. "What do you think of that?" I asked.

"Well, unless I ask questions, she doesn't tell me things. I have noticed that more."

"I must write to Uncle and ask A.J. for the address. I can post your letter if you write too." A.J. was calling us, standing at the door. "Too much chatter. We need to go!" We hurried downstairs. She had the door open. We were on our way to clean the chapel. When we had finished, and were at home, I thanked U.S. for what he had done for me. I asked, "Has A.J. heard from our uncle?"

"I think so."

"Can we have his address?"

"You will have to ask A.J. later, in the front room." A.J. came into the kitchen. I asked, "I have to get the early bus. Can you find the letter before I go?"

"It will take me a while. You'll have to wait till your next visit."

"Did Uncle mention that he is coming to see us?"

"I need to find the letter, to read it. I don't think he mentioned that." Lydia asked, "Do you want me to help you find the letter?"

"I think I can do that by myself, thank you." I ran upstairs to pack my things. Lydia said, "I'm going to have to ask her more."

"Yes, do that. If I get the address, I can write, and he will write to me."

"I hope she finds the letter." We were sitting on the bed. Lydia didn't want me to leave. I didn't want to go either. I wasn't sure about seeing Dennis. I sort of did and didn't. I needed to get back on time. It would be against me if I was late. Lydia said, "Well, we had better get moving. Let's see if she has found the letter, and I'll come with you to the bus stop."

"Thanks." I gave her a hug. "Life is changing for us."

"Don't worry about me. I can still do more homework. I'll be OK."

"Right. Let's go downstairs and see. Hope she has found the letter." We went into the kitchen, and they were sitting at the table, talking. I asked A.J., "Have you found the letter?"

"No, I haven't been able to put my hand on it yet. You will just have to wait until you're back again."

"Can't we help you look? I need the address."

"Well, no, if I haven't got the letter, I can't give you the address."

"Would you have it written down somewhere?"

"No, I don't." I asked, "Where are all the letters he wrote to you?"

"Sylvia, I will not have you speak to me like that. They will be all together in a safe place. You will just have to wait until the next time we see you." Lydia said, "We'd better go. You'll miss the early bus."

"Goodbye. See you in two weeks. Hope you find the letter by then!" U.S. said, "Have a good two weeks."

"Thank you." Lydia said, "Come on. I'm walking to the bus stop with Sylvia." I picked up my things and walked to the front door. I closed it with a bang. I said, "How about that?"

"I have noticed A.J. is forgetting things. She didn't tell me that she had had a letter."

"Can you remind her every so often, or try to find the letter?"

"I'll do my best." We could see Dennis standing at the bus stop."

"I hope it goes well with him. He doesn't look very happy."

"Thanks. Look after yourself. See you in two weeks." We had reached Dennis. He said, "Hello." He took some things from Lydia, who was carrying them for me. We could see the bus coming. It was on time. I gave Lydia a hug and said, "Bye." Dennis said goodbye. The bus stopped and we got on. He was quiet. I think he was upset about Friday night. I didn't bring it up. We went to the same café as last time. He bought me an ice cream. "Thank you," I said.

"What are you going to do about A.J.?"

"Well, it's difficult. I am hoping she will come round."

"I don't know if that will happen."

"Sorry. I can only take it slowly. Please try and understand."

"I am trying. She will find out, and stop you from seeing me."

"I will really try and tell her next time."

"Yes, you should!" We chatted a bit more about it.

"Do you really have to get back on time again?"

"Yes, I do. Please don't put pressure on me. I can't be late – it will go against me."

"Well then, we had better start walking back."

"Thank you." We had reached the gate. I said, "See you in two weeks." I hurried through the gate, not looking back.

Chapter 98

Once I was back in my room, I sat on the bed. I was out of breath. I thought about things: I will really have to tell A.J. next time I'm off, if I want to see Dennis. I was hoping U.S. might say something to her. That would be really good. I unpacked and got my books out, to do some study. I heard Rosalind in her room and wondered how her time off had gone. I decided to go and see her. She said she had had a great time. Everything had gone well. "Mum and Dad get on really well with Paul, and have met his parents. Everybody is happy."

"You are so lucky." I chatted about myself.

"Dennis is right. You must let A.J. know, if you want to see him."

"I will do, next time. Hope she will be all right with me."

"She will have to get used to it. Now, we must switch off. We have to study, remember?"

"You are right. Go and get your books, and bring them here, and I'll get organised."

"Thanks," and I left the room. I was so fortunate to have had her for a friend. She was a bit bossy, but I didn't mind. We were coming into our second year and no longer the beginners. We got on so well, and she really helped me to get through. Doctor Tom did call in to see me from time to time, and gave me news of the family. Catherine wrote me letters, which he gave me. I was so pleased to hear how she was getting on.

Our next time off, Rosalind talked with me. "I will be staying home and seeing Paul. What are you going to be doing?"

"I've made up my mind I'm going to speak with A.J. I'm seeing Dennis. I'm not looking forward to it, but I know it's the right thing to do. He wants to take me out from youth group, which finishes late."

"That will be a very late night, then."

"Oh, I know."

"You might have to miss youth group."

"I really enjoy that, and I'm with my sister then."

"Well, I'm sure you'll work something out. Just leave from there, and let A.J. know you will be late." I thought, if only she knew how hard it is for me. It would be nice to have a mum like hers. The day arrived for our time off, and Rosalind said, "I hope it all works out for you."

"You too. Enjoy your time off."

"Thanks. Will do." I was going to Lena's first, to have a chat with her. I was looking forward to that. I would tell her my problems and see if I could find out any more about why A.J. didn't like Dennis. I got off the bus and was walking down her street. I could see her in the front garden. She was pleased to see me. "Come in." She was busy planting something. We went inside. "I'll just get out of my gardening clothes." She handed me a drink. "I won't be long." I sat and looked out at her lovely garden, with lots of lovely different-coloured flowers. I knew she would be picking some for the chapel on Saturday afternoon. Lena came in. "I'll make you some lunch. Would you like that?"

"That would be nice. Thank you." She asked me how I was getting on. After a while, I told her about Dennis, how he was taking me out, and asked, "Why is A.J. the way she is about Dennis?"

"Oh, it's a long time ago, when there was a family feud. She doesn't want to have anything to do with that side of the family, and she won't talk about it."

"I know. I have tried to talk about it with her, and was told the subject is closed."

"Oh dear. She is not going to like me going out with him."

"No, she won't. She will try and stop you."

"How can I go about it?"

"You will have to be honest with her."

"Yes, I will. I might go and talk with U.S. and see what he says."

"That's a good idea. Dennis is a nice boy. It's a pity it's turned out this way." After a bit more talking, I said goodbye. "You're welcome any time. Goodbye!"

I walked in the back gate and saw U.S. He was surprised to see me. "You're early."

"I've been to Lena's for lunch. I need to talk to you." We sat in the kitchen, and I explained about Dennis wanting to take me out after youth group. "I will be home late."

"Well, well. We didn't know things would work out like this. A.J. will not be happy about it." I tried to find out what the problem was, but U.S. refused to go into it. "What should I do?"

"Just tell it like you have told me."

"She will try and stop me."

"Yes, that could happen."

"I think it would be unfair if I'm not told the reason, and you won't tell me either! I was hoping you would, so I can make my mind up for myself." I opened the back door and said, "I'm going to meet Lydia off the school bus and talk with her," and slammed the door. I was really cross, upset and disappointed. When I got to the bus stop, Lydia got off, and asked, "What's the matter? You look cross." I went through it all while we walked home.

"I understand how you feel. Just come out with it and tell A.J. how it is, and see what happens. I'll stick up for you."

"Thanks," and I gave her a hug. "Do you really like him?"

"Yes. He's nice, and it's best you tell her, before she finds out from somebody else. "

"You're right. Dennis is taking me out after youth group, so I will be late in. Hope I don't disturb you when I get into bed."

"Just don't wake me. Tell me in the morning."

We got home. U.S. said, "Sylvia, please understand. It's up to A.J. to tell you things, if she feels you need to know."

"Of course, she needs to know if she is going out with him."

"Let's just see what happens when you tell A.J." Lydia changed out of her uniform and we went for a walk to the woods. We were able to chat about everything that had happened since we saw each other. It was so good. When we got back, A.J. was in the kitchen.

"Hello girls. Dinner is ready." We ran upstairs and washed our hands. Lydia said, "Good luck with your talk."

"Thanks." We ate in silence. Once we were in the front room, Lydia was asked about her day. "I'm getting good marks."

"Are you organised with your homework?"

"I am, thank you."

"That is good to hear. Sylvia, what news do you have to tell us?"

"I'm doing well with my nursing. I want to know, have you heard from our uncle? Did you find the letters?"

"Oh yes. I have another letter. I will go and get it. He has written to both of you."

"That's the best news."

"Do you have anything else to tell us?"

"Dennis has asked me to go out with him this evening after youth group." A.J.'s face changed.

"That's not a good idea. I don't want you to go."

"Why not?"

"I don't need to go into it, just to say, I don't want you to go out with him."

"Well, it's only right and fair that you should tell me the reason."

"I don't have to do that. It should be enough for me to say I don't want you to go."

"Well, it's not. He seems nice, and I want to be able to go out with whoever I want to, otherwise, you should tell me the reason. Has he done something bad, or been unkind?"

"Not that I know of, but I do have a reason. I do not want to go into it anymore."

"I don't want to be rude, but I am going out with him tonight." Lydia said, "Dennis is always polite when we see him. When Sylvia's not at youth group, he walks me home. If Sylvia wants to go out with him, she should, unless you have something against him. Surely you can see that is the right thing to do."

"Lydia, thank you for your input and your point of view, but I choose not to go into details. Sylvia has to accept that."

"Why do you feel this way? I am going out with him tonight, and I'm being honest and telling you. I'll get to know him and make up my own mind about him." Lydia said, "We'd better go now, or we will be late for youth group. Can you please go and get the letters?" A.J. got up, gave Lydia a look and walked out of the room. I thanked Lydia for supporting me. U.S. just sat there, not saying a word, twiddling his thumbs. A.J. came back into the room and gave us a letter each. We thanked her and got up. Lydia said, "We need to go. We will be late." We said goodbye and closed the door. We could hear them talking as we walked away. We ran upstairs and got our coats. We hurried, taking our letters with us.

Once we were outside, I said, "Lydia, thank you for your support again. Let's see if we can read our letters underneath the street light." We stood, reading. I said, "Uncle is coming to see us."

"That will be good. It will be a Saturday."

"Oh, I hope I can get that time off." We were excited. We had reached the hall. "Have fun tonight. I'll see you in the morning." Betty was outside the door, waiting for us. She told me her news, and I told her I was going out with Dennis that night. We walked inside, and could see Dennis sitting with some boys on the other side of the room. He raised his hand to me and I did the same. We had a nice evening and a yummy supper. When the evening finished, Dennis walked up to me, and asked, "Did you tell A.J.?" I said yes. We said goodbye to Betty, then we walked Lydia home. "See you in the morning!" She said, "Goodbye. Have fun."

Dennis and I walked to the bus stop. He said, "I thought we could go and see a film."

"Oh, that would be good." I really enjoyed the film. I had never seen one before. We caught the late bus back. "I hope A.J. has left the door unlocked." The street lights were on. We opened the gate, which squeaked. Dennis walked up to the front door and opened it. He gave me a hug and a kiss, and he whispered, "I hope to see you in two weeks," and he closed the door. I quietly went up the stairs and opened the bedroom door. The moon was out, and I could see to undress. Lydia had left the curtain open a bit. I carefully got into bed without touching Lydia. I managed to lie on my side, and straight away fell asleep. Lydia had to wake me in the morning, and started asking me questions. "What time did you get in, and what did you do? Thanks for not waking me."

"I am tired. Give me a chance to wake up, and I'll tell you."

Chapter 99

I was happy telling Lydia about my time with Dennis. U.S. called, "Breakfast is ready!"

Lydia said, "We'd better hurry. You are going to help me with these jobs?"

"Of course. I feel better now. I'm more awake." We ran down to breakfast. U.S. said, "I didn't hear you come home."

"Oh, that's good. It would be awful if I woke you."

"What time was it?"

"I'm not sure. We caught the late bus back." Lydia asked, "Where did you go?" I told Lydia. U.S. was listening to our conversation. He asked, "Are you going out with him again?"

"Yes. He told me he works in the old part of the hospital, and he's a plumber."

"I didn't know that."

"He rides his bike everywhere." Lydia said, "I like him. He walks me home from youth group when you're not around." U.S. said, "That is the right thing to do. I am pleased. Now you had better get into the jobs." We got up from the table and thanked U.S. for breakfast. He said, "I'll do the dishes."

"Thanks," we said, and ran upstairs. We hurried, and got into the jobs. "I think U.S. is all right with you seeing Dennis."

"I wish he would tell us what happened."

"Well, you can find out more from Dennis."

"I did ask him, and he said he didn't really know. He thought it was a family feud or something."

"I'm glad it's out in the open, even if A.J.'s not happy about it. When are you going to see him again?"

"Not until two weeks."

"That's good. We have some time together this afternoon."

"Yes. I wonder how A.J. will be with me when she gets home?" We had finished our jobs, and told U.S. we were going to visit Mrs. Taylor. "I'll come with you, to see if she needs any help," as he closed the greenhouse door. "I'm ready to go."

We walked to Mrs. Taylor's. She was pleased U.S. was with us, and was glad of his help. Mr. Taylor left for work very early in the morning. Elizabeth came out of her bedroom, asking, "Can we go to the park?" Mrs. Taylor said, "Yes, for half an hour." It wasn't long before we were in the park. Nobody else was there. Elizabeth jumped on the swing, calling out to me, "Please give me a push!" Lydia sat on the other swing. She was almost too big to do that. Elizabeth had fun, and we walked back to her home. U.S. was waiting for us and ready to leave. Mrs. Taylor asked me, "Before you go, are you enjoying your job nursing?" She told me that when she went to the doctor's, Doctor Tom gave her news of the children, which she passed on to me when she saw me, and they sent their love. We said our goodbyes and started walking home. I asked U.S., "Do you think A.J. will be all right about me seeing Dennis again?"

"She is not happy about it."

"How do you feel?"

"I really don't mind."

"Well, I like him, and I'm seeing him again. I wish I knew why she feels this way. You know, and won't tell me. It doesn't seem right that I'm not told."

"Sylvia, it's up to A.J. to tell you herself, not me."

"That's so stupid. If she told me, I might not want to go out with him again, although he's polite, and I do like him." Lydia said, "I think he's nice, and he is your grandson. Is it because something happened in the family?" We had now reached home. He said, "I am not talking any more about it."

We helped to make lunch.

Chapter 100

I settled back into my nursing and enjoyed it. I was looking forward to seeing Uncle when I was off next. I told Rosalind how things were. She thought, like me, that I should be told. She said, "It can't be that bad, or U.S. wouldn't mind you seeing him."

"Yes, you're right. I'm so looking forward to talking with my uncle."

At last, the time came round, and our uncle would be at A.J.'s when I would be home on Saturday. I was excited. I met Lydia off the school bus on Friday afternoon. We had lots to talk about. We were looking forward to youth group, where I would be seeing Dennis. I was not going to be seeing him on Saturday afternoon. A.J. hardly spoke with me, only to say, "I will have words with Uncle about this situation." He was coming for lunch on Saturday. She was hoping to get back early from her job. She told us we had to make sure everything was tidy, and had done all our jobs. It didn't take us long. A.J. came home early, and was pleased we were organised. I asked, "Can we walk to meet the bus?" We knew when it would be coming. She said, "We will wait. You don't need to do that." Lydia said, "We want to." She reluctantly agreed. We ran all the way to meet the bus and saw Uncle walking towards us already. The bus must have been early.

There were big hugs and squeals of excitement. We were both talking nineteen to the dozen. "One at a time, please! I can't understand what you're saying." Lydia said, "You go first. You have more news than me." So, I quickly told him what was happening. He said, "I'm proud of you, doing nursing, and what you have been doing with the doctor's family. You have done well. Now, what's this about the boy, Dennis, you have met?" I went into it all, talking as fast as I could, as we had reached home. Uncle said, "We will go out, the three of us, and we will talk about things." I said, "A.J. has lunch ready."

"Well, we will go out after that." A.J was standing at the front door, which was wide open. "Do come in. Girls, leave your uncle alone for a while. We need to have a talk." I asked, "Is lunch ready?"

"I will call you when it is ready." They went into the front room. We ran upstairs. "Well, I'm so happy. Uncle is proud of me, and doesn't seem to mind about Dennis."

"I didn't really get to talk with him."

"Sorry. Well, when we see him next, you can talk first." We chatted between ourselves. It seemed a long time before the front room door opened, and we were called. I asked, "I wonder how it went?"

"We will be able to tell by how they are."

"Yes, you're right." We sat at the table. Uncle sat between us, and said grace, then asked Lydia, "How are you going at school?" A.J. spoke, "We have our meals in silence." Uncle said, "Oh. I forgot. I will respect that." I thought that was funny and almost burst out laughing. I gave Lydia a look. She tried not to giggle. When we had all eaten, Uncle said, "I will take the girls into town and spend some time with them. I will be going back to London this evening."

"Oh. What time had you in mind?"

"Well, straight away. We only have a few hours together." I knew A.J. wanted us to help with cleaning the chapel, and it would mean she would have to do it on her own. That would be a first, I thought. That's great. I said, "I'll go and get my things." Then I asked Uncle, "Can you take me back to the nursing quarters?"

"Yes, of course."

A.J. was just standing there, in a state of shock, I thought. Lydia followed me upstairs and whispered, "Well, I can't believe I don't have the chapel to clean. It's so good that we can leave straight away." We ran downstairs, carrying my things, and left them at the front door. Everybody was in the front room. I opened the door and said, "We're ready to go." A.J. said, "We are talking. It's rude to interrupt."

"Sorry. I thought we were going straight away." Uncle got up. "Yes. I think we should get going." After a bit more talking, we eventually reached the front door. I said, "Goodbye. Thank you for having me." U.S. said, "Have a good two weeks." A.J. said, "Goodbye." Lydia said, "I'll see you later today." A. J. asked, "What about your homework?"

"I'm organised, thank you." I opened the front door, picked up my things, and started walking down the path. Lydia followed and Uncle was in the rear. I could hear the front door close. At last, we were on our own, walking to the bus stop. Lydia was chatting to Uncle, telling him how she always had to help clean the chapel, "Sylvia helps when she's here. This is the first time I won't have to do it." Uncle was surprised, and glad she was having time off from it.

We had the best time together, and talked and talked. Uncle was interested to know how I met Dennis. I told him it was through the youth group. He seemed pleased for me, and said he was proud of both of us. He asked Lydia how she was getting on with A.J. We laughed together when Uncle tried to make conversation while we were eating lunch. He said he had forgotten we had this strange silence at mealtimes. He spoilt us. We had afternoon tea in a cosy little tearoom. It was so good. The best thing was, he gave us his address, so we could write to him on our own, without A.J. being involved. He said, "I will try and keep in touch more," and explained how busy he was. He gave us news of Alice, Marion and Peter. "They all send their love."

Time went fast, and Lydia was the first to get back on the bus. We said our goodbyes. Then Uncle walked me back to the nursing quarters. He said, "I hope you get through your next exam." He said goodbye and gave me a hug. When I reached my room, I unpacked, then I went to see Rosalind. I couldn't wait to tell her my news. She was still unpacking. We sat on the bed, chatting. She had had fun too. She was happy for me, that my uncle was pleased with us, and how it all went. "He said he would like to meet Dennis one day."

I found it really hard to get back to my studies. If it hadn't been for Rosalind, who pushed me, I was sure I would not have been able to manage. I think she enjoyed pushing and bossing me. I thanked her after we did another exam. I just got through. We became inseparable. She shared her home life with me, and I felt I helped her. When we chatted, she would say, "Thanks. I didn't see it that way." I enjoyed it when we were on the wards. Some patients would show they were grateful, and others didn't. We were taught to have a smile on our faces, no matter what, and do whatever was asked of us. You had to have a lot of patience, and never show you were cross or tired. By the end of the shift, I was really tired, and was glad to sit down, but it felt good, knowing you had helped people.

On my next days off, I was wondering how A.J. would be with me after our uncle's visit. I met Lydia off the bus and asked, "How was A.J. with you?"

"The same. Nothing has changed." We walked home. U.S. was in the garden, and asked, "How are you getting on?" I told him what our uncle had said about seeing Dennis and being happy for me. "He said he would like to meet him one day."

"Well, it's because of the past and what did happen, that A.J. doesn't want you to see him."

"You won't tell me, so I'm continuing to see him. I like him a lot. I asked Dennis, but he doesn't know what it's all about. Some family upset, he thinks. I asked why we should we have to suffer for it."

"I can understand your point of view, but I can't do anything about it." We helped him with dinner. We could hear A.J. come home. She came into the kitchen and said, "Hello." She was polite, and said, "We will talk after dinner, in the front room." We ate dinner in silence, of course. I chatted with U.S. while helping with the dishes, telling him about being on the wards. I think he really enjoyed me talking to him. He was s different from when we went into the front room. He hardly ever spoke, just sat there, twiddling his thumbs.

We went into the front room. A.J. asked Lydia about her day. She said she was getting top marks now. A.J. said she was proud of her. Then I was asked. I told her I was coping well and enjoying what I was doing. "I'm on the wards now." She was surprised. "Are you not finding it too much?"

"No, I'm enjoying it, and it's rewarding."

"Well, what are your plans?"

"I'm going to youth group, then I'm seeing Dennis, and I'll help Lydia with the jobs and cleaning the chapel tomorrow. We'll get the bus back in the afternoon."

"Very well. I'm pleased you will help your sister, and not just think of yourself." Lydia said, "We'd better get ready to leave. We'll be late." She got up and walked out of the room. I followed. We ran upstairs, chatting, and got our coats. We called out, "Goodbye."

Lydia said, "You did well, talking to A.J. and mentioning Dennis. I expected her to say something."

"Maybe she accepts it now."

We arrived at the hall. Everybody was inside. We were a bit late. Betty walked towards us. She had saved us a seat. We listened to the speaker, then our evening started, with games and some exercise, which we enjoyed. Dennis was with his friends, and waved. At suppertime, Betty was asking me about him. "Is it serious?"

"I don't know." She chatted about the boy she was going out with. We had lots to talk about while having supper. Lydia said, "I'll see you in the morning, and don't wake me."

"No, I won't. It's worked out well so far." After supper, Dennis came over and talked with us, saying we would walk Lydia home first. He introduced us to his friend, Roy. He seemed nice. Betty's mum was outside. She spoke with me for a while, then we said our goodbyes and started walking home. We said goodbye to Lydia, "I'll see you in the morning." We were on our own. We caught the bus into town and went to a hall where there was music. We sort of danced, which I had never done before. I enjoyed it – my first experience of trying to dance. We got the last bus back, and Dennis walked me home. He gave me a hug at the front door and a sort of kiss, and opened the door. I crept up the stairs. I opened the bedroom door. Good. Lydia had remembered to leave the curtain open, so I could see a bit. I managed to get into bed without touching her. I was so tired I fell asleep straight away.

Chapter 101

During my time off, I was seeing more of Dennis. I was helping Lydia as much as I could. A.J. didn't speak with me about Dennis any more, but knew I still was. Things were going sort of all right. I was still finding studying hard, but with Rosalind's help, I was getting a pass. She got higher marks. We kept it a secret that we had boyfriends, and only talked about it when we were on our own. She told me that when she got her certificate, she would be getting married, and hoped to work at the hospital. I was finding things between Dennis and me hard. He was becoming more serious, and told me he really loved me and wanted to see more of me. I spoke with Lydia about it. I didn't want to change anything in my routine. I wanted to spend the same time with Lydia as I had been doing. We chatted about it.

Lydia said, "You will know when you want to see Dennis more. I will understand. I would miss you heaps, but it will happen one day. I won't be the one to stop you." I gave her a big hug. I was no longer able to get to youth group. My time off had changed to the middle of the week. I would visit Lena and take my books with me. Lena would help me by asking me questions. I was only staying over one night. A.J. was polite, but didn't speak much to me. She knew I was seeing Dennis, but did not mention it again. Lydia told me she had not been very well, and didn't work as many days. She had managed to get someone to clean the little chapel, which was good for Lydia, as she had been finding it difficult.

She also told me that Dennis had been looking for me. "I told him you'd be off on Wednesday night. He said he would come round to see you."

"Oh. That won't go down well with A.J."

"He needs to talk to you, he said."

"I will have to explain that I can't do anything about my time off changing. That's how it is. I'm not sure how long it will last for."

"I think he really loves you and wants to see you more."

"Well, you understand. I can't do that."

"I know, but you will have to tell him that's how it is."

"Yes, I will."

We had just finished dinner. I was helping with the dishes, when there was a knock on the door. U.S. said he would go. I stayed in the kitchen. I could hear U.S. talking with Dennis, saying, "Come in, and wait near the door. I'll get her for you." U.S. called out as he walked into the kitchen, "Dennis is at the door! You had better go and see him."

"What happened? You don't come to youth group anymore."

"I can no longer get the time off. My days have changed. I have Wednesday and go back on Thursday evening." Now A.J. came out of the front room. Dennis said "Good evening," to her. "I've come to see Sylvia."

"I can see that," she turned to me. "Are you happy to see him?"

"Yes. I'm explaining why I can no longer go to youth group."

"Have you finished tidying up in the kitchen? You need to go outside to talk. You are disrupting Lydia with her studies."

Dennis opened the front door, and I followed, closing it. We talked for a while. He said, "Maybe after your dinner next time, when I call round, we can go out for a while."

"All right. I'm not sure how long this will last."

"You'd better go in. It's too cold to stand here talking."

"Goodbye. I'll see you next time." Lydia was still doing her homework when I went inside. She said, "It didn't worry me, you talking. I've nearly finished. Let's go in the front room together." When we walked in there, A.J. said, "Well, you won't be seeing much of him now."

"It won't be the same, but he wants to see me on the Wednesday nights, when I'm here."

"Does he, indeed? We'll see how long that lasts." She then asked Lydia, "What have you got to say?"

Lydia spoke about her day, "And it wasn't disturbing me when Dennis was talking with Sylvia." A.J. then asked me, "How do you think this will work, if you only have a Wednesday night off?"

"I don't know. I will just see him after dinner for a little while."

"I don't think this will last long, and I think it's just as well, how things have turned out."

"You are being unkind, saying this."

"I am saying it how I see it, and it's for the best." Lydia said, "You have no feelings for my sister, and I think Dennis is a nice person. He's always polite to me."

"Lydia, I know you're standing up for your sister. Time will tell. We will talk no more on the subject." I said goodnight and got up to walk out. Lydia did the same, and followed me. We ran upstairs. Lydia said, "She has no feelings on how you feel."

"Well, it's nearly always been like that." We sat on the bed and chatted. I said, "In a way, she is right. If Dennis doesn't come around on a Wednesday night, we just won't get together, so we'll have to wait and see what happens. I have to get the early bus in the morning. We can have breakfast together. Are you sure you want to get up that early? You don't have to."

"I want to. I'm not seeing as much of you either."

"Sorry. It's how it is. It's getting harder for me with my studies, and I need Rosalind's help more. I hope I can keep passing. She is clever, like you."

"I hope I can get to meet her one day."

"We'd better get ready to get into bed, or I'll never wake up early."

Chapter 102

I was finding my days off in the middle of the week more difficult than I had thought. I so missed Friday nights. I missed Dennis too. He still called in on Wednesday nights, although A.J. hoped otherwise. We had to talk outside the front door. It was so cold. She was making it as difficult as she could, hoping Dennis would stop calling in. I spent my days off with Lena, bringing my books with me. She was lovely, and helped me. Then I would meet Lydia, and she had lots to tell me about the youth group and Dennis. He was really missing me, "He can't wait for you to have weekends off again."

"I don't know when or if that will happen."

"Well, Dennis wants to take you out tonight when he comes round."

"Oh. So, I'll have a late night."

"Yes, I think so. Just don't wake me! I have school tomorrow."

"I won't. A.J. won't be happy about it." U.S. was pleased to see me, and wanted to know how I was getting on. I told him I was finding it much harder with the studies, but enjoying the practical side, "I do miss having the weekends off. Dennis is coming round tonight to take me out."

"Really? He seems as keen as ever."

"So, I will be late home."

"Well, be as quiet as you can."

"I will."

We went for our walk to the woods and chatted for a while. It was getting darker and colder in the afternoons. We decided to run back. Dinner was nearly ready. I said hello to A.J. in the kitchen. She barely said hello, just muttered, "Lydia, dinner is ready." We ran upstairs and washed our hands. Lydia said, "She's being rude to you."

"I know. I'm not going to be here long. I think U.S. would have told her that Dennis is coming to take me out."

"Have a nice time. I'll see you in the morning."
"Don't let her upset you in the front room."
"I'll try not to."
We ate our dinner in silence. Dennis knocked on the door. I had just finished eating. I said, "Sorry I can't help with the dishes," and got up, saying goodbye. A.J. said, "If he calls round, it needs to be a bit later. It's not convenient. Will you tell him that?"
"Yes."
I got up and left. I opened the front door. Dennis said, "How about we walk to my place? It's about twenty minutes' walk. You can meet my mum and dad, and I have a brother who is a lot younger than me."
"All right."
It was a fine but cold evening. We walked fast, holding hands. His parents made me welcome, and knew how A.J. was treating me. His father said, "It's a shame that she feels this way. She is making it difficult for us." His mum said, "Say hello to U.S."
"Why is it this way? Can you try and fix it?" His father said, "Unfortunately it has been this way for a long time. She doesn't want to talk, or fix the situation." I asked, "What is it all about?"
"It wouldn't do any good. There's no point in discussing it. We have to accept how it is." It was getting late, and it was time to go home. Dennis and I talked as we walked back. I said, "Your parents are as bad as A.J. They don't want to talk and try and make it right." Dennis didn't agree. We had an argument about it. I said, "Well, if nobody wants to talk about it, how will it get resolved?"
"It won't."
"You're just accepting it." I got quite upset and cross. "Can't you get your dad to talk to A.J. to try and sort it out?"
"It won't happen." We had arrived home. I was really cross with him. Dennis opened the front door. And I went in. No goodnight kiss tonight! That was my first argument with Dennis.
The next day I told Lydia about meeting Dennis's parents, and what happened. She agreed, "It won't get fixed if you don't talk about things."
"It would be nice if it got sorted."
"Just see Dennis. Don't worry about it. A.J. can't stop you."
"You're right. Well, it'll be another two weeks, and we'll see what happens if Dennis comes round again."
"Of course he'll come around. I don't think your argument will stop him." I felt better about things after talking with Lydia. I had two weeks to know how I felt about Dennis. Would I be upset if he decided it was all too difficult? I must not think about it anymore. I really needed to study if I wanted to pass and get my nursing degree. Rosalind was such

a good friend and helped me as much as she could, but there was only so much she could do. I knew I was struggling, but I was not giving up. She was able to switch off, and had no worries with her home life. I guessed that must have made a difference. I decided to do my best. Rosalind said, "Think about it, make a decision, then let it go. Concentrate on your studies. You can do it." That is what I did. I knew what the answer was. Leave it now, until you are off again. You can't do anything about it till then.

It was a hard two weeks, but I felt better prepared for my next exam, with Rosalind's help. It was two days before our time off. Rosalind asked, "How do you think you went?"

"All right, I think."

"I found it easy."

"I couldn't say that, but now it's a waiting game to find out."

It was now Tuesday night. Rosalind and I were getting organised for our day off.

"Well, have you decided about Dennis?"

"Yes, I know I would miss him if he stopped coming around. I'll just have to wait and see if he comes tomorrow night."

"Follow your heart. Don't let anybody stop you."

"Thanks. Enjoy your time off."

"You too."

"I will."

"Good luck."

I did my usual routine. I saw Lena, who was always pleased to see me. We chatted, and I told her about Dennis. "I met his parents, and afterwards we argued about them not doing something about the situation. I thought his parents could sort things out with A.J. His mum said to say hello to U.S. She is his sister, isn't she?"

"Yes." Lena understood, and said, "It's a difficult situation." She helped me with my studies and gave me some lunch. Then I said goodbye and left, and went to see U.S. I told him what had happened when I went to see Dennis's parents. "Oh, his mum said to say hello to you, and she is your sister, isn't she? You don't see her or talk with her. How can that happen?"

"It's not an easy situation."

"Well, I'm just passing the message on. I want to keep seeing Dennis, and hope he will come round tonight. Because of the argument we had, I'm not sure whether he will. I hope we can sort it out. Can you try and talk to A.J. about him?"

"Thank you for telling me. I will talk with A.J. but I don't think it'll make any difference."

"You can change it, if you really want to. We could be a big family. I'm going now, to meet Lydia."

I felt so much better about things. I had made my decision. I knew I had feelings for Dennis. The bus was in. Girls were getting off. Then I saw Lydia jump off the bus with her big schoolbag. She said, "So good to see you."

"Me too." I quickly told her about what I had said to U.S., and asked, "How was Dennis at youth group? Did he talk with you?"

"Yes. He said he was looking forward to seeing you."

"Oh. I'm so happy. I was worried about the argument we had."

"Don't worry about what A.J. thinks. She can't stop you. Remember, it's what you want. You should do it." We chatted more and I gave her a hug.

We had just finished dinner. A.J. was in the front room, barely speaking to me now. I was wiping dishes in the kitchen. Lydia was doing her homework on the dining table. There was a knock on the door. I asked, "Can I go? It will be Dennis."

"Yes. You go." I ran towards the front door. A.J. came out of the front room and got there first. And opened it. She saw Dennis. "This is not convenient. Sylvia is helping in the kitchen." I was standing behind her and said, "I'm here." Dennis said, "Sorry." Then A.J. closed the front door in his face. She told me to go back to the kitchen and finish tidying up. She went back to the front room, leaving Dennis waiting outside. I asked U.S., "Do you need me to finish in the kitchen first?"

No, you go." I left the kitchen. Lydia said, "A.J. was so rude."

"Look, I'll see you in the morning."

Dennis was waiting for me. It was so cold, and it was raining. He said, "Let's go into town and sit somewhere where it's warm, and talk." That's what we did. He said, "Let's stop worrying about what the grownups think. We will do our own thing. I wish I could see more of you. How much longer do you have with your nursing?"

"Another year and a bit, and I should be finished."

"When are you getting the weekends off again?"

"I don't know if it will change. I can't do anything about it."

"I'm not happy in my job. I'm looking for something else. I don't know what at the moment. I'm looking to see what there is." After a hot drink, we caught the bus back, and he walked me home. He said, "See you in another two weeks." He gave me a hug and a kiss. "Goodbye."

Chapter 103

I settled back into studying, feeling happier, knowing that Dennis and I were together. Rosalind asked me, "Are you in love with him?"

"Oh, I think so. It's so nice having somebody who says he loves me and wants to see more of me. I find I can concentrate more, knowing we are in a good place together. We have both decided we are going to let the grownups get on with it and leave us alone. They can't stop us being together."

"Wow! Good on you."

My exam results were a bit better. I was so pleased, and thanked Rosalind.

"I told you that you could do it." We celebrated in her room, eating chocolate. She had a wireless, and we had music on. We danced and jumped around until Matron was doing her rounds. We were told to end the celebration and get ourselves to bed. They were happy times. Rosalind and I were the best of friends.

The weeks passed and my days off were just the same. I missed youth group and my friends. The weather was becoming warmer. I would still meet Lydia. We chatted. She told me that A.J.'s health had deteriorated somewhat, and she wasn't working as many days.

"Oh, did I tell you? A.J. has managed to find someone to clean the chapel. I am pleased. It was getting difficult for me too. I missed your help."

"Sorry. We don't see as much of each other now."

"Dennis is calling around after dinner, he told me. "

"Oh, that's all right." We had now reached home. She changed out of her uniform. U.S. was in his greenhouse, and we went and chatted to him. He said, "A.J. has a meeting tonight, so it will be the three of us."

"That's great." He gave me a look. I asked, "Is it all right if we go to the woods?"

"Yes. We will have something easy for dinner."

"We will be back to help you soon."

Lydia said, "Don't forget, Dennis is coming around after dinner. He's looking forward to seeing you, he told me at youth group." U. S. said, "So it's sorted out, the argument you had?"

"Yes. We have talked about things and we want to continue seeing each other. We are not going to worry if you grownups don't want to make things right. It's so stupid. We could be a big family, which we would love." Lydia said, "That would be so good. Can you please talk with A.J. and try and fix it?"

"Well, girls, I can understand how you feel, but this has been like it for years, and I don't think it will change." I said, "If you really wanted to, you could try hard to talk about it."

"Girls, go for your walk. I will give it some thought."

We chatted as we walked to the woods. Lydia said, "We have tried. It's up to U.S. to talk to A.J."

"Yes, you're right."

We had now reached the woods. The bluebells were out. It was so lovely to see. We picked a few to take back. It was nice without A.J. U.S. had already organised dinner. We chatted until we sat at the table, then it was still eating in silence. It wasn't long before there was a knock on the door. He said, "Off you go," and opened the door. I said, "Come in. A.J.'s not here. I'll just say goodbye to Lydia and U.S." U.S. came and had a chat with Dennis. I ran and got my coat. Lydia was also at the door, talking to Dennis. He said, "I'm on my motor bike. I thought you might like to have a ride." He had a helmet, and one for me to wear. He had mentioned to me about having a motor bike, but no more was said. I was not really interested.

"Oh. I'm not sure I want to." I was feeling a bit nervous. U.S. was still at the door. He said, "Don't go too fast. It's good that you have a helmet."

"Are you going to come and see me sit on the bike?" Lydia came to have a look. She asked, "Where are you going?"

"Not far. It's such a nice evening. We'll just go for a spin." The bike was outside the gate. Lydia and U.S. watched me get on the bike. I held onto Dennis and he started the motor. We were off, calling out, "Goodbye!" It was a bit scary at first. After a while, I enjoyed it. We didn't go far, just down a few lanes. It was a lovely evening. We stopped near a field and got off the bike. Dennis had a rug in a bag attached to his bike. We walked onto the field. He put the rug down and we sat on it. He seems excited, I thought. Then he said, "I have something to tell you."

"Have you found a job?"

"Not really."

"Tell me what it is."

"Well, it could be a job. What I'm about to tell you – I don't know how you will feel. This is what I want to do."

"Tell me, just tell me!"

"I don't know how you'll feel about this. They are wanting tradesmen in Australia. I found out the process will take about twelve months, filling in forms, and you should be finished your nursing in twelve months. We can get married before we leave. What do you think?" I was in shock. Go to another country and leave my sister? I was not excited.

"I don't want to leave Lydia."

"Well, she could always come later. She will make a life for herself."

"I know that, but I wouldn't see her, and what about my nursing?"

"Well, you should be finished by then. If not, you could finish it in Australia. I'm so excited. Just think, we can make life for ourselves in another country."

"What about your parents and your brother?"

"Oh, I'd miss them, but they could come for a visit. It's exciting!" I think he was disappointed about my reaction. I said, "Sorry. It's a lot to take in, and you know how close Lydia and I are."

"Well, when she finishes school, she will make a life for herself."

"I know that, but going to another country? When will I see her?" He gave me a hug and said, "I'll stay in my job. You will have to decide, because we need to fill the forms in and get married, if we are leaving together. I really want to do this. If you really love me, you will want to come with me. It's so exciting. We can have a new life together. I have decided I want to do this, even if I have to go by myself." It was time to take me home. I hopped on the bike, and thought, I had no idea about any of this when I was on the bike last time. This is huge for me. Dennis said goodnight to me when we reached home. "Have a big think about this. It will be so good, starting a new life in a new country." He gave me a hug and opened the door.

I hopped into bed. I wanted to talk with Lydia, but knew I must not wake her. I couldn't sleep. Why does Dennis want to do this? Surely, he would miss his parents and friends. He felt excited and happy to go into the unknown I was so unsure about this. I didn't want to leave Lydia. When would I see her again? He really doesn't understand how I feel about this. He just kept saying, if I really loved him, I would want to go. He just said, it's so exciting – we can build a house together and make a new life, make new friends, and have fun. I must have fallen asleep. Lydia tried to wake me, asking, "What time did you get in? Are you all right?"

"Yes. I'm tired. I'm going back to sleep."

"You have to get up," and she pulled the covers off me.
"It's time to get up."
"Yes. I'm getting up. I have something to tell you."
"Well, it will have to wait till when I walk to school, if you're coming with me."
"Can I tell you now?"
"No. We have no time now to talk. What's the matter with you? Have you broken up with Dennis?"
"No." She was asking me while getting dressed.
"Well, good. We will talk while walking to the bus. Hurry up and get dressed, if you're coming with me. Are you unwell?"
"No."
"So please get moving!"

I got myself together. I felt in shock still. Why was this happening? I wasn't hungry. I managed to eat a bit of breakfast. Lydia was worried about me. U.S. said, "Just as well you have the rest of the day off." I was catching the bus back in the afternoon, and was going to Lena's, after walking with Lydia to the bus. When I had finished breakfast, I said goodbye to U.S., and went up and got my things together. Lydia was waiting at the front door. "Hurry up!" As soon as we had closed the front door and were walking to the gate, Lydia said, "Tell me! I'm worried about you." I quickly went into it, watching Lydia's face, to see how she was taking it.

"Wow! That's big!"
"Yes."
"How do you feel?"
"I don't know if I want to do this. I would miss you so much."
"If you want to do it, I'd understand." We had now reached the bus stop. There were children everywhere.
"You will have to decide."
"Dennis wants to know in two weeks."
"Why the rush?"
"Well, it won't happen for approximately twelve months."
"Well, then you've got plenty of time."
"Don't let me stop you. It's your life. I don't know what I'll be doing when I leave school. I could always come for a visit, to see you and see what it's like."

A bus had arrived. We gave each other a hug, "Go back earlier and get some sleep," she said, as she got on the bus. "Yes, I think I will," I waved as the bus left.

I walked to Lena's. It was still early. She was expecting me. She said, "Come in." I followed her into the kitchen and sat at the table. She made me a hot drink. "You look tired, Sylvia."

"I am. I will get an earlier bus back than I normally do, and try and have a bit of sleep." Lena asked, "What has been happening to you?" I went into it all.

"Goodness me. That is very adventurous for Dennis to want to do this. I can understand how you must feel. Of course, you wouldn't want to leave your sister."

"I am torn, not knowing what to do, and I have to make a decision in two weeks."

"That must be a difficult decision for you."

"It is. Dennis says he will still go, if I decide to stay. I want to finish my nursing, although we wouldn't be leaving for another twelve months, approximately. That's the time they are saying. Dennis said I can always finish my nursing in Australia."

"Well, you certainly have a lot to think about. Let me make you something to eat, then go and get the bus back, and have some sleep." I thanked her, "Yes, I really need to. I'm so tired."

I got back to my room. The first thing I did was to put a note under Rosalind's door – "Don't disturb me. I need to sleep. Will explain when I wake." I quickly unpacked, and lay on the bed. It didn't take me long to fall asleep. When I woke up, it was dark. I looked at the clock. It was coming up to midnight. I got into my PJs and checked the roster. I set the alarm and got back into bed properly. I started thinking about things again. I couldn't sleep any more. I was looking forward to talking to Rosalind in the morning. I couldn't believe I had slept for so long.

My alarm went and I got up quickly and dressed. There was a note under my door from Rosalind. "Hope you're all right. Come round when you want to." I knocked on her door. She opened it. She asked, "What's happened? It's time for breakfast." We walked together to the dining room. I was telling her about Dennis. She said, "That's exciting."

"But it's another country, and I don't want to leave my sister."

"I can understand that." We were now in the dining room, sitting at a table on our own. "Have you spoken to her about it?"

"She says I must do what I want to do. She has no idea what she will do when she finishes school, and she said, of course she'll miss me, and will come for a visit. I said, but it's another country, not here in England."

"What about your nursing?

"That too. Dennis seems to think I could finish my training in Australia, if I haven't finished here. It's all so hard."

"You have a lot to think about. We have a lecture soon, and you need to try and focus."

"Yes, you're right." We got up and walked to our rooms.

Chapter 104

A few days passed. I was barely managing. My thoughts were all about not knowing what to do. Every spare moment I spent thinking about it. I was trying to forget, but knew Dennis would want an answer when I got my days off. Rosalind said, "You must make a decision, and then you can concentrate. You will fail if you keep going the way you are." She was trying to help me, I knew. She said, "Let's have a talk tonight. I'll help you to decide."

"Thanks. I would like that." She was really concerned for me.

At the end of the day, I went to her room. We both sat on the bed. She said, "I know it's hard for you, but first of all, do you love Dennis?"

"I think so."

"How would you feel if he wasn't around? Would you miss him?"

"Yes, I would miss him, but I would miss my sister too."

"Of course you would, but she wouldn't want you to stay around for her. Like she said, she doesn't know what she wants to do when she finishes school. She could come for a visit, or you could come back after a while, if it doesn't turn out. If you never go, you will never know what you would have missed out on."

"Yes, I think you're right. She wouldn't want me to stay for her. We will always be close, if not in distance, and somehow, we will keep in touch and hope to see each other."

"I know it will be hard for you, but you can now see it's the right decision, and Lydia will understand, when you tell her." I thanked her heaps for our talk, and gave her a hug. She made me see clearly and helped me move on with a decision. "You will now have a clear head to concentrate on your nursing, and after all, I don't want you to fail, with all the help I've given you – ha ha!"

"I don't want to, either. Thank you so much. We will always be close and keep in touch."

"Yes, for sure," and we did a pinkie with our little fingers. I felt so much better after our talk, and thought, it will be an adventure. I am sure Lydia will understand and be happy for me. I was able to study better, and we were back to giving each other tests to help us both, with what we had ahead of us.

Rosalind and I were packing for our days off. She asked, "When you see Dennis, are you going to tell him?"

"Yes. I'll see Lydia first, and tell her. Wonder how she will take it? Then I'll mention it to U.S."

"How are you feeling about it really?"

"Well, as long as Lydia is happy for me to go, I think – all right. Oh, I'll have to write to my uncle about it. Wonder what he will have to say?"

"Enjoy your time off."

"Yes, thanks. You too."

I couldn't wait to meet Lydia off the bus, to see how she would be with me, now I had made my decision. I knew I'd feel better if Lydia was really all right about it. I was at the bus stop early, waiting. I saw the bus come in. Lydia was one of the first to jump off, and pleased to see me. "How are you? What have you decided?" I watched her face. We were walking home.

"It has been a hard two weeks, but I have decided to do it." She dropped her schoolbag and gave me a hug. "I'm happy for you." I looked at her. "Are you really sure you want me to go? Won't you miss me?"

"Of course I will miss you, but I don't want you to stay just for me. I have no idea what I will be doing, and I can come and see you, or you could come back after a while."

"Yes, you're right. Did you see Dennis at youth group?"

"Yes. We talked. He can't wait to see you." We had now reached home. U.S. was in the front garden, and pleased to see me, asking if I was feeling better. "Yes, thank you. I've had a big decision to make, and was in shock about it."

"Well, are you going to tell me?"

"Yes. Well, Dennis is wanting to emigrate to Australia, and for us to get married, and me to go with him." U.S. was taken aback. "That is a big decision."

"Yes. I haven't seen him yet. He is coming round tonight, and wants an answer, because there are forms to fill out, and it's only applicable for a certain time."

"Goodness me. I wouldn't have thought it of him, wanting to do something like that. So, do you want to do that?"

"Well, I feel I do love Dennis, and would miss him if he went. Even if I say no, he is still going on his own, but I'm going to miss Lydia so much." Lydia said, "Me too. But I can come for a visit. I'm not sure what I'll be doing when I leave school, and I don't want Sylvia to stay because of me. She has to live her own life and be happy." U.S. said, "Well, well. Who knew things would turn out like this? It's a lot to take in. You will let A.J. know."

"Yes. She will probably be happy to see me go." U.S. said, "I don't know about that."

"When we go in the front room, I will tell her." Lydia asked, "Is it all right if we go for a walk?"

"Yes. I will make a start on dinner."

Lydia ran up to get changed. I took my things up to the bedroom, then we left. We talked. Lydia said, "Dennis spoke to me at youth group."

"What did he say?"

"Not much. Just that he was looking forward to seeing you, and hopes the answer is what he wants."

"Did he say that? Nothing else?"

"No." We had now reached the woods.

"I'm pleased you are doing what you want to do. You shouldn't let anyone stop you. It's your life."

"Yes, I know, but it will be hard for me, not having you to see or talk with."

"And for me too, but we are becoming adults. We will always be close, and I can write to you."

"And I'll answer you straight away. Talking of writing, I must let our uncle know. Hope he can come again soon, and meet Dennis."

"Yes, you'd better write straight away."

"I will. We'd better start walking back. I wonder how A.J. will take it?"

U.S. had made our favourite dinner. A.J. was home when we got back. I was asked to say grace. I helped with the dishes, then went to the front room. Lydia came with me. She wanted to hear what A.J. had to say. "Have you finished your homework already?"

"I can do it when Sylvia has left."

"Oh. I believe you have something to tell me."

"Yes." I went into it all, "Dennis wants me to emigrate to Australia, and wants me to go with him, and for us to marry."

"Goodness me! What next! I hope you're not serious about wanting to do this. As for getting married, I'll have to write to your uncle. This is ridiculous!"

"I will write to Uncle and explain. I'm hoping he can come and meet Dennis. He only has a certain time to fill out the forms and apply to emigrate."

"I think that would be foolish of you. What about your sister? You're just thinking of yourself, and are happy to give up your nursing for a crush you have on a boy."

"Lydia and I have spoken. I wasn't sure I'd want to do this, because I wouldn't see my sister."

"Sylvia needs to do what she wants to. It's her life. I can visit later, or she might come back after a while, and we can write to each other."

"I can't believe I'm hearing this. I don't think your uncle would approve. I must write to him straight away."

"I'm going to write and explain, and see if he can come soon and meet Dennis."

"He is a busy man, you know." We heard a knock on the door. "Oh, that's Dennis. I'll go and open the door." I ran out of the front room. "Come in. I was telling A.J. about things."

"How do you feel? Will you come with me?"

"Yes." He put his arms around me. "That is so good."

"I'm going to write to my uncle and see if he can come and meet you. We can see what he says about everything." We were talking in the hall. A.J. came out. "You have caused quite a commotion with your fancy ideas. Why would you want to do this?"

"Because it's a new start in life in another country, and they are needing and asking for tradesmen."

"Well, it's disrupting for Sylvia, and you haven't really known each other very long. It will cause an upset with Lydia." Lydia came out of the room. "I'm all right with it. I will miss Sylvia, but we can write, and I can try and come for a visit."

"We will see what your uncle has to say on this matter." U.S. came out of the front room. We were all standing in the hall. U.S. said, "This is a big decision. What are your parents saying on the subject?"

"They feel, if that's what I want to do, it could give me a good start in life, and they wished me every success."

"Well, I never!"

"They are going to help me fill out the forms. They need to be posted by the end of the month." A.J. said to me, "You will need to speak with your uncle before you do anything."

"Yes, I hope he replies quickly." Dennis said, "I could help you send a telegram, which gets there faster than a letter."

"That would be good." A.J. looked at Dennis. "I don't know if Sylvia's uncle would appreciate a telegram. That is only for something urgent."

"It really is urgent, because the forms have to be filled out and posted, and they have a closing date on them." A.J. said, "It looks like you'll be going on your own, then, if you're set on doing this." I said, "I'm going to let Dennis send a telegram for me." A. J. said, "He will be concerned, to get a telegram."

"Yes, but when he reads it, he will know I want to see him as soon as possible, and say I want him to meet Dennis."

"Well, there's nothing else to say. We will wait to hear from your uncle." She walked back into the front room with U.S. Lydia said, "I'm all right with it. I'd better get my homework done." I ran up to get my coat, and left with Dennis. We caught the bus into town, and sat and talked about things in a café and got a hot drink.

Chapter 105

A week passed and I got a telegram from Uncle. Matron gave it to me, saying she hoped everything was all right. She told me to take it to my room and read it. I sat on the bed and opened it. It said, "I will be down on your day off, for a quick visit." I was so pleased. I went and told Rosalind all about what was happening, and she was happy for me. Now it was a waiting game for my next day off. Rosalind asked, "Do you think your uncle will be all right with you doing this?"

"I hope so. He hasn't met Dennis. I hope they get on."

"I hope you will finish your nursing before you go."

"So do I. Dennis said it will be approximately 12 months from the time we fill in the forms until we leave."

"Well, it will be longer than that before you finish nursing."

"Paperwork usually takes a lot longer than they say."

I felt excited about seeing Uncle soon. I was still concerned. Did I want to go to Australia, another country, not just another place? I would miss Lydia heaps, I knew. She was putting on a brave face, saying I must do what I wanted to do. I didn't really know what I wanted. It was hard for me to concentrate. Rosalind said, "Once you have seen your uncle, you will feel better, and talk about everything."

"Well, I don't know if I really want to. Sometimes I do and sometimes I don't."

"Why can't Dennis find a job here?"

"I agree."

At last, the time came for my days off. I said my goodbyes to Rosalind. I was meeting Uncle in town, at the café where I had been with him before. I found it and went in. A few people were there, but not Uncle. I sat and waited. It felt strange, sitting on my own. Half an hour passed, before he came in. He apologised. I was so pleased to see him. He ordered us a drink and asked me to tell him what it was all about.

I went into the details. "How do you really feel about Dennis? Do you love him? That is the most important thing."

"I think so."

"I will meet Dennis later in the evening, and we will talk about the situation."

Uncle knew I didn't want to leave Lydia. "Sooner or later your lives will be changing, and decisions will need to be made. Again, you really need to be sure of your feelings for Dennis." We were going to meet Lydia off the school bus, and Uncle could have a chat with her before going to A.J.'s for dinner. It was so good being able to talk with him. He was happy for me, as long as I was sure of my feelings for Dennis, whom he would be meeting soon. We were waiting for Lydia to jump off the bus. When she saw us, she gave a big squeal of excitement. There were big hugs. Uncle chatted to her, and asked how she felt about me emigrating to Australia. "Of course, she will miss me. I'm all right with it. We will always keep in touch, one way or another." We had now reached home.

U.S. opened the door, and was pleased to see us. He chatted to Uncle, and in a few minutes, A.J. came home. She turned to us. "Girls, your uncle and I are going to have a chat in the front room."

"Can we go for a walk?"

"Yes, that's a good idea."

It wasn't long before we were doing our favourite walk in the woods. I was telling Lydia about my time with Uncle. "It will be interesting when A.J. finds out Uncle is all right with me going to Australia."

"Yes, she thinks he wouldn't want you to go."

"I know. He said a few times to me that I must be sure of my feelings for Dennis."

"Well, you are, aren't you?"

"Yes, it's just that I'll be away from you and my friends, and I won't know anyone."

"I know what you mean. It's another country. We will write to each other, and I will come and visit you for a holiday."

"That will be good. Dennis is so excited about it. I don't feel like that. He doesn't seem to mind leaving his mum and dad and brother."

"Well, when Uncle meets Dennis, he will find out about everything. We'd better hurry home."

"I wonder how everyone will be when we get back?" We ran to the back gate and up the path, and opened the kitchen door. U.S. was doing dinner. "Girls, dinner is ready. A.J. and Uncle are still in the front room. I will let them know that you're back." We hurried upstairs and washed our hands. We heard the front room door open, and voices. "Well, let's see how it is."

"Yes. Good luck with later, with Uncle meeting Dennis."

"Thanks." We hurried downstairs. Uncle asked, "How was your walk?"

"It was good, thank you."

"Have you finished your talk?"

A.J. said, "Yes. It seems your uncle is happy about your going to Australia, much to my disagreement. You must be sure of your feelings for Dennis. I will meet him soon, and we will have a talk about things."

"Thank you."

U.S. said, "Dinner is ready. Can we all sit at the table?" Uncle sat between us and said grace. Of course, we ate in silence. Uncle and A.J. went back into the front room. We helped with the dishes. U.S. asked, "How do you feel about going to Australia?"

"I am not sure about going to another country, and leaving my sister and friends. That's a hard thing. It will be so far away." Lydia said, "I want to visit when I finish school." U.S. said, "Now you must write, so we know how you are."

"Yes, I will. Dennis is so excited." We had just finished putting the dishes away when there was a knock on the door. "It's Dennis. I'll go." I ran to the door and opened it. He gave me a hug. "My uncle is here, and in the front room with A.J."

"My parents have made a supper that we can have." A.J. and Uncle came out of the front room. Dennis said, "Good evening." I Introduced Dennis to my uncle, who said, "Pleased to meet you." A.J. went back into the front room. U.S. came to the front door to say hello to Dennis. "I hear you're wanting to go to Australia."

"Yes. I'm so looking forward to it. I will have a job to go to when I get there, and we will live in a hostel for a while." U.S. shook Dennis's hand, saying, "Hope all goes well for you, and please keep in contact with your parents."

"Oh, I will."

Lydia said, "You'd better make my sister happy. I want to come and visit when I've finished school." Uncle said, "We had better get going." He turned to thank U.S. A.J. stayed sitting down in the room. He opened the front room door, calling out to her, "I am leaving now. Thank you for your hospitality and dinner, and sorry we can't agree on this matter. It could give them a good start in Australia, a new life together."

Dennis, Uncle and I walked to Dennis's house. Uncle was chatting to Dennis. I was listening. We reached his parents' house. They made Uncle welcome. Everybody was getting on well. "I would like to have a talk to Dennis on his own." I went into the kitchen with his parents, and helped get supper ready. I asked his mum, "How do you feel about Dennis leaving?"

"It is going to be hard for me, but if it means he will get a good start in life, job-wise, and get a house, then that's fine with me. They call it The Lucky Country. We hope to be able to go for a holiday."

"That's what my sister wants to do when she finishes school. I am really going to miss her."

"I expect you will, my dear." I was asked to knock on the door and say supper was ready. Uncle said, "That's nice. Thank you." Everybody was talking about emigrating, and Dennis asked, "Can I go and get the forms? They need to be filled out." He got up to get them. His parents had already seen them. Uncle took them and had a read. "Well, it all seems straightforward," and showed them to me. He asked me, "How you feel if I fill it in for you, and you can sign it?" Oh, I thought, this is it.

"If we don't like it, can we come back?"

"Of course you can, but with this scheme, you must stay for two years, and you will have to pay your own fare back. It only costs ten pounds each to emigrate." Dennis said, "That's what's so good about it. I will have a job to go to, and we can stay in a hostel until we find a place to live." I hadn't asked about any details. So, I asked, "We won't be leaving for twelve months. Is that right?" Uncle said, "That is approximately. They will give you a firm time later."

"I really want to finish my nursing."

"Yes, that would be good, if you can." Dennis said, "You can always finish it in Australia. Can we please fill the forms out, as they have a closing date? I don't want to miss out!" Uncle asked me, "How do you feel about it? Do you want more time to think?" I could see Dennis looking at me. He said, "The closing date is only two weeks away." I knew Dennis was really wanting it to be signed. I thought, would I really feel any different in two weeks? I didn't think so. I was nervous. "No, that's fine." Uncle said, "I notice we have a problem," and he looked at me. "You haven't completed a qualification." Dennis interrupted, "We will need to get married, then." Uncle said, "Yes, you will, if you're going together."

"Oh. It's all happening too fast."

"You don't need to get married yet. You have time. We will organise it in a while." He had the papers in his hand and showed them to me, and pointed out where to sign. I was so nervous, but I did it. Dennis had already signed them. He was so excited. I thought, what have I done? Uncle seemed pleased. He was getting on really well with Dennis, saying, "Leave it to me to make more arrangements. I will come down from London in a month, and we will meet and talk about things." He thanked Dennis's parents for supper and shook Dennis's hand. "I must get going. I don't want to miss the last bus." Uncle was walking me back home, and was chatting to me. He then said, "You are quiet."

"There's so much to think about. It's all happening so fast."

"Well, yes. We had to fill the forms in, or Dennis would miss out. He's a nice boy, and really does love you, and will take care of you."

"I just wish it wasn't another country, and having to stay for two years. I'm going to miss Lydia so much."

"Of course, she will miss you too. You can write to each other – that's something you can look forward to, receiving letters." I was back home now. Uncle gave me a hug and said he would write to me, telling me when he could come for a visit. He gave me another hug and said, "Goodbye. Do well with your nursing." He opened the door for me. I crept up the stairs. It was very quiet. I got myself into bed. Lots of thoughts were going through my head. I eventually fell asleep.

In the morning, Lydia woke me, asking questions. "What happened? Are you walking with me to school? You can tell me everything." U.S. had our breakfast ready, and he was asking me questions about the night before. I told him that Uncle had read the papers and checked everything, and Dennis and I had signed them. "Goodness. So, you are going to Australia?"

"Yes. It will be in about twelve months."

"Oh. You have a bit of time before that will happen."

"Yes. I hope I can finish my nursing by then." Lydia said, "That's good. You're not going for a while yet." U.S. served our porridge and said grace. We ate in silence. I said my goodbyes to U.S. and walked with Lydia to school. We talked. I told her that I had to be married, or have an occupation. Since I had not, when I signed the form, Uncle would organise for us to marry before we went.

"Wow! So that will happen later in the year?"

"Yes. He will write to me, letting me know when he will be down to talk about things." We had reached the bus stop. The bus was there. Lydia gave me a hug. "See you in two weeks! So much is happening!"

"Yes, I know."

Chapter 106

I walked to Mrs. Taylor's. She was pleased to see me. "I do have an appointment in an hour with Dr. Tom. Why don't you come with me, and you can get to see him?" I thought, that might be good. I waited with her in the waiting room. When Mrs. Taylor was called, Doctor Tom saw me and asked Mrs Taylor if she would mind if I went in with her. She said that was fine. I sat on a chair while he talked with Mrs. Taylor. When he had finished, he asked me, "How are you getting on?"

"So much has happened. Have you got time for me to tell you?" I went into it as quickly as I could. He said, "I'm happy for you. It's just a shame that this has happened in the middle of your training. I do hope you can complete it before you leave. Please keep in touch."

"Yes, I will. Oh, don't say anything to Matron."

"No, that wouldn't go well for you. I'm sure the children would like a visit from you. I will be in touch." I thanked him.

When we were walking back, Mrs. Taylor said, "It's a difficult situation for you."

"It is. I hope Doctor Tom doesn't mention it to Matron."

"He said he wouldn't. Now, don't go worrying about that." I said my goodbyes and decided to catch the bus back. I returned earlier than I usually did. I needed time to think about how my life was changing. I had mixed feelings about leaving. I couldn't concentrate on study, but knew I should. I heard Rosalind come back, and gave her a few minutes, then went to see her, to let her know how things were. I knocked on her door. "Come in!" She was pleased to see me. She had been away with Paul, and had a lovely time. "How was your time off?" I told her about Uncle's visit, and everything that had happened. She said, "I can't believe it! You are getting married before me?"

"Well, I hadn't planned it like that. It's because of the dates of the scheme. You have to have an occupation or a qualification. This is the only way I could go with Dennis."

"When is this happening?"

"Uncle is going to arrange it when Dennis hears about a date when we will be leaving."

"It's so exciting, getting married, going on a boat to another country!"

"Sometimes I am excited and sometimes I'm not sure about it all. It's just that it's all happening so fast for me."

"Yes, it is, and you can't really tell anyone about it, only me."

"I saw Doctor Tom today."Please tell me you didn't tell him!"

"Well, I had to, because…"

"You didn't! Why?"

"The lady I was with had an appointment with the doctor, and I went with her. She was the one who recommended me for the job with Doctor Tom."

"Oh! If Matron finds out, I didn't know what will happen to you."

"I know. I asked him not to tell Matron, and he said he wouldn't say anything."

"Well, what else did he say?"

"He said it's a shame it's happened in the middle of my training. He did wish me well, though."

"Yes, the timing is all wrong. It's a shame for you."

"I can't do anything about it."

"Hope it's longer than twelve months before you hear when the leaving date is." We talked more about things.

"Doctor Tom wants me to visit the children again, which will be nice. He will let me know when."

We both had an early night, which was much needed. Then it was back into study. I said to myself, I must get through my exams, and try not to think about my life outside the hospital. We were back on the wards, which I really enjoyed. Some patients showed how grateful they were, and loved to have a chat. We were taught to help people feel at ease if they were very nervous. That was part of our training, how you reacted to patients. I did get good marks on my practical, but theory I found difficult. That's where Rosalind shone. She was so good, and she helped me so much, with tests she would set up between us. She would say, "This will help you. If you don't understand it, ask me." She worked hard helping me. She really cared and was a true friend. She knew how hard my home life was. I really appreciated her help and friendship.

I settled into studying and life in the hospital. It was going smoothly. My days off were almost here. I was looking forward to them and seeing Lydia and Dennis again. Rosalind was having a quiet time with her mum. In the evening, we were chatting and packing our things. I said, "I'm going to see Lena. I haven't told her what's happened, and about Uncle's visit."

"She has been a friend to you."

"Yes. It would be nice to let her know about everything." We said our goodbyes, both going in different directions. We said, "Enjoy your time off."

I caught the bus, then walked to Lena's. She was so pleased to see me. She had heard that my uncle was down, and that I might be going to Australia. There was some talk when she went to chapel, about Dennis and me. She hadn't heard from me for a while. I apologised, saying, "So much has happened." I told her everything. When I had finished, she said, "Well, I will miss you, and would never have thought it of Dennis, wanting to do this."

"Dennis heard they want tradesmen in Australia. He is so excited. We are waiting to hear when this will happen. We will leave in about twelve months." She understood how hard it was for me, leaving Lydia, with me in the middle of training.

"It's such a pity I have to sign with the closing date so soon. He is looking forward to it so much. He is happy my uncle approves. They got on well when they talked about things."

"When are you seeing your uncle again?"

"He said, in about a month, and it has been two weeks now. I will keep in touch with you when I know more."

"Thank you." I said my goodbyes. I was looking forward to seeing Lydia. I walked to meet the school bus. It was early, and she was already walking home. "So good to see you. I was getting worried when you weren't at the bus stop." I told her I'd been to see Lena. Lydia told me what had been happening at home. A.J. hadn't been well, and had had time off, staying at home. She was in bed at the moment. She hadn't been to work all week. We chatted more about things at home. Lydia was managing better with A.J., as she was now getting top marks, which A.J. was very pleased about, and proud of her. I was too, saying, "You are a clever girl!"

We had now reached home. Lydia ran to get changed, and went to see A.J., who was still in bed. I could hear them talking. In a while she came out of the bedroom and ran downstairs, saying, "A.J. is getting up for dinner. She is feeling a bit better." She turned to me and said, "She will see you then." I was talking with U.S., who asked me how I was getting on. I told him I had been to see Lena and had told her my news. "She has been a good friend to me, and sometimes helped me with my studies. I take my books with me, and she asks me some questions from them."

"Well, that's nice of her."

"Yes, it does help me." I chatted about being on the wards, which I had just finished, and how I was enjoying doing that. I asked, "Can we help with dinner?"

"Yes. That would be nice. I need the peas to be shelled."

"I'll help."

"Well, girls, don't go eating them like you used to do when you were younger. We don't have that many to shell." We helped prepare other vegies, then asked, "What else can we do?"

"Thank you, girls. That's been a great help. It's just a matter of cooking them, and the meat." We set the table. U.S. said, "You have time for a quick walk." We said thanks and ran out the back door. I said to Lydia, "U.S. is looking very tired."

"Yes, he has been up and down the stairs seeing to A.J., and doing everything. I help as much as I can when I'm home. Did you tell him Dennis is coming round?"

"No, I didn't mention it. Oh, that won't go down well with A.J."

"Oh, I think she is getting used to it, now that it's official you are going out together. Have you mentioned that you might be getting married later in the year, before you leave for Australia?"

"No, I haven't. I think it's better not to, for a while, till I hear about a date when we will be leaving. That's when Uncle will make the arrangements."

"Well, I won't say anything, then."

"No, don't. Thanks."

We had reached the woods. It was so quiet there. You didn't hear any traffic, only some birds, and rabbits scurrying to their burrows. It was peaceful. We had always loved our walks here. We didn't stay long, and decided to run back home to help U.S. A.J. was up when we walked into the kitchen, and said hello to me. I asked, "Are you feeling better?"

"Yes, thank you." U.S. said, "It's good timing. Dinner is ready." We ran to wash our hands. Lydia said, "A.J. is trying to be a bit nicer to you, I think."

"It did seem like that," I agreed. "She won't like it when Dennis comes round, though."

"Well, have a nice time, and we will walk together in the morning."

"Yes, thanks." I was asked to say grace, and we ate in silence, of course. I helped with the dishes. Lydia joined me. She had very little homework. A.J. went into the front room. We chatted with U.S. He asked me, "When are you going on the motor bike again?"

"I don't know. Dennis hasn't mentioned it. I'm not sure where we are going."

"You will be quiet, won't you, when you come home?"

"Yes, I always am."

"Good to hear." Lydia said, "I'd like a ride on the bike."

"Well, we can ask Dennis. He will take you for a spin. If he brings the bike, you can get on it."

"He won't mind?"

"Of course not." We had finished the dishes and put them all away. We went into the front room. A.J. asked me first, "What have you got to say?" I told her I had just finished doing duty on the wards, which I enjoyed. "It's very rewarding." A.J. seemed really interested. "My marks are better in Practical. The theory I find difficult, but I have a lovely friend who helps me."

"Well, that's nice to hear." A knock came on the front door. Lydia jumped up. "I'll go," and ran to open the door. I followed. Dennis was standing there with his helmet on. Lydia asked, "Will you take me for a ride?" Dennis looked at me. "Lydia would love you to take her for a spin. It's all right with me." He had a helmet in his hand. Lydia ran into the front room, saying, "Dennis is going to take me for a ride. I won't be long." Then she ran up the stairs to get her coat. I waited at the front door. A.J. and U.S. came out, and were standing at the front door. A.J. said, "I don't know if this is a good idea."

"I have my coat on and a helmet to wear. I'll be fine." Dennis said, "Good evening. We won't be long." I followed Lydia and Dennis to where the bike was, and watched my sister get on. She waved. "This is fun!" Dennis had started the motor, and they were off. A.J. turned to me, "Did you organise this?"

"No. I didn't know Dennis would be on the bike. I knew Lydia would love to have a ride one day."

"I don't really approve." U.S. said, "He is a sensible boy. She will be fine."

"It was my first time on the bike not long ago, and I enjoyed it in the end." We all stood at the door. It was a lovely evening. I wondered where Dennis would be taking her, and what he had planned for us. About fifteen minutes later, we heard a motor bike. I thought, this is them, and saw it was. Lydia jumped off the bike, smiling. "It was so good." She thanked Dennis and gave him a hug. A.J. was not impressed. She said, "Well, I'm glad you are all right."

"Of course, I am." Dennis said to Lydia, "Glad you enjoyed it," asking me if I was ready to leave. I said my goodbyes to everyone. A.J. said to Dennis, "I hope you will be careful. I don't think it's very safe."

"Thank you for your concern. The bike has been checked and is in good condition, and I do stick to the speed limit."

"Well, I'm glad to hear it." We walked down the path. Lydia came with me, and watched me get on the bike, saying, "It was fun. Where are you going?"

"Just down a few lanes, somewhere we can talk."

"Have fun!" I waved and we were off.

Chapter 107

After a while, Dennis stopped the bike and we got off. He had the rug with him again and we sat in a field and talked about everything. "I can't wait to leave. I'm not happy with work. There have been changes made which I don't like."

"I want to finish my nursing before we leave."

"I don't think that will happen, as it is only twelve months before we leave."

"Well, it could be longer."

"Oh. We will just have to wait and see what happens. I like your uncle. I got on well with him."

"That's good. I should get a letter soon to say when he's down again."

"Yes. I hope I get to meet him again." We chatted a bit more.

"How do you feel if we ride into town?"

"Oh. Have we got time?"

"Yes, if we go now, we can have a drink and sit down in that café and talk." I hadn't been on his bike that long, and was nervous about riding in traffic. I found it scary. We stopped outside the café, and I was glad to get off the bike. We walked in. It was nearly empty. We sat down, and Dennis ordered a hot drink and something to nibble. It was nice and warm inside, and I found myself relaxing. We talked more about our future, which was all so new to me. It was getting late.

"I think we'd better get going."

We sat back on the bike and put our helmets on. It wasn't long before we were off. It was completely dark now – another new experience for me, on the bike in the dark. I was so glad when we finally arrived home, and I could get off. I was amazed at how my legs felt – a bit wobbly. Dennis walked me to the front door, gave me a hug and a kiss, and said goodbye. He opened the front door and closed it for me. I crept upstairs. All was quiet. It wasn't long before I was in bed and fell asleep.

Lydia woke me in the morning, saying, "We have to be quiet. A.J. will still be asleep in bed." We quickly got up, dressed and went down to the kitchen. U.S. was making breakfast. "Good morning, girls." He served it.

"Were you late home? What did you do?" So, I told her, "We ended up in town."

"On the bike?"

"Yes, with the traffic. It was new to me, and was scary." U.S. said, "That would be, for you." I was asked to say grace, and of course, we still ate in silence. Lydia said, "We haven't got time to talk. We have to hurry."

"Oh." I said my goodbyes to U.S. "Have a good two weeks."

"Thanks." I asked, "How is A.J.?"

"She will need to rest."

"Can you tell her from me, I hope she feels better soon?"

"I will. Thank you." Lydia said, "Come on, and be quiet. I'll be late if we don't hurry." I quickly got moving and collected my things. It wasn't long before we were out of the door and walking to the bus. We talked about things. "Do well with your studies."

"Thanks. I'm going to go back to my room to do that. Dennis seems to think I won't get my nursing finished before we go."

"Well, if it is only twelve months before you leave, he's right."

"I hope it's longer than that."

"The longer the better for you. Just do your best. You can't do anything about it." The bus had arrived. We gave each other a hug and said goodbye. Lydia said, "See you in two weeks."

I waited, and decided to get the early bus back. Once back in my room, I got my books out and had a look at them. I knew I would need Rosalind's help. She would give me some tests, which would help me heaps. After a while, I heard her come into her room. I'll wait a little while, and then go and see her, I thought. I was finding that I could concentrate now my decision had been made, and it was now a matter of waiting for the date when we would be leaving. I hoped I would hear from Uncle to say when he was coming to see me again. I thought, I must go in and see Rosalind now.

I told her my news. "That will be nice for you. I wonder if your uncle has made any arrangements?"

"Well, we haven't got a date yet."

"But he knows it's going to be twelve months, or round about, and it's now eleven months."

"Oh, you're right. It will be when I see him again." We chatted more about things. "You did well with your last exam."

"Thank you."

"It's also good for me, us working together."

I had got a letter from Uncle, saying to meet him in town, where we had met before. I was counting the days until our time off again. At last, it came. I said my goodbyes to Rosalind. I found the café and again, I was the first there. Uncle apologised – the train was late. He ordered lunch for us and asked me how I was. He said, "I'll tell you what I have organised. I feel it would be a good time to get married, at the end of the year, and it will probably be early January when you leave, if that works out. You should be able to get time off then, and if you have a longer date for leaving, it will work out all right. What do you think of that?"

"Oh. I thought you were going to wait until you heard a date before you organised anything."

"That might not give us the time we need. We have been told approximately twelve months, so December is probably the longest we can organise it for. You will be leaving sometime in the new year. At the end of the year, you should be able to get some time off."

"Yes. I hadn't thought about it like that."

"You have had a lot to think about. How do you feel about the arrangements?"

"Thank you. I can understand it. That could be the right time."

"Yes. You will hear a departure date, and it won't be this year. So, how about a few days before Christmas for the wedding?"

"That seems nice, thank you."

"Now I can organise it. Would you like a church wedding?"

"I hadn't really thought about it. That sounds nice."

"It would be in London."

"Really?"

"Yes, and I can solemnise the wedding."

"What does that mean?"

"I can marry you."

"Oh." I got up and gave him a hug. "Can you do that?"

"Yes. It will be in the Church of Scotland, where I attend." I was overwhelmed. I found it hard to believe that this could be happening soon. The waitress brought our lunch, and we ate, talking between mouthfuls. It was so nice. I asked, "Is there any way we could leave at a later date, so I could finish my nursing?"

"Well, no. It seems, when I read the forms, that this was the only date given. This is a new scheme that the government has organised and approved." I told Uncle about Doctor Tom saying that it was a pity that this was happening in the middle of my training.

"Yes. It is hard for you, but you can take it up again in Australia, I'm sure." After more talking, we finished our lunch. We caught the bus to meet Lydia from her bus. She was thrilled to see Uncle, who told her the arrangements he had made, while we were walking home. Lydia said A.J. was feeling better, but hadn't been back to work yet. We told Uncle that we hadn't mentioned about marriage yet. He agreed, "There is no need to tell her at this stage. We haven't finalised the date yet, anyway. I will see Dennis after dinner, let him know what we have arranged, and see how he feels."

"He is coming round to see me tonight, and we can walk to his parents' place, to let them know."

We arrived home. U.S. had a chat with Uncle. We ran upstairs. We could hear them talking, and A.J.'s voice as well. We could hear the door close. When we got downstairs, nobody was about. We decided to go for our walk. Lydia said, "I'll write a note to say what we are doing."

"Let's go and see if Betty is home. I haven't seen her for so long, now that I can't get to youth group."

"It's a longer walk. I don't know if we have time for that."

"Yes, we can. We'll hurry."

"All right. Let's go." We arrived. Betty was so pleased to see me, and I her. We talked about everything that had been happening in my life. "I don't think I'll be able to come to youth group again." It was so good catching up with her.

"We'd better go. I can give Betty your news." We said our goodbyes and hurried back. Everybody was in the kitchen. A.J. said, "You are late. We were waiting for you."

"Sorry. We have been to see my friend Betty, and the time went fast. "Are you feeling better?"

"Yes, thank you." We sat at the table, with Uncle between us. He said grace. He remembered that we ate in silence. As soon as dinner was over, Uncle started talking. A.J. gave him a look. We were not in the front room yet. They went into the front room. Lydia and I helped U.S. tidy up and do the dishes. We chatted away to him while he was doing them. He wanted to know any more news we had. It was difficult, because there were things I couldn't say.

"We are going to see Dennis's parents." When we had finished in the kitchen, we joined Uncle and A.J., who asked me, "How are you feeling about what's happening?"

"I'm managing. There is so much to think about, and it's busy. It's nice that Uncle is here and organising everything."

"Well, yes. I feel it's all moving too fast. I think you should stay and finish your nursing." Uncle said, "Ideally, I agree, but this is the only date there is for emigrating to Australia." A.J. said, "It's a risky thing to do. How do you know they will be happy there?"

"It's a good opportunity to take advantage of, job-wise, and there is the chance of owning a house."

"What if they don't like it?"

"Well, they will need to save money to come back, but they must stay for two years before they can do that."

"I still think it is risky."

"They would have had the experience of travelling and seeing a bit of the world." We heard a knock on the door. It was Dennis. I ran to open it, saying, "We are all in the front room!" He waited at the front door. Uncle said, "We had better get going." He thanked A.J. for dinner. Lydia came out with me. I said, "Goodbye. See you in the morning." I also said goodbye to U.S. Lydia gave me a hug. U.S. spoke to Dennis, "Say hello to your parents."

"I will. Thank you."

"We had better get going."

We walked fast to Dennis's. It was starting to rain, and it was so cold. Uncle was chatting to Dennis while we walked. We arrived without getting too wet. Uncle told Dennis and family what he had organised. Dennis said, "We couldn't have organised it ourselves. Thank you." Dennis's father said, "We have a trip to London to look forward to." They had never travelled anywhere before. Uncle said, "I will organise accommodation if you need it." There was more talking. His parents had made supper again, and we all sat to eat. The evening went well. Uncle said, "I'd better walk you home, so I can get the last bus back."

We said our goodbyes to Dennis and family, and started walking home. It was still raining. We hurried. When we got there, Uncle said, "I'll write to you again. Do well with your nursing and be happy." He opened the door for me, and then closed it. All was quiet. I got myself into bed. I was starting to feel excited. I made sure I didn't disturb Lydia. It took me a while to get to sleep. Everything was going around in my head again. Lydia had a job to wake me, saying, "A.J. will still be asleep. She is not going to work. We need to be quiet." We dressed quickly and crept downstairs to the kitchen. U.S. said, "Morning, girls. Sit down. It's all ready to serve." We thanked him. I asked, "How is A.J.?"

"She is still sleeping. I think she is feeling better." He asked me, "How did it go with Dennis's parents?"

"It went well. Uncle has organised so much. Now we have to wait till we hear a date."

"Hope you have a good two weeks."

"Thank you." We said our goodbyes. I walked to the bus stop with Lydia. We chatted. I told her what Uncle had organised. Lydia said, "There's nothing else to do but wait till Dennis gets a letter giving a date."

"No, I hope it doesn't happen for a long time." She agreed: "I want you around as long as possible."

"Thanks. Me too." We said goodbye and gave each other a hug. The bus was pulling in. "Where are you going now?"

"I'll see Lena for a while and tell her what's happening."

I walked to Lena's. She was pleased to see me. I gave her my news. She was happy for me. She helped me with some questions from my books, then invited me to stay for lunch. We chatted until it was time for me to leave. I said goodbye and caught the bus back. When I arrived in my room, Rosalind had put a note under my door saying to go and see her. I knocked on the door. "Come in!" She asked, "Is everything all right?"

"Yes. I just want to hear all the news. I have been thinking about you."

"Oh." We sat on the bed, and I told her everything I knew.

"This means it's all arranged, with nothing else to do until you hear a date?"

"Yes."

"Wow! Well, you really do need to concentrate and get through all the exams."

"Yes."

"We should have eleven months together."

"And more, I'm hoping." She started telling me about her time off with Paul, working out a date to get married. "It would be good if you could come to the wedding."

"Well, I'd like that, and you could come to mine, but it's in London." We talked for a long time.

Chapter 108

The days went by. I settled into studying and lectures. Rosalind was my constant friend, and we had a routine working together. I heard from Doctor Tom. He organised for me to visit during my next time off, which was coming up in a few days. I was looking forward to it. I chatted to Rosalind about it, "It will be nice to see the children again, and I have so much news to tell them."

"Yes. You will be having a busy two days."

I caught the bus to Aldham, and Margaret met me. I spent time with her before we picked the children up from school. She gave me their news. "They are doing well. Catherine is really looking forward to seeing you." It was nice seeing Ethel again. She made lunch for Margaret and me. We walked the grounds and down by the river. Margaret asked me how I was getting on, and I told her my news.

"Goodness! Does Tom know?"

"Yes. He said he would keep it quiet. We don't want Matron to know until I tell her I'm leaving."

"Well, he certainly has kept it quiet. He hasn't mentioned it to me."

"I expect he wanted me to tell you myself."

"It is a shame you won't finish your training, though, by the sound of it."

"I know. I'm hoping it will be a longer time before it happens."

"Goodness. And you will be getting married at the end of the year? Catherine will be so excited when you tell her your news."

"It will be in London. My uncle has organised everything." We chatted while walking. We had now reached the house again. It was time to pick the children up. We arrived outside the school. Margaret said, "Catherine is always the first to come to the car. The boys take their time to get here." I was sitting in the car, looking out of the window. There were children everywhere, walking and running. I spotted Catherine.

She looked just the same, maybe a bit taller. She opened the car door. She was so pleased to see me. We gave each other a hug. I asked her how she was, and she chatted nineteen to the dozen, telling me what she was doing, and that she loved maths and English.

The boys had arrived, and Luke was still quiet. He didn't have much to say. Mark chatted a bit. Catherine never stopped talking, asking me to stay for dinner. "I've had lunch with your mum." She then turned and asked her mum, "Please can Sylvia stay for dinner as well?"

"Yes, if she would like to do that." I thanked her. "That would be lovely." We had arrived back at the house. "Come to my room, please." I followed her, and the boys came too. We went up the twisty stairs, which brought back memories of when I was there, working and living. Nothing had changed. Catherine's room was tidy, and she showed me some things she had made at craft. The boys' rooms were a bit messy. They started to chat to me, though. It was good to hear what they had been up to. Catherine asked, "Come back to my room, please." She closed the bedroom door. "I want to talk to you on my own. How is your nursing going? Tell me all your news."

"Lots has happened since I saw you last." So, we sat on the bed, and I went into it all. She was so happy for me, and gave me a hug. "I want to come to your wedding."

"It's in London, so I don't think you'd be able to."

"I'm going to ask my dad. He might take me."

"That would be lovely, but you will have to wait and see."

"So, why doesn't Matron know?"

"Well, we are not supposed to have boys in our lives, and it wasn't that I was looking. It just happened, the way I told you." Catherine thought it was like a fairy tale. "So, my dad mustn't let Matron know."

"No. It looks like I might have to leave before I've finished my training, and I will have to tell Matron. That won't be easy for me." Margaret called out, "You are staying for dinner, aren't you?" Catherine said yes. "Thank you. I will." I asked Catherine, "Have you got homework to do?"

"Yes, it's maths. It's easy. I'll show you." I watched her doing it. The boys had very little homework. I organised them. They all had their homework done before dinner. I felt like I was working there again. I really enjoyed being with them. Ethel called us, saying, "Dinner is ready!" We all went downstairs and walked into the dining room. Catherine said, "It is a special occasion, because you're here, and we're eating in the dining room." Doctor Tom said, "Nice to see you join us for dinner. How are you?"

"Good, thank you." There was a lot of chatter. They really made me welcome. Doctor Tom said that he would run me home. Catherine asked, "You will write to me, won't you?"

"Of course. I will let you know my news." I thanked them for having me. Margaret said, "You must keep in touch." It was time for me to leave. Margaret said, "Now, children, you need to get your homework done."

"We have already done it. Sylvia organised us." She turned and thanked me. The children watched me get into the car, and waved goodbye. Doctor Tom spoke with me, asking how I was managing. I told him, "Better now. I did have a lot on my mind. My uncle has organised things, for when I get a date. It's all planned."

"That's good. You can concentrate on passing."

"Yes."

"Let me know when you hear, and I will discuss with you how Matron should be told."

"Oh, thank you. I'm just hoping it will be a longer time than they say."

"That would be good." We had arrived. Doctor Tom dropped me outside the house. I thanked him for the ride. "You're welcome." We said goodbye.

When I walked in, A.J. came out of the front room. "Whose car was that I saw you come out of?"

"Doctor Tom's. I have spent my time with the children, and he said he would take me home. "That's very nice of him."

"Yes. He has been caring and kind to me."

"Come into the front room. Don't talk in the hall. You have missed out on dinner."

"I had dinner with the family, thank you." Lydia came out of the kitchen. She had just finished helping U.S. "Sorry I couldn't let you know what was happening. I've had a lovely day." U.S. joined us, and I was asked first to tell my news. A.J. said, "Mrs. Taylor has told me how happy she is with her doctor. He is a caring man."

"Yes, he is. All the family are. It was so nice being with them again, and being back in the house where I worked. Catherine was so happy to see me." Lydia said, "It's a lovely place, and the children are too." A.J. said, "Well, you are fortunate that it turned out all right. Does the doctor know that you are giving up your nursing and going to Australia?"

"I did tell them my news. He knows I want to finish. It's just the timing before we leave."

"Well, I feel you are doing the wrong thing, and you will regret deciding to leave."

"It is a difficult decision, but I have made it, and I can always come back after two years if we really don't like it." Lydia said, "It's an adventure, and I want to visit for a holiday."

"Well, we will have to see how things turn out."

"Has Dennis been round?"

"Yes. He was on his bike, and he will call round later to see if you are here. He was off somewhere." A. J. asked, "What are your plans?"

"I'll just have to see if Dennis comes. Can I spend time with Lydia?"

"She has homework to do."

"It doesn't need to be done tonight. Can we go to my room now?"

"Very well."

"I'm glad you're feeling better."

"Thank you." We left the room. We ran upstairs.

"Dennis asked where you were. I didn't know."

"Sorry. I was organised with Doctor Tom, and I had no way of telling him or you about it." We chatted, and I caught up with Lydia's news. "Has A.J. been back at work?"

"Only two days a week. She isn't that well, really. U.S. does everything, and I help where I can." We talked more about things. It was now dark. "I don't think I'll be going out with Dennis." We decided to play a game. It was getting really late.

"I really need to get to bed."

"I do too. I'll have to catch up with Dennis when I'm off again. I wonder where he went?"

"That's the first time I haven't seen him."

"I know. I am happy to have an early night, and I'll walk with you tomorrow."

The next morning, I woke up first, then woke Lydia, "So, you didn't go out last night."

"No, I haven't heard from Dennis. I wonder if he's left me a note under the door?" We quickly got dressed and crept downstairs. There was no note on the mat. We opened the kitchen door. U.S. was making breakfast. I asked, "Was there a note for me on the mat?"

"No, I haven't seen anything." We chatted to U.S. "This is the first time you haven't been out with Dennis, since you first met. Have you had an argument?"

"No. It's just that I couldn't let him know where I was, and I expect he was waiting for me to let him know, which I really couldn't do."

"Oh well, it will sort itself out when you see him."

"That's another two weeks away."

"When I see him at youth group, I'll tell him what happened. All right?"

"Thanks. That will be good. Try and find out where he went." We kept talking. U.S. served breakfast, saying grace, and we ate in silence. I said my goodbyes to U.S., and walked with Lydia to the bus stop. She asked, "What are your plans now?"

"I'll go and see Lena for a while, and then catch the bus back." We said our goodbyes. "See you in two weeks."

Lena was pleased to see me. I told her my news, and where I had been the day before. She was pleased for me, that I was still in touch with them. She wished me well for my studies. I said goodbye and caught the bus back. I walked to my room and started unpacking and had just put everything away. I heard a knock on the door. It was Rosalind. "Can I come in?'

"Of course. Is everything all right?"

"I need to talk with you."

"What is it? You look upset."

"I haven't told anyone, and I know you won't."

"What's wrong?" We sat on the bed. "I don't know what to do. I haven't told my mum."

"Tell me. What's wrong?"

"I think I might be pregnant.""Oh. How? I thought you knew what to do!"

"I know. I can't believe it. I haven't had my period."

"You might just be late."

"Well, it's over a week." She started to cry. I had never seen my friend like this. I put my arms around her. "You really need to tell your mum. Have you told Paul?"

"Yes. He is happy about it. He just says we will get married. It will be fine, but I want to finish my training and work for a while before we have a family." We talked more. "You must tell your mum. How are you feeling?"

"I'm worried how my parents will be about it."

"Are you feeling well?"

"Yes."

"No morning sickness?"

"No. I thought we did the right thing." After more talking, I was in shock about Rosalind being in this situation. She asked me, "What should I do?"

"You must tell your mum. You get on well with her, don't you?"

"Yes."

"So – you're very lucky. You have a mum who will look after you."

"Thank you. I will."

"How is it going with Dennis?"

"I haven't seen him." I told her what had happened.

"You haven't been away together yet?"

"No. I won't be until we are married, which will be in December." We talked more about things. Rosalind said, "I will have to tell Mum when we have our next days off. I might to leave before you." I was finding it hard to understand how things were changing. We talked till it was time to walk to the dining room for dinner.

Chapter 109

We settled into studying, and Rosalind still gave me tests, based on questions she had worked out from the books. I could see she was worried about things, and she was looking forward in a way to telling her mum. We went to lectures and everything seemed just the same. If Rosalind hadn't told me, I wouldn't have known anything was different. She looked really well, only every so often, she would say to me, "I find it hard to believe I'm in this situation."

The days went by, and it was coming up to another exam. We had been preparing, and I felt more confident. Rosalind asked, "How did you think you went?"

"I think, all right."

"I found it easy." She was clever, and I wondered how it would all work out for her. Our time off had arrived. We were packing our things. Rosalind said, "Wish me luck."

"I hope it all works out well for you with your parents."

"You too, with Dennis."

"Yes. I haven't seen him for a month. See you in two days."

We walked into town together, and then went our separate ways. I met Lydia off the bus.

"Did you tell Dennis?"

"Yes. He will call round tonight and talk with you."

"He felt you could have let him know."

"Well, I don't know how I could have done that."

"I did tell him that."

"Thanks." We talked more about things while walking home. I asked about youth group. "Sylvia said she would like to see you."

"That would be nice. I'm not sure how we can organise it."

"Sylvia said when you are off next time, her mum can pick you up, and you can have dinner with them."

"That will be nice. I'd like that." We had reached home. U.S. was in the garden as we walked in the back gate. "I'm just going to the allotment." He had the wheelbarrow with him. "Would you like to come?"

"Yes. I will just take my things up."

"I need to change. What are you going to be doing there?"

"I am hoping there are some vegies for dinner." We hurried, and walked with him. I hadn't been to the allotments for quite a while. It was very tidy. U.S. pulled carrots out, and dug up potatoes. There were some peas growing. We helped to pick them. I asked, "How is A.J.?"

"She is slowly coming good, but has to take things easy now."

"What is wrong with her?"

"It's up to her to tell you." Lydia said, "I've tried to find out, and she just says she gets tired easily."

"That is true. I make sure she rests, and doesn't overdo it. I help when I can. We all do our best. Is Dennis coming around?" We were walking home.

"Yes. He told me at youth group, and said Sylvia should have let him know when she was off last, that she wouldn't be there." U.S. agreed.

"Well, how could I do that, when I didn't know about it myself, when I saw him last?"

"Maybe you should have said you couldn't go, but made it another time."

"It was organised for me."

"Yes, well, it's a difficult situation. I'm sure you'll sort it out."

"Thank you for letting me know. So, he is cross with me."

"Yes. He wasn't happy. We spoke at youth group."

"I know what to expect, then."

We had arrived home. I asked, "Can we help you with dinner?"

"Yes. That would be nice, thank you." It didn't take long with the three of us.

"I know you want to go for your quick walk, so off you go."

"Thanks." We ran out the back door. "It's nice have our chats on our own."

"I tried to tell Dennis you didn't know. I had never seen him cross before."

"Me either. Oh well, thanks. I'll soon find out how he is with me."

"Stick up for yourself."

"I will. I didn't do anything wrong."

"I agree."

"Thanks." Lydia told me about her friends, and wanted my opinion. It was so good having time on our own, even if it was short. We ran, and were out of breath. A.J. was up, and said, "Hello. Dinner is ready." We quickly washed our hands. U.S. served, and I was asked to say grace. While we helped U.S. with the dishes, I asked, "Did you speak with Dennis when he called round?"

"Yes, I did. We were a bit worried when you didn't come home."

"Oh, I hadn't thought about it like that. I can see your point of view, but it was organised for me."

"You just need to explain it like that."

"I will."

In the front room, A.J. had words with me about not coming home, and not letting anyone know. I started to talk and was told, "Stop interrupting. I haven't finished. I brought you up better than that. Don't just think of yourself." I tried to explain and was told, "You were in the wrong." I had to admit I could see that I should have thought about other people, who would wonder where I was. I did end up apologising. "Doctor Tom organised it."

"Yes, and you just went along with it, only thinking of yourself. That has to stop, if you want to get along in the world." Then I was asked how I was getting on. "I have had another exam since I was here, and got better marks."

"I am pleased about that."

"My visit with Doctor Tom and the children was really good, and they were pleased to see me."

"Well, if there is a next time, I hope you have learned your lesson and know what to do."

"Yes, thank you." Lydia looked at me. There was a knock on the door. I knew it was Dennis. I got up. Lydia came with me to open the door. He said, "Hello. You're here this time."

"Yes. Sorry. A visit was organised by Doctor Tom. Sorry. I hadn't thought about you being worried if I wasn't here."

"I hope you won't do this to me again. You need to let me know."

"I didn't know about it when I saw you last, and there was no way I could let you know anything." Lydia said, "It was difficult, when Doctor Tom had organised it."

"Thank you, Lydia. I can see that now. Let's get the bus into town."

"All right. I'll just say goodbye." I went back into the front room. A.J. and U.S were still there.

"I'm going into town with Dennis. I've just come to say goodbye. Thank you for dinner. I'll see you in two weeks."

"Very well. Goodbye." U.S. said goodbye too. As I went down the hall, Lydia whispered, "He's all right with you now?"

"Yes. See you in the morning for breakfast."

We caught the bus. Dennis said he had missed me. I asked, "What did you do?"

"I saw my mate Roy, and caught up with him."

"That was good."

"Yes. I told him our news. He said, if I like Australia, he would like to come. He's really interested."

"That will be nice for you." We had arrived, and went into our favourite café. It was nice and warm, and we were able to sit in the corner, where it was quiet, and talk. Dennis told me about work. "I can't wait to leave. I have told a few people now, and my boss called me in. He had heard about it, and he's happy to keep me on until it's time to leave."

"That's good. You could have lost your job. I haven't been able to tell anybody. Only Rosalind knows. She won't say a word. We are close friends."

"We could hear any time about a date. I'm so excited. How do you feel?"

"Sometimes I am, and other times I'm unsure. I have mixed feelings. You haven't got anyone you will really miss."

"No. You're right. Yes, it does make a difference."

"It sure does, to your feelings, and you're not happy in your work, whereas I am. I wish the timing was better."

"Once it's sorted, you'll be happy. We can make our life together. It will be exciting! I can't wait."

"I know." After more talking, we caught the last bus back.

In the morning, Lydia woke me, whispering: "Is everything all right between you?"

"Yes, thanks. I think at last Dennis understands why I have mixed feelings about leaving."

"Hurry, please. We can talk more while walking to the bus."

We opened the kitchen door. U.S. was pleased it had been sorted out between Dennis and me. We ate our breakfast. After we had finished, I also told him that Dennis's boss had heard our news. "Now he knows about Australia. He says he will keep Dennis in his job until it's time to leave, and wished him all the best. He doesn't know that Dennis is unhappy, and can't wait to leave." We talked more before it was time for me to say goodbye. While walking to the bus with Lydia, I told her about Rosalind. "Oh no. What is she going to do?"

"She is going to tell her mum. I'll find out about it when I get back."

The bus was coming. We said goodbye and gave each other hugs. I decided to catch an early bus back, and wondered how Rosalind had got on. I walked to my room and sat on the bed, and was pulling stuff out of my bag to put away. I had just finished, and lay down on the bed. I was feeling really tired. I must have fallen asleep, when I heard a knock on the door. I quickly opened it. Rosalind said, "You're back. Good."

"Come in. How are you? What happened when you told your parents?" We sat on the bed.

"Mum is all right with me. I've seen a doctor, and I am pregnant. I feel really well."

"So, what's going to happen?"

"I won't say anything till I show I'm getting bigger, then I'm going to have to leave. Mum will let Matron know. I'm not sure what she will say, or how. They are both happy they are going to be grandparents. It's sooner than they would have liked, and for me too, but I can always go back later and finish my nursing."

"So, that's good they are fine with you."

"Yes. They want me to be careful what I do, and keep it quiet, until I'm starting to show, and get fat."

"Oh. I hope that won't happen for quite a while."

"Me too."

"I am so happy for you, that your parents are good about it." I gave her a hug. "You must feel a lot better, now that you have told them."

"Thanks. I do, and it's so hard to believe I'm going to be a mum soon." We spoke more about things, "Ask me if there is anything you find difficult. I can help. It's our secret."

"Yes, thanks. Please don't tell anyone."

"No, I won't." She asked about Dennis, and I told her what had happened. "Everything is fine now," she said. We walked to the dining room for dinner.

Chapter 110

As the weeks went by, everything was going smoothly for Rosalind. She was looking and feeling really well, and it was hard for me to believe that she was pregnant. She did say that when she had been on the wards, she felt rather tired, and would put her feet up and rest when she got back. When our days off came around, she told me she got really spoilt, and her mum made sure she rested. She had taken her and Paul shopping for baby things, and they had a big house. They would be able to live with them until things sorted themselves out.

Her mother said, "Paul has a good job, and his parents are looking forward to being grandparents." On my days off, I would spend time with Lena and Mrs. Taylor, and see Lydia when she finished school. Dennis would come round in the evening. Sometimes he would come on his motor bike, and Lydia would ask, "Can I have a ride before you go?" Then we would leave and go into town on the bike. I was actually starting to enjoy it.

Everything was going along fine, only A.J. was not very well. U.S. was managing to do everything, with Lydia's help. Whatever A.J. wanted, he did. I did get a letter from Uncle, and I would write back. I was still passing, only just, sometimes, with Rosalind's help. She was amazing. She didn't look any different. We were getting ready for our time off. Rosalind said, "I will walk with you into town. I'm meeting Paul. He has a day off. Why don't you come with me to meet him?"

"Thanks. Yes, I'd like that." Paul was waiting where they had arranged to meet. We went into a coffee shop, and we all talked. He was a nice boy, and said, "Rosalind has told me lots about you." I congratulated him. He said he was excited, and worried that Rosalind was doing too much.

"She is amazing, and is resting when she can. I try and help, and make sure she doesn't carry too many heavy books."

"Thank you. I know about Australia. Are you looking forward to it?"

"Yes and no. It sounds silly, but I don't want to leave my sister."

"That wouldn't worry me. I have a sister." I thought, I won't go into that, and changed the subject: "What are you going to do this afternoon?"

"We are looking at prams."

"I'm so happy about the baby, and Rosalind doesn't look any different. I keep asking her, "Are you sure you're pregnant? Rosalind said, "Yes, it's good, isn't it? I want to keep up my training as long as I can." We had so much to talk about -- "I must go and catch the bus. See you in two days. Have fun."

"Thanks. You too."

I met Lydia off the bus, and told her where I had been, "She's lucky she doesn't show with her tummy."

"Yes. You wouldn't know." We chatted away, "Dennis is looking forward to seeing you, he told me at youth group. He seemed excited."

"Oh no! Maybe he knows something."

"You mean, he has heard?"

"I'm just guessing. Why would he be excited?"

"Just to see you!"

"Oh! I didn't think about it like that."

"Oh well, we'll know when he comes round."

"Hope he has his motor bike. I would love a ride."

We had reached home. It was nice to see U.S., who was pruning the roses in the front garden, and was happy to see me. "A.J. is resting, so be quiet when you go upstairs." We hurried silently. Lydia changed. I dropped things on the floor, and quickly went down the stairs and outside. U.S. asked, "Are you going for your favourite walk?"

"Yes."

"Don't be long."

"We won't. We will help you with dinner when we get back."

"Thank you, girls." We walked to the woods. "I have a feeling Dennis knows something."

"You could be right. He was really excited, and was telling Roy something."

"Well, I'll know soon."

"So will I." We didn't stay long, and ran home. We helped prepare the vegies. U.S. asked, "How are you getting on?" He enjoyed hearing what I had been up to.

"How is your friend?"

"Oh, Rosalind? She is well. She got top marks in her exams. She says she finds it easy. I just managed to get through, with her help. We study, and she sets questions for me and marks me."

"She is clever. You're lucky you have a friend like that."

"I know."

A.J. came in. I asked, "Are you feeling better?"

"Yes, thank you." I thought she had lost weight, but didn't say anything. U.S. said, "Good timing. Dinner is ready!" I helped to serve. A.J. sat down. I noticed U.S. only put a small amount on her plate. I thought, I must ask Lydia about her. I was asked to say grace. We ate in silence. When we were helping with the dishes, I spoke to U.S. "A.J. is not eating much."

"No, she has lost her appetite."

"What does the doctor say?"

"I can't talk about that. It's up to A.J. to tell you."

"I'm going to ask her." Lydia said, "I have done that. I got nowhere with it."

"Well, I'll try."

Later, in the front room, I asked A.J. and was told, "I have lost my appetite. No more to discuss."

"You need to get checked and find out why."

"Thank you, Sylvia, for your advice. It has been taken care of. End of subject."

"Please, can you tell us what the problem is? Lydia and I would like to know. Why are you keeping it a secret?"

"It is my decision. It will do you no good to know about it. Now, Sylvia, how have you been getting on?" I gave her some news, saying "I am enjoying it."

"That is good to hear. What are your plans?"

"Dennis is coming round, and I'll go back tomorrow." Lydia said, "Ooh, I can hear a motor bike. I would like a ride before you go!" She got up and walked towards the door. A.J. said, "Lydia, behave yourself! Dennis isn't here to give you rides!"

"I know that, but he won't mind, will he?" She turned to me.

"No, he won't." We heard a knock. We ran to open it. Dennis had his helmet in his hands and was smiling. Lydia asked, "Can I have a ride before you go?"

"Yes, that's fine. Just a short one." He said to me, "We need to talk. I have some news."

"Oh, really?" I thought, this is it. I do hope it's not too soon. My heart was racing. I was nervous. It wasn't excitement, I told myself. I went back into the front room. A.J. said, "That is kind of Dennis, to give Lydia a ride, but I'm not entirely happy about it."

"He rides safely. He doesn't do anything silly."

"Well, I'm glad about that."

"I am starting to enjoy it."

"Just as well. He brings it round quite often." After a while, we could hear the motor bike. I quickly said my goodbyes and walked to the front door. Lydia was coming up the path.

"It wasn't very long. He wouldn't go any further. He is so excited, and can't wait to talk with you. He's on his bike still, out the front. You'd better go." I gave her a hug. "See you in the morning."

"And you can tell me EVERYTHING!"

"Will do!" I ran down the path and got on the bike, then Dennis started the engine and we were off. He didn't speak to me. After going down a few lanes, we ended up in a small village. Dennis stopped the bike, and we got off. He still didn't speak. We walked to this small pub, and were able to get a table and sit down. He ordered drinks. "We need to celebrate!" It was my first time having a drink, which I didn't like. I ended up with just water.

"I need to tell you. We have a date."

"When?"

"We are sailing out of Tilbury on January the fourth."

"Oh. That's not long after Christmas."

"Isn't it exciting?" We clinked our glasses. "I can tell my boss and everyone now."

"Well, I can't. I don't want Matron to know. I will write to Uncle."

"No -- I'll send a telegram to your uncle. We need to be organised. He must know as soon as possible." We discussed things.

"Uncle has organised a date for the wedding, and he thought we would be leaving in the new year. He was right."

"Yes, I will send the telegram to ask him to come here, so we can finalise everything."

"Thanks. That will be good. I can still write."

"Uncle will contact you, so wait for that."

"Yes, I will."

"So, now you have to work out when you will be leaving the hospital."

"I will talk to Uncle about it. I need to keep it quiet for now. It's going to be hard for me."

"Well, I can shout it from the rooftops. We should have a going-away party."

"Who will do that?"

"I will see what I can find out. How do you feel? Are you excited?"

"Sort of. It's really hard to believe that this is going to happen. Now we have a lot more news."

"Yes, it's really happening. You can let Lydia know."

"I will, in the morning. What do your parents say about it?"

"They are pleased for me."

"They will miss you."

"They think it's a good thing, what we are doing." After some more talking, he took me home.

In bed, I couldn't sleep. Everything was going round and round in my head. It wasn't long before I had to leave. I thought, I must let Doctor Tom know. Lydia was sound asleep, snoring. I would let her know later. In the morning, she woke me. "Are you right? Did Dennis have a date?"

"Yes," and I told her.

"Oh. Uncle was right. He thought it would be early in the new year, so you can let everyone know."

"Yes, except, not Matron, yet. I will talk with Uncle and Doctor Tom, who said he would help me when I have a date." We quickly got dressed and crept downstairs. In the kitchen, U.S. said, "Morning, girls."

"Sylvia has news to tell you." "

"Dennis has heard – we have the date when we are leaving.

"Goodness, already!"

"Yes. It's January the fourth, and we have sent a telegram to Uncle to come. We need to finalise everything. I want to keep it quiet till I talk with Uncle, and I need to let Doctor Tom know too." U.S. said grace. We ate our porridge quickly. Lydia said, "We need to hurry. Come on, and be quiet." Once we were out of the house and walking, Lydia asked me questions. "Are you feeling happy? Do you want to go?"

"I can't quite believe it's going to happen soon. I'm nervous about everything, and how it's going to work out."

"I can understand that, but are you excited?" "I'm not sure what it is. I'm a bit excited and a bit nervous. I must keep it quiet. We don't want Matron to know, and I need to talk with Uncle about how to do things." The bus was there. "Be happy. See you in two weeks." We quickly gave each other a hug, and she jumped on. I decided to call in to Mrs. Taylor's and tell her the news. She was happy for me. "You have a lot to organise."

"Yes. Please don't tell Doctor Tom. I will, myself, but you can say I'd like to hear from him."

"I'll let him know when I see him next." I said my goodbyes, and thought I'd better walk to Lena's and tell her the news. She said, "Oh. I will miss you. It's exciting, and you must keep in touch. I will write down my address." She had a little notebook for addresses, and gave it to me. "Thank you." We chatted for quite a while. "I'd better go now."

"I'll see you in two weeks."

"Yes."

I caught the bus, and was glad when I reached my room, and could think. I was looking forward to telling Rosalind. It wasn't very long before I heard her come in. After a few minutes, I knocked on her door. "Oh. Did you come back early?" She opened the door.

"I have some news to tell you." We sat on the bed. "I have a date when I'm leaving."

"Already? When?"

"January the fourth."

"Well, you're not going to finish your nursing."

"I'm like you, having to leave."

"When will you do that?"

"I'm going to talk with Uncle, and Doctor Tom said he would help me tell Matron. So, keep it quiet until I have spoken with them. Uncle is coming to see me." We talked more about everything.

"We could end up leaving at the same time." I looked at her. "Yes, it could happen." She started talking about her time off. "We bought a pram, and I'm feeling excited about everything. I'm feeling really well. Mum said I'm lucky I don't have morning sickness."

"Yes, you are."

"Oh. You won't be here when the baby is born."

"I can't believe I will be in Australia."

"That is so sad. I won't see you. Promise you will write, and keep in touch."

"Of course I will, and you too." We talked about how our lives would be changing, and we both had secrets to keep. We walked to the dining room for dinner.

Chapter 111

We got back into our routine of study and lectures. I always looked forward to time for us to be on the wards, which I enjoyed. Being with people, I felt I was helping, in a small way. I got a letter from Uncle, saying he would meet me in the café on my day off. I was looking forward to that. I talked with Rosalind, telling her that after my days off, I would be able to tell her the date when I had to leave. "I will be sad about it."

"I know. I will be too."

"Who knew, when we started nursing, that this would happen to us? We both thought we would do three years, and have our training done. Yes, I can now understand why Matron didn't want us to see boys."

"Yes, I guess so, but I'm glad I met Paul. You are too, with Dennis?"

"Yes, but I wish it had been a bit later. It would have been good."

"Well, we can't change things."

"No, you're right. We will finish our nursing another time." We did a pinkie with our little fingers.

The day arrived for our time off. I packed and walked into town with Rosalind. Then we went our separate ways. I said, "Enjoy your time off."

"You too. We will have lots to tell."

Uncle was already there, sitting at a table. "Are you hungry? Let's order some lunch." It was good to see him. "Well, you have a date. It was like I thought it would be. How do you feel about it?"

"I wish it wasn't so soon."

"Even if it was later, you still wouldn't complete your nursing."

"I know you're right. I'm sorry I will have to leave, though."

"Yes, I can understand that. We must look forward, not back, because you can't change what's happened, only what can happen. Remember that." We talked more, and our lunch arrived. It was so nice, being able to eat and talk. I asked, "When do you think I should leave?"

"Well, in November, the beginning of the second week – I think that's the latest. There is a bit to organise, and you will need to come to London and stay with us. Alice will help you with a wedding dress, and I must find out from Lydia when she finishes school, and see if you can come together. Do you want her to be your bridesmaid?"

"Oh yes, I do."

"Also, we must let people know the wedding is on the twentieth of December, and will be in London. You must understand, a lot of people won't be able to travel because of that. We can't do it any differently."

"Thank you. I do understand. I will have to say goodbye before I go."

"Yes, you will now. How do you feel?"

"Nervous. Thank you for your help. That sounds lovely."

"There's only four months of your training left. Are you starting to feel excited?"

"I'm unsure about it."

"So, have you spoken to your friend who is helping you?"

"Yes, and she has confided in me. She has a problem herself, and will need to leave about the same time."

"Really? That's a shame. She isn't able to complete her training? She is clever, you told me."

"Yes, she is, and hopes, like me, to be able to complete her training later."

"So, Matron is going to lose two of you?"

"Yes."

We met Lydia at the bus stop. She gave big hugs to Uncle and started chatting about her day. Uncle asked, "When do you start your holidays?"

"I'm not sure. I can find out." He gave Lydia the news and plans for what would be happening. "Sylvia will be leaving in the second week of November. Hopefully, you will have broken up and you can come together to London."

"This is so exciting, and I will be your bridesmaid!"

"Yes. Alice will help you both with dresses." We had arrived home. Uncle said, "I must tell A.J. and U.S. I wonder if she will be well enough to come to London?" Lydia said, "She is up and down, and sometimes she is really well."

"We will have to see what they think of the plans."

A.J. was in the front room, and pleased to see Uncle. We went into the kitchen. U.S. was organising dinner. I asked, "Can we help you?"

"That would be nice."

"Uncle has some news. Why don't you go into the front room too?" Lydia said, "We can do the vegies."

"Please go into the front room. We can do this."

"Thank you, girls. Are you sure?"

"Yes." He went into the front room. I made a start on the potatoes. "I'm going to get out of this uniform. Give me your things and I'll take them up."

"Thanks."

"I'll be down soon."

There was meat in the oven. I put the potatoes round the meat, and made a start on the carrots. Lydia came down. "You must be excited about the plans Uncle has made." She told me what was happening at school. "I know we get longer holidays than the other schools. I will find out when they are."

"There's only four months left before I have to leave. I must tell Doctor Tom. He said he will tell Matron for me."

"Will you be sad?"

"Yes. I'll have to say goodbye to everybody. A lot of people can't come to London. Uncle said that. After dinner, when Dennis comes, we must tell him the news and go and see his parents."

"It's all happening. I'm excited, but I really don't want you to leave. I will miss you so much."

"Me too. I wish it wasn't so far away – another country!" We talked more, and had dinner all cooked when everybody came out of the front room. A.J. looked better, I thought, and thanked us for making dinner. U.S. said, "It's nice for me to have a night off."

"You all sit down." We served, and I started cutting the meat, but couldn't. U.S. said, "I think I need to help you with that." Uncle said, "You sit down. I'll do this. You have a night off."

"Thank you. That's nice of you." A.J. gave Uncle a look. When it was all served, Uncle said grace. He remembered to eat in silence. When the last mouthful had been eaten, he said, "Very nice. Girls, you did well." He said thank you to U.S. and A.J. for having him for dinner. I said to U.S., "We can do the dishes. This is your night off." Lydia said, "Yes. Please go into the front room. We can do this."

"Well, thank you, girls, very kind of you," and they all walked into the front room to talk. Lydia said, "This is giving us more time together to talk, as well." We chatted until we had done everything and put it all away. Then we went into the front room. A.J. asked, "How do you feel about things?"

"I didn't think we would hear for a while, but now I'm feeling a bit excited." Uncle started talking about the plans, and was hoping they would be able to travel to London. He would organise accommodation. A.J. said, "That is kind of you, but I'm not sure if we'll be able to come."

"We will talk more the next time I'm down." Lydia said to A.J., "you must get plenty of rest a few days before the time. Then you should be fine. I'm going to be bridesmaid, and it will be a long time before you see Sylvia again."

"Thank you, Lydia. We just have to wait and see how things work out." We heard a knock. I got up. Lydia came too. It was Dennis. "How is everybody?" Lydia said, "Come in."

"Well, I'm not sure if A.J. will like that." I said, "Our uncle is here, and we will walk up to see your parents." Everyone came out of the front room. Dennis said, "Good evening." U.S. said, "You must be feeling pleased with yourself."

"Yes, I am, and really excited about everything." Uncle said, "Yes. We can see it on your face. Now we will go and see your parents and tell them of the plans." We said goodbye.

"See you in the morning!"

"Yes." I said goodbye to U.S. and A.J.

"I hope you start feeling well again."

"Thank you, Sylvia. Goodbye."

We walked up to Dennis's parents' house. Uncle was talking to Dennis, and I was listening. Dennis's parents welcomed us. Uncle told them the plans he had made, and about the accommodation arrangements, which they were happy about. The evening went well. Uncle had to catch the train back to London. It wasn't going to be a late night. We had to walk back. We said our goodbyes. Dennis said, "Wait a minute.", and took me into the front room. He wanted a few minutes on our own. He gave me a hug and said he loved me very much, and hoped I would start feeling happy.

"Once Matron is told and I have left, I can look forward to everything, but I have to get through this to say my goodbyes to my friend, Rosalind, and Doctor Tom's family and other friends. It's a difficult time for me."

Uncle was calling – "We need to leave. I have a train to catch!"

"Sorry." We quickly said our goodbyes. When walking home, Uncle asked, "Is everything all right?"

"Yes. Dennis said he wished I looked happier. I told him it's not an easy time for me, having to say goodbye to my friends and Rosalind. Once it has happened, I can start looking forward to things, and hope to feel happier."

"You're right. You have a lot to sort out first, and your circumstances are so different." We talked about things. "Just do your best. It's all you can do. You need to contact Doctor Tom and give him the details about when you will be leaving. I am not sure what notice is required."

"I will." We had reached home. He gave me a hug, "Write and keep me informed. I will be down again soon."

In the morning, Lydia asked, "How did it go with Dennis's parents?"

"It went well, and Uncle is organising accommodation for them. They are happy with everything."

"That's good. I think U.S. and A.J. will try and make it."

"Hope so." We hurried downstairs for breakfast. U.S. was asking me questions. I replied. He was pleased that everybody was happy with the arrangements.

"I hope you will both be able to make it."

"I will certainly try my best, and hope A.J. will be well enough." Lydia said, "You must come. You won't see Sylvia for who knows how long."

"It would mean a lot to me if you could come."

"Thank you, Sylvia." It was time to say goodbye. "See you in two weeks."

"Yes, thank you." It wasn't long before we were walking to the bus. "I will find out when our holidays are."

"That will be good. You can let me know next time I see you." We chatted more. There were children everywhere. The bus was late. "Where are you going now?"

"I will see Lena for a while, and let her know how everything is for me. She is so easy to talk with, and likes seeing me." The bus had arrived. We quickly said our goodbyes and hugged.

Lena was glad to see me, and interested to hear my news. "I would like to come to the wedding." I gave her a hug. "I am thrilled. You are the first person who has said they can come. Oh, Dennis's parents will definitely be there. If A.J. is well enough, they will come. Not sure if U.S. will come on his own."

"Well, you could ask him. He might be happy to come with me, if A.J. is unable to. It's still a while away." We talked more. She wished me well, asking, "How is it all going for you?"

"I have to let Matron know I'm leaving. Not looking forward to that." It was time to leave. We said our goodbyes, and I caught the bus back.

In my room, I sat on the bed, thinking. My life will be changing. I will miss the friendships I have made, and being here with Rosalind. It's been good. Now I'm going to spend my time saying goodbyes. I will find that difficult. I will need to start saving some money for a holiday, so I can come back and see everybody. I could hear Rosalind was back. It wasn't long before she knocked on my door. She asked me, "How did it all go?" We talked, and I told her what had been planned by Uncle, and when I would have to leave. It wasn't very far away. "I know." After more talking, Rosalind told me her news. Then we walked to the dining room for our meal.

We soon got into a routine again. The days rolled by. I still hadn't heard from Doctor Tom. I would have to see Mrs. Taylor on my next days off. I wanted to find out why Doctor Tom hadn't contacted me. I was hoping I could visit the children one more time. I must make sure I let Dennis and Lydia know when it was being organised. Rosalind was helping me still, and we enjoyed our time together. I noticed she had put a bit of weight on. It was not with her tummy, but was all over. You would never know she was pregnant. She would talk about leaving, "But I would like to leave when you do, and we can leave together. I hope I don't get too big too soon."

"I don't think we can leave together. I hope I can leave first, because I will find it difficult without your help."

"No, when you have told Doctor Tom, and he has told Matron, I will ask my mum to come and tell Matron."

"I don't know how that's going to work."

"Oh, it will."

My days off were coming around again. I had a lot to organise. I would see Mrs. Taylor first, and see if she knew anything about Doctor Tom. She said she had passed the message on, and that she didn't need to go for another few weeks. I thanked her. "I will walk in and see if I can get an appointment, or I could write a note and leave it at the desk for him."

"That's a good idea. I'm sorry, I won't be able to come to your wedding, but I would like you to come and have dinner with me before you leave."

"Thank you. That would be nice."

"Now, come and sit down." She handed me pen and paper to write my note, and an envelope. "You can go and leave it at the desk." I said my goodbyes and walked to the surgery. I went up to the desk and left it for Doctor Tom. Then I walked to Lena's and spent time with her. She had everything written down – when I would be leaving, and the date of my wedding. "I am definitely coming. Have you spoken to U.S. about whether A.J. can come?"

"No. I will have to, when I'm on my own with U.S. That's not easy, but I will try and do it today."

"Have you made a list of the things you need to do?" She handed me a little notebook. "Write things down, and cross them off when you've done them."

"Oh, thank you. That will help. There is so much I need to think about, and to ask Uncle when he comes down next."

"Please keep in touch." It was time for me to leave. I said goodbye, and walked to meet Lydia off the bus.

She was already walking home, and pleased to see me. I gave her my news and told her what Lena had said. "She is definitely coming."

"That's great. You must let U.S. know if A.J.'s not well enough. He can go with her."

"I will, tonight." We chatted about what had been happening since we had seen each other. "Uncle will be down soon, and we can talk about last-minute things and finalise them."

"Yes, it's getting close now." We had reached home. U.S. was in his greenhouse. "I'm going to talk with him now, and let him know what Lena said."

"Good idea. Give me your things. I'm going to change." I opened the greenhouse door. U.S. hadn't seen me. "Oh. Is it that time already? How are you?"

"Good, thank you. I've been to Lena's," and told him what she had said.

"Oh, that is kind of her. I will give it some thought."

"How is A.J.?"

"She is better at the moment, and has had some good days."

"That's great."

I chatted away, telling him how I had been. I told him that Mrs. Taylor was unable to come, but I had been invited to dinner to say goodbye. Lydia was here now. She asked, "Have we got time to do a quick walk? Then we will help you with dinner."

"Yes. Off you go. Is A.J. still asleep?"

"I haven't seen her yet. She is still in her room."

"I will come in now and check on her." We walked out of the back gate. A few children were playing and called out to us. We waved and kept walking. Lydia was telling me about school and different friends.

"How's your friend, Rosalind?"

"Really well. She has put on a bit of weight, though, mainly all over, but you wouldn't know she is pregnant."

"When do you think she will leave?"

"Oh. She wants to leave when I do, hoping she won't get too big before then. That will be good for me. It will be really hard if she leaves much earlier than me. I would miss the help she gives me."

"It will be interesting how it all works out." We walked in the woods. There was nobody about. It was so peaceful. Lydia said, "We'd better not stay long – we said we'd help U.S. with dinner. Where are you going with Dennis tonight?"

"I don't know. He never said when I saw him last."

"Hope he brings the motor bike." *

"You really like it?"

"Yes. I wish I could go on a really long ride."

"I don't think that can happen. We don't have much time together. Sorry."

"I know." We hurried home.

A.J. was in the kitchen with U.S. I asked her, "Are you feeling better?"

"Yes, thank you."

"We will help with dinner. You go and rest."

"Thank you, Lydia. I might just go and do that." She walked out of the kitchen. We gave U.S. a hand, and it was good – we were able to talk with him. I asked, "Did you speak with A.J. about the wedding?"

"Yes, I did mention it. She did say she hopes to be able to come if she's well enough."

"Oh, that's good. Of course, it will be a last-minute decision."

"Yes. I'm afraid that's how it will be."

"I'm sure Uncle will understand about the situation. When he is here next time, we will talk about last-minute things." We enjoyed talking with U.S. He was so different on his own.

Later, in the front room, I was asked to speak first. A.J. was interested in what I had been doing. I told her little things that had happened. I think she was feeling a bit better towards me. She asked, "Are you organised?"

"I'm getting there. I have written a note to Doctor Tom, to let him know when I will be leaving, and left it on his desk at the surgery. He did ask me to let him know when I have a date. He said he would talk to Matron about me leaving."

"Well, that's good to hear. I hope you will let us know if and when you are spending time with him and the family, and not do what you did last time."

"Yes, I will let you know first, and make sure Doctor Tom gives me enough time to do that. Oh, Mrs. Taylor told me she is unable to come to the wedding, and has asked me to stay to dinner one night."

"That's nice of her. I didn't think she would be able to come."

"Oh, Lena is coming, which is nice, and I think Uncle will be here when I'm off next."

"Yes. I have that written down. Lydia, how was your day?"

"Everything is going well, thank you. I found out about the holidays, and I will be on holiday the first week in November."

"That's great, because that's when I'm leaving. Uncle will be pleased."

"Well, it looks like it's all working out for you. You are fortunate that's how it is."

"I can hear a motor bike," and she ran out of the room. A.J. said, "Lydia can't expect a ride every time Dennis comes." I walked out of the room. Dennis was talking with Lydia. I asked, "What are we doing tonight?"

"We will go into town. All right if I give Lydia a ride?"

"That's fine." Lydia already had her helmet on. "Thank you. We won't be long, will we?" He gave me a hug and walked down the path. Lydia was already there, waiting by the bike. I watched them leave and went back inside. A.J. said, "I'm not happy that Lydia is getting rides."

"Well, it won't be for much longer. Dennis will have to sell his bike soon."

"That will be a good thing, and you will have to walk everywhere."

"We won't be here for long after that." A.J. was still carrying on about Lydia not being safe on the bike. She wasn't worried about me.

After a little while, I could hear the bike, so I said my goodbyes. "Thank you for dinner."

U.S. said, "See you in two weeks."

"Yes," and I left the room. Lydia was at the door. "That was so good."

"Glad you enjoyed it. A.J. is not happy about it."

"I can manage her, thanks. See you in the morning. Have fun!"

We went into town on the bike. I was getting more used to it, weaving in and out of the traffic. I still found it scary. We sat in the corner of our favourite café, with a hot drink, and talked about our wedding plans. Dennis said, "I've organised a honeymoon for us. We will be going away after the wedding, and be back just in time, before we leave."

"Oh. Where are we going?"

"It's a surprise. Your uncle has helped me organise it."

"I must thank him. I hope I can get help to pack."

"Don't worry. It will be taken care of. When you have left, I have asked at youth group that on the first Friday, they are going to have a farewell night for us, with food and drinks."

"Oh – that's great."

"You can see your friends and say goodbye. The lady who runs it is having a paper printed with the date and time on, so those who want to say goodbye to us can come."

"Thank you so much. It will be good to see friends I haven't seen for a long time. "

"So much is happening. It's exciting. Don't you agree?"

"I must admit I am starting to feel a bit excited now."

"That's good to hear. I can't wait till you leave, to see more of you." It was time for him to take me home.

In the morning, I had lots to tell Lydia. "It will be good that you can come to youth group. They're doing it specially for you and Dennis." I told U.S. at breakfast. He thought that was very nice of them. He would tell A.J., who was still asleep. We talked a bit more, before it was time to walk with Lydia to the bus.

"Where are you going now?"

"To Mrs. Taylor's." We quickly said goodbye. Her bus had arrived. I called in to Mrs. Taylor's. She hadn't heard anything from Doctor Tom. She suggested I walk to the surgery. "I will give you pen and paper and an envelope, and you can write a note." I said thank you, and quickly left and walked to the surgery. I sat on the seat outside and thought, I'd better write down when I'm off again on the back of the note. I went inside, and asked, "Can I leave this at the desk, please?" I asked the receptionist. She smiled, "Of course." I left, and decided to go and see Lena, and tell her my news.

While I was walking, I thought, that's good – I can let Dennis, Lydia and A.J. know when I will be at Doctor Tom's, because I've asked him. Lena saw me coming and opened the door. "Come in and tell me all your news. Sit down. I'll make you a drink while you talk to me." Of course, there was lots to tell, and it was nice being able to confide to her all my thoughts about what was happening.

"Have you written down important things in that writing pad I gave you?"

"Oh. Some, I have, but not recently."

"You'd better go and do it now, before you forget. You have a lot going on that you need to remember."

I did as I was told. She was right. It was getting really busy, and it was good to refer to the notepad. Time went fast. I had spent all day with Lena, when she told me that Lydia would be getting off the school bus soon. I couldn't believe it! I thanked her for her help, and for having me. "Come and see me again soon."

"I will, thanks."

I hurried to the bus. Lydia was walking towards me. "Have you been at Lena's?"

"Yes. I have so much to tell you." We chatted all the way home. U.S. was working in the garden. He told us to be quiet inside. A.J. was sleeping. Lydia went inside by herself. I talked with U.S. and told him what had been happening.

"Later, in the front room, just let A.J. know the news."

"Yes, I will. I know when I'm going to say my goodbyes to Doctor Tom and the children, so I will give A.J. the dates when I won't be here." Lydia was back. "Is it all right if we go for a quick walk?"

"Yes. That's fine." We left, saying we would be back soon. "A.J. hasn't been the best, again, and refuses to tell me what is wrong. U.S. makes meals, and takes them up to her room, so I don't know if you will see her. She's hardly eating."

"Well, I'll ask. I might be able to take her dinner up."

"Yes. I often do it. It's a lot for U.S., going up and down the stairs all the time."

It was so peaceful in the woods. We hardly saw anyone in the late afternoons. We enjoyed our walk, and it was nice to catch up with our news. We arrived back. U.S. said, "It will just be the three of us. A.J. will have a little on a tray."

"May I take it up to her?"

"I think that should be all right, but please be careful what you say. She can't have any upsets."

"I will make sure that doesn't happen." U.S. served dinner and put a little on a plate for her. I took it up on a tray. I opened the door. She was sitting up in bed, and was surprised to see me.

"Hello. Sorry you're not feeling well."

"Thank you, Sylvia. How are you?"

"Good, thanks. Can I come up later to collect the tray? If you'd like me to, I can talk with you for a little while."

"Yes. You can do that before you leave."

"Thank you," and I closed the door. I came downstairs. I said to U.S. and Lydia, "A.J. was sitting up in bed, and said I can go up later to collect the tray and talk with her."

"That's good. Mind you don't upset her, when you talk."

"I will be very careful." We ate our dinner and helped with the dishes.

"You should be all right to collect the tray now."

"I can go up too."

"Yes. Just be careful. Leave if it's getting too much for her." We walked upstairs. Lydia knocked, and we opened the door. Lydia asked, "Are you feeling a bit better?"

"Yes, thank you."

"I'll just take the tray and come back to talk with you for a little while."

"Very well." U.S. was pleased that most of the dinner had been eaten. I said, "I'll just stay for a little while," and I left. I could hear Lydia talking, and went into the room. A.J. asked, "What news do you have to tell me?" I told her all about what had happened.

"The youth group is making a Friday night dinner for Dennis and me, and I can say goodbye to my friends. That's really nice of them."

"Yes, I have heard that is being organised for you. It is kind of them."

"I haven't been able to come for such a long time. I'm really looking forward to it. Oh, and Doctor Tom has invited me to see the children and stay for dinner, and say goodbye. And I have the date. It will be next time I'm off, so you know I won't be here for dinner."

"Thank you, Sylvia. You have now told me. You need to make sure you tell anybody else who needs to know."

"Yes, I will." We could hear a motor bike. "It sounds like Dennis is here." Lydia said, "I'll get a ride first!" and she ran out of the room. I spoke with A.J. a bit longer.

"How do you feel about leaving your training?"

"A bit sad, but I hope I will be able to continue in Australia. It's hard saying goodbye to everybody."

"Well, you know how I feel about it, and you have chosen to do this. I hope it all works out for you, and that you will be happy."

"Thank you for that, and for what you have done for me. I do appreciate it, even though we have our differences."

"Yes. We will leave it at that. I need to rest now. Goodbye."

"Goodbye." I left the room and closed the door. I could hear the motor bike. U.S. asked, "Is everything all right?"

"Yes. A.J. wants to rest now." Lydia was full of chatter when she came inside. We went a bit further this time. Dennis asked, "Are you ready to leave?"

"Nearly. I won't be long." I ran to get my coat.

"See you in the morning. Have fun!"

"Thanks."

"Was everything all right with A.J. when I left? You didn't upset her?"

"No. We just talked. She is resting now."

"OK. See you in the morning."

U.S. was chatting to Dennis at the door. I said, "Goodbye. See you in the morning," and I walked down the path with Dennis.

Chapter 112

My last few weeks at the hospital were sad. I was also nervous about how it was all going to work out with Matron, and how she would be towards me after Doctor Tom had spoken with her. I had said my goodbyes to him, Margaret and the children, which I found hard. I promised to write. I knew the day when Doctor Tom would be seeing Matron, and also the time. Doctor Tom said he thought two weeks' notice would be fine. I told Rosalind.

"Why are you leaving so soon?"

"My uncle wants me to go to London with him. There's a lot to organise, and my wedding dress and the bridesmaid's dress too."

"I can't believe it's going to happen next week."

"Yes. Then I have two more weeks left."

"Have you worked out when you will be leaving?"

"No. I am getting more tired now."

"You have done so well, and nobody knows, only me."

"Yes. I feel I should be leaving soon. So, you have three weeks left? I would really like to leave with you."

"Oh. I don't think you can do that."

"Why not?"

"Well, it won't go down well with Matron."

"I can't stay much longer than you."

"Anyway, I'm starting to get really big, and I need to rest more."

"Well, I can understand that."

"I'm going to ask Mum to come and see Matron. I want to leave with you. Tell me, what day is Doctor Tom seeing Matron?"

"Oh, I don't know if I should."

"Please tell me when it will be. It will be good to leave together." After some more pleading, she started to get upset. In the end, I told her.

"It wasn't planned to be like this. It's just the way it has turned out."

"I guess that is true." I could see Rosalind was getting quite big. Nobody had said anything about her weight. I was sure it had been noticed. I thought she was keeping well, and getting though her exams. She had helped me so much. We had had our last exam two weeks before.

"I don't have to study anymore."

"No, you don't, and I don't either. I can't believe this is going to happen so soon." We talked more about it all.

"Well, I won't be here when our next exam is due."

"Are you sure you want to leave, then?"

"Yes. My mum has been saying it's getting too much for me, and she is worried about it. I should be resting more."

"That is true, but leaving together –"

"Stop worrying about it. My mum will talk with Matron, and anyway, I want to come back and finish my training after I've had the baby." I did enjoy Rosalind's company, and I could see she was getting very tired, and would lie down on her bed more often, and I would help her where I could. I also knew it was time for her to go. I told her she was overdoing it.

The day arrived when Doctor Tom would speak with Matron. I wondered if he would come and see me afterwards. He didn't say he would. I was feeling stressed. Rosalind said her mum was coming later that day. It was lunch time. We were walking to the dining room. I couldn't believe it. Doctor Tom was walking with Matron in the corridor. He smiled and said, "Hello. Are you off to lunch?"

"Yes." Matron just nodded. We sat in the dining room. Rosalind asked, "Do you think he has told Matron, or is he on his way to tell her?" We talked about it. Matron didn't look happy. I think he might have told her. "You could be right. Matron might come and see you."

"I'm so nervous about it."

"I can understand that. I'm feeling the same."

"I wonder how Matron will be about it?" We ate our lunch, chatting. When I got back to my room, there was a note on my door, saying to go to Matron's office.

"Tell me about it when you get back." I was so nervous. I reached the office and knocked. "Come in!" Matron and Doctor Tom were sitting there. "Well!" Matron said. "It seems you are leaving us."

"Yes. I feel sad it's turned out this way. I would have really liked to finish my training."

"We don't have students leaving in the middle of their training. It has been explained to me, and I understand you don't have any option, under the circumstances."

"Sorry about the way it has turned out."

"So, you will be leaving us at the end of this month. I hope you will be happy in your new venture, and that you will continue with your nursing."

"Thank you, Matron, and Doctor Tom, for all your help." Matron stood up and shook my hand, and then Doctor Tom did. Matron said, "You may go now." I walked back to my room. I was still feeling nervous and uptight. I sat on the bed and thought – it's over. Matron knows now. I tried to relax. I felt upset about it all.

Rosalind knocked on my door, came in and sat on my bed. "How did it turn out?" I told her all.

"I'm feeling sad and will miss this." Rosalind gave me a hug. "Well, I wonder how Matron will be with me? My mum has arranged a time to see her later this afternoon."

"How do you feel?"

"A bit nervous, like you. I will be glad when it's all over. I'm feeling so tired now."

"You have been amazing, to be still here." We talked more about things. Rosalind would let me know after her mum had been.

It was late afternoon before Rosalind came to my room. She looked upset.

"What happened?"

"She was shocked about my situation, and said it was a health risk for me to have been still working. I should leave straight away. She is not happy with me."

"Oh, sorry. When are you leaving?"

"Tomorrow morning."

"Really?"

"Yes."

"I will miss you so much. I have two more weeks here." We talked about it all, staying up really late. Our last night together. Rosalind left in the morning. I had arranged to see her in town, after I'd left, to say my last goodbye. She promised to keep in touch. I gave her U.S.'s address, and I would ask him to forward letters to me. She gave me her address.

I did not enjoy my last two weeks. I missed Rosalind a lot. It was so quiet. I spent my time packing and writing things down that I needed to do. There was no need for me to study any more. I left on the day that had been arranged, saying my goodbyes to the place. My new life was now beginning.

I arrived home in the morning with my case and bags. U.S. was pleased to see me, "So it's done now."

"Yes. It feels strange and sad."

"You have new things to look forward to. Take your belongings to your room, and come down and talk to me." It wasn't long before I was sitting in the kitchen.

"Dennis will be pleased to see you tonight."

"Yes." After we had talked, U.S. made me some lunch, and it was just the two of us. I don't remember that happening before. It was so nice. "Where is A.J.?"

"She has an appointment and will be back later in the day."

After more talking, I left to meet Rosalind. She was sitting in the café. It was so good to see her. We chatted lots, catching up. She had seen her doctor, and everything was going well for her. "I left this morning. It's hard to believe I won't be going back. I missed you a lot in the last two weeks. I did not enjoy those weeks." Paul came into the restaurant to take Rosalind home. We said our goodbyes and hugged. We promised to write, and wished each other all the best. "Be happy. Goodbye."

Chapter 113

It was Friday night. I was really looking forward to it. I walked down to the hall with Lydia for the last time. So many people were there. Dennis arrived on his bike and said hello. "So glad you have left!" There were people I hadn't seen for such a long time, who all wanted to talk to me. An announcement was made, saying Dennis and I were leaving, to get married in London, and going to live in Australia. There were some speeches. I didn't realise we were expected to say a few words.

Dennis spoke first, then I thanked everyone for coming, and those who had organised it. I also said, "I will miss my friends." It was so good seeing everybody, and my friends Sylvia and Betty again. They gave me their addresses -- "We will write." They wished us all the best. There was lots of lovely food and music, and a bit of dancing. It was a great night. It finished really late. I enjoyed it so much. Dennis walked Lydia and me home. "I'll see you tomorrow."

"Yes, only for a short time. Uncle is arriving, and Lydia and I will be going back with him, to stay for a few days, finalising wedding details and dresses."

Lydia said, "It's all happening, and we have to pack and be ready. I don't think there will be time for you to see Sylvia."

"Well, I'll just pop in for a little while." He gave me a hug and started cycling home. There were no lights on in the house. We were very quiet. It wasn't long before we got into bed.

In the morning, U.S. woke us, saying, "I'll make breakfast for you, so hurry up, girls, and be quiet. A.J. is still asleep." We went into the kitchen and sat down. "How was last night?"

"It was really good. A lot of people were there."

"The food was great. Is A.J. awake? Is she still in bed?"

"Yes, I have taken her some breakfast." We chatted to him while he was making our breakfast. Lydia said, "We will do our jobs quickly, then we have to pack. Uncle will be here before lunch time, and we'll be going back with him, to stay a few days, to sort out last-minute plans."

"Goodness. Does A.J. know about this?"

"Yes. I think so."

"Well, I didn't know about it."

"She might have forgotten to tell you. She hasn't been well. I should have woken you. It's getting late. You will have to hurry with breakfast."

We hurried and got into dusting and chores. There was a knock on the door. We ran to open it. I said, "Sorry we got up late, and we haven't really packed." Lydia said, "Our uncle will be here shortly. We need to be ready." Dennis gave me a hug. "Have a nice time. I'll go and let you get organised."

"Thank you." Lydia said, "Please. We must be ready!" I said, "Yes. Sorry. See you when I'm back. Goodbye." Lydia closed the door, saying, "Come on. We need to hurry!" She ran up the stairs. I followed.

We had just finished our packing, and ran to put our bags at the front door. U.S. called, "A.J. wants to see you both." We went into her bedroom. She was sitting up. "What is all the noise about? Running up and down the stairs!" Lydia said, "We have been packing, and have just put our bags at the door."

"Where are you off to?"

"We are staying at Uncle's for a few days to organise last-minute things, and he will be here soon."

"Why wasn't I told?" Lydia said, "You were. It was a while ago, and it was talked about. You haven't been well. You must have forgotten."

"Lydia, I do not forget things. You have planned this, without me knowing." We looked at each other. A.J. was getting cross and upset. "You thought you could do this without me knowing!" U.S. came into the bedroom and looked at us. "You are upsetting A.J. Please leave now!" Lydia said, "See you when we are back. Hope you will be better soon." We ran downstairs. There was a knock on the door. We opened it. Uncle had arrived. "Are you ready, girls?"

"Yes," Then Lydia ran upstairs again to say "Goodbye. We are off now." U.S. came downstairs to speak to Uncle, explaining about A.J., "She cannot remember about this arrangement, and is not well."

"Sorry to hear this. Yes, it was arranged quite a while ago. She wrote it down in her black book."

"Oh. She has been confined to bed, and hasn't been looking in her black book. Nor have I. Thank you. I will take the book up to her." We said our goodbyes to U.S. Uncle said, "Enjoy the quiet time without the girls around."

"Yes, thank you."

We left, chatting to Uncle. "One at a time, please!" Lydia told him, "A.J. has been in bed a lot, and we don't know what is wrong. She won't tell us. U.S. just says it's up to her to tell you, if she wants you to know."

"Well, that is true."

"U.S. does everything – all the meals. I help where I can, and he is up and down the stairs all the time. He gets very tired."

"I can understand that. Let's hope she will get well soon."

It was so good being with Uncle again. We enjoyed the train trip. I told Uncle about my last few weeks at the hospital, and how difficult it was for me, also about my friend, Rosalind. "I miss being there." Uncle said, "This is a new chapter in your life. There is lots to look forward to."

"I know, and I am feeling some excitement now, but also nervous. So much is happening so fast."

"I'm excited. I'm going to be your bridesmaid." We talked about my wedding plans. Uncle was letting me know about the format of the service.

Chapter 114

We had now arrived in London, carrying our bags and getting on the escalators, which I still found difficult. We walked for quite a while before we reached the park. I could see the swings that Lydia and I sat on when we were younger. Uncle said, "No sitting on the swings now!" We walked a bit further, and I could see the house. We kept walking. Alice was standing at the door, watching us. There was a lot of talking and hugs. She was so pleased to see us. "It has been a while. Now I have food all ready. You must be hungry." She talked so fast. "Take your things to the room. Do you remember the way?" "Yes, thank you."

We walked to the room. Lydia and I chatted while walking. Lydia said, "Alice is so nice."

"I wonder where Peter and Marion are?"

"They are both out, I should think," said Lydia. We left our things on the bed, then walked back down the passage to the kitchen. Alice was asking me a lot of questions, and talked and talked. She made us very welcome, and had made something to eat. Uncle said, "Help yourselves, and eat whatever you would like." Alice continued to talk with us. We did too. It was so good being able to eat and talk together.

Afterwards, Alice took us to visit a lady nearby. We walked. She would be making our dresses. She measured us, and had lots of materials for us to choose from. We had two weeks left before the wedding. Alice helped me choose. Because it was so cold, I had a dress with a velvet bodice and three-quarter sleeves in white brocade. Lydia chose pink satin for her dress, with short sleeves. We were told to come back in two days for a fitting. Alice said, "She is very good, and I have had clothes made by her." Alice took us to look at the shops and the big stores. We had a lovely time. We bought some pretty things.

When we got back, Peter and Marion were there. It was nice catching up with them. We helped Alice to prepare dinner. She chatted away to us, asking me how I was feeling. "A bit excited and a bit nervous about everything."

"That's understandable. How about we have a girly talk?" Lydia asked, "Does that include me?"

"Yes. I think you are old enough now."

"Oh, that's good. I'm included!"

Later in the evening, after dinner, we all sat and chatted, and got to know each other more. It was really good, and it was late when we got to bed. Lydia and I talked about our day. How nice it was all being together again. We were tired, and it wasn't long before we fell asleep. We woke up really late, and went into the kitchen. Alice asked, "How did you sleep?"

"Really well. Sorry it's so late."

"Just relax. We have nothing planned. Uncle is in his study. Now I'll get you something to eat." She talked away to us, "Please sit and talk to me," which we did. She had made us a lovely brunch, and said, "How about we go for a walk and visit the Gardens? Would you like that?" We said, "Yes. That's lovely."

We set off in the early afternoon. The weather was fine, and it was just the three of us. There was more talking, and after a walk, we sat on a seat overlooking the Gardens. Alice asked, "Tell me about Dennis. What is he like?"

"Well," I started telling her how we met. "He is caring, and I was attracted to him." Lydia said, "I like him, and he really loves Sylvia."

"Do you love him?"

"Yes, I feel I do."

"Well, marriage is a lot of give and take. You will have ups and downs, and it's not a bed of roses."

"I understand that."

"The main thing is, to sort it out as quickly as you can. Do not sleep until it's sorted."

"I'll remember that." We talked more. "Do you want to ask me anything?"

"Well, I'm not sure how to put it. Dennis told me he and Uncle helped to organise our honeymoon. I don't know where I'm going. Dennis won't tell me anything. It's a surprise, he says. When we get back, we will be leaving the next day for Australia. It's all happening so fast."

"Yes, Dennis has planned it well, with Uncle's help. You won't be going to A.J.'s anymore."

"Oh, so I'll say goodbye to them at the wedding."

"Yes. The boat will be leaving from Tilbury, and we shall see you off."

"That will be nice, but I haven't been told anything. I would like to know some of the plans."

"Just enjoy it and be happy."

"Thank you. I want to." Lydia asked, "What about me? When will I be going back home?"

"I think Uncle will take you back, or you might go with U.S. and A.J. It just depends on how it works out."

"I'm really going to miss my sister."

"Me too."

"Yes. You both will, and your lives will be changing. You must keep in touch and write to each other."

"We will."

"I will want to know how you are getting on, so you're going to be busy writing to everybody."

"Can I ask about the honeymoon?" I looked at Lydia, and said, "No!"

"Well, do you know what happens?"

"Yes, I do." Then I told Alice about my friend Rosalind. "I don't want to have children for quite a while."

"I am pleased to hear it. Yes, I will buy what's needed for you, and you must talk with Dennis, and make sure you both agree."

"But I'm sure he will feel like me about it." Alice asked, "Lydia, do you know what we are talking about?"

"Yes. I have learned at school, in biology, which has helped me understand the workings of the body. I know that stuff."

"Well then, that's sorted. I don't expect A.J. has spoken to you about the subject." We looked at each other and I said, "No. We couldn't ask any questions about that. They would think we were being rude." Alice said, "You have lived a very strict and sheltered life, but you have turned out lovely girls. We must give them both credit for that. They have done what they felt was the right thing." She asked, "How are you getting on with them now?"

"U.S. I am fond of. He is easy to talk with, and understanding, but only when A.J. isn't about. Otherwise, he just sits there. A.J. makes all the decisions."

"What about A.J.?"

"I feel she has been very hard on me. I couldn't get on with her. I did the best I could, but since I got into nursing, she has been interested in what I have been doing. She feels I should finish my nursing, and not leave. She is not happy about Dennis and me. Since I have grown up more, I'm feeling sorry for her. She is not at all well, and seems unhappy. She wants her own way on everything, but she has taught us the correct way to behave, and has cared for us and given us a home. We have been fortunate she took us in. We could have been somewhere so much worse."

"That is true." Lydia said, "I appreciate what she has done for me, and because I started school at the right age and found school work easy. Sylvia struggled. She didn't go to proper school till she was nearly eight. I have got on better with A.J. She is proud of me." I said, "Yes, she is."

"Well, I'm pleased you get on better with A.J. You have a bit longer at school. I think we will start walking back home."

Chapter 115

We really enjoyed our time with Alice and Uncle. We played board games in the evenings, and it was so good to be able to talk about anything, and listen to what others were saying. Uncle asked, "can you come into the study, please? I will let you know what we are doing tomorrow. We will visit the church, where I will be marrying you, and afterwards we will visit the reception rooms, where you will go after the ceremony, and have a buffet lunch, which is helping yourself to food, and then sitting down to eat. After that there will be music, and anybody can get up and dance."

"Really? I didn't know about any of this."

"Dennis and I have been organising it for you both."

"Thank you. That sounds lovely. What time does it finish?"

"Dennis and you will leave about 4 p.m. and catch the train for your honeymoon."

"Oh, how—"

"It's all taken care of, and we will put you both on the train."

"Where --"

"No, I'm not telling you where you are going. Dennis wants it to be a surprise for you."

"I know that, but I would like to know. How will I know what to take with me?"

"Alice is taking care of that side of it. Do not worry, please."

"That is lovely of you both. Thank you."

"All you need to do is be happy and enjoy it. He is a nice boy and loves you very much."

"Yes, he does tell me that."

"I am pleased that he does. And how are you feeling?"

"I do love him, but I'm nervous about going to another country."

"It will be strange at first. You will soon make friends. It will be an adventure. New things to see and try! It's exciting."

"That's what Dennis always says."

"You will enjoy it, I'm sure. It's just a bit daunting for you right now."

"I'm going to miss Lydia so much."

"Yes, you will, and she will miss you too. You must keep writing to each other, and you never know, when she has finished her schooling, she might decide to come, at least for a visit."

"Yes, she did say she wants to come and see me."

"Well, I think it's time for bed." I said goodnight and gave him a big hug.

I found Lydia talking with Alice. "We have a big day tomorrow. We are seeing the church," I went on to say what was happening. Alice said, "It's going to be a busy one. How about I wake you, so we can have breakfast before you leave?"

"Thank you. That would be good. Uncle has just told me the plans for my wedding day. Thank you for helping me and packing for me. I don't know where I'm going, and Dennis wants it to be a surprise for me."

"Yes, now don't worry about anything. I have it all under control. I'm looking forward to meeting this Dennis chap. Uncle is very taken with him." Uncle heard us talking, "Girls. You need to get to bed. Alice, stop talking to them, please. We all have a big day tomorrow." Alice said, "Yes. Now off you go and get yourselves to bed." We said goodnight and left.

In bed, Lydia was asking me questions, "What else is happening?" I quickly told her, "We'd better get to sleep." It took me a while, with lots of thoughts going through my head. I must eventually have fallen asleep. Alice woke us in the morning. We hurried and got dressed, then walked into the kitchen. We could smell breakfast cooking. "Good morning, girls. Good timing. Sit yourselves down." She served breakfast. We all sat down and enjoyed it. Uncle asked, "Are you ready for a big day?" We said, "Yes."

"We will leave in twenty minutes." We quickly helped Alice with the dishes, and got ready to leave. It was a good walk to this very old church. It was beautiful – constructed of bluestone blocks, and had stained glass windows. The interior was made of wood. He took me through the order of service, and asked, "Have you thought about who you would like to walk you down the aisle?"

"I wonder if U.S. would like to?"

"We need to ask him. Otherwise, I can do both."

"I would like to ask him when I see him. That might be nice."

"If for any reason he is unable to, I will do it." We spent quite a time at the church. Then we had another walk. We were going to the reception rooms. It was upstairs, and there were lots of stairs to climb. We opened the door to a large room, with tables and seating. There were large windows, through which you could see lots of buildings. Uncle pointed out the church we had just come from. We left there. He asked me, "How are you feeling about everything?"

"It is lovely, what you have organised. Thank you. I'm really happy, and feeling excited now."

"That is very good to hear." Lydia said, "You have done such a great job, Uncle!" We went to a little café for a drink and something to eat, and chatted about our morning. Alice said, "Tomorrow you will have the fittings done on your dresses."

"Yes. It's exciting to see how they will look."

"Then we will go shopping and get something for your honeymoon."

"Really?"

"Well, I don't think you will have anything suitable at A.J.'s."

"No, not really." Lydia said, "You are being spoilt."

"Thank you so much. I didn't realise how much there is to do, and what's involved in getting married." Alice turned to Lydia. "Your turn will come."

"Oh. It won't be for a long time. I'm not really interested in boys. I will miss Dennis, though. He takes me for rides on his motor bike." Both Uncle and Alice said, "Goodness! We didn't know he had a motor bike." So, I told them all about it, "And now I'm enjoying it." Lydia said, "I enjoyed it from the start. I will miss having rides."

"Dennis said he was looking at selling it while I was away, so he might not have it when we get back."

"I hope he still has it."

"Well, it won't be coming to Australia with us." Uncle said, "Not a good idea. Best to sell it and have the money, maybe, to put towards a car, when you get to the land of Oz." We chatted more about things, before we headed for home.

Chapter 116

Later, after dinner, we played games, and enjoyed it so much. Alice said, "Tomorrow, we have another busy day. Both of you have your fittings, and they might need to be altered, in which case, there'll be two visits. We still need to go shopping for your honeymoon clothes."

"Thank you. We will need to have an early start, so I think an early night is needed." It wasn't long before we got ourselves into bed.

"I will wake you in the morning. Goodnight."

"Thank you." We did talk about our day in bed, saying how nice it was, staying with Alice and Uncle. We eventually went to sleep.

Alice woke us, and we got moving. She had made breakfast and was organised. It wasn't long before we were on our way. Off to the dressmaker! I tried my dress on, and it was lovely. It just needed a little bit of altering. Lydia's fitted really well. She loved it. Alice said, "You both look gorgeous. I am pleased with how they have turned out. One more quick visit tomorrow, and that's one item off the list. You will need shoes, both of you, then clothes for the honeymoon. Have you anything at A.J.'s that is suitable?"

"No, not really, and I don't know where I'm going, so how do I know?"

"That is true," still not telling me.

"Well, you will need something warm, the way the weather is, and you feel the cold."

"Yes, I do. We did a lot of walking in the shops, and I tried quite a few different clothes and shoes on. We didn't buy anything."

"We really need to think about this. We will go shopping again tomorrow."

We had two more days left with Uncle, and there was still a bit to finalise. The next morning, we were up early again. Alice said, "Let's go to the dressmaker first, then that's done. Then we will go to the big stores. We are running out of time. We don't want to come back empty-handed this time." My dress fitted beautifully. Lydia looked lovely in hers. She asked, "After the wedding, can I take it with me?"

"Yes, of course. It's yours. You could wear it to a party."

"I haven't been to one yet."

"I'm sure you will, at the end of your school year. When you leave school, I think they call it a formal."

"Oh, well, it would be good if I can wear it more than once."

"You will find an opportunity to wear it again, not like Sylvia. I'm not sure whether that would be possible. You might be able to get it altered so you can. It's a lovely dress."

"Thank you."

"Now, off to the shops. Let's see what we can buy." We walked and walked, trying different clothes on. Eventually I tried a matching skirt and jacket. Alice thought it was suitable. "If you get warm, you take the jacket off."

"I need something to wear underneath."

"Well, yes, you do." We did find something after a long search. There were still a hat and shoes to find. We managed it all in the one day, but we were so tired. Alice said, "We have done well. It's all done now. Tomorrow is your last day, and you can have a relaxing one. We don't need to go to the shops anymore."

"Thank you very much for all you have done for us."

"You are very welcome."

It was our last day with Alice before we would be leaving to go back home. We didn't get up until late, and just relaxed at Alice's. We spent a lot of time talking together. Uncle wanted to leave really early in the morning. Alice made sure we were organised, and in bed early. Lydia and I talked about everything. Both of us realised that we wouldn't be doing this for much longer, promising we would write, and answer each other's letters straight away. We said, "We'd better try and get to sleep. We must be up really early."

Alice woke us and got us moving. Our breakfast was organised. It wasn't long before we were ready to leave. Our bags were at the door. A taxi was taking us to the station. We said our goodbyes to Alice. She said, "I will see you in a week's time, for the big day." I didn't have much to take with me. Uncle asked, "Are we ready to go?"

"Yes. Thank you for everything, and for having us." There were big hugs all round. Alice opened the door. Our taxi was outside. We said goodbye and hopped in. It wasn't long before we were at the station, waiting for the train. Uncle said, "We will be doing this again in a week's time." Within a few minutes, the train arrived, and we were able to get a carriage on our own, so we could talk. I thought, I wonder how A.J.

is? Uncle asked, "How are you feeling, girls?" I said, "Good. I wonder if A.J. and U.S. will come to my wedding?" Lydia said, "I think she will, if she is well enough." We talked with Uncle about things. He said, "I will stay for a few hours. I want to catch up with Dennis, and I expect you want to see him too."

"Yes, that would be good." Lydia said, "I hope he still has his motor bike, and I can have one more ride." Uncle laughed. "You will have to find a boyfriend with a motor bike." I said, "That wouldn't go down well with A.J."

"I'm not looking for a boyfriend," Lydia said. "I just want to concentrate on my school work." Uncle asked, "What would you like to do?"

"It depends on my marks. I'm not sure. I will get back into studying after the wedding. We still have more holidays, which is good, and I'm really going to miss my sister."

"Me too."

Nobody came into our carriage, and part of the journey was express. We arrived in Colchester on time. It was still quite early. Uncle said, "Let's go and get a drink, and then we'll have to wait for the bus." We then walked home.

"Well, try and settle in and be helpful. Go along with things."

"I will. I would like it if they can both come to my wedding."

"Yes. It is a memorable day, and nice to look back on, as they have been part of your life."

"Yes, that is true." We had reached home. Lydia opened the door and called out. U.S. came to the door. "It's nice to see you." We were all standing there. "Come in." I asked, "How is A.J.?"

"She is in the front room, and better than she was." He whispered, "Just be careful how you talk. No upsets."

"No, of course not. I will be careful." He took us into the front room. A.J. was sitting in her chair. I thought she didn't look well. Lydia went up to her to give her a hug. "Nice to see you. I won't get up. You understand," she said to Uncle.

"Yes. Please stay where you are." I asked, "Are you feeling better?"

"As well as I can be, thank you."

"Nice to see you up."

"Thank you. Do sit down and tell me your news." Uncle spoke, telling them what had been happening, and the arrangements that had been finalised. A.J. said, "I'm pleased it's all gone well for you. What are your plans now?"

"Well, I want to catch up with Dennis, and Sylvia would like to see him too. I will catch the train back, but not too late. I hope you enjoyed your quiet time and are feeling stronger."

"Thank you. I have some days when I'm better than others, and today is a better one."

"That's good." After more talking, Lydia and I left the front room and took our things to the bedroom. She said, "She is really not that well."

"I know. She has lost weight. We will have to be really careful how we talk, me more than you."

"Yes."

"U.S. looks tired. We need to help more."

"Yes, agreed. Maybe we can make dinner for everybody. I don't know what food there is."

"We'd better ask."

We went down to the kitchen. "Now girls, are you able to help me?" I said, "Let us do dinner. Tell us what you have."

"Well, there are lots of veggies, and I have meat all cut up." Lydia said, "We can do this. You go and talk with Uncle." I said, "Oh, first, I want to ask you something." He looked worried. "Would you like to walk me down the aisle? I really would love you to, if you would like to."

"Goodness me!" He had tears in his eyes. "That would be an honour. Are you sure?"

"Yes, thank you." He was overcome. "I must go and tell A.J." I asked, "How is she really? Is she going to be well enough to come?"

"We are hoping so. She gets upset very easily, so you will have to be extra careful how you talk," he said, looking at me.

"I will, I promise. I will think more before I speak."

"Thank you. We will have to see how it all goes."

"Do your best. I know it won't be easy. Now I'll go and let A.J. know my news."

As soon as he left the room, Lydia said, "Well, he's right. It's not going to be easy for either of us. It's you, really."

"I know I can do it. Don't worry. Let's make the casserole and get moving." We put it all together and put it in the oven. We were tidying up when U.S. came back in. "Thank you, girls, for your help. A.J. thought that was very kind of you to ask me, and she is happy about it."

"I am pleased. Dinner is in the oven and will take a little while yet."

"Come back into the front room when you have finished." Then he left.

We chatted and Lydia set the table. Everything was ready when it was cooked. "We'd better go into the front room. Be careful." Dinner was a success. Lydia and I did the dishes. The grownups went into the front room. Lydia said, "Well, so far, so good."

"Yes. I'm going with Uncle to see Dennis. I know, find out if he still has the motor bike."

"Thanks. We had better go into the front room now."

Uncle asked, "All finished?"

"Yes. Are you ready to go and see Dennis?"

"I am. I will say my goodbyes now, as I will get the bus to the station after leaving Dennis, and of course I will walk Sylvia back, but I don't want to disturb you both. I hope to see you next week at the wedding."

A.J. asked, "Is it next week?"

"Yes, only a few days to go now." Uncle and I walked to Dennis's, talking all the way, "A.J. has deteriorated, and U.S. is finding it difficult."

"I know. He is looking tired. I will help as much as I can."

"Yes, that will be good. It's not going to be easy for Lydia once you have left. I will try and keep in touch more."

We had arrived. Dennis was so pleased to see me. There was a lot of talking from Uncle, telling him what had been organised. Dennis's parents were interested, and looking forward to the big day. Everything was ready. I asked, "Have you still got the motor bike?"

"Yes. It has been sold, and he is picking it up in the week. Do you want to go for a last ride tomorrow?"

"Yes, that would be good, and I know Lydia would like to. She really enjoys it. I was hoping you hadn't sold it yet."

"Well, it's still mine. They haven't given me any money. I can do it. They will, when they take it." Uncle said, "A.J. is not at all well, so you might have to check with her when you can do that." He turned to me. "You will need to help while you are there."

"I will. It's only five days."

"So, Dennis, I'm sure you understand. You won't see much of each other until you're married."

"Oh, I understand. I'll keep well away. I don't want to upset anybody."

"Maybe the girls can walk up to your place and have a ride from there."

"That's a good idea."

"I will be helping as much as I can. I would really like them to be at the wedding."

"I'm fine with that," Dennis said. After more talking, Uncle said, "It's time to leave. I have a train to catch." We said our goodbyes. Dennis gave me a big hug. "See you soon."

While walking back with Uncle, he said, "I know you will do your best. We will have to wait and see how everybody is on the day."

"Yes, you're right. It's not long now, and I will be getting married." Uncle gave me a hug. We were now back home. "See you soon, and do your best."

Chapter 117

The last five days were really busy for Lydia and me. We did everything. We prepared meals, kept the house tidy, and did anything A.J. needed. U.S. thanked us, "I might have to get someone to come to the house and help, when you have left. Lydia will be at school and have homework to do." We took it in turns. A.J. would ring a bell, and we would run up to see what she wanted. U.S. was so grateful, and was glad of the rest from going up and down the stairs.

Lydia asked A.J. at lunchtime, "Do you want us to wake you, or not?"

"No, let me sleep."

"Is it all right if we walk to Dennis's early in the morning? He still has his motor bike." A.J. pulled a face.

"I can get my last ride, also Sylvia will, so you won't hear the loud noise it makes, because we'll be at Dennis's."

"That is very considerate. Thank you." Later, while A.J. was asleep, U.S. said, "Go for your favourite walk. I will keep an ear out." We had been twice already, and each time we said this could be the last one. We would really miss going to the woods together.

Three days had passed. We asked U.S., "Is it all right if we walk to Dennis's today, and get our last motor bike ride? We don't want to miss out." U.S. said yes. It was early in the morning when we left to walk to Dennis's. He was so pleased to see me. "I'm glad you came, as the bike is going tomorrow."

"Really? Take Lydia first." She was buckling up the helmet. She asked, "Can we go for a longer one?"

"All right, but you will have to wait while I take Lydia."

"I will." I saw them leave, and spent time with Dennis's parents. I found them easy to talk to. His younger brother was there. I asked him, "Will you miss Dennis?"

"I don't see him that much. Will you come back for a holiday?"

"Yes, one day. It's a long way. It won't be for quite a while."

"Oh. I can come and see you."

"Yes, you could." I heard the motor bike. "It's my turn for a ride." He came and watched. Lydia jumped off. "That was so good." She handed me the helmet. "This is Gordon, Dennis's brother. You can talk with him."

"Thanks." She was not impressed. Dennis said, "Hop on!" and we were off. We went into the country, down lanes with hedges on either side. There was hardly any traffic. It was lovely. He stopped outside a farmhouse. We got off. "Let's go and have some scones and tea."

"Did you take Lydia here?"

"No. We stuck to the main roads. I want to talk to you." We walked in and sat at a table overlooking the garden, which was peaceful. We chatted. He asked, "How are you feeling? I'm so excited. I can't wait till we are on our own and married. Are you organised?"

"Yes. Alice has been great. She has bought clothes for me. I've seen the church, and it is lovely. I have no idea where we are going for our honeymoon. "

"Good. I want all this to be a surprise for you."

"It is. Nobody has told me anything." We talked more, then I said, "We had better go. It's difficult with A.J. So far, it's all going OK, but she is not at all well. Lydia and I do everything, and we have dinner to make. "

"Two more days left, and we will be leaving to get married!"

"I know. Won't you miss your parents and brother?"

"Not really. I will have you. It will be so good."

"I know what you are going to say -- I'm so excited!"

"Aren't you?"

"I am a bit, but I'll miss Lydia."

"I can understand that."

"Come on, let's go!"

"Do we have to?"

"Yes." He gave me a hug and kissed me. We got on the bike again. Lydia was pleased to see me. "You have been a long time." Dennis said, "Sorry. It's my fault."

"We'd better go." I said goodbye to Dennis and his parents. He gave me a hug and Lydia one too. "See you at the wedding."

"Thank you for the rides." We quickly walked home. Lydia was talking. "You were ages!"

"Sorry. Dennis wanted to talk with me."

"Hope A.J. is all right." She opened the front door. U.S. met us in the hall. "I've made lunch. Did you enjoy your rides?" Lydia said, "Yes, it was great!"

"A.J. is awake and wants to see you." Lydia went upstairs. It was a little while before she came down. I asked, "Is everything all right?"

"Yes. A.J. is going to get up and come down for lunch." U.S. said, "We will wait for her. She wants me to help her with the stairs." She was ringing her bell. Lydia hurried upstairs. "Just be careful how you talk. No upsets, please."

"I will." Lunch was ready. Lydia was helping A.J. down the stairs. She came and sat down, and U.S. sat beside her. I asked, "Are you feeling better now?"

"Not really. I thought I'd see if I felt better being up."

"That's a good idea." I passed the plate of sandwiches to her, and she took one. I watched her eating. She said, "That was nice." When we had all finished eating, we went to the front room. U.S. said, "That's good – you're eating."

"Thank you. Girls, what have you been up to?" Lydia said, "Remember – I told you we were having rides on the motor bike."

"Yes, well, that will stop, now Dennis and Sylvia are leaving. I don't like you being on that motor bike. So, that's one good thing that will happen!"

"It has been sold, and it will be gone tomorrow."

"Good to hear. What are you going to do now?" Lydia asked, "Is there anything you would like us to do?"

"You seem to be organised. What needs doing?"

"We have a few hours. We might go for a walk, and Sylvia and I will make dinner." "Sylvia, when are you leaving for the wedding?"

"Uncle will be here, not tomorrow, but the next day, to take both of us, and you and U.S. will be coming to the wedding on Saturday morning."

"I only have today and Friday morning left here."

"Goodness! Is it that soon?"

"Yes, it is."

"How do you feel?"

"A bit sad. I will miss you all, my sister the most."

"Well, this is your doing. It is your choice. You only have yourself to blame."

"Oh." I thought really hard before I spoke – no upsets, remember.

"Well, what have you got to say for yourself?" A.J. looked at me again. "Well?"

"It has been a hard decision, and, like Uncle said, we can stay for two years and return if it's not what we wanted. We will have had the experience of seeing another part of the world."

"I feel your uncle has encouraged you, and you have made the wrong decision." Lydia said, "We will be writing to each other all the time, and I might go for a holiday after I have finished school."

"We will see about that, young lady. I hope you will be happy. You will have to make the most of it, if it turns out otherwise. That is life. You will learn through your mistakes and the choices you make. I hope you will write to me."

"Yes, I will, to both of you."

"Good." Lydia asked, "It's a sunny day. Would you like to walk round the garden?"

"I haven't been outside for a long time. Yes, that might be nice."

We both got up to help A.J., who was weak on her legs. U.S. hadn't said a word, but now spoke, "The roses are out. I'm sure you'd like to see them." He opened the front door for us, and we slowly walked A.J. into the garden. She managed to bend down to smell a rose, and turned to U.S. "That is beautiful. You have done well." We walked round the front garden. She seemed to be enjoying it. We walked A.J. back inside. "I need to rest now, girls. Why don't you go for your walk?"

"Yes, we'd like that. Thank you." U.S. got up and followed us. "Take your time. Enjoy it."

"We will. Our last one together, before I leave tomorrow."

We went out of the front door. Lydia said, "I thought there was going to be an upset."

"I didn't know how to answer. It was so hard, but it went all right, don't you think?"

"Yes, I'm glad that's over."

We ran to the woods. The bluebells were out. "Do you think we should pick some?"

"Yes. Let's put them in a vase in the middle of the table, and look at them at dinner." We chatted about different things. I asked, "Did you check what we are cooking for dinner?"

"Yes. We are going to make toad in the hole. I have never done it before."

"We will follow the recipe. It's easy. It's in A.J.'s book. Then there is ice cream. U.S. must have got it in." We were talking while picking the bluebells. I said, "And we have to pack. We are going to be busy!"

"We can pack in the morning. Wonder if A.J. will still be up when we get back?" We put our bunches together, making one large bunch, and started walking home. "Goodbye, woods!" I called.

"Come on! You are getting upset, and you mustn't, or I will too."

"I'm all right. Let's hurry, and see how the land lies." We raced home.

U.S. was in the garden, coming out of his greenhouse. "That is a big bunch of bluebells."

"Yes," I said, "They are everywhere, and it's looking lovely. We will put them in a vase on the table."

"Where is A.J.?"

"She is having a lie down. She will be up for dinner."

"We are going to make a start on dinner now."

"Do you want me to help?"

"No. It's your rest time from cooking, while I'm here."

"Thank you." We walked inside. It wasn't long before we were organised, chatting away together whilst getting out the ingredients. We enjoyed making it. Lydia said, "I'm going to check on A.J. and tell her it will take about half an hour to cook." It wasn't long before she returned.

"How is she?"

"She is reading, and wants me to come up and let her know when dinner is ready."

"That is good." We could smell it, and were hungry. We tidied the kitchen. "I'll go and get A.J."

"All right. I'll tell U.S."

He was in the front room. "It smells good." He walked to the dining table and sat down. Lydia and A.J. walked in, and A.J. sat next to him. Lydia helped me to serve. It turned out really well. A.J. asked me to say grace and we started eating. It wasn't until we had all finished that A.J. said, "I enjoyed that. Thank you, girls." U.S. said, "It was good." I said, "You both go into the front room. Lydia and I will do the dishes. See you soon." After they had left, I asked, "That did turn out well, didn't it?"

"Yes. I will make it again. It's quite easy." We chatted away while doing the dishes, then went into the front room. There was more talking about me going to Australia. A.J. asked, "Is it tomorrow when you are going to London?"

"Yes. Uncle will be here late morning. We both will be leaving, and you will be coming the next day, to my wedding."

"Is it so soon?"

"Yes. Time has gone fast." A.J. asked Lydia, "I will get you to put my clothes out, ready for me to wear."

"Yes, I can do that."

"And write down the time when we need to leave. Thank you." U.S. said, "Goodness. I'd better have myself organised." A.J. looked at him. "Yes. Make sure you are. You will be walking Sylvia down the aisle." I asked, "Do you need any help?"

"I'm not sure."

"Uncle will be here late morning. He won't mind if you ask him for help."

"Thank you, Sylvia. I just might run it past him."

"That's a good idea. So much is happening now. It's hard for me to believe I will be married in two days." A.J. said, "Yes. Where has the time gone? Well, I really hope it works out for you, and you will be happy."

"Thank you. So do I." U.S. said, "I agree with that." Lydia said, "Me too. Dennis loves you very much. He told me that."

"He tells me that a lot, which is nice." A.J. said, "So he should." After more talking, we said goodnight and got ourselves to bed.

We chatted in bed. I said, "This is our last night in this bed together."

"Yes. We will have one more night at Alice's. A.J. is nicer to you now."

"Yes, she is, now that she won't be seeing me till who knows when."

"I will save money when I get a job. I might see if I can do some work in the holidays, then I can come and see you, because you can't come back for two years."

"I know. That would be good, if you can." After more talking, we said we'd better get to sleep.

Chapter 118

In the morning, when we woke, which was later than we wanted -- we should have asked U.S. to wake us – we had to hurry. We had a late breakfast. I looked in my wardrobe. I had a few things to pack. Lydia said, "I will wear what you don't take."

"Yes, that's fine. Some of it might be a bit big." I had one more look, and took my things down to the front door. There was a knock. It was Uncle. "How are you, and are you ready?"

"Yes. It's just that I think A.J. is still in bed." I called out to Lydia, "Uncle is here!" U.S walked down the hall. "Oh," I said to him, "You want to ask Uncle about what you plan to wear."

"Thank you for that." Uncle asked, "How can I help you?" U.S. explained what he had chosen to wear, and asked Uncle's opinion on it. He walked upstairs to bring it down. Uncle said, "That is fine. We had better get going, or we will miss the train." I asked U.S., "How is A.J.?"

"She is still in bed, but feeling better, so we are hoping she will be all right for tomorrow."

"If she is awake, can I go and say goodbye?"

"I will go upstairs and see." Lydia was upstairs, and called out, "You can come up!" I ran up and went in. "I just want to say goodbye. Uncle is here and we must go now." A.J. put her hand out to me, "I hope to see you tomorrow. I hope all goes well for you." I held her hand."

"Thank you. We have to go now."

"Yes. Off you go!" We ran downstairs. I was saying to myself – the last time. I said goodbye to U.S., who was chatting to Uncle. He said, "We will see you tomorrow." Lydia and I said goodbye to U.S. "See you tomorrow." We walked down the path. I was thinking, I wonder when I'll be here again.

On the train, we chatted. Uncle said, "It looks like A.J. will make it."

"Yes. She has been really nice to me the last few days, although, every so often, she comes out with something unkind. I nearly answered her back, but stopped myself – no upsets, and let it pass." Lydia said, "It has been really hard for me too. We have managed, and there wasn't one upset."

"I'm pleased to hear it." We had arrived at Alice's. She was pleased to see us. "Take your things to the bedroom, and come and talk to me. Tell me how it has been for you since you went home. I'll make you all a drink and something to eat." She chatted away to us, talking fast. We walked to the bedroom and left our things on the floor. We could see our dresses hanging up. "Oh, they look lovely," I said.

"Yes, they do. In the morning, you will be getting married."

"I'm nervous and excited."

"You will be fine." Alice was calling us. She had drinks and food on the table. "Now, sit down and tell me how it has been for you both." We both started talking. "One at a time, please."

"A.J. is hoping to be there. She is quite weak, but wants to come. She has been much nicer to me, now that I am going."

"Well, she realises that she'll miss you, I'm sure." We both talked about our time at home. Lydia said, "U.S. is going to see if he can get somebody to come and help. I will have to do a lot of study in my last years at school."

"That is good. Don't overdo it. You can't do much, with school and study going on."

"In the holidays, I'd like to get a little job to save and have some money, so I can come for a holiday and see Sylvia." Uncle said he would keep in touch with A.J. more. There was a lot of talking about last-minute procedures for the next day. My case needed to be packed for my honeymoon. Alice said, "You will be away for four days, and Lydia is staying with us. She will be here when you get back, and the following day, you will be leaving for the Land of Oz!" Lydia said, "I will see you get on the boat and wave till you're out of sight."

"Oh. Everything is so organised. Thank you."

"You will have to be up early in the morning. Someone is coming to the house to do your hair."

"Really?"

We had a busy afternoon, getting everything ready for my big day. We helped Alice make dinner, and chatted. We had a lovely dinner. Uncle asked, "How do you feel? Anything you want to talk with me about? Let's go into my study." He had a talk with me about being happy and keeping in touch. I thanked him for everything he had done for Lydia and me. He ran through what would be happening next day. "Now, you need to get to bed early. Is there anything else on your mind?"

"No, I don't think so. I'm nervous."

"You will be fine." I gave him a big hug. We said goodnight.

Lydia was talking with Alice when I came out of the study, "I'd like you to get ready for bed now. We will need to get breakfast out of the way before the lady comes to do your hair. I will wake you. Come down for breakfast in your PJs." We said goodnight. I thanked her for everything she had done for me. "Now, get some sleep. Please don't talk for long in bed."

"We won't."

Once we were in bed, Lydia asked, "How are you?"

"Good, I think. I'm nervous, though."

"So am I. I wonder how many will be at the church?" We did talk for a little while. "Well, this is the last time we are sleeping together."

"Will miss you, big sister."

"Me too. I'm glad you will be here when I get back from our honeymoon."

"Me too. We'd better get to sleep. Good night."

"Goodnight!"

Alice woke us in the morning, "See you soon for breakfast." Lydia said, "Come on. You have to get up. It's your big day."

"Yes, I'm getting up." It was a really cold morning. I had a peep out of the curtains. "It's not snowing. I wouldn't mind if it was."

"Hurry up!" We went into the kitchen. Alice had our breakfast organised. There was a knock on the door. It was the lady to do our hair. Lydia got hers done first, then it was my turn. Alice helped us into our dresses. She said I looked beautiful, and Lydia looked gorgeous too. We were ready to go to the church. It was a fine day, but really cold. Uncle had already gone. He had a car organised to pick us up. I was on time when I arrived at the church. I could see people standing at the wooden door.

Then I saw U.S. Alice said, "You go to him. I will go inside now." Lydia followed me. U.S. said, "Oh my! You look lovely." Lydia asked, "Is A.J. here?"

"Yes, she is sitting inside. You look lovely too." I asked, "Have you seen Dennis?"

"No. I think he must be inside." An organ was playing. U.S. said, "I think we are meant to walk down the aisle now." I held his arm, and we walked into the church, with Lydia behind us. It seemed a long walk. Dennis was standing at the altar. Uncle was in his robe, with his white collar on. Then the service started. It was so quick, I thought. Dennis had a ring, and put it on my finger. Then we started walking out of the church. There were people outside throwing confetti at us. Lydia said,

"I'm going to look for A.J." People were talking to us. Lena came out and talked with me. Dennis's parents were talking, saying how lovely I looked. His brother was there. I found A.J. and Lydia inside the church. A.J. said I looked lovely. "It was a nice service." Uncle came and spoke with A.J. and U.S. He thanked U.S. for what he had done. "You did a good job."

After a little while, we were driven to the reception rooms. The seating was organised. Dennis and I were in the middle of the long table, with Lydia. There were speeches, and I got a telegram from my friend Rosalind, who wished me all the best and was thinking of me. That was so nice to hear from her. I could see Lena talking with A.J. and passing food to her. I thought that was nice. U.S. was talking with Lena too. I thought, maybe things might improve. The wedding could make a new start for all of them.

The food was good and it was a lovely day. After everybody had eaten, there was music. Dennis took my hand and we did a waltz. Other people got up and danced. I could see Lydia too. I didn't know who he was. I went and spoke with A. J., who said it was a lovely wedding and she was glad she had made it.

I said, "I will be leaving soon. I don't know where we are going. I hope your health improves." She gave me a strange look, and I said, "I'm glad you were here to see the wedding." She took my hand, "I hope you will be happy."

"Thank you." I spoke to U.S., who said the same, "You will write to us?"

"Yes, of course I will." The music stopped. An announcement was made: "Sylvia and Dennis will be leaving for their honeymoon, and have a train to catch." There was a lot of clapping, and people came up to say goodbye. Lydia gave me a hug. Alice said, "You need to go now." Lydia gave me another hug, and said, "See you when you get back from your honeymoon."

"Yes, see you then." Lena said, "You will write to me." I said yes. Dennis's parents came to say goodbye. Lydia said, "I will see you in four days." Dennis's parents were going to wait until after the honeymoon too. I was not sure who else would be here when we got back. Alice said, "We need to leave now." Uncle had a car ready to take us to the station. Lydia ran to give me another hug. "Goodbye. I will see you board the boat!" Uncle had put our cases in the car, and we got in. It took us to the station. We got on the train with little time to spare. Uncle said, "See you when you are back from your honeymoon. There will be people staying to watch you get on the boat, the Orcades, and set sail for Australia!" We both said, "Thank you for a lovely wedding. And for all you have done for us." The whistle blew, and the train started pulling out of the station. We waved out of the window till they were out of sight.

This is the end of We Made It, Sylvia Moss's story.

www.ingramcontent.com/pod-product-compliance
Lightning Source LLC
Chambersburg PA
CBHW030258080526
44584CB00012B/362